THE
TERROR
NETWORK

THE TERROR NETWORK

THE SECRET WAR OF
INTERNATIONAL TERRORISM

CLAIRE STERLING

HOLT, RINEHART AND WINSTON

Reader's Digest Press

New York

Published by Holt, Rinehart and Winston, 383 Madison Avenue,
New York, New York 10017, and by Reader's Digest Press,
200 Park Avenue, New York, New York 10166.

Published simultaneously in Canada by Holt, Rinehart and
Winston of Canada, Limited.

Library of Congress Cataloging in Publication Data.

Sterling, Claire.
    The terror network.

    Includes bibliographical references and index.
    1. Terrorism—Case studies. I. Title.
HV6431.S73   303.6′2   80-24845

ISBN: 0-03-050661-1

Designer: Robert Bull

Printed in the United States of America

10   9   8   7   6   5   4   3   2

FOR TOM

"You think it's absurd that I should go out and shoot a man just because I'm ordered to? That's your bourgeois mentality. Don't you think it's absurd that you're ordered to go out and write an article?"

—an anonymous member of Italy's Red Brigades,
    to the Roman weekly *Panorama*

CONTENTS

Eight pages of photographs follow page 182.

ix

PROLOGUE

As I was writing the last pages of this book, somebody planted a bomb in Bologna's railway station. It was a Saturday morning in midsummer, and ten thousand travelers were going, coming, or waiting. Eighty-four died and nearly two hundred were hurt. It was the worst terrorist assault in Europe since the last world war; and right-wing, or Black, terrorists were responsible. Six weeks later, another Black bomb killed twelve and injured more than two hundred holiday-makers at Munich's crowded Oktoberfest. The next week, yet another Black bomb ravaged the Paris Jewish Synagogue in Rue Copernic. These were unmistakably concerted hits, orchestrated by a Continent-wide Black Terrorist International which has been lying low in Europe for most of the 1970s. The spectacular reemergence of these former SS officers, neo-Nazis, Fascists, professional anti-Semites, revived nightmare memories for all of us.

My book deals with them only obliquely. Black terrorism had long been receding when I set out to write about left-wing, or Red, terrorists, who dominated the world scene in the harrowing decade between 1970 and 1980. The distinction is important, but only up to a point.

Many young people in this story set out with blazing revolutionary faith, only to reach the arid conviction that somehow, tragically, they had gone wrong. They wanted to make things better, and made them worse. In the end, they found a grotesque identity of interest with Black terrorists, their hideous mirror image. Both were joined in a single-minded effort to disarticulate and eventually destroy the democratic order wher-

1

ever they found it. The higher their rank, the more clearly they perceived this common objective. They even talked it over together, at the top.

It would have been easier for me to write about Black terrorists, always a virtuous pursuit—and now, once again, becoming a singularly urgent one. Writing about left-wing Red terrorists did not make me feel virtuous: it saddened me.

Few of us, in my generation or my children's, can easily shake off the belief that Left is always and necessarily Good. The feeling is particularly strong in situations where Right is so obviously Bad. There are plenty of such situations in Latin America, Africa, and Asia, where vicious right-wing dictatorships seem unlikely to be dislodged by any pressure but their own savage kind. Time and again, authentic left-wing liberation movements have slipped over the line from brave organized resistance to terrorist violence. All too often—not always, happily—their success in overthrowing an oppressive regime has simply led to installing another just like it. Whether Black or Red, the results for the population are much the same.

I have not tried in this book to indicate when or where terrorist violence might be justified. The more I learned about it, the more impossible it seemed to draw a line like that. My own conclusion was that, Black or Red, right or left, there are no good killers and bad killers—only killers. Readers may draw their own conclusions.

In October 1980, fifty-two Americans seized the previous November were still being held hostage in Iran by people calling themselves students. Very little could be learned about these students, who might have been Black or Red or both. Whatever their political coloration, they shocked the American people into some sense of what the terror decade was about. It was mostly about destabilizing the West, by extending the classic Von Clausewitz definition of war as the continuation of politics by other means. Terrorism, during Fright Decade I, became a continuation of war by other means: cheaper, safer, and no less portentous. Its uses were nowhere plainer than in Iran, where the simple seizure at gunpoint of a single building in Teheran, with its fifty-odd American occupants, became an instrument not just of effective if informal war on the United States but of internal government policy, Islamic politics, international finance, and planetary counter-diplomacy.

The Teheran hostages were America's trauma in Fright Decade I. West Germany's was the kidnapping (and subsequent murder) of industrial leader Hanns-Martin Schleyer by the Baader-Meinhof Gang—on September 5, 1977, the fifth anniversary of the Palestinians' Black September massacre of eleven Israeli athletes at the Munich Olympic Games. Italy's was the identically executed kidnapping and murder of Christian Democratic statesman Aldo Moro by the Red Brigades the following spring. Britain's was the bomb assassinating the octogenarian war hero Lord Mountbatten on his fishing boat in the summer of 1979. Austria had its trauma around Christmas time 1975, when "Carlos the Jackal" led a German-Palestinian team into the OPEC headquarters in Vienna, taking eleven Arab oil ministers hostage, representing the bulk of the Western world's oil supplies. Saudi Arabia had a trauma of its own in December 1979, when three hundred devout Arab Moslems, led by professional, impeccably trained guerrillas—trained in the Russian satellite state of South Yemen, according to reliable reports— seized and occupied the holiest of all Islamic mosques in Mecca.

Most countries in the strategic Western crescent under terrorist fire had their trauma sooner or later. Slow to recognize the nature of the threat, they began at last toward the decade's end to close ranks in the face of an inexorably advancing enemy.

Some have suggested that the CIA was egging on the enemy all along. A surprising number of people abroad still think there are no limits to the CIA's capabilities in this regard. I had no access at all to the CIA while gathering material for this book, since its agents were formally forbidden to talk to journalists abroad. I couldn't swear, then, that the CIA had no connection whatever with the planetary wave of terrorism I've described here. But it was certainly not the CIA that ran guerrilla training camps for tens of thousands of terrorists in Cuba, Algeria, Libya, Syria, Lebanon, South Yemen, North Korea, East Germany, Hungary, Czechoslovakia, Bulgaria and the Soviet Union. The CIA could not have provided, and evidently did not, the colossal supplies of weapons employed by the terrorists of four Continents in Fright Decade I, or sanctuaries for their fugitives, or intelligence information for their operatives, or diplomatic cover in the United Nations.

This is not a book of fiction. It deals with facts.

—CS
October 1980

1

1968, WHEN IT BEGAN

"I killed two," the girl said, glancing up at her bulky companion with a small smile of content.

"Quite right; I killed one myself," he replied.

Which of them was Sheikh Yamani, she wanted to know, and he nodded toward the Saudi Arabian oil minister who had just come out from hiding under a desk. They were pleased with the way things were going (though she would be less pleased the next day, when he told her they wouldn't be killing Sheikh Yamani after all. "Fuck," she remarked on that occasion).

They were chatting in the Vienna headquarters of OPEC, the Organization of Petroleum Exporting Countries, where they had come in a mixed team of six to kidnap eleven Arab oil ministers for a firmer Arab commitment to annihilate Israel. The girl was short, slight, smart in a furred gray wool jacket and matching knitted cap pulled down like an absorbed child's to her eyebrows; her Makarov automatic pistol was still warm. She had fired it into the stomach of an Iraqi security guard, and before that into the nape of the neck of an elderly Austrian plainclothesman. "Are you a policeman?" she had asked, and when he said yes, she shot him dead from four feet away, shoveling his body into an elevator, and pressed the Down button.

Her game-name for the day was "Nada." Her companion, suitably dressed as team leader in beret, dark glasses, and belted white raincoat, was "Salem." In real life, she was Gabriele Kröcher-Tiedemann of West Germany, and he was Ilich Ramirez Sanchez of Venezuela, referred to in the press as "Carlos the Jackal." "You know who that is, don't you?" he had asked his assembled OPEC captives with a pardonable hint of swagger. Indeed they did.

The OPEC affair, which looked like a hot story at the time— December 1975—has long since been buried under stories that keep looking hotter. Even the Mecca affair, with its three hundred precision-tooled captors of the world's holiest mosque, is a fading memory. Carlos has never been seen in action again. He could be lying low in Moscow, or hiding out in Baghdad, or living it up in Libya, in the villa he was given after the Vienna operation by his grateful patron, Colonel Muammar Qaddafi, who added a cash bonus of $2 million. Wherever he is, he no longer appears to count. His generation of terrorists is washed up.

Gabriele Kröcher-Tiedemann, who went on to use her Makarov once too often, is in a Swiss jail, where the courts have ordered her to remain until 1993. She is washed up too. So is her ex-husband, Norbert Kröcher, whose plans for the city of Stockholm might have put Vienna in the shade if the Swedish police hadn't caught up with him. The Kröchers, who were small fry when Carlos became The Man on the international scene, are spoken of as second-generation terrorists in West Germany, where third and fourth generations have already overtaken them. Their peculiarly exigent revolution is quick to devour its young.

They are unfailingly replaced. The very considerable defeats inflicted on the world's terrorists in recent years have forced many changes in faces, methods, pressure points. All told, though, there are more of them around than ever. Nothing in history could equal the bands of professional practitioners dispensing violent death in forty-odd countries on four continents today.

Methodically trained, massively armed, immensely rich, and assured of powerful patronage, they move with remarkable confidence across national frontiers from floodlit stage to stage, able at a word to command the planet's riveted attention. A planeful of captive passengers, a kidnapped statesman, an embassy held at gunpoint, a cathedral occupied and barricaded, can bring them money, recognition, immunity, absolution, forcing government after government to its knees. Governments too have learned to use them, as instruments of diplomacy or to wage surrogate wars—employing the power of impotence to expose the impotence of power, as a Western diplomat described the Iranian seizure of the American hostages in Teheran.

In just the past ten years—the decade of the 1970s—the lawful restraints of centuries have fallen away—and not merely, or even mostly, in countries with not much law to speak of. Some with none at all, the most lawless dictatorships on earth, have been left in perfect peace. But hardly a surviving democracy has been spared, from the United States and Canada to Great Britain, West Germany, Italy, Sweden, Holland, Belgium, France, Spain, Portugal, Austria, Switzerland, Greece, Turkey, Japan. More than half of the international terrorist attacks since 1968 have taken place in the industrialized democracies of North America and Western Europe. The most deadly have come in a strategic crescent from the Black Sea to the Atlantic—Turkey, Italy, Spain, Great Britain, Federal Germany—half encircling the European continent. The terrorists are the first to say that they hope someday to close the circle.

There is nothing random in this concentrated assault on the shrinking area of the world still under democratic rule. Not only is it easier and safer to be a terrorist in a free country than it is in a police state, it is ideologically more satisfying. The Italian Red Brigades, who like to think that they speak for many or most of their kind, have made it plain that theirs is a war for the destruction of Western democracy. They have even published a terror timetable.

In their Resolution on Strategic Direction of 1978, Italy and West Germany were singled out respectively as "the weakest and strongest links in the Western democratic chain" and thus as the front-line states. Circumstances permitting—the governments and peoples under siege permitting, that is—the next stage was supposed to be the formation of a Continent-wide "Organization of Communist Combat," striking at the West's "vital centers of multinational imperialism." Then would come the final storming of the imperialist heights: the United States, forever in the gunsights of the worldwide revolutionary left, supreme target in the "long and terrible war" that Ernesto "Ché" Guevara once urged upon his followers.

It was three years before the opening of the terrorist decade when Fidel Castro's companion in arms died in wretched obscurity in the Bolivian Andes. The last of the old-fashioned *guerrilleros,* Guevara was a larger-than-life hero to a generation in revolt, and a romantic failure. His attempt to lead a popular uprising in Bolivia was doomed from the start—he never managed to recruit more than fifteen Bolivians—and nothing else he did came to much after he helped Castro to take Cuba. But his parting advice was sound. "We must above all keep our hatred alive and fan it to paroxysm," he wrote shortly before the end; "hate as a factor of struggle, intransigent hate of the enemy, hate that can push a human being beyond his natural limits and make him a cold, violent, selective, and effective killing-machine." [1]

His successors are proof that it can be done. Gabriele and Norbert Kröcher, and others uncannily like them in Italy's Red Brigades and Front Line, the Turkish People's Liberation Army, Northern Ireland's IRA, Spain's ETA-Militar, the Popular Front for the Liberation of Palestine, are all good haters who have made it across those natural human boundaries. They rarely betray emotion: the Palestinian who kneeled to drink the blood of Jordanian Premier Wasfi el-Tal after gunning him down in Cairo was an anachronism.[2] They do not kill in anger; that is the sixth of seven sins they are expressly warned against in Carlos Marighella's *Mini-Manual for Urban Guerrillas,* the standard terrorist textbook. Nor do they kill on impulse: haste and improvisation are fifth and seventh on Marighella's sin list. They kill as a matter of course, since that is "the urban guerrilla's sole reason for being," his textbook says. What matters is not the identity of their corpse but its impact on their audience; "the purpose of terror is to terrorize," as Lenin once reminded the forgetful. Their use of violence is deliberate and dispassionate, carefully engineered for theatrical effect, and it takes a lot of doing.

Operations like OPEC, the Teheran hostages, the mosque of Mecca, would never even have crossed the minds of Guevara's campfire and muleback militia. The terrorists of the seventies shifted right away from the rural hinterland with its backward, illiterate, and generally hostile peasants—most of whom ran away at the sight of Ché Guevara in Bolivia—preferring the political backdrop and logistic convenience of big cities. They took to shopping on a prodigal scale; traveled in fast cars, yachts, helicopters, jets; and had only to pick up a telephone to flash a message around the globe by satellite television.

IBM electric typewriters, electronic monitoring gear, walkie-talkies, oscilloscopes, high-powered transistors tuned to police frequencies, soundproofed guest rooms for kidnappees (fitted with intercoms and video-television cameras), shoulder-borne ground-to-air heat-seeking missiles that can knock a moving plane out of the sky from six miles away, all became part of their working kit. Intensive courses in weaponry, marksmanship, karate, commando tactics, hijacking, kidnapping, sabotage, explosive devices, forgery, disguise, photographic reconnaissance, intelligence gathering, prisoner interrogation, and psychological warfare completed their preparations.

By now they are mass-produced. The machinery practically runs itself, and anybody who wants to be a terrorist can get to be one. But it wasn't so easy when this fright story began. There is a lot to be learned from inquiring into how so formidable a secret army could have come into being in just ten years.

Those who live in this subterranean world are not given to explaining much. The very density of their prose betrays a hopeless incapacity to communicate by any means save the barrel of a gun. "Terrorism is the most degraded form of language," says a French criminologist, capturing in a phrase their sad dependence on the primitive language of gunspeak. The most knowledgeable among them are rarely caught, or if caught, will rarely talk. The few disposed to talk are likely to get a bullet through the brain or, in Northern Ireland, a hole bored through the kneecap with a Black and Decker drill. The veil of mystery drawn around them is a practical necessity for the hunted men they are. But it is also a part of the act, helping to cast the spell that makes them look ten feet tall.

There are interested parties in all the target countries who would just as soon keep it that way—because they can turn terrorist violence to their political advantage or lack the Olympian detachment to overlook the implications of angering Colonel Qaddafi in Libya, or other Arab oil producers, or wandering Palestinian hit-teams, or the Russians in what remains of détente, SALT II, and Ostpolitik. I heard a number of bland lies in all ten of the countries I visited for this book, from unimpeachable sources: the U.S. State Department's Office to Combat Terrorism, the Bundeskriminalamt in Wiesbaden, the Interior Ministry in Ankara, the Ministry of Police and Justice in Berne. The lies were mostly of the familiar dampening sort meant to talk a reporter out of being a troublemaker and a pest. "You don't really believe this bunk about international terrorism, do you?" President Carter's adviser on terrorism in the National Security Council asked me, before Teheran.

Well, yes: I do.

For a fellow in his position, the president's adviser was as earnestly persuasive as a Sicilian building contractor swearing that there is no such thing as the Mafia. The fact that there is such a thing as an international terrorist circuit, or network, or fraternity—that a multitude of disparate terrorist groups have been helping one another out and getting help from not altogether disinterested outsiders—is hardly classified information anymore. There is enough evidence lying around to pole-ax the reader. It does not prove a closely planned and centrally commanded worldwide conspiracy. But if these terrorist bands may not all be welded, they are linked.

By CIA count—and a more cowardly source would have been hard to find—over 140 terrorist bands from nearly fifty countries or disputed territories were connected in some way one to another by 1976.[3] The number is probably larger now. The tangled lines pass from guerrilla training camps to thefts and shipments of arms, stolen and forged documents, safehouses, safe passage in transit and sanctuary abroad, regional summit meetings, hot-money laundering services, straightforward cash transfers, swapping of cadres, and contract killers borrowed from the criminal underworld. There is no following them all through a deep underground maze. But it is no longer so hard to see where the broader lines begin, and end.

The Terrorists we are talking about are not the right-wing neo-Nazi sort. There are plenty of those scattered across the map, many engaged in an intricate game of thrust and parry with their left-wing antagonists. Their sinister terror underground, largely dormant through the seventies, has evidently made big plans for the eighties, well worth a book on its own. Nevertheless, the past decade belongs to the emerging forces of the radical left, in Africa, Asia, South and North America, Europe, the Middle East. They come from the generation of 1968, an amazing year.

In that single year, the earlier student sit-ins at Berkeley swept like a grassfire from California across the United States and around the globe to the Orient. Columbia University became a specter haunting a shaken nation. Robert Kennedy was assassinated and so was Martin Luther King. Vietnam had its Tet offensive, bringing the antiwar movement in the United States and abroad to its convulsive climax. President Lyndon Johnson sued for peace and renounced a second term. The students of Paris had their May on the barricades, very nearly destroying Charles de Gaulle's Fifth Republic. Federal Germany reached the brink of insurrection when a crazy young rightist shot the New Left student leader Rudi Dutschke in the head, throat, and chest. An exotic young German named Andreas Baader burned down his first department store in Frankfurt.

Uncontrollable rioting swept Tokyo, led by the left-wing extremist Zengakuren, which became the notorious Rengo Sekigun, Japan's Red Army. Wave upon wave of street fighting and rioting broke over Turkey until temporary martial law was imposed in 1970, reimposed for two more years in 1971. A sudden flare of violence erupted in Spain's northern Basque provinces, forcing Generalissimo Franco to proclaim a state of emergency there. Northern Ireland moved to the threshold of civil war, with a Catholic civil-rights march that would eventually bring the IRA Provisionals out, guns blazing. The Czechs threw caution and Stalin to the winds for their brief Prague Spring, cut off by Soviet tanks. In China, Chairman Mao gave a first official sign of sanction to the Red Guards of the Cultural Revolution.

Several other things happened that year, less widely known but full of portent. In Beirut, a Palestinian Christian physician named George Habash exported terrorism from the Middle East to Europe for the first time, sending his commandos to hijack an El Al plane in Rome. Also in Rome, an Italian friend of his named Giangiacomo Feltrinelli, millionaire publisher and world traveler, issued Europe's first open call for armed guerrilla warfare. In Rio de Janeiro, an expert on that subject named Carlos Marighella, son of an Italian father and black Brazilian mother, finished the text of his *Mini-Manual* and sent it off to the printers. In Havana, Fidel Castro, the guerrilla leader who had shown the world what a small but inflexibly resolute armed band could do, lost the last of his independence. First the Russians cut off shipments of oil and vital industrial supplies until Castro gave in to their wishes. Then they installed five thousand Soviet technicians to oversee the Cuban economy and KGB Colonel Viktor Simenov to supervise the Cuban intelligence service, DGI.

Starting in 1968, the news deriving from these developments could be transmitted by satellite television.

There is no simple way to sum up this remarkable string of events. All the same, 1968 was clearly the year when a generation born after the last world war declared its own war on society, with a brief but stunning show of strength. For a while, the whole planet seemed to be lurching leftward toward a revolution none too well defined but momentarily expected. Then, almost as abruptly as it began, the dramatic interlude of mutual discovery and messianic revelation was over. Nine out of ten who went through the experience have long since put it behind them. But those with a true vocation for violence had found each other while it lasted, and others found them.

It doesn't take much dabbling in the political occult to guess that the radical left would have had to be infiltrated right around then, by the KGB, CIA, British MI 6, French SDECE, German BND, and so on. The colossal force released by a bunch of beatnik kids once dismissed as a lunatic fringe knocked the breath out of the world's various Establishments. Not only did it drive President Johnson out of the White House and de Gaulle out of the Elysée Palace, but it turned the Vietcong's military defeat after the Tet offensive into a political conquest that ended the Vietnam War. Certainly it was a force to be watched; possibly it could be harnessed. Every country blasted by that 1968 gale must have felt a need to know. Soviet Russia, caught by a staggering gust in Prague, certainly did. Indeed, the Russians seemed to feel more of a need than others.

There is strong evidence of a significant change in the Russians' unofficial foreign policy after 1968. Officially, they continued to show fastidious contempt for a gang of disorderly infantile leftists threatening the world's carefully balanced stability, not to mention the peace of mind of the world's orthodox Communist Parties. Unofficially, however, the Kremlin took an avuncular interest in terrorist "adventurers" of every alarming shade. Nothing was too good for armed "national liberation movements," however improbable in geography or politics, even if dominated by visceral anti-Stalinists—or worse, by Trotskyites, long regarded in conformist Communist circles as ritually impure if not certifiably insane. Practically every other sort of armed guerrilla group bent on destroying the vital centers of multinational imperialism has been able since then to count on a discreetly sympathetic ear in Moscow.

The policy was consecrated in 1971 with an article in *Kommunist* by Boris Ponomariev, the Kremlin's director for international Communist affairs.[4] He conceded that the New Left was "neither ideologically nor organizationally homogeneous," embracing as it did "various types of adventuristic elements, including Maoists and Trotskyites." Its members were "easily affected by revolutionary phraseology" and "clearly contaminated by anti-Communist prejudices." Nevertheless, their "overall anti-imperialistic direction is obvious." To neglect them, therefore, would be to "weaken the anti-imperialist struggle . . . and the prospects for a united front against monopolistic capitalism." He closed with a brisk reminder: "The

Communists always remain the party of socialist revolution, a party which never tolerates the capitalist order and is always ready to head the struggle for the total political power of the working-class."

The prospects looked especially good from Ponomariev's standpoint because luck, or foresight, had guided the Russians' hand well before 1968 broke upon them. During the Prague Spring of that same portentous year, General Jan Sejna of Czechoslovakia defected to the United States, thoughtfully taking along documents accumulated over his twenty years as military counselor to the Central Committee of the Czechoslovak Communist Party. He revealed, proof in hand, that as early as 1964 the Soviet Union's Politburo had decided to increase spending in the field of terrorism abroad by one thousand percent.[5] The secret services of all the Communist bloc countries were involved in recruiting spies and infiltrating the world's nascent left-wing terrorist movements; special guerrilla training schools had been set up in Czechoslovakia, East Germany, and Cuba for "selected terrorists from all over the world."

Two years later—in January 1966—a Tricontinental Conference opened in Havana, attended by 513 delegates representing eighty-three groups from the Third World. The like of it had never been seen since the Bolshevik Revolution of 1917, and the world would never be the same. Its General Declaration reminded proletarians everywhere of the need for close cohesion between the "Socialist countries" (the Soviet kind) and "national liberation movements," providentially including "democratic workers' and students' movements" in capitalist Europe and North America. Its purpose was to devise "a global revolutionary strategy to counter the global strategy of American imperialism." [6]

The conference demanded more than just a Vietnam apiece for each continent. The list of candidates for armed liberation struggles included the former Belgian Congo, the Portuguese colonies of Angola and Mozambique, Rhodesia, South Africa, South-West Africa, southern Arabia (the Yemens), Palestine, Laos, Cambodia, South Korea, the Dominican Republic, Venezuela, Guatemala, Peru, Colombia, Cyprus, Panama, and the Indonesian province of northern Kalimantan.

The gathering ended with an African, Asian, and Latin

American Solidarity Organization. Its permanent secretariat was based in Havana. Its secretary-general, Osmany Cienfuegos Goriaran, was a long-standing Moscow hard-liner on the Central Committee of the Cuban Communist Party.

Some saw the Tricontinental simply as a mirror of Castro's desire to export his kind of revolution to the Third World. Sovietologists detected a deep strategic move by the Kremlin to counter Red China's successful penetration in Africa and Asia. Western diplomats said it was in any case the beginning of a massive thrust against Western capitalism generally and the United States in particular, through formation of a Guerrilla International. Ten months later, in fact, a whole new chain of training camps for guerrilla fighters on four continents—Europe along with the other three—opened in Cuba under the supervision of Soviet KGB Colonel Vadim Kotchergine.[7]

All the world's emerging terrorist bands in the 1970s were indebted to the Cubans and their Russian patrons for that honeycomb of camps around Havana. None could have started without rudimentary training, and those who didn't train in Cuba were trained by others who did. The Palestinians, soon to become a second great magnetic pole for apprentice terrorists, began sending their own apprentices to Cuba in 1966; Cuban instructors have taught in Middle East *fedayeen* camps since the early seventies. The third pole closing the triangle was Soviet Russia itself, arming and training Palestinians on its own territory and turning out other professional terrorists by the thousands—European, South and North American, African, Asian—inside Russia or in the satellite states of Czechoslovakia, East Germany, Hungary, Bulgaria, North Korea, South Yemen.

Over the seventies, the line of camps reached down into Africa. Many thousand more rookies from the same First, Second, and Third Worlds trained in liberated Angola and Mozambique, Russia's new Communist client-states; in Algeria, for the Palestinian cause and with Libyan money; in Libya itself, in the Palestinians' name and with several billion dollars worth of Soviet armament. Cubans taught in most of these camps, East Germans in many, North Koreans in some. It was all in the family. (Red China, an alternate magnet in the early years, dropped out after the Gang of Four fell from grace.)

A lot more indispensable assistance was forthcoming over

that decade, from one or another part of that triangle. Weapons turned up when and where they were needed, traveling protected routes through Eastern Europe or carried by Arab diplomatic pouch; promising terrorists got more advanced training; hit-men were assured of a fast getaway and privileged sanctuary. The more help the terrorists received the more advanced their technology became, and the more advanced the technology the more help they needed. By the decade's close, there was not much going on at the handicraft level.

Not all those who took the Cubans and Russians up on their aid offer were for sale, or even for rent. Many have proved to be a headache to their former benefactors. Others never cared where the help was coming from and never went anywhere to get it, content to have the necessary skills passed on to them. Their value to the Soviet Union has been their capacity to disrupt the West in whatever way they might see fit, always stopping short at the outermost borders of the Soviet empire.

They made an incredible assortment by the end of the 1970s: ethnic and religious nationalists and separatists, anti-colonial patriots and anti-racists, Sardinian bandits and Mafia thugs, anarchists, Trotskyites, Maoists, unregenerate Stalinists and otherwise unclassified Marxist-Leninists. No single label could be pinned on them; but they had all come to see themselves as elite battalions in a worldwide Army of Communist Combat.

They have entered the 1980s still fighting for a Communist society they have yet to define. Beyond alternately reviling and soliciting the aid of orthodox Communist Parties, they have scarcely hinted at the kind of communism they are after. They may not even know, and don't appear to care. Nowhere in their voluminous ideological tracts does the subject get more than a negligent nod in passing. In sixty pages of their famous Resolution on Strategic Direction, the Red Brigades devoted four lines to the question.

Their immediate purpose, wherever they are, has been to dismantle whatever society they are in. The aim has a certain stripped-down simplicity, but the choice of targets doesn't, quite. They have never tried to dismantle a society under Soviet sponsorship. They haven't lifted a finger against some of the most appalling tyrannies on record, either. Uganda under the maniac rule of Idi Amin did not make their list. (In fact, Palestinian guerrillas volunteered to act as his personal bodyguard.) [8] Nor did the Central African Empire under the cannibal reign of Emperor Bokassa (unseated not by the worldwide revolutionary left, but by the imperialist French).

Yet the nearly empty desert sultanate of Oman in the Persian Gulf has been high on their list, and so has a stretch of Saharan sand staked out by the Polisario guerrillas, demanding statehood for a population of eighty thousand—these two side by side with the most sophisticated industrial societies on earth.

These terrorists make no political, economic, social, or cultural distinctions between, say, the sultan of Oman and the queen of England or Polisario's patch of the Sahara and the Federal German Republic. Nor do they concede a grade of difference between Germany's opulent consumers and a Turkish population afflicted by pathological inflation, unemployment, and slums. All are lumped together in a single Multinational Imperialist State, to be told apart only by the roles assigned to them. (For the Red Brigades, Italy is "the garbage pail of Europe.") Germans and Turks, the Dhofar tribesmen of Oman, and Polisario guerrillas train in the same camps, carry the same Makarov and Kalashnikov weapons, pursue the same stated objectives. The idea that all of them are emanations of the same sick society is popular in some progressive quarters, but it is not easy to see why.

More often than not, these Armed Parties are surprisingly small and unrepresentative of the proletariat they claim to speak for. The Symbionese Liberation Army in California had twelve members when it kidnapped Patty Hearst, providing one of the more gripping TV thrillers of our day; its commanding general was an ex-stoolie on the Los Angeles police payroll, and his chief lieutenants were college girls with emotional problems.[9] The German Red Army Fraction, offspring of the Baader-Meinhof Gang, had less than a hundred hard-core activists when it abducted and murdered industrialist Hanns-Martin Schleyer in 1977, bringing a nation of sixty million to a paralyzed standstill. The Fraction's sole working-class member willingly got himself arrested to be quit of it long before then. Even the Tupamaros of Uruguay had only three thousand members, a tenth of one percent of the population, when they successfully demolished Latin America's freest democratic republic.

The Tupamaros, who invented the original model for what has become the planetary fashion in urban guerrilla warfare, make a wonderfully instructive case.

Having terrorized their nation straight into a military dictatorship in 1972, they are widely accepted abroad now as freedom fighters opposing a military dictatorship. This seems hard on the authentic kind. The world is full of places in need of freedom. Three-quarters of the human race lives under colonial or racist rule, or capitalist or Soviet imperialist domination, or in indigenous police states embracing much of Latin America and nearly all of Africa, or in the Soviet-style real Socialist states. Many have no freedom fighters around, whereas others have regrettably few. Most of us may think we would know one if we saw one, but the case of Uruguay shows how far we can go wrong.

Named after Inca Prince Tupac Amaru, who fought Spanish rule in the eighteenth century, the Tupamaros fought the good fight in Uruguay for only a few stirring years of the twentieth. Their Movimiento de Liberación Nacional (MLN) was founded in 1963, in a country mercifully free of Latin America's prevailing misery and rankling injustice. A minuscule parliamentary republic wedged between turbulent giants—Brazil to the north, Argentina to the south—it was fiercely proud of its liberty and social enlightenment. If Uruguayans had their share of political corruption and a devastating plague of inflation, nine out of ten were literate; their health care was the best in Latin America, their infant mortality the lowest, their social insurance system the oldest in existence outside of Sweden; and practically the whole working class belonged to trade unions.

The Tupamaros never got far in the unions, though not for want of trying. Their ranks consisted of teachers, lawyers, doctors, dentists, accountants, bankers, architects, engineers, a model, a radio announcer, and an actress.[10] They were radical Marxists, committed to profound revolutionary change, who unmistakably started out with fine intentions. They lived in a politically worldly society open to the winds of change and given to voting social-democratically left. Like middle-class revolutionaries everywhere, they were plainly moved by a strong sense of social guilt and an uplifting political vision. Even later, when they started to kill, they wept.

But that didn't happen for five or six years. Until then, the Tupamaros robbed from the rich to give to the poor. They would hijack a truck bound for some supermarket and hand out the free food in humble districts, or stick up a gambling casino for a quarter of a million dollars and parcel out the boodle to the workers, or kidnap a prominent citizen for an overnight stay, just to make a point. Not until 1969 did their leader, Raúl Sendic, hint that the age of Robin Hood was over. "We now have three hundred kilometers of streets and avenues at our disposal to organize guerrilla warfare," he said, whereupon he did.

It took just two years, starting in 1970. The Tupamaros bombed, burned, robbed, kidnapped, and killed with a dazzling display of nerve, skill, discipline, inventiveness, and bravado. They took off with verve by murdering Dan Mitrione, U.S. adviser to the Uruguayan police force. There followed the abduction of a Brazilian diplomat, an American cultural adviser, and the British ambassador, Sir Geoffrey Jackson, confined to a cage six feet long by two feet wide for the next eight months. By 1971, they held the all-time record for multiple and cumulative diplomatic kidnappings.[11]

In three hundred other recorded assaults over those two years, the Tupamaros invaded and occupied airstrips, police stations, telephone exchanges, and radio broadcasting studios; kidnapped for huge ransoms as well as political display; blew up cars, shops, private homes, public buildings; and murdered with increasing clarity of intent. From Dan Mitrione, their selected victims advanced in quick succession to the head of internal security for Punta Carretas prison, a former undersecretary of the interior, two high-ranking police officers, a naval captain—all in the armed forces and engaged in counter-insurgency operations. They couldn't have planned a better way to unnerve a frightened left-wing government so that it would ask the army in.

The army did come in. Civil rights were suspended in Uruguay in the summer of 1970 and again the following January. Midway through 1972, the National Assembly proclaimed a "state of internal war," in effect turning power over to the armed forces. They had massive popular support by then. Four-fifths of the electorate had voted against the Communist Party's Frente Amplio, backed by the Tupamaros, in Uruguay's last free election, in November 1971.[12] By that winter, tens of thousands were demonstrating in the streets against the spreading terror. The army thereupon did what armies usually do in such situations; its "energetic and professional interrogation of prisoners," to use its own words, conveys the nightmare idea. But—or and—it got results. At the close of 1972, 2,600 Tupamaros (real or alleged) were in prison; another 40 were dead; hundreds had fled the country; and Raúl Sendic, though altered by plastic surgery to elude detection, had been captured in a shootout with the police. It was all over.

In a matter of months, the army had uncovered an extraordinary underground apparatus. Scores of safe-houses and military bases were found, air-conditioned, stocked with food, books, and television, and fitted with human cages, or "people's prisons." Other facilities included an electronics laboratory, a forgery factory, a hospital with operating table and X-ray equipment, a foundry with machinery to make grenades, and a printing press for counterfeit bills. Impounded documents showed running expenses of $138,000 a month, nearly $2 million a year. Captured equipment and supplies could have maintained a combat army of four thousand.

The reward for this conspicuous expenditure of money and talent was a decree by Uruguay's new military rulers, depriving all members of all traditional parties of their political rights for the next fifteen years.

The Tupamaros, though resourceful, did not dream it all up out of nowhere. They had been sending their people to Havana for training since 1968, after Raúl Sendic met personally with

Fidel Castro to arrange it—two years before he stopped playing Robin Hood.[13] Whatever they missed in the Havana camps could be found in the all-purpose *Mini-Manual* published in 1969 by Carlos Marighella. An intimate of Castro's and assiduous visitor to Cuba, Marighella was an apparatchik in Brazil's pro-Moscow Communist Party for forty years.

In forty-eight densely packed pages, the *Mini-Manual* says it all. It explains why cities are better than rural areas for guerrilla operations, and how to behave there: no "foreign airs" and "normal" occupations when possible. It suggests how to drill in urban courtyards; blow up bridges and railroad tracks; raise money by kidnap ransoms and bank "expropriations" attacking "the nervous system of capitalism"; plan the "physical liquidation" of ranking army officers and policemen; deal with spies and informers, to be summarily executed, preferably by "a single sniper, patiently, alone and unknown, operating in absolute secrecy and cold blood."

It stresses the importance of learning to drive a car, pilot a plane, sail a boat, be a mechanic and radio technician, keep physically fit, master photography and chemistry, acquire "a perfect knowledge of calligraphy" to forge documents; to be a practical nurse, amateur pharmacist, and field medic "with some notion of surgery." It goes into careful detail about choices of weapons, and the need to "shoot first," at point-blank range if possible: "shooting and aiming are to the urban guerrilla what air and water are to human beings." [14]

It is also a clinical study of the step-by-step tactics in the strategy of terror whereby the Tupamaros deliberately destroyed democracy in their country.

First, wrote Marighella, the urban guerrilla must use revolutionary violence to identify with popular causes, and so win a popular base. Then:

> the government has no alternative except to intensify repression. The police roundups, house searches, arrests of innocent people, make life in the city unbearable. The general sentiment is that the government is unjust, incapable of solving problems, and resorts purely and simply to the physical liquidation of its opponents. The

political situation is transformed into a military situation, in which the militarists appear more and more responsible for errors and violence. When pacifiers and right-wing opportunists see the militarists on the brink of the abyss, they join hands and beg the hangmen for elections and other tripe designed to fool the masses.

Rejecting the "so-called political solution," the urban guerrilla must become more aggressive and violent, resorting without letup to sabotage, terrorism, expropriations, assaults, kidnappings and executions, *heightening the disastrous situation in which the government must act.* [Italics mine.]

These carefully articulated steps, concludes Marighella, are bound to end with "the uncontrollable expansion of urban rebellion."

The Tupamaros were the first outside Marighella's native Brazil to apply his words literally. By then, Marighella was dead. Killed in a police ambush soon after his *Mini-Manual* came out, he had ended up as a striking example of the flaws in his own logic. By resorting without letup to sabotage, terrorism, expropriations, assaults, kidnappings, and executions, Marighella did not achieve the uncontrollable expansion of his urban rebellion in Brazil. He never got past the stage of provoking the militarists into intensified repression, whereby they have retained power ever since.

Some might consider this a failure, but not Marighella's disciples. For terrorists of whatever country, rich or poor, backward or enlightened, freely governed or despotically ruled, his *Mini-Manual* continues to be revolutionary scripture. Translated into a score of languages, found in the cars, pockets, hideouts of celebrated terrorists from Stockholm to Beirut to Tokyo, it is their strategic blueprint. Short of actually achieving the Communist revolution—something which, they generally calculate, could take thirty or forty years—his strategy of inviting intensified repression and a right-wing military takeover is unmistakably their idea of the best interim solution.

The Tupamaros, pioneers in this field, are homeless exiles now. Many have taken refuge in Cuba, and hundreds more are scattered abroad. Their fugitive leaders travel freely around the free world, honored guests of a thousand committees, commissions, boards, parties, committed to the defense of political decency. Their imprisoned fellow Tupamaros, two thousand or more still in maximum-security detention, are on all the best lists as victims of Yankee imperialism. Their posters of protest may be seen on walls throughout Europe.

Their influence on the growth of worldwide terrorism has been enormous. The first Germans to have a go at it in 1969 called themselves the Tupamaros of West Berlin. The first patron of Continent-wide terror, the itinerant Italian millionaire Giangiacomo Feltrinelli, went to Montevideo in 1971 to watch them at work. The U.S. Weathermen's Bernardine Dohrn happily announced her group's "adaptation to the Tupamaros' classic guerrilla strategy" in 1970. If anything, their political charm has grown with defeat.

They are on intimate terms with the ETA-Milis in Spain, the IRA Provisionals, the German and Italian undergrounds, the whole army of Palestinian terrorist formations. To follow them from Montevideo to Buenos Aires and Havana, and on to Paris, Rome, Berlin, Madrid, Stockholm, and Beirut is to draw one of the broader lines on the global terrorist map; and I will follow it in this book.

Crisscrossing so many other lines, it will give us repeated glimpses of young urban guerrillas who started out with selfless and generous intent, only to be corrupted—by the power they discover in the mouth of a gun, or by outsiders with something less selfless in mind, or by growing estrangement from the society they wanted to improve. Often they are rejected by an overwhelming majority of their countrymen, reduced to a minority so absurdly small that tragedy almost becomes black comedy. Their response is to kill with increasing ferocity—to punish the profane, and because nothing else is left for them to do. From killing for a cause, they slip into killing for their vested interests. Nobody's freedom but their own inspires them.

The murderous pace they have set has brought a change incomparably for the worse. If there was some quality of intellectual quest, or revolutionary conscience, or moral scruple, or even a touch of glamour in the first terrorist generation—Ulrike

Meinhof of the German Red Army Fraction, now dead; Renato Curcio of the Red Brigades, jailed until the twenty-first century—it is rarely to be found now. The latest recruits are not just younger—though, at fourteen or fifteen, in Belfast, Bilbao, or Istanbul, some are pretty young. They are less encumbered with political memories, bored by the past, uninterested in the niceties of theory, more and more brutalized after ten years of mounting planetary violence, struck by the opportunities beamed nightly into their living rooms by satellite television, fascinated by the improved machinery for killing at their command and the power to be had from it. Theirs is a high-technology, high-risk generation.

2

FELTRINELLI, THE PATRON

On March 15, 1972, just as Italians were settling down for the long weeks of rhetoric leading to the national elections that May, their morning papers reported the discovery of a burned and mutilated body beneath a high-tension pylon in Segrate, on the bleak northern outskirts of Milan. The pylon, spattered with blood and torn flesh, was taped with forty-three sticks of dynamite. Another stick seemed to have blown up in the man's hands, hurling him heavily to the ground. The force of the explosion had flung one of his legs ten yards away, and bits of bone as far as fifty yards. A peasant had stumbled on the body, led by the bark of his mongrel dog, Twist.

The death of "Vincenzo Maggioni," according to clumsily forged papers on the corpse, did not cause much of a stir. Bombings and explosions of this sort were averaging about one a day in Italy, and accidents happen. Twenty-four hours later, however, the nation was stunned to learn that the dead man had been identified as Giangiacomo Feltrinelli. Publisher of the renowned *Dr. Zhivago* and *The Leopard,* scion of an immensely rich Milanese family, and one of Europe's wealthiest men himself, Feltrinelli was a name to be reckoned with.

Within hours, the machinery of state was in position. Roadblocks went up all across the north. Twelve thousand policemen and carabinieri combed the countryside, raiding the homes and hideouts of right-wing and left-wing extremists in Milan, Turin, Genoa, and Rome. Dozens were picked up for questioning. Sinister coded documents, marked terrorist maps, and huge caches of arms—several thousand machine guns, three tons of explosives, half a million Molotov cocktails—turned up in the police dragnet. For seven consecutive weeks, until election day, vigorous champions of democratic law and order saw to it that the case made daily front-page headlines. Alive, Feltrinelli had done his obsessive best to destroy the Establishment. Dead, he assured its victory in a critical election. In effect, he died for his country. How he would have hated the epitaph!

The Italians were sure they would never find out how it happened. "No crime involving political power in Italy can touch the shores of truth," said the noted Sicilian novelist Leonardo Sciascia; impenetrable fog shrouded this one. Nevertheless everybody who was anybody among the Italian version of the radical chic—writers, academics, journalists, lawyers, politicians, the well-heeled middle-class keepers of *Milano-bene*'s intellectual salons—took it for granted that the CIA, or the Italian secret service, or some right-wing cabal, or all three, had done him in.

It was said that he was killed somewhere else and dumped at the scene, or else set up for an ambush. The Communists' daily *L'Unità* spoke of "dramatic suspicions" and likely "Fascist infiltration" of the "radicaloid left." The dissident Communists' *Manifesto* hinted at "the most murky aspects" of a political structure dominated by "the American power system." Italy's leading author, Alberto Moravia, asked, "What is provocation? For the left, it is a form of action that seems revolutionary but is in reality meant to justify repressive measures." A lengthy list of intellectual luminaries signed a letter to the Socialist weekly *L'Espresso* saying flatly that this was "a monstrous assassination" with "International Reaction behind it." [1] "What proof do I have?" demanded columnist Camilla Cederna, among the signers. "But what does that matter? The proof will come along later." [2]

Proof of a somewhat different nature did come along, much later. At the time, however, there was at least no mistaking Feltrinelli's intentions. He had driven to Segrate fully conscious, undrugged, and climbed twelve feet up the pylon, as his fingerprints and bloodstains showed. Not only did he plainly mean to blow it up—that would have been just the beginning.

At San Vito di Gaggiano, on the other side of Milan, police found another high-tension pylon taped with the same dynamite (a product called Dynamon), unexploded only because of a fluke in the battery-wired timer. In the Volkswagen Camper that Feltrinelli had driven to Segrate were maps of northern Italy marked with crosses and arrows at the sites of other power pylons, bridges, airports, military barracks. Five of his safehouses were discovered around Milan's working-class districts, containing an arsenal of weapons and ammunition, more dynamite, forged passports, an exact copy of the carabinieri's nationwide communications system, coded correspondence, and a long letter to an unknown "Saetta" annotated in Feltrinelli's hand, proposing a joint high command for an underground Army of National Liberation.

Not long afterward, police made a spectacular predawn raid on two more hideouts. One was yet another arsenal, with enough weapons for a small army. In the second was Feltrinelli's authentic passport—he had five fakes as well—along with hundreds of stolen identity cards; four radio receivers tuned to police wavelengths; assorted documents in Chinese; a thick file on candidates for kidnapping in political, industrial, and financial circles; and, below a trapdoor, a six-by-nine-foot "people's prison," stoutly built, padded and soundproofed, fitted with hidden microphones, a magic-eye peephole and handcuffs. The arrest of several people turning up with keys revealed that these last two hideouts belonged to a group barely more than a year old and as yet almost unknown: the Red Brigades, they called themselves.

The revelations that followed were a clue begging to be noticed, pointing to what was in store for all Western Europe. But scarcely anybody would have believed it at the time.

In Italy, in 1972, it was a hardy soul who would venture to suggest that terrorist violence could come from anywhere but the neo-Fascist right. The kneecappings, kidnappings, and killings shortly to bring the Red Brigades world fame had not yet begun. The only violence attracting attention—a succession of bloody bombings starting in 1969—was commonly believed to have been mounted artfully by the far right to put the blame on the far left so as to shift public opinion rightward. Predictably, in a country justifiably suspicious of the far right, this "strategy of tension" was if anything shifting public opinion leftward. Not until Feltrinelli died did credible evidence come to light suggesting that all wasn't so well on the left either.

Leftward of the country's known ultra-left fringe, the evidence showed, was an eerie political underworld where ex–Communist Party Communists, anarchists, Maoists, Trotskyites, and Marxist-Leninists of every other description commingled in a cult of terror with Fascists and former Fascists, lumpen proletarians, and common crooks. There seemed to be no end of them: the Red Brigades in Milan, the XXII October Band in Genoa, the XXII March anarchist circle in Rome, Proletarian Justice in Padua, the FARO-ML (Workers' Revolutionary Action Front, Marxist-Leninist) in Turin and Rome. The busiest and noisiest was the Proletarian Action Group (GAP), preparing for "armed struggle against the bosses . . . and Fascist pigs." [3]

Implanted in Milan, Turin, Trento, and Genoa, GAP's members were armed to the teeth, kept in trim by a doctor-comrade prescribing a spartan diet and long, brisk walks; trained in remote Apennine camps by ex-partisans and German instructors using Carlos Marighella's *Mini-Manual*; and committed to bombing, arson, dynamite, robbery, kidnapping, and killing for atonement or simply as an instructive exercise. That was Feltrinelli's group.

Nobody had dreamed he might have a group of his own, until the semiclandestine Workers' Power (Potere Operaio, more familiarly Potop) announced it. Ten days after he died, its newspaper (also called *Potere Operaio*, and subsidized by Feltrinelli, it turned out) declared proudly that he really had betrayed his class. He was "Osvaldo," a "militant Communist" with the rank of column commander in GAP, to whose needs he had adapted himself "as skin to flesh." "A REVOLUTIONARY HAS FALLEN IN BATTLE," ran *Potop*'s black headline. It was the only radical voice in Italy to say so, then and for a long while to come.[4]

Seven years later, when spreading terrorist warfare would bring Italy to the verge of collapse, chastened democrats would regret the blind eye a whole nation had turned at the time. "Within a few hours of Feltrinelli's death, the democratic-progressive intelligentsia and the entire left began a complete operation to remove the facts, retarding our consciousness of reality," wrote the democratic-progressive *L'Espresso* in 1979. "In those years, we journalists understood nothing of the armed left," added the popular Socialist columnist Giorgio Bocca. "When those incredible safe-houses of GAP were turned up with all those guns, we smiled. Instead, that is just how it was: the safe-houses were true, the guns also, and so was Giangi Feltrinelli's tragic game."

To the day he died, Feltrinelli had never persuaded his friends and countrymen to take him seriously as a professional revolutionary. Ardent, yes. The heat of his devotion to the cause had sent many a pulse racing in elegant drawing rooms up and down the Continent, and brought fellow class-traitors from all Europe to his funeral in their Bentleys. Despite spectacularly successful books like *Dr. Zhivago,* his publishing house was forever in the red, because he persisted in printing so many unsalable radical tracts.

He was the first to publish Marighella's *Mini-Manual* in Italian and the first in Italy to print a simple diagram showing how to manufacture a Molotov cocktail. He had long been a sugar daddy of far-left fringe groups, who treated him as sugar daddies are customarily treated. He revered Fidel Castro and Ché Guevara, was given to slogans like "In Every Corner of Italy, a Vietnam!" and, toward the last, had adopted the Uruguayan Tupamaros' style of military dress. That, with his earnestly bespectacled gaze and luxuriantly bushy mustache, was all he needed to become a cartoon image. To the average Italian, he was a slightly nutty left-wing millionaire, nothing more.

Yet addled as he was—and he was—Feltrinelli could afford to live out his fantasies with such extravagant abandon that a good part of them came true. The fortune he squandered could never buy him the place he coveted in history; no amount of money could have made a Fidel Castro out of him. He slipped into history as Tolstoy might have put him there: an otherwise forgettable man who, with his wealth and delusions, at the right moment and in the right setting, could, unknowingly, affect the course of great events.

And that is what he did. A figure to be mocked and a "cow to be milked," as an ungenerous comrade remarked, he was nevertheless the first to put together a fully operational terrorist network in Europe, the first to get it moving across national frontiers, the first to set the scene and provide the props for the glittering cast of international killers soon to burst upon the worldwide stage.

He could hardly have seemed more improbable for the part. The "Giangi" known to his family and friends was no intrepid warrior. Born to one of the nation's great families and endowed with a bottomless bank account, condemned to a frozen childhood under a succession of Teutonic governesses and his mother's wintry eye, sexually impotent, intelligent but untalented, evidently driven by social guilt and God knows what private furies besides, he was, says Leonardo Sciascia, "very ingenuous, very discontinuous, very disarmed."

From his birth in 1926, he grew up in ceremonial solitude. The Feltrinellis, with their huge stands of timber in Eastern Europe, vast cattle ranches in Brazil, banking, real estate, and industrial holdings, lived in style. The writer Luigi Barzini, Jr., married for some years to Giangi's widowed mother, Giannalisa, has described his own uneasiness in "a grand house full of servants, regulated and staffed like a small court. . . .

"In the early years of his life, Giangi was always isolated from others of his own age like a prince of the blood royal in olden times," recalled Barzini in *Encounter* after Segrate.[5] "It was I who sent him to a state school for the first time, in Milan, plunging him among boys of every class and cultural level. He caught colds the whole time. . . .

"From his lonely and harshly disciplined childhood, he inherited a curious incapacity to tolerate any form of control, to distinguish between people or behave as if others were his equals. He would be deferential with superiors and arrogant with inferiors, was seldom courteous and matter-of-fact with his peers. He ended by preferring always the company of the illiterate, the fanatic, and those who were in some way dependent upon him."

While still in his teens, continued Barzini, "Giangi was an ardent fascist. He wore the uniform of a mounted *avanguardista*, and papered the house with posters singing the *Duce*'s praises. If he had caught me listening to foreign broadcasts, I'm sure he would have denounced me without a qualm; and so his mother and I used to lock ourselves into a small study when the broadcasts began." Then, "a gardener converted him to the Revolution and he embraced his new faith with the same blind fanaticism. . . . What the gardener taught him was surely not Marxism and Leninism but a utopian socialist enthusiasm which, when the revolutionary situation ripened, was to prepare for the great bloodletting: political purges and quick killings similar to those Giangi had approved and dreamed of earlier when he wore his black shirt. It was hard for me, who believed in reason, to cope with this kind of romantic apocalypse."

No layman could say how big a part emotional deformities played in drawing Feltrinelli toward political violence, whether Black or Red. His troubles in that connection were all too plain. Fatherless and oppressively mothered, unbearably lonely and starved for affection, he was also born with a shriveled penis. Not for all the Feltrinelli money could he purchase the normal sexual pleasures enjoyed, say, by his stepfather or the gardener. He ran through four wives in a rising frenzy of frustration: a stern proletarian named Bianca delle Nogare, a ripe young Communist named Alessandra de Stefani, the attractive German radical Inge Schoental (who bore his only son and still runs his publishing house), and a much lighter-headed German cover girl named Sibilla Melega. The first two divorced him for nonconsummation of the marriage. The other two understandably don't discuss the problem. But his sex life would be loudly revealed when he turned up a phonograph to recordings of gunfire and martial music.

Still, his politics weren't necessarily just a matter of neurotic stress. "Only later did I understand why a boy like Giangi could gravitate to an extreme leftwing proletarian party immediately after the war," wrote Barzini. "He was not alone. There were many others. A few had possibly made a conscious choice; some were finding explanations and consolations for the collapse of their youthful dreams of an Italian victory; others were in revolt against the suffocating Buddenbrooks atmosphere of their families, frightened of the name they bore and the terrible burdens of wealth. . . ."

Dissuaded by his stepfather, the still teen-age Giangi did not join up with the partisans when the Allied Armies advanced up the peninsula in 1944. But he did volunteer for the Italian Liberation Army, and fought with honor.

By all accounts save one, he then went on to join the Socialist Party in 1946 and switched to the Communist Party in 1948. But according to the paper he financed, *Potere Operaio*, he had in fact been working for the Communist underground since 1942, joining the Socialist Party "as an agent of the Communist Party's secret service." [6] This illuminating detail offered more than merely a glimpse into Feltrinelli's early conspiratorial bent. It also showed when and how he met up with his lifelong friend, a very particular Communist named Pietro Secchia.

A leader of the partisan Resistance, Secchia ran the Communists' entire "parallel" apparatus after the war, including a secret intelligence service and military force—in effect, an Armed Party within the Party. He would send his millionaire friend on several clandestine missions abroad. As early as 1950, an Italian police circular warned that Feltrinelli was heading for Prague with "important documents dealing with military espionage." [7]

As a Communist Party member, paying assessed dues of $200,000 a year and driving around in a baby-blue Cadillac, Feltrinelli was inevitably an exotic object of attention. He was asked to handle a number of the Party's business affairs, which he was always good at. He was also steered tactfully toward setting up the foundation bearing his name—Europe's best documentation center on working-class movements—and, strategically, into the publishing trade.

He was not the most congenial of publishers, tending to treat writers with arrogance or contempt. (The brilliant novelist Giorgio Bassani, an editor at the publishing house, was dismissed "like an unsatisfactory footman," wrote Barzini, after Feltrinelli forced open his desk drawers and read his private letters.) Nevertheless, he was a bold newcomer in the field who, by throwing his doors open to new writers of the left, soon cut a swath at Europe's annual Frankfurt Book Fair. In 1957, he brought out *Dr. Zhivago,* after going to Moscow personally to get the rights from author Boris Pasternak. It was a literary sensation, and it annoyed the Russians sufficiently to terminate Feltrinelli's orthodox Communist career. He resigned from the Party in a blaze of publicity, telling the *Herald Tribune*'s Ralph Chapman: "The Italian Communist Party has disappointed me."

But he hadn't wasted his time. Guided by his patron and counselor Pietro Secchia, he had rapidly found his way through the Party maze to a clandestine Communist band calling itself the Volante Rosso, or Flying Red Squad. Not to be confused with the Party's own secret armed militia, which Secchia was supposed to keep in reserve for emergencies, the Volante Rosso was made up of former partisan fighters who refused to accept the Party's postwar collaboration with a capitalist state. From 1945 to 1949, they fought a struggle within the Party, against its leaders' constitutional illusions. From killing off ex-fascist higher-ups and big landowners, they spread out to vicious intimidation in factories, "proletarian expropriations" (bank heists), and the murder of fellow Communists short on Bolshevik zeal. They were the precursors, down to a T, of the Red Brigades who would make the Communist Party's life miserable twenty years later, and they made its then secretary-general, Palmiro Togliatti, nervous.

Eventually, he packed them off to Czechoslovakia, where a Communist regime with impeccable Stalinist credentials had just been installed (in 1948). There, two decades later, Feltrinelli would often drop in on his old friends of the Volante Rosso. He would enter the country in his own name or with a forged passport made out to "Giancarlo Scotti," behaving as if he were very much at home. Indeed, he was running his own guesthouse near Prague by 1971, offering hospitality to "comrades from all over the world," many if not most on the run.[8] This was in occupied Czechoslovakia, three years after the Russian invasion. The Kremlin's omnipotent security service, the KGB, was not in the habit of letting anybody entertain comrades from all over the world there without its knowledge and consent.

The fact that a notorious Communist renegade like Feltrinelli must have had some understanding with the Russian secret services in Prague—that he was allowed to play host, in an inflexibly controlled Stalinist state, to terrorist fugitives from his own and other Western countries—went unexplained for many years. Not until 1980 was a plausible explanation presented.

It came from General Jan Sejna, the Czech Communist military counselor who had defected to the United States in 1968. In an interview with Michael Ledeen of the Georgetown Institute for Strategic Studies in January 1980,[9] he spoke of the Soviet decision in 1964 to step up spending on terrorism abroad; of the KGB's training camps set up at Karlovy Vary for beginners; of the Soviet military GRU's special school at a parachute camp thirty miles south of Karlovy Vary, an enormous forest of two thousand acres in Doupov—the serious place where top foreign terrorists from Europe and the Third World were trained. The Czech formally in charge of the Doupov camp was General Sejna's army colleague, Colonel Burda, representing his country's security service (the STB) in the Czech Communist Party's Politburo. General Sejna had the names of thirteen Italians trained at one or another of these schools between 1964 and 1968.[10] Feltrinelli himself had taken one course at Karlovy Vary and two at the GRU camp in Doupov, studying sabotage, weaponry, electronic telecommunications, and urban guerrilla tactics. Too impulsive and nervy to be reliable, he was considered "hard to control" by his Czech instructors. His life story might be told in those three words.

According to General Sejna, the KGB did not trust the Italian Party's top leaders to handle such delicate questions of "alternative" Communist policy. The choice of Italians for the Czech training schools was made from a list of "eligibles" in Potere Operaio and its fellow radicals in Lotta Continua (Continuing Battle), drawn up by "trustworthy" Italian Communists designated in Moscow. Pietro Secchia's name leaps to mind.

What became of Secchia and his Armed Party within the Party is another thing Italians may never learn the truth about. Until his mysterious death in 1973 (by poison, or so he said while dying), he was the emblem of revolutionary restlessness in the Italian Communist Party.[11] An acid critic of his more domesticated fellow Party leaders, he nevertheless remained in the Party's top official circles to the end.

He also remained in the Kremlin's good graces, though the revolution he refused to renounce had been ruled out by Stalin in person. It was Stalin who had imposed the whole Italian Party line of renunciation, after his wartime agreement with Churchill and Roosevelt left Italy on the wrong side (the Western capitalist side) of the Yalta line. Yet nobody in Moscow, or Rome for that matter, made Secchia officially disband the Italian Party's secret military arm until Stalin died in 1953. Some say it wasn't really disbanded until Secchia died himself.

Certainly, Secchia's keen interest in such formations never flagged. He kept in close touch with old-timers in the Volante Rosso and he did not allow Feltrinelli's thunderous break with the Party to interrupt an intimate friendship that would last for thirty years. Beyond being grieved, he was evidently distraught when the publisher died. No sooner did he hear the news than he sent his own trusted men to the scene—to investigate on his private behalf "the incredible version of Feltrinelli as a terrorist" and to recover the apparently scorching correspondence he had left in Feltrinelli's safekeeping.

Still, it wasn't necessarily Secchia who arranged for somebody to break into and ransack Feltrinelli's Piedmont mansion, Villadeati, just after the funeral. A lot of other people might have done it. The Red Brigades sent couriers to Switzerland even before the funeral, to empty Feltrinelli's safe-deposit box there.[12] The secret services of a dozen countries were equally anxious to get their hands on his papers: Israelis, West Germans, Swiss, French, Bolivians, Americans, as well as his fellow Italians. So was NATO, whose intelligence service met in emergency session. So were the Russians, whose embassy in Rome was in a visible flurry. That same spring, Italy's counterintelligence service, SID, demanded the immediate expulsion of twenty Soviet bloc agents accredited to their embassies "for their collusion with Feltrinelli and the subversive movements gravitating around him." [13] Prime Minister Giulio Andreotti vetoed the proposal, for reasons never disclosed. (See chapter sixteen.)

There is no way of knowing everything Feltrinelli did to deserve so much attention. But the trail begins in Cuba.

He first went to Havana in 1964, and was hopelessly smitten. Barely five years had gone by since Castro had won his guerrilla war, the first such spectacular triumph in the land of the Monroe Doctrine and the Yankee dollar. Those were Castro's golden years. The romance of his revolution was still warm. The Russians still weren't quite sure what to make of it. The gallant Ché Guevara was still at his side. Intellectuals were flocking to his capital from everywhere, to watch an enthralling chapter of Communist history unfold. Feltrinelli, talking for hours with a Communist leader who was every inch his vision of a fighting revolutionary hero, came back to Italy as Castro's man.

He returned to Havana again and again, to stay a few days, weeks, months. At first, he went as a publisher. Having given Castro a $20,000 advance for an autobiography, he would sometimes inquire about it, until he was obliged to give it up. Castro, who said that he was "too busy making the revolution to write about it," spent the money to buy a prize breeding bull named Rosafé instead. [14]

By 1966, however, Castro and Cuba had become something more than a romantic attraction, with the opening of the Tricontinental Conference. Naturally Feltrinelli was there, meeting the major protagonists of the terrorist decade to come.

Back in Italy, he opened a matchless era of inflammatory prose. A chain of Feltrinelli Bookshops in Rome, Florence, Bologna, and Milan featured his Italian edition of *Tricontinental* magazine; edited in Havana, it was Castro's first official voice on the Continent offering among other things the first full text of Marighella's *Mini-Manual* in Italian and French. Side by side on display were Feltrinelli's own paper, *La Sinistra* (The Left), and scores of throwaways for those "who want to make a revolution, not in words."

Browsing through his bookshops, a generation drifting toward the tremendous *contestazione* barely two years ahead could find not only the works of Guevara, Mao, and Marcuse but all sorts of do-it-yourself numbers: how to make primitive hand grenades (gummed paper, tin cans, metal fragments, black powder); how to construct a homemade grenade launcher with a shotgun (recommended by Guevara for firing from balconies, terraces, and courtyards in street fights); how to beat up a cop; how to "Paint Your Policeman Yellow," with spray cans conveniently on sale in the Feltrinelli Bookshops.[15]

Though the mutinous young flocked to his bookshops, they would prove ungrateful when the momentous confrontation came. In May 1968, with Italian universities under riotous student occupation, thirty-foot red banners streaming from their flagpoles and Maoist Tatzebaos papering the walls, Feltrinelli made a speech at the University of Rome. Amid hoots, whistles, and jeers, students demanded a percentage of the money he'd earned from them in his bookshop sales:

"Hey, Feltrinelli! Instead of talking, give us a million lire!"

"Aaah, Feltriné! Throw us two!"

"Make it three!"

"We want four!"

"We earned it! And you? Give us ten!" [16]

In a sense, he was asking for it. He still cut the figure of a trendy publisher, enjoying the shock waves he could set off among the bourgeoisie, and was not above appearing in *Vogue* to model the latest men's fashion in furs (Persian lamb double-breasted military overcoat, with matching Russian hat). "I'm no Milanese *commendatore*; I don't need the sound of speedboats to make me happy," he would say. But he still kept two yachts of his own and lived in every other way like a millionaire: custom-built cars, a cadmium yellow office furnished with Mies van der Rohe armchairs, a magnificent villa on Lake Garda with sumptuous gardens and half a mile of private beach, his mansion in the Piedmont for weekends, a hunting lodge in the Carinthian forests of Austria for winter sports.

Nevertheless, he was way ahead of Rome's wildly undirected student *contestatori* when they booed him down.

In January of that year, Feltrinelli had published a paper entitled *Italy 1968: Political Guerrilla Warfare*.[17] Restricted for debate to selected Communist Party cells and Rome's small but elite San Saba circle of leftist intellectuals, it was Europe's first proper call for an Army of Communist Combat. Italy's Red Brigades, the German Red Army Fraction, the Spanish ETA, the Turkish and Iranian undergrounds, would not catch up with it for some years.

The "imperious need," he said, was not just for organized terror but for "intensive provocation" to "reveal the reactionary essence of the state." The guerrilla's task was to "violate the law openly . . . challenging and outraging institutions and public order in every way. Then, when the state intervenes *as a result* [italics mine], with police and the courts, it will be easy to denounce its harshness and repressive dictatorial tendencies." Carlos Marighella, whose own thoughts were not yet committed to print, could hardly have put it more neatly.

Feltrinelli also broke new ground in urging "militant Communists" to work with anybody else trying to destabilize the state; ethnic and regional minorities and even right-wing terrorists. This meant accepting their methods, "striking indiscriminately at passengers on a train, etc."—the unselective killing of innocent victims.

As if in a self-fulfilling prophecy, right-wing terrorists began to do just that in earnest barely a year later, bombing crowded banks, open-air meetings, and eventually Italy's fast *Italicus* express. By then, Feltrinelli had written a sequel about how useful such raw violence could be, to force "an authoritarian turn to the right . . . opening a more advanced phase of struggle." [18] The "brutal intervention of repressive forces . . . would end any lingering idea that a socialist revolution is possible without resorting to arms," he said. A right-wing coup in Italy had become his "delirious obsession," wrote Judge Guido Viola, assigned to investigate his death. "He awaited it, desired it, almost invoked it, so as to lead the guerrilla resistance" inevitably following. [19]

But Feltrinelli was preparing for something more than a mere right-wing coup in Italy.

Starting soon after the Tricontinental Conference, he moved in rather special international circles. He had sought out the implacable Palestinian nationalist George Habash in Beirut in 1967 and persuaded him to "go international"; [20] it was with Feltrinelli's money that Habash sent his first commando into Western Europe in 1968, opening the international terrorist age with a bang. He had discussed the future with West Germany's New Left student leader Rudi Dutschke, too. "Feltrinelli came to me in 1967 and said he was ready to help financially," Dutschke revealed twelve years later. "We talked about actions to take, how to organize, and we asked him for concrete support in making useful international contacts." [21]

He had also started to make plans with Horst Mahler, soon to launch West Germany's Red Army Fraction, which would in turn soon be going off to train in the Palestinians' Middle Eastern guerrilla camps. He had entertained Ulrike Meinhof and her husband Klaus Rainer Röhl for an idyllic few days at Villadeati, in the summer of 1967. There, "in a millionaire's castle with cooks, fancy chauffeurs and trusty servants," wrote Röhl afterward, the couple was "wined and dined" on vintage champagne and caviar while Giangi and Ulrike talked about revisionism and the revolution. The two were kindred souls, said Röhl, and Feltrinelli's urging went far to help Ulrike make her final and fatal terrorist choice.[22]

No sooner did she and her husband leave Villadeati, returning to Hamburg by Rolls-Royce and private plane, than Feltrinelli took off for Cuba.[23] After an exhilarating week of touring the island, with Castro as his personal guide, he flew on to Bolivia. Then he cabled his New York office to send him "an exorbitant sum," according to his fourth wife, Sibilla Melega, who was there.[24] He may have wanted the money for Ché Guevara, bogged down in the Bolivian Andes with a motley Cuban-trained and -equipped guerrilla force (fifty Cubans, fifteen Bolivians, fifteen other Latin Americans). But it isn't certain that Feltrinelli went to Bolivia to help Guevara. Not only was the guerrilla leader's picaresque style of rural warfare proving a burdensome flop for Castro, but his anti-Soviet sentiments were getting on the Russians' nerves. (He was in fact betrayed to the police by a famous Russian agent called "Tania," Tamara Bunke.) Feltrinelli, coming directly from a week's intimate conversation with Castro, would have understood all that.

He may have gone just to visit Guevara's best French friend, Regis Debray, in a Bolivian jail at the time. But Sibilla Melega seemed to doubt that; something more suspicious would probably have been needed to land Feltrinelli himself in jail for two days during that visit, interrogated by none other than the chief of Bolivian security, Roberto Quintanilla.

It was Quintanilla who captured and killed Ché Guevara that November. And it was Feltrinelli's Colt Cobra Special that killed Quintanilla four years later, when he was the Bolivian consul in Hamburg.[25] The gun was fired by a German terrorist named Monika Hertl. But, as *Potere Operaio* later revealed, Feltrinelli's underground GAP had sentenced the Bolivian to death; Feltrinelli himself had then seen to the execution. It was the beginning of a fruitful Italo-German terrorist friendship.[26]

Though Feltrinelli had a lot to say about his forty-eight hours in a Bolivian prison—*My Prisons* was the title of his pamphlet—he failed to explain how he wound up in one. The true reasons may never come to light. But the circumstances suggest that he was up to his neck in revolutionary conspiracy when the Year of the Big No began.

Nobody would argue that Feltrinelli had the brains to be a prime mover in the extraordinary events of 1968—"A brain is just what he didn't have," observed the irreverent editor-historian Indro Montanelli, who had known him since youth. Nevertheless, he had what it took in other ways. Every country caught up in that insurrectionary surge of 1968 had its cluster of young Marxists impatient to push on from instant rebellion to armed revolution. But they did not have arms, or money, or practical preparation, which is just what Feltrinelli did have, or could arrange to provide.

He was ready. In January 1968, he was in Cuba again, for Castro's International Cultural Congress. From his luxurious suite at the Hotel Habana, he had come before the delegates to deliver a speech in incomprehensible Spanish. "I understood," wrote Enrico Filippini, an editor he brought along from Milan. "He wanted to signal to the Cubans that his function as a publisher was over, that he saw himself as an anti-imperialist fighter." [27]

In West Germany two months later, he proposed to Rudi Dutschke that they blow up an American ship in Hamburg loading supplies for Vietnam, and he brought along a suitcase full of explosives to do the job. Dutschke, saying he would "never use violence against people, only against things," refused.[28]

In Berlin that May Day, flanked by Ulrike Meinhof and Horst Mahler, he made a flaming speech in praise of armed violence. Hardly a month had passed since Rudi Dutschke had been shot and Andreas Baader had burned down that Frankfurt department store; Feltrinelli drew fervent applause. From there he went straight on to join the students behind the barricades in Paris bombarding de Gaulle's Fifth Republic. He was promptly thrown out of France. Expelled over the next few weeks were 115 other foreigners accused of infiltrating student ranks during the Paris May. Three Cuban diplomats were so deeply embroiled that they were hastily recalled to Havana. The episode, though awkward, did not deter Castro from bringing two thousand French students to Cuba for a work-study program that summer, along with six thousand others from elsewhere in Western Europe.[29]

On throwing him out, the French warned members of his family that Giangi was getting into trouble: he was recruiting young Frenchmen and Italians for guerrilla training in Habash's Middle East camps, they said. Clearly, Feltrinelli was on close terms by then with the man who would soon become the most intractable leader in the Palestinian's Rejection Front. Late in 1968, he went to singular lengths to cement the friendship. He borrowed a million dollars from an Italian financier named Giuseppe Pasquale, ostensibly to produce some films but actually to buy a shipload of weapons for Habash in Beirut. When the Israelis intercepted the ship and seized its cargo, Feltrinelli told Pasquale that he couldn't (or wouldn't) pay the money back; Pasquale went bankrupt.[30]

It was during the same year that he opened his famous payola account no. 15385 in a Swiss bank, under the name of "Robinson Crusoe." [31] Court investigations later revealed that the account served mostly to finance a *"centrale"* in Zurich, coordinating services for South Americans, Palestinians, Germans, Spanish, French, Greeks, and Italians. Several checks went to a German terrorist who taught radio communications to Feltrinelli's underground GAP commandos. Substantial payments went to the German June 2 Movement, flanking the Baader-Meinhof Gang. The June 2 people would send their jaunty Michael "Bommi the Bomber" Baumann to Milan and he had only to enter that cadmium yellow office for Feltrinelli to pull out his checkbook and ask, "How much?"[32]

A sizable sum flowed into France, to build up a Continent-side network. Jean-Edern Hallier, a French Gauchiste and a millionaire himself, has told me of Feltrinelli's persistent efforts to finance such a network "starting after the Tricontinental Conference." Early in 1970, Hallier said, he played host in his own Paris home for a three-day meeting with Feltrinelli, Baader, Curcio (just forming the Red Brigades), and leaders of the French Gauche Prolétarienne (Proletarian Left) "to organize European terror."

He had quite a few expensive propositions going in Italy too, from 1968 onward. Apart from bankrolling half a dozen erratic Trotskyite or Marxist-Leninist formations there, he subsidized a string of heavily indebted left-wing publications and Potere Operaio, perennially broke but an inexhaustible source of terrorist recruits over the next ten years.

In the summer of 1968, he also tried to whip up a separatist uprising in Sardinia. He put the idea to the most famous multiple murderer and kidnapper on that poverty-stricken and bandit-ridden island, Graziano Mesina, offering him 100 million lire (nearly $200,000 then) to head a Revolutionary Sardinian Army. The meeting was picturesque. Feltrinelli showed up in tweeds, with a retinue, dispensing largesse to poor peasant women on the road. Mesina came incognito, and the whole bunch trooped off to hunt capriola, Sardinia's prized roe buck. But Mesina did not care to give up his thriving business for the sake of a hypothetical Cuba in the Mediterranean; Feltrinelli returned to the mainland disappointed.[33]

The press made a big joke of his Sardinian escapade, but his ghost had the last laugh. Eleven years after that expedition of his to the island, a secret band of Sardinian separatists played host in Cagliari to twenty-one foreign armed underground parties—or so we are told by the president of the IRA

Provisionals' Sinn Fein, Ruairi O'Bradaigh, who says he was there.[34]

Meanwhile, the millionaire publisher was working with some anarchist bombers calling themselves the Individualists. At the same time, he was trying to persuade the semiclandestine Potere Operaio to go clandestine altogether and arm itself. "Let the heads fall! For risks we are second to none!" he wrote to its ideological guru, Antonio Negri.[35] Someone present at a meeting between Feltrinelli and Potop's top men—all imprisoned celebrities now—has told me that Feltrinelli proposed to put up the initial folding money for the underground apparatus, through his "Robinson Crusoe" account; to help procure weapons in Switzerland; and to assure refuge in Czechoslovakia when needed. That was in 1969, a year after Soviet troops had settled down in Prague.

That summer, Feltrinelli spent a whole month in Cuba.[36] His wife Sibilla "joined one of those youth camps, where they work in the fields," she said, while "he had his own itinerary, meeting Cuban leaders." A few months later, he went underground for good.

Nobody made him do it. A judge had questioned him about an allegedly false alibi he gave for some anarchist bombers, but no warrant was out for him. Nevertheless, he left Milan on December 4, 1969, never to return as Giangiacomo Feltrinelli.

He dropped in many times as "Jacques Matras," "Jacques Fisher," "Andreas Pisani," "Giancarlo Scotti," "Vincenzo Maggioni"; those last two clandestine years of his life must surely have seemed to him his best. In that short while, he founded GAP (1970), set up twenty-odd safe-houses for it, assembled a huge arsenal of weapons, established his paramilitary camps in the Piedmontese hills, generated a series of pirate radio programs, and sponsored thirty bombing and arson attacks on factories and army barracks.

He sent off a young Swiss named Bruno Breguet with dynamite to blow up the Israeli port of Haifa (caught red-handed, Breguet is still in jail there).[37] He dispatched a Milanese girl and a Cypriot to blow up the U.S. embassy in Athens (using one of his faulty timers, they blew themselves up).[38] He even managed, while in deep clandestinity, to organize one of the earliest international terrorist conferences: in a Jesuit college in Florence, early in October 1971, attended by sixteen underground groups, from the IRA and ETA to the Argentine Trotskyite ERP and the Palestinians.[39]

All this while, he traveled incessantly. From Milan that December he flew to Cairo and on to a guerrilla training camp in Jordan. Then he rushed back to Milan, when its Bank of Agriculture was bombed by Black terrorists, leaving seventeen dead. That Christmas Eve, Reuters news agency signaled his presence in Prague, and soon afterward, in North Korea— where the Russians had their biggest training camps for foreigners at the time. From there, his wanderings were largely lost to view.

He surfaced in Czechoslovakia many times after that. (After his death, police found twenty-two stamped entry visas for Czechoslovakia in a false passport.) [40] Once, on May 30, 1971, he drove to Prague with the Italian fugitive Augusto Viel, who settled in with "other comrades" at Feltrinelli's villa there for the next five months.[41] Since he was wanted for murder in connection with a bank "expropriation" in Genoa, Viel's presence in Prague must have been known to the Czech security police and the KGB. That October, Feltrinelli returned to Prague and brought Viel back to Milan, putting him on the GAP payroll.

Meanwhile, Feltrinelli was going back and forth to his *centrale* in Zurich, staying in different seedy hotels. He was a frequent visitor to Liechtenstein, the Continent's most wide-open arms market. He spent months in Paris studying with a master forger. He went to Chile, and again and again to Cuba, and once, in 1971, from Cuba to Uruguay, where the Tupamaros— just finishing their demolition job on the democratic republic— gave him a warm welcome, generous advice, and, presumably, his final military wardrobe.

He was certainly acting oddly toward the end. A friend who spotted him on a Milan-Rome express says he ducked furtively into the train corridor from his compartment. Another who offered to put him up for the night says he insisted on pitching a tent in the garden instead. He had taken to going without baths for weeks, in order to toughen his hands and look like a worker. He always carried a gun, and let it show, and he was wearing his Tupamaro uniform. "If you don't hear about me for a while, and then you read in the papers about a naked and mutilated body found under a bridge, that body will be me," he told a publishing colleague. No wonder people thought he had cracked.

Yet whatever Feltrinelli may have been—neurotically unbalanced, sexually distressed, vain, weak, imperious, exalted, frustrated, rash, sadly vulnerable to flattery, given to irrational dreams and preposterous ambitions—he was still shaping the history of a decade.

The ferocious terrorist assault on Western Europe didn't really get off the ground until several elementary conditions were met. The principal performers had to make contact, acquire elementary training and weapons, learn about reconnaissance and intelligence gathering, pick up rather a lot of money, and assure themselves of a safe haven. Feltrinelli could put them in the way of all that. The Palestinians' entrance into the Western European theater of operations was indispensable to their takeoff, and there his help was priceless. The Cubans, with their rich revolutionary experience and all those guerrilla training camps supervised by Colonel Kotchergine, could offer invaluable aid, and few men could have conveyed their message better than Feltrinelli did.

There is no firm evidence that Fidel Castro ever entrusted Feltrinelli with direct responsibilities or delicate political missions. We have only Feltrinelli's astonishing word for how things stood between them: "On a cozy evening around a fireplace in Havana, Fidel talks of a new decree to re-educate and suppress homosexuals, prostitutes, and pimps," writes Klaus Rainer Röhl of the story Giangi told him at Villadeati. "Feltrinelli, in a rush of courage, says, 'Fidel, I don't approve of this,' and gives his reasons. Everybody is stricken with shock; Castro isn't used to open contradiction anymore. But then Castro says, 'Maybe you're right,' and homosexual artists are rehabilitated in Cuba." [42]

No doubt Castro would tell it differently, if at all. Nevertheless, there is ample evidence about Castro's close and frequent contacts with this otherwise forgettable man, whose wealth and delusions, at that time and in that setting, could do wonders to translate the principles of the Tricontinental Conference in Havana into practice on the continent of Europe.

Seven years after his death, he received some of the homage due him. The Italian Red Brigades, a tiny and penniless band while he lived, owed a lot to their late millionaire patron. No sooner was he gone than they picked up his entire arsenal of weapons, most of his activist followers, everything in his Swiss safe-deposit box and, reportedly, a windfall in hard cash.[43] In the spring of 1979, they thanked him.

Thirty Italian terrorists came before the court in the so-called Feltrinelli trial, involving his close accomplices. Most were in jail on other counts already, and manacled in the dock with the Brigades' founder Renato Curcio was Feltrinelli's murderous protégé Augusto Viel. The trial opened with the Brigades' ritual warning to judge and jury: "We'll crush you like dogs! You won't come out alive!" Curcio shouted. Then Augusto Viel rose to read out the Red Brigades' belated eulogy for a dead comrade.

Though they had said all along that Feltrinelli was assassinated by imperialist reaction, they took it back. "Osvaldo was not a victim, but a revolutionary fallen in battle," they declared. He died because of a banal "technical error": one of his faulty timers was to blame. The "sole authentic revolutionary among many opportunists," he was a valorous figure in the "Party of Communist Combat, whose supreme contribution was to develop a Continental strategy . . . of long-lasting and decisive importance." [44]

It was decent of the Red Brigades to clear the names at last of so many villains in the piece, from the CIA and NATO to the whole Italian governing class. But the truth about Feltrinelli's death had been known for some while. The Red Brigades themselves had the story on tape, found in a safe-house of theirs at Robbiano de Mediglia near Milan in 1974.[45]

The story is told to one of them by two young Italians, still unidentified, who were with Feltrinelli at Segrate. They met him before the Vox Cinema in Milan, and drove off together in his Volkswagen Camper.

On this night, "Osvaldo" is tense, very nervous, almost gets into an accident twice. We must remember that he has always been a bad driver, so it isn't surprising if he is clumsy tonight. . . . Undoubtedly he is going into a big action, alone, with two inexperienced kids; the expert comrades who could have helped him were somewhere else [planting Dynamon at the other end of town].

Their relations with him are strange. "Osvaldo" is a person who does everything to prove he is more proletarian than they are. The two friends are fascinated by this personage, an important man whose name is on everyone's lips, though they have to pretend not to know who he was. . . . They get to the place and park the camper five hundred yards away. "Osvaldo" is wearing an elegant overcoat. He goes into the back of the camper alone; the others look at him stupefied as he comes out. He is wearing a military-style uniform, like a Castroite, they say. The pants and jacket are full of big pockets, like a Castroite. It is stupefying, but in character, they say.

They unload things from the van. It's drizzling, the night is damp; the two can see lights in the distance but don't know exactly where. They have trouble carrying the stuff to the pylon, their shoes sink in the mud. . . . Then the two start tieing dynamite sticks in packets of eight, around the first leg of the pylon. . . . An electric wire dangles and "Osvaldo" sees it is too short to be pulled up the pylon. He is furious, he swears, he decides to do two explosions in one, to do something really big. . . . He goes to the camper and brings back more material. . . .

They decide the stuff should be tied higher up. "Osvaldo" decides to climb up. It's hard to climb. He gets up and perches on a crossrail, with his legs dangling, and the two pass the material up to him, ten or twelve feet up. . . . "Osvaldo" gets one leg of the pylon mined, with his legs hanging, and he holds on with his right arm, trying to attach the timer. The timer doesn't work, it seems the soldering is no good. "Osvaldo" swears, throws it to the ground, asks for another timer. He tries to tie the pack of dynamite sticks, holding them between his knees. He isn't comfortable, he tries to move and swears because he's stuck. . . . He shifts the dynamite sticks, they get caught under one of his legs . . . that is, the left leg . . . and he's in this position, trying to set the timer, arrange the wires, and attach the bomb. . . . At this moment, one of the two halfway up the pylon hears a tremendous explosion. He's shaken, he feels a terrible pain in his ear and falls to the ground. . . . He looks around and sees "Osvaldo" breathing with a death rattle. . . . He thinks both legs are gone. The other one feels a terrible pain in his thigh, more like a burning hot thrust, and he falls. The one who fell first comes to him and says, " 'Osvaldo' . . . 'Osvaldo' is no more, he blew up."

The problem of the legs. . . . One says, "He lost both legs," then they remember the right one is under his body. The left one isn't there, it's torn off. They can't understand how it happened, they're terrified, they run away screaming . . . ten or fifteen yards, then they go back to "Osvaldo." His breath is rattling, he breathes once more, then they don't hear anything. . . .

The whole thing happened in forty minutes. . . .

The tape ends there.

Judge Guido Viola, presenting the full text of his findings, concluded that Feltrinelli had destroyed himself by attempting to set an explosive device "with an inexpert hand." He was within sight of a warehouse belonging to the Feltrinelli Publishing Company. Half of Milan was Feltrinelli property. He died on his own land.

3

THE STRANGE CAREER OF HENRI CURIEL

"Revolutionaries around the world, including terrorists, mourn the assassination of Henri Curiel, leader of a Paris-based support apparatus that funneled money, arms, documents, training and other services to scores of leftist groups." [1] Thus, as if in a trade paper's in-house column of Births, Deaths, and Marriages, did the CIA note the passing of a true craftsman.

Henri Curiel, a gray and fatherly-looking figure in half-rimmed glasses, was shot dead on May 4, 1978, in the elevator of his Left Bank Paris apartment, by two featureless gunmen wearing gloves—the only detail his neighbors noticed. A stateless Egyptian Jew, he had been living in Paris for twenty-seven years. For nearly all that time, he was listed as foreign agent S 531916 in the files of the DST, the French internal security service. Every major counterespionage agency in the West had a file on him, and almost anybody in the trade reading through these would assume he worked for the KGB. Nevertheless, he had a foolproof system for evading arrest. "My dossier is the thickest one in the DST, but they can't do a thing about it," he once remarked, rightly.

Only four months before he was murdered, Curiel had been released from enforced exile in the small Provençal town of Digne. There, from late in the previous October to January, he had stayed at the Hôtel Saint-Jean with six DST operatives and twelve plainclothesmen watching him in shifts, around the clock. Forbidden to communicate with outsiders, he was followed by two policemen at five paces wherever he went, flanked by police at the next table when he ate in the hotel restaurant, and sent to bed at eleven in the evening, when police would lock the hotel door and stand guard through the night. No charges had been lodged against him. He was simply picked up in Paris and bundled off to the south of France on the strength of "information received," authorities said.[2]

The timing was suggestive. Two days before Curiel was taken into custody on October 22, 1977, the German industrial leader Hanns-Martin Schleyer had been found with three bullets in his head in the trunk of an abandoned car, in Mulhouse, near the French-German border. Forty-nine letters from his kidnappers had been mailed in Paris during his forty-five days in captivity. The colossal manhunt for Schleyer's kidnappers and killers—members of the Baader-Meinhof Gang—would mean they were urgently in need of shelter. Fugitives in their particular situation would know where to turn for help in France.

Henri Curiel ran something politically chic and vaguely charitable called Aide et Amitié (Help and Friendship). He liked to say that it was meant for people working against "undemocratic countries in the Third World," and he would often confide that the operation was slightly illegal. The added spice of breaking the law just a little bit in a worthy cause made it all the more attractive. A hundred or so young volunteers of various nationalities were on his helpful and friendly team, including Catholic worker-priests and Protestant pastors. A Dominican priory in the Rue de la Glacière gave him houseroom for meetings; a group called France, Terre d'Asile (France, Land of Asylum) gave him hostel facilities just up the street; the Protestant aid mission Cimade gave him the use of its refugee shelter in the suburb of Massy. The foreigners he bedded down for the night, the nocturnal visitors, the couriers to and from distant lands—Africa, South America, the Middle East—attracted little public attention. It was all part of his benevolent if rather indistinct image as a doer of good works.

Not until 1976 did the French public get an idea of what

Curiel had really been up to for the previous quarter of a century. The lid was lifted by Georges Suffert, a respected journalist who spent three months investigating the story he wrote for the weekly *Le Point*. One alluring glimpse from Suffert and the lid was clamped down again, unmistakably from somewhere above. "I have the feeling that Henri Curiel will not be arrested, that he will not be found if looked for, that he will disappear for a while and his network will be put to sleep," wrote Suffert at the end of his long account.[3] He was not far wrong.

Two personal stories gave Suffert his lead.

In the summer of 1968, a Parisian woman named Michèle Firk went to Guatemala with a false passport in the name of "Isabelle Chaumet." A member of the French Communist Party for some time, she had evidently chosen a more active life of revolutionary combat. After several weeks in Guatemala, she rented a car there on August 22. The American ambassador was assassinated six days later. Her hired car, used in the attack, led police to the hideout of the Cuban-backed FAR (Armed Revolutionary Force), which claimed credit for the killing. Rather than face interrogation, Michèle Firk committed suicide. Her FAR comrades claimed to know nothing about her, except that she had worked in Paris with an "important" man known as "Julien," or "Raymond."

Seven years later, the South African poet Breyton Breytenbach (also traveling on a false passport) returned to his country from Paris after a long stay abroad. He went there to set up a secret printing press for the South African underground and was soon arrested under the antiterrorist laws. But just as an international campaign was getting under way to free him, he pleaded guilty. The campaign stopped abruptly, and Breytenbach settled down in oblivion to serve his nine-year prison term.

The behavior of this talented young poet had puzzled reporters at the time: he seemed to *want* to go to jail. Once there, in fact, he confided to his brother his nagging suspicion that he had been "manipulated" in Paris. An ardent opponent of apartheid, he had attended several meetings on "aid to underdeveloped countries," whereupon he was recruited for undercover activities. Over the next two years, he worked in an organization called Solidarité (later to become Aide et Amitié). Its chief was known as "Julien," or "Raymond."

Clearly a professional, "Raymond" had an impressive quantity of false passports on hand, was often absent without explanation for days or weeks, and held countless meetings heavily attended by Catholic and Protestant intellectuals. Gradually, the conviction grew on Breytenbach that Solidarité fronted for a deep underground apparatus providing technical services to international terrorist groups. He had the impression that its main purpose was to collect information on the terrorists' plans and movements. But he had no idea who wanted the information or who was paying for it—in short, exactly who he was working for. Nor could he say just who this "Julien," or "Raymond," was. All he knew was that the man was a Sephardic Jew from Egypt, who had once helped to found the Communist Party there.

Only one man in Paris answered the description. With that for starters, Suffert went on to piece together the first account ever published of the real Henri Curiel. He couldn't hope to get it all, nor could others of us who have kept trying; the police are still reluctant to talk, and witnesses are afraid to. But there is no doubting the nature of Curiel's mission by now. He was running a triple-tiered service network, probably unique in the world, and catering to the carriage trade.

Paris was the perfect place for it. France has long been proud of its traditions as a haven for political exiles. For centuries, historic victims of oppression—nihilists fleeing the tsar's wrath; White Russians fleeing the Bolsheviks; anarchists fleeing Franco; fugitives from Communist, Fascist, military, monarchic, colonial, or tribal rule; anti-Establishmentarians of the right or left; and even ordinary delinquents on the lam—have naturally gravitated to the French capital. Claiming their ancient right of political sanctuary, they have usually been free to fight their national battles from a distance, provided they leave France itself alone.

For the world's emerging Armed Parties, starting around

1968, a city like that had magnetic charm. No other Continental capital could match it for freedom to hide, meet, mingle, swap ideas, experience, and equipment, plan and organize actions on a continental if not global scale. By the mid-1970s, practically every terrorist and guerrilla force to speak of was represented in Paris: Iranian, Turkish, Greek, Japanese, Spanish, German, Italian, African, Latin American, Palestinian. The Palestinians especially were there in force, running a snappy Europe-wide operation under the flamboyant leadership of Ilich Ramirez Sanchez, better known as Carlos the Jackal.

There was no limit to the opportunities for an enterprise providing specialized services, discretion guaranteed; Solidarité was in a class of its own along those lines.

It made no bones about its illicit activities. Its statute declared: "Experience proves that clandestine work of a certain dimension cannot be carried out seriously except by a secret organization." Its working rules began with the warning "Solidarité's activities entail risks. It is indispensable that members understand this clearly." To limit such risks, the organization "abstains from all actions on the actual terrain of liberation struggles" whenever possible. "Exceptions . . . can only occur if members are fully aware of the particular risks they assume." [4]

The minimum risks merely involved "traveling" to and from South America or Africa, bearing messages and money. But members who looked more promising would be invited to attend Solidarité's annual congress for screening. They would be given no address, instructed simply to gather at a suburban railway station where cars would be waiting to carry them off to a country house. Those who passed muster at the congress would then get an eight-day course of training. Four or five to a group, they would meet morning and evening with expert but unidentified instructors. Some extremely knowledgeable German, say, would fill them in on the latest police methods and liberation struggles in West Germany, a Brazilian would do the same for Brazil, and so on for Chile, Morocco, Tunisia, the Middle East. (Who were they liberating in West Germany?) Then they would learn a little about how to forge a passport, behave in clandestinity, use the funds they would be carrying abroad, respond to interrogation in case of arrest. In effect, they were taught just enough to become efficient couriers without losing their valuable amateur status—valuable because, as amateurs, they were still respectable in the progressive religious circles they were largely drawn from, and unknown to the police.

The rock-bottom organization lay beneath, in deep submersion. Its members were sworn to obedience as Soldiers of the Revolution. It used all the familiar underground paraphernalia: invisible ink, codes, letter drops, camouflage, disguise. Its operatives gave training in explosives, sabotage, weaponry, map making, map reading, wire cutting, secret communications. Its assorted services ranged from such limited guerrilla training to intercontinental couriers, safe-houses, money, false papers, temporary jobs, and safe passage across frontiers.[5]

The services were free and dispensed with largesse. American deserters from Vietnam could count on a welcome at Curiel's hostels anytime. So could American hijackers, moving on from their hideouts in Algeria. Black Panthers returning from North Africa might be put up a few nights in Paris, then passed on through Quebec's underground Liberation Front to the United States. Or else they could stay on in Paris for special training courses (Black Panthers only) given by Curiel's staff in 1973 and 1974. A mixed international terrorist team plotting to snatch a cabinet minister for a four-million-dollar ransom in Stockholm, in 1976, could send a messenger to Paris to pick up fake identity papers. Other selected groups could ask for more.[6]

The separatists in Canada's French-speaking Quebec province were among the select: a Curiel aide spent months among them sorting out their Marxist hang-ups, and two of them wanted for the kidnapping of British diplomat Richard Gross hid out with Curiel for a full month in Paris, after sheltering in Cuba for several years. Italian terrorists had two safe-houses reserved for them. All the Palestinian formations operating in Western Europe could have help for the asking. (Curiel knew George Habash well, and his liaison with the Palestinians, Sophie Magarinos, also doubled as his link to the Tupamaros.) So could the front-line guerrilla forces of southern Africa, regularly supplied by Solidarité with funds and clandestine equipment. For the Polisario guerrillas, fighting Morocco for the former Spanish Sahara with massive Soviet armament passed on by Libya, Curiel's group ran the main French show. (Madeleine Rebeirioux, George Montaran, and Robert Davezies, directors of the Paris-based Friends of the Sahraoui Republic, were all attached to Solidarité.) And nothing was too good for Iranians fighting the shah. The fanatic Sadegh Ghotbzadeh, spokesman for Ayatollah Khomeini in Paris and, after the Islamic Revolution, the Ayatollah's foreign minister in Teheran, was one of Curiel's valued clients.[7]

All in all, his list of clients was impressive. Suffert was able to track down twenty groups, some terrorist and others not. They included the Basques' ETA and GRAPO's urban guerrillas in Spain, Israel's two Communist Parties, the outlawed Communist Parties of Iraq, Haiti, Morocco, and Sudan, and four or five Latin American guerrilla bands, including the Tupamaros. Informants have since tipped off the French and other Western intelligence services to quite a few more. They include the IRA, the German Red Army Fraction (RAF), the Japanese Red Army, assorted urban bands in Belgium, Holland, Sweden, Portugal, Greece, Iran, and Turkey, and Kurdish separatists of Iran, Turkey, and Iraq—for whose sake Curiel's second-in-command, Joyce Blau, learned to speak the Kurdish dialects.[8]

For Latin America, Curiel appears to have offered not just personalized services but a wholesale arrangement. In 1976, at a safe-house of the Trotskyite ERP in Argentina, police found documents revealing a plan to launch a "Europe Brigade" for a strategy of tension on the Continent. Described in chapter six, it was sponsored by the Junta for Revolutionary Coordination (JCR), formed by the Tupamaros of Uruguay and fellow terrorists of Argentina, Bolivia, Chile, and Paraguay. According to the confiscated documents, the brigade was to be armed and financed by Cuba and mounted from Paris. Its intermediary there was to be France, Land of Asylum, Curiel's serviceable front-group.[9]

The most damning proof of his shadier international connections came along by pure chance. On July 26, 1974, an unusually conscientious French customs inspector at Orly airport opened the briefcase of a well-dressed Japanese passenger from Beirut. The name on his passport was Furuya Yukata. But three other forged passports in different names were found in his briefcase. So were $10,000 in counterfeit bills and a number of coded messages. One, on scented rice paper, said: "Little Miss Full Moon. I am ill with desire for you. Let me embrace your beautiful body again. Your love slave, Suzuki!" "Little Miss Full Moon" was a ranking member of the Japanese Red Army cell in Paris, one of the deadliest bands of killers on earth. Another of the coded messages was for the head of the cell, Taketomo Takahashi.[10]

When police came for him, Taketomo tried in the best B-movie style to swallow slips of paper bearing the pseudonyms "Achème" and "Jean-Baptiste." Both turned out to be in regular contact with Taketomo, the one providing his Red Army cell with weapons, the other with fake papers and money.

It was easy to find "Jean-Baptiste," who had been under DST surveillance for months. He was André Haberman, a microphotographer believed to be turning out quantities of those beautifully made passports and phony dollar bills for Solidarité—Curiel's master forger.[11] Arrested at once, Haberman refused to confess and was eventually released. Nevertheless, the French Interior Ministry would state flatly three years later, when Curiel was packed off to the south of France, that his organization did provide the Japanese Red Army with false documents. Questioned about it by a reporter then, Curiel answered with a smile: "I see you've been reading up the documents. You surely cannot expect me to say anything likely to prolong my exile in Digne." [12]

Spotting "Achème" took longer. In real life, he was a Brazilian by the name of Antonio Pereira Carvalho. But his occupation became known only a year after Furuya's arrest, when a tremendous shootout with the police obliged Carlos the Jackal to clear out of France. In his haste to make a getaway, the man whose multinational terrorist squad was savaging the Continent—bombing, murdering, kidnapping, hijacking from one end of Europe to the other—left a fertile collection of notes and diaries behind. A search of Carlos's flat in Rue Toullier revealed that "Achème" was in charge of his network's arms supply throughout Europe. Several other aides of Carlos's were found to be in regular touch with members of Curiel's staff.

The Furuya Yukata arrest provides a fascinating diagram of the international circuit in action. The Japanese terrorist, flying in from a Palestinian base in Lebanon, was on his way to kidnap a wealthy Japanese businessman in West Germany, with logistic support from the German Red Army Fraction and with fake papers and funds from Curiel's group in Paris. Upon Furuya's arrest at Orly, the action on the circuit switched. From Paris, his fellow Japanese terrorists moved into The Hague to occupy the French embassy there, holding five French diplomats at gunpoint, demanding Furuya's release from jail and a million-dollar ransom. They had planned the job with Carlos, who met them in Amsterdam to hand over the necessary money and weapons. The weapons included explosives stolen by a Swiss anarchist group from a military depot in Zurich (the Swiss takeout service, reported in chapter four) and hand grenades stolen by the German RAF from a U.S. Army base in Mesau. To underscore the Japanese message from Holland, Carlos personally blew up Le Drugstore on the Left Bank in Paris, with a grenade from the same batch stolen by the Germans. "If the government does not do what it should, we will attack a cinema next," warned a mysterious caller to the French news agency, Agence France Presse. At long last, the French government freed Furuya, gave him $300,000 as ransom, and put him in a plane that, after a circuitous itinerary, landed in Damascus.

Neither in this or any other case did Henri Curiel initiate a terrorist action. Violence was distasteful to him. "I have a horror of terrorism," he said after *Le Point*'s front-page story broke, adding that he had often "managed to prevent young people from participating in revolutionary actions." He had the opportunity, he explained, because he was a "public relations counselor on Third World problems, which means I meet a lot of people." His overriding concern, he went on, was to help "militant liberation movements fighting to transform societies in the Third World." [13]

But Japan is not in the Third World. Neither is the United States, or Canada, or Northern Ireland, West Germany, Sweden, Italy, Spain. In all these countries, his services were available for armed violence of every sort: ethnic, religious, nationalist, ideological. Yet he denied the same services to several seemingly authentic revolutionary bands in the Third World itself. His instructions to Solidarité's staff on the subject are arresting.

In a bluntly worded document he wrote himself, Curiel defined "the attitude to be taken toward pro-Chinese forces" by his network.[14] "If we are dealing with pro-Chinese groups who receive concrete aid from China, their action must be considered as purely interior to the state in which it is applied. No interference from our organization will therefore be tolerated," the document said. "On the other hand, if local activities should opt for a Maoist approach to national problems, simply on a theoretical basis, the assistance of our apparatus becomes perfectly possible."

Accordingly, Curiel's staff was forbidden to have anything to do with the Marxist-Leninist Communist Party of Spain, the Workers' Party of Haiti, certain factions of the Tudeh Communist Party of Iran, and similar groups anywhere else—Guyana and the Antilles, for instance—receiving "concrete aid" from Peking. There are not too many plausible explanations for so categorical a refusal of assistance from an organization otherwise broad-minded and generous to a fault. The simplest is that Communist China is, or was until Mao's recent eclipse, Soviet Russia's single biggest rival for the hearts and minds of revolutionaries the world over. And that fits.

When Curiel first hit the headlines in 1976, the far-left Parisian daily *Libération* chose an odd way of coming to his defense. The idea that his network might be helping terrorists was preposterous, it said; but it added: "You could die laughing at *Le Point*'s article if the distinguished investigator had not given us to understand that the Curiel network is nothing but an antenna of the KGB, mounted to infiltrate left-wing terrorist groups who are independent of Moscow. In fact, this theory has circulated several times in recent years, among different liberation movements, leading to the reduction of Solidarité's activities." [15]

There certainly was some defection going on. Like the Afrikaner poet Breyton Breytenbach, dozens of committed leftists outside Moscow's orbit began to suspect that they were being used. Those willing to talk about it (not all, by any means) believed that Solidarité was cleverly designed to extract information from terrorist groups and national liberation movements in exchange for prodigal handouts. Some suggested that the recipients even knew this and didn't mind, considering the arrangement of mutual benefit. By and large, in any case, they felt that Solidarité bore an unmistakable Soviet imprint.

The most ingenuous of Curiel's helpers couldn't quite laugh that off. Most seemed to think of him as a quietly knowing and hardworking man, growing old before his time in pursuit of a lifelong cause. It was the cause itself they couldn't be altogether sure about. Who were some of the Bonnies and Clydes passing through his doors? Why should a Frenchwoman he sent haring off to Guatemala have killed herself rather than face interrogation? Where did Curiel go when he vanished from Paris for days or weeks at a time? How could he afford the prodigal sums he spread around on a labor of love? Where did he get the money?

The questions still nag at Western security agents, who to this day haven't been able to pin a piece of totally incriminating evidence on Curiel. "The Agency kept telling me the fellow was KGB; but I don't buy it," one senior CIA operative in Europe remarked to me. "The man was a pro, and he was incredibly good. He had plenty of leeway, and he didn't make mistakes. But he was KGB, all right," said another, closer to the scene and, judging from the only kind of evidence around—the circumstantial kind—probably closer to the truth.

The known history of Henri Curiel is notable for its missing parts. Cultivated, composed, polished, austere (he didn't even drink or smoke), he himself was the soul of discretion, and he had elaborate protection. Nevertheless, practically everything coming to light about him now suggests that the greater part of his life was spent in the active and conscious service of the Soviet Union.

He was born in 1915, the son of a wealthy Jewish banker in Cairo, and became a Communist in his early twenties—an orthodox Communist undeviatingly loyal to Moscow, then and forever after, as he kept telling whoever asked.[16] If he never went to live in Russia, during a quarter of a century as a stateless, homeless, and passportless wanderer, it was only because he felt he could be "more useful" outside, as he also told reporters toward the end.[17]

The Egypt of his youth, still under British rule, simmered with novel Marxist thoughts. Sheltered by his father's position and fortune, young Henri would entertain privileged middle-class leftists like himself in the family villa on the Nile and drift on to the flyblown Arab cafés where early Marxist grouplets were forming. He could count on support from both quarters when he helped found the Egyptian Communist Party in 1942.

Before long, he was making connections that would come in wonderfully handy. Wartime Cairo abounded in spies and informers in the pay of one or another Axis or Allied power, or both. Henri's father had died by then, and his mother had opened a Communist bookshop near the Rond-Point. It soon became the "in" place to go for literary buffs and radicals alike, offering invaluable encounters and gossip as well as the only Russian books available in Egypt—or anywhere else around the Mediterranean, for that matter. Henri and his future wife Rosette could pick up any amount of information there. They shared it partly with British intelligence, spotting the pro-Nazis who also abounded in Cairo. And they helped to find and screen recruits for the Free French Mission, a favor that would later bring handsome rewards.

Imprisoned by King Farouk from 1946 to 1948, Curiel then took off for Europe until a military junta deposed the king in 1952. Details about his four-year interlude on the Continent are hazy. He is known to have traveled quite a bit, returning again and again to Prague, fresh from its Communist coup. Reportedly, he spent most of 1951 in Italy, getting acquainted with Communist leaders like Pietro Secchia, head of the Party's secret "parallel" apparatus and Feltrinelli's particular friend. He also appeared to have shuttled to and from Paris, meeting frequently with the French Party leader Jacques Duclos, who was working for the Cominform in those days. Old-timers in French inner-Party circles recall that they used to speak of their Egyptian visitor as the "White Wolf," on the prowl for the Russian secret service.[18]

No sooner was Farouk thrown out of Egypt than Curiel went home, only to be thrown out himself. Colonel Gamal Abdel Nasser, a great favorite in Washington at that sunny stage—"a vile tool of American imperialism," is how Europe's Communist press described him then—wanted no truck with Communists, and Curiel became a lifelong political exile.

He did his best to unseat Nasser in the 1950s (as he would do again in the 1970s, to dislodge Sadat). An Italian Communist leader of those days has told me of a visit he had from Curiel asking urgently for arms and money to back a pro-Communist army coup in Egypt. He made the same demands on the French Communists, in repeated meetings with Léon Feix of their Politburo and the late André Marty, former secretary of the French Communist Party.[19]

It was during those blurred early years of his in Europe that French police found the first hard evidence of his Russian ties. In a raid on the Casablanca villa of the Moroccan Communist Party's general secretary, they discovered the minutes of a secret meeting held near Algiers on November 5, 1951. Attended by several North African Communist leaders and the same Léon Feix from Paris, the meeting was chaired by a "Monsieur Marcel" on behalf of Mikhail Suslov, then heading the Cominform's IV Division—the Kremlin's Arab network. The discussion dealt with special training for anticolonialist officers and students in Algeria, whose war for independence from France would break out three years later almost to the day. The meeting's organizer was Henri Curiel.[20]

That was when the DST gave Curiel the number S 531916 as a foreign agent. Twenty-seven years would pass before the public heard a word of it. Even then, the word came from the *Economist Foreign Report* of London, not the French press.[21]

Shortly after that secret Algiers meeting, Curiel settled down in Paris for good—a refugee with no papers, no profession, no visible source of income, and, for the first nine years, no residence permit. (Even from 1960 onward, when he finally got the permit, he had to renew it every three months.) He could thus draw on personal experience for his later work in training recruits to "live clandestinely." Learning how to "manufacture identity papers" was indispensable, he would assure them. "What is the first thing someone needs who is living outside the normal set-up in a country? Documentation, of course. Even before he needs food, he needs papers, because without them he cannot get food," he explained to the press during his brief exile in Digne.[22] He did not explain whether or how he was providing such documentation, or for whom.

In the course of the Algerian War for independence from France (1954 to 1962), Curiel evidently learned whatever he might have to know about clandestine living. He was a key man in Paris for the Algerian National Liberation Front (FLN), providing information, cover, and sizable sums of money smuggled into France from unidentified sources in Switzerland. Broad sympathy for the Algerian cause brought him into contact especially with Catholics and Protestants strongly motivated by religious sentiment. Many became his lasting allies, helping him out when somebody needed a night's sleep, no questions asked, or sending a friendly priest to ease some fugitive's passage across a national border. Among others, the Dominican Father Maurice Barth and Protestant pastor René Rognon were his intimate collaborators to the end.

As usual, it was by pure chance that he got into trouble. In the autumn of 1960, the DST picked him up for routine questioning about his FLN activities. A casual check at the home of a close collaborator led to discovery of documents having nothing to do with the Algerian War. They were photocopies of the minutes on secret talks between the French and German governments, which could only have come from classified files in the Quai d'Orsay. Curiel's refusal to explain how he had come by the documents led to his imprisonment for two years at Fresnes.[23] When the Algerian War was over, though, he was free as a bird again.

He formed Solidarité in 1963. But it did not get cracking until 1966, a vintage year. It was in 1966 that the Tricontinental Conference in Havana launched its global assault on Western imperialism and, with Soviet blessings, opened an era of international guerrilla warfare. For the next fifteen years, Solidarité perfectly reflected the policies laid down at Havana.

It was not a combat force, and it didn't meddle with the operational plans of its clientele. The Russians would hardly have expected that, if all they wanted was to keep tabs on a motley ideological crowd. Where ideology was concerned, an auxiliary outfit like Curiel's couldn't be too careful about showing a bias. The world's national liberation and terrorist movements are shot through with heretics of an unimaginably varied range between, say, the Trotskyites and the Maoists and anarchists. Except where they have actually taken money and arms from Russia's Chinese competitors, the Russians have not blacklisted any of them. Solidarité didn't either.

The faithfulness of the pattern alone might have been enough to arouse suspicion. On top of it, though, was the weighted presence in the network's top echelons of hard-lining pro-Moscow Communists and their all too familiar brand of sympathizers, not to mention the peculiar state of the network's finances. Apart from Curiel, who wore his heart on his sleeve, there were his indispensable assistants Father Barth and Pastor Rognon: both were long-standing activists in the World Peace Movement, one of the hoariest Soviet front groups still around. Michèle Firk, before going to Guatemala for Curiel, had worked for the French Communist Party's daily, *L'Humanité*, a Stalinist journal if there ever was one. Two other orthodox Communists turned out to be the answer, at last, to the eternal question of where Curiel's money could be coming from. They were Raymond Biriotti and Bernard Riguet, both on Solidarité's board of directors.

According to authoritative French sources (who confirmed it privately to me), Biriotti and Riguet were largely responsible for funneling the funds into the network. They were, respectively, the founder and commercial director of the Société d'Echanges et de Représentation, an export-import firm with offices at 2, Rue Colonel-Driant.[24] Their company maintained a current account at the Banque Commercial pour L'Europe du Nord (BCEN) in Paris, owned outright by the central bank of the Soviet Union. The BCEN, which also handles the account of the French Communist Party, is the Soviet Union's paymaster bank abroad. It has been notorious for years as the Kremlin's instrument for distributing illicit funds throughout Western Europe.[25]

What with one thing and another, then, the cracks in the network were bound to come. By the mid-1970s, defectors like

Breyton Breytenbach were adding considerably to a meager store of knowledge; what they had to say, when they were willing to say it, tended to confirm the prevailing view of Curiel in Western security circles. But two decades and more of laborious police surveillance had yielded little in the way of legal evidence. There were a few sure facts. Curiel did once work for, or with, Mikhail Suslov (now the Soviet Communist Party's chief theoretician, who insists that détente must in no way lessen the "ideological struggle" against Western democracies). He did get caught, in 1960, with secret French government papers that were none of his business. He was careless enough, just once, to be observed visiting the Soviet embassy in Paris. His trusted aide, Robert Davezies, had been seen visiting the Cuban embassy more often, while his second-in-command, Joyce Blau, had made a rather extended visit to Moscow in 1974. He had a number of veteran Stalinists on his staff, and his only known income depended on managerial ties with an export-import company drawing money from a pretty special branch of the Russian central bank.

He happened also to have a remarkably interesting family connection, though that didn't come out until very late in the day. In all those years of watching Curiel so warily, nobody in a dozen Western intelligence services seems to have associated him with a younger cousin he once took under his wing. The son of Henri's mother's brother in Holland, George Bihar was sent to Cairo in 1936 after the breakup of his parents' marriage. The Curiels had agreed to take him in and see to his education at the fashionable English School. He was an impressionable fourteen when he arrived and was given a room next to Henri's. His fascinating cousin was almost twenty-two. They became fast friends, with Henri patiently explaining the intricacies of radical politics and letting George tag along on those absorbing rounds of Cairo's left-wing salons and Arab cafés. The dazzled younger boy would tell his mother long afterward that those few years with the brilliant and dedicated Henri Curiel were the most meaningful in his life.[26]

From George Bihar, he went on to become "George Blake" in London—a member of Britain's MI 6 who betrayed forty Western spies and every state secret he could lay his hands on to the KGB before he was caught—the most stunningly success-ful double agent in modern history.

We are unlikely ever to discover whether "Blake" made his first contact with the KGB directly through his cousin Henri. The cousin is dead, and "Blake," lounging in the club for re-tired British spies in Moscow, is hardly the man to tell. He never did explain how he got into the trade, beyond confessing with some amusement that he did it all "for nothing." Since he didn't do it for money, or love, or blackmail, he must have been moved by boredom, or spite, or perversity—or political convic-tion, as his wife concluded when she divorced him. He was certainly a Communist, she said, though where and how he got to be one was a mystery. Such was the tingling shock he sent through the entire British Establishment that the matter is not just evaded, it is simply not discussed. He testified behind closed doors and was sentenced to forty-two years in prison, the longest such sentence on record. After serving barely four, at Wormwood Scrubs, he climbed over a wall on a ladder con-trived mostly of knitting needles and escaped. In good time, for he was not to be hurried, he proceeded on his leisurely onward journey to Moscow.

He stopped off in Cairo on the way, mailing a letter from there to his mother.[27] Curiel was long gone by then, but the association must have been strong for "George Blake," if for no one else. (Even then, nobody had yet connected the pair.) He could scarcely fail to recall another occasion when he had gone out of his way to drop in on that particular city.

On his first British secret-service assignment to South Korea, in 1948, "George Blake" had asked for leave to stop off in Cairo "to see a cousin." Though the leave was granted, he did not get to see Henri, who was in jail at the time. But it is hard to imagine that, with so warm an attachment, he would never try to see the cousin again. By his own account, he began to pass information systematically to the KGB from Hamburg in 1951, just about when Curiel opened shop in Paris, an hour or two away by plane. Did they ever meet, somewhere on the Continent, from then on until Blake was arrested a decade later? (Curiel did tell reporters once that he often crossed over into Germany, "borrowing a friend's passport and changing the photograph.") [28] "Blake" escaped from Wormwood Scrubs in 1966 with the help of a fellow prisoner, Sean Bourke of the IRA. Did Curiel, a valued benefactor of the IRA by 1966, have a hand in that? "Blake" was decorated in Moscow with the orders of Lenin and the Red Flag in 1970, honors never bestowed upon fellow club members like Philby, Burgess, McLean, but reserved solely for civilians on active service. What sort of active service might "George Blake" have been active on, in Moscow?

The dumbfounding question is how British intelligence could have hired "George Blake," knowing nothing of the cousin he held in such admiring esteem—the man representing the most meaningful political experience in his life. Everything else about his family and relations was in his dossier for his chiefs to see. The one fact that might have warned them escaped them, "precisely because it wasn't there," observed Lord Radcliffe, who headed the security commission of enquiry. It remained for *Le Point*'s correspondent, ten years after "Blake's" escape, to unearth his birth certificate as George Bihar, grandson of a Smyrna merchant, nephew of the Cairo banker Daniel Curiel, cousin of foreign agent S 531916 in Paris.[29]

That's that. You can't blame a man for his relatives, and nothing else known or still likely to be uncovered in the story proves a thing about Curiel. He denied all knowledge of "Blake's" nefarious double life, as was only natural. He also denied all the other lurid charges against him in the press, as did his associates. Indeed, they all threatened to sue, but none did.

Three months after *Le Point*'s exposé, Solidarité disappeared. The Aide et Amitié group that replaced it was carefully laundered. A bullet took care of Curiel barely over a year after that.

He died a free man. The material gathered so painstakingly against him was never enough to bring him to court. Even upon sending him briefly into forced exile, the French Interior Ministry did not make its charges public. It could only send a confidential note to the council of state responsible for refugees, summing up the main ones: operation of a "very sophisticated clandestine organization" supporting "revolutionary move-ments—some of them engaged in armed struggles," especially but not exclusively in the Third World; "active participation" in terrorist operations by providing false documents to the Japanese Red Army; "constant and concealed intervention in French affairs and centers of tension, especially in the Middle East conflict"; "extremely dangerous activities conducted from French territory," threatening to "undermine" French diplomacy in several countries "and to create a situation . . . harmful to public order." [30]

The circumstances of Curiel's murder in May 1978 are wholly mysterious. Somebody claiming to speak for something called "Delta" sent a statement to the press: "The KGB agent and traitor Henri Curiel ceased his activities at 2:00 P.M." But Delta, an assassination squad of the right-wing French extremists in the OAS during the Algerian War, had been defunct for more than fifteen years. Who else might have wanted him dead just then?

It was not an ordinary moment. For the first time since 1952, he was preparing to leave France not as "Julien" or "Raymond," but as Henri Curiel, with valid papers. For all anybody can tell, he might have been planning no more than the little holiday in Greece he said he was looking forward to, or getting out for good. He was going under murky circumstances either way.

Among the more singular features of Curiel's career was the delicate handling he received in high places. Kept under more or less continuous DST surveillance since 1953, he had nevertheless gone about his business without a single leak from the French authorities to the press until 1976. The leak evidently caused distress in certain official quarters, since the French press was thereupon given to understand that it was expected to lay off the subject. Access to further information about him has required heroic effort, as I for one can testify.

A possible clue goes back to those wartime days in Cairo, when he had given a hand to the Free French Mission. It is not unreasonable to assume that French Resistance leaders would remember Curiel's wartime services and reward them with a measure of indulgence. Nor would it be poor form to speculate on the chances of his having discreetly furnished information in return. Nobody gives anything away for nothing in this business. There seems little doubt, in any event, that his special relationship was with the Gaullists. When the general himself retired from the national scene in 1968, Curiel's position in France "changed dramatically": or so he told the *Economist Foreign Report*'s Robert Moss shortly before his death.[31]

That alone could have caught him in the perpetual crossfire of rival secret services in France—assorted official kinds or the eternally elusive "parallel police." Somebody in those quarters might have felt obliged to stop Curiel before he could get out of the country—either to silence him because he knew too much or to punish him because, all too plainly, the French courts never would.

If so, it wouldn't have been the first time. The French services have often been known to employ the tough old *barbouzes* of Algerian War days for a swift killing to expedite the solution of some tricky case. The practice became an international scandal in 1966, when the Moroccan leftist Ahmed Ben Barka vanished from Paris. A political menace to French interests (and King Hassan II) in Morocco, and organizing secretary abroad for Havana's imminent Tricontinental Conference, Ben Barka was kidnapped in broad daylight on the Boulevard Saint-Germain, never to be seen again.

Any number of others, dying in obscurity, have gone the same way. One of my more memorable conversations in France was with a personage of vast charm and qualified experience who assured me that he would brand me a compulsive liar if I quoted him. If, now and then, I should notice a small news item about a body washed up on a beach, he said, it might well be that of some trained and unregenerate professional terrorist, sent on "a long, long voyage—very long, madame," in the interests of preserving public order.

On the other hand, the French might have had nothing to do with the cessation of Curiel's activities. If he did work for the Russians, he was of no use to them once his cover was blown, and what he knew could hurt them. The hasty dismantling of his network within three months of its exposure suggests how worried somebody must have been about any more leaks like that. Somebody has also made sure, since then, that we are never going to find out anything more about Solidarité from the only man who knew all about it.

There is hardly any need to point out how little trouble it would give the KGB to take care of a problem like this—if it had to, of course.

With the death of Henri Curiel, a public that never got a chance to learn much about him is bound to forget him. But his file is still open in the DST, as it is in all important Western security services. By now, they have cross-indexed it with his cousin George's—not so much a mark of intent as an expression of regret.

4

"ANNABABI"

"Anna Maria Grenzi," alias "Marina Fedi," alias "Waltraud Armruster," known to her band as "Annababi," born in Berlin as Petra Krause, was described by the Swiss police as "the terrorist of the century" when they caught her.[1] But that was in 1975, before the police of a dozen countries caught up with some of her friends. She was no killer, like the rest. All she did was mind the store.

"Annababi" has retired now, living in Naples more or less in the odor of grace. She walked away from her Zurich jailers long ago, without even standing trial, whisked out of the grip of stern Swiss justice by a committee of indomitable Italian lady deputies who believed she was a victim of monstrous persecution. She certainly looked and acted the part, and the ladies did not inquire too deeply into her record. It wasn't done, in those days.

A citizen of Italy by marriage, Petra Krause was of German-Jewish birth. Both her parents died in Hitler's gas chambers. Her first three years of childhood were passed in the Nazi concentration camp of Auschwitz, within hearing distance of the laboratory where Nazi scientists experimented on children her age. She was spared by pure chance, exchanged along with a batch of two thousand babies for a shipment of Swedish steel. She always said afterward that she was being hounded for her anti-Fascist beliefs. It was ungallant to doubt her.

She did seem to be forever on the run. Both the Federal German government and the Italian government had warrants of arrest out for her when she was picked up in Switzerland,

and the security services of France, Spain, Austria, Greece and Israel would have liked very much to have had a word with her. Frail-looking as she was—with her slender frame, her thin, wan face hidden behind huge dark glasses, her air of troubled and weary womanhood—she eluded them all.

She was running a weapons takeout service in Zurich for a select European terrorist clientele when she was caught. Her customers included Greeks, Iranians, Spanish Basques, Irish Provisionals, the Baader-Meinhof Gang, Italy's Red Brigades, the French Gauchistes, the Palestinians' European Directorate led by "Carlos" in Paris. They would book their orders, and her band of young anarchist accomplices would then steal the specified items from Swiss Army depots, holding the merchandise for pickup in Zurich or shipping it by car or train. On special occasions, she would take care of deliveries in person.

The Swiss anarchists' takeout service was nothing so grand as Henri Curiel's Help and Friendship network. Though the band did try a bit of everything, from bombing consulates and multinational banks to plotting the shah of Iran's assassination, it stuck mostly to procuring and distributing weapons. Its stocks, drawn largely from Switzerland's armed forces, were excellent—one of its specialties was a heavy panzermine that could blow up a fifty-ton armored tank—but necessarily limited. The band could never have kept up with its clients' increasingly exigent demands as the fright decade advanced.

Nevertheless it was a godsend while it lasted—in the right place, at the right time. Nowhere else in Europe could neophyte terrorist bands turn for such bespoke logistic suppliers. By the time it more or less closed shop, halfway through the seventies, the Swiss takeout service had provided the guns and explosives for some of the Continent's biggest terrorist hits; and its work was done. A bigger and better supply and distribution system was ready to take over then, assuring a copious flow of arms to the European underground from the Soviet bloc, Libya, and the Middle East.

Though listed as the "Petra Krause Band" on the CIA's international terrorist chart, her Zurich ring was founded before she got there.[2] A few teen-age Swiss anarchists had gotten started on their own in 1970, with AKO (Anarchistische Kampforganisation). Very young, intensely earnest and unworldly, they dreamed of following somehow in Ché Guevara's footsteps. Before long, they hit on the idea of raiding Switzerland's loosely guarded armories to keep their fellow revolutionaries in weapons all over Europe (especially in Spain, where they longed to help overthrow Franco).

They started off with a bang on the burglary side, stealing a ton and a half of explosives, more than 200 rifles, 525 revolvers, and 346 grenades in their first three operative years.[3] But they were doing poorly on the distribution side before Petra Krause joined them. Once she came along, the ring's underground office in Zurich became the hottest address in Europe.[4]

Her Swiss accomplices told the whole story in court. She wasn't present, having been rescued by the Italian lady deputies in the summer of 1977. But the others who stood trial that year—Peter Egloff, Urs Staedeli, Daniel von Arb—confessed everything.[5]

They began to pass on explosives in 1971, they said, through a French anarchist who was soon jailed in his own country for gunrunning. Left in the lurch, they went to Milan in search of better international connections. There they found an Italian anarchist named Roberto Mander, or he found them.

Active in Italy's ultra-left circles since the mid-sixties, Mander was deeply involved in what was fast becoming Europe's most elaborate and advanced revolutionary-terrorist movement. The Organization emerging in his country not only needed weapons urgently for itself but was working closely with others in the same fix. (See chapter eleven.) Mander, meeting Egloff, Staedeli, and von Arb in Milan, knew a good thing when he saw one. Within weeks, he dropped in on his new friends in Zurich. With him was a German girl, from the inner circle of the Baader-Meinhof Gang, named Brigitte Heinrich.[6] One thing kept leading to another from then on.

Mander explained that his Italian comrades were strapped for guns and explosives. So were Brigitte Heinrich's comrades in West Germany. So were Mander's Spanish Basque friends and a lively Marxist-Leninist guerrilla group in Madrid called FRAP. The Swiss takeout service booked its first commissioned orders and opened shop.

Mander returned to Zurich often, bringing Brigitte Heinrich along, and the pair never left empty-handed. When West

German police raided two Baader-Meinhof safe-houses early in 1974 (in Hamburg and Frankfurt), they found an arsenal of grenades, antitank mines, machine pistols, shotguns, handguns, and explosives traceable to the Swiss takeout service.[7] It was a modest find, compared to others.

That was the year Petra Krause joined the ring. Roberto Mander produced her, at a secret meeting with the Swiss trio in Milan, in April 1974. A mature divorcée, with red-blond hair and rather more of a cold eye than her deceptively feminine manner suggested, she plainly knew her way around. Mander introduced her as "Anna Maria Grenzi."

She was thirty-four then, with a long political trail behind her. The horror of her childhood had naturally inclined her to left-wing views, which grew more pronounced as she grew older. "I started out as an orthodox Marxist-Leninist and passed from complete non-violence to a point where I understood that non-violence is a bourgeois luxury," was how she put it to *Newsweek* upon her retirement.[8] Drifting into Italy while still in her teens, she joined the Communist Party and, before long, slipped into the twilight zone of clandestinity.

Her assignments were modest at first: she would "lend" her passport, say, to fugitives from Franco's Spain or Salazar's Portugal or put such people up in her Milan apartment. Then she was sent on mysterious missions to Africa—Algeria and the Portuguese colonies of Angola and Mozambique, all three magnets for European revolutionary missionaries in the sixties. "I was helping the natives to understand the realities of their country," she explained.[9] Back in Italy, she wound up working for Giangiacomo Feltrinelli, as an interpreter-translator. By 1968, she was wholly caught up in the exuberant surge of New Left politics and ready for the approaching decade. "The police were getting after me," she told the press years later. "I began to see the need for other instruments to fight the bourgeois state, and my reservations about violence fell away." [10]

She went underground, acquired a new name and fake passport, took a faceless clerical job in Milan, and traveled a lot on the side. There was not much she didn't know about Europe's subterranean terrorist circuit when the ingenuous Swiss trio met up with her.

She appears to have bowled them over. If they never did

trust her entirely, von Arb explained after his arrest, they deferred to her judgment and were enormously impressed by her international contacts. (They would be sorry someday. "The defendants insisted that they had always wanted to be independent. But once they got into the international net, they could not get out," wrote the *Neue Zürcher Zeitung* reporter covering the trial.) [11]

For some months, she commuted between Milan and Zurich, briskly expanding the service. At one meeting in her Milan home, she presented to her Swiss partners a Greek with the game-name "Alexis"; he became the ring's go-between for arms consignments to Greece and Spain. Soon afterward, she and "Alexis" met again with the Swiss trio in her Milan flat, to introduce "André." He turned out to be the Lebanese Michel Moukarbal, chief aide to Carlos the Jackal in Paris, who promptly entangled the Zurich band with the whole Carlos network.

"This 'André' asked us if we had explosives available and were possibly prepared to give him some," von Arb told interrogators, describing the fateful meeting in Petra's flat. "Then he said he had several connections with left-wing extremist groups in Europe, and he would need explosives for them. . . . He told us he was working for the Palestinians, for Dr. George Habash. . . ." [12]

Within a couple of weeks, "André," or Moukarbal, sent couriers to Zurich to collect twenty antipersonnel mines, a scatter mine, and one of those devastating panzermines, stolen by the Swiss anarchists from an army depot at Hochfelden.[13] Von Arb himself led them on foot over a "Green" (or unguarded) border, to smuggle the material back into France. From then on, the Carlos network shopped regularly in Zurich for mines, explosives, and firearms, passing them around to its own multinational terrorist team in Paris, the IRA Provisionals, the Spanish Basques in ETA, and the Japanese Red Army on the Continent.

When Carlos sent his Japanese commandos over to seize the French embassy in Holland—the first such spectacular assault of the decade—"André" tried to get the Swiss in deeper, but they balked. Three Japanese, shipped out for the hit from

Aden and Baghdad, were stranded briefly in Switzerland on their way to meet Carlos and Moukarbal in Amsterdam.[14] " 'André' asked us to smuggle them across the Green Border, but we refused," von Arb told the police. "Then he called us up two weeks later to say proudly that the French Embassy hit had come off." It was the first clue they had to the shadowy "André's" extravagant operational ambitions. He had also asked them to back up the Holland operation by bombing Japan Airlines in Zurich, "if possible during the day, when its office in Pelikanstrasse had the most people in it," said von Arb. "But we didn't want to do it."

Clearly, the ingenuous Swiss anarchists were getting leery of Moukarbal, though they had no idea who he really was. Not until his boss, Carlos, drilled him between the eyes more than a year later did they identify a photograph of the dead Moukarbal as their "André." Petra Krause knew all along, though. Indeed, she had hired a Ford Escort for Moukarbal from Avis in Geneva, just three days before his death. French police found the contract, signed by "Anna Maria Grenzi," among his papers.

She had changed names again by then. In October 1974, a car of hers was found at the scene of a ten-million-dollar fire, set by Italian terrorists to destroy an electronics plant owned by the multinational ITT. With the carabinieri at her heels, she slipped over the border into Switzerland and settled in Zurich for good. She was "Marina Fedi" now, with a brand-new fake passport.

To von Arb, Egloff, and Staedeli, she quickly became "Annababi," the band's acknowledged leader, and things began to hum.

Within a month—the single month of November 1974—they were up to their necks in three different terrorist conspiracies of the highest order.

For one thing, Brigitte Heinrich showed up again. This time she came without Roberto Mander, bringing along an Iranian student instead. He was Mehdi Khanbaba-Teherani, who, with a band of fellow Iranians in Frankfurt, was interested in assassinating Shah Reza Pahlevi. "Annababi's" Swiss ring was all for it. Months of intricate German-Swiss-Iranian plotting followed. The shah was going to be blown up in his ski chalet at Saint-Moritz, exactly as Spanish Premier Luis Carrero Blanco had been blown up in Madrid a year before—by tunneling underground and planting a hundred or so pounds of explosive, that is. (In that case too, the explosives had come from the Swiss takeout service.) [15] The plans, meticulously drawn and well advanced, were found accidentally when Swiss police stumbled on a cache of stolen arms and secret documents that December.

Meanwhile, Petra had her Italian friends to think of. The autumn of 1974 was to have marked a decisive stage for Italy's terrorist movement. The Red Brigades, in collaboration with a broader ultra-left Autonomous Area, had plans for proliferating violence in the industrial north, leading to popular armed insurrection—or so they hoped. The documented evidence would come out in Italian courts at the end of the decade (see chapter eleven), whereupon this particular episode clicked into place.

"About November 10, 1974, 'Annababi' told us she needed explosives for her Italian left extremist connections and asked for some of our stolen mines," von Arb told his interrogators. "She said we wouldn't have to transport the mines. She would do it herself, with 'Andrea,' alias Sergio Spazzali."

A celebrated lawyer for Italy's Red Brigades, Spazzali was no stranger to the Zurich ring. He had come up in person the previous summer, to collect a sizable assortment of mines and grenades.[16] Now, on November 17, he came again to join "Annababi" and von Arb for a smuggling run vital to the Italian underground's audacious plans. They all took off in a car loaded down with forty-two heavy antitank mines—enough to blast a good part of downtown Milan into rubble—but the car never made it across the border.

"When we got to Altdorf, near the Italian frontier, our driver ran into a traffic light pillar," von Arb told police later. "Spazzali and I managed to drag the mines out of the car before the police came. But the accident was reported, and we couldn't use the car anymore." Another Italian comrade, summoned urgently by phone, rushed up from Italy to collect Spazzali and his precious cargo, while "Annababi" and von

Arb nipped back to Zurich. Once over the frontier, though, Spazzali and his driver fell right into the arms of Italian police. (Brought to trial six years later, Spazzali was sentenced to seven and a half years in prison. So was Petra Krause, tried *in absentia* because she was allegedly too unwell to appear in court. Neither has actually gone to prison on this count so far, however. Their appeals are still pending as this is written.)

Within days of "Annababi's" narrow escape at the border, another celebrated lawyer came to see her in Zurich. Siegfried Haag was a fixture of West Germany's Legal Red Aid Society, Röte Hilfe, just as Spazzali was of Italy's comparable Soccorso Rosso. Like Spazzali, he was apparently overcommitted to his imprisoned terrorist clients. Indeed, lawyer Haag would soon be taking over the active direction of the Baader-Meinhof Gang he then served as legal counselor. By the spring of 1975, Haag was the new second-generation leader of the entire West German terrorist underground. (By 1980 Petra's own lawyer, Maître Rambert of Swiss Red Aid, was jailed as well for receiving "stolen goods" in the form of several thousand blank identity cards. He was arrested August 20, 1980.) [17]

Petra Krause had worked closely with Haag and his Röte Hilfe for years. No sooner was she moved to Zurich, in fact, than she obliged her Swiss band to provide sanctuary for the noted German terrorist fugitive Astrid Proll. It was "Annababi" who saw to smuggling Astrid Proll from Germany to Switzerland to Italy to England. Now, in November 1974, Haag came to enlist her aid again for his most distinguished client. Languishing in West Germany's maximum-security prison at Stammheim, Ulrike Meinhof, Andreas Baader, Gudrun Ensslin, and Jan-Carl Raspe were making imperious demands for action to get them out.

Carlos the Jackal had shown the way barely two months before. By seizing the French embassy in Holland at gunpoint, he had sprung a Japanese terrorist from a prison cell in Paris. Lawyer Haag's idea was to seize five German embassies: in Amsterdam, Berne, Copenhagen, London, and Stockholm. (He chose them in alphabetical order, confided a retired German terrorist to *Der Spiegel*.) [18]

Berne being Switzerland's capital, Haag naturally asked the

Swiss anarchists to give him a hand there. A grain of caution led them to refuse. As von Arb observed later, though, "It was hard for 'Annababi' to turn her old German friends down." She agreed, at least, to provide the weapons for what turned out to be one of the decade's most grotesque and calamitous terrorist assaults—on the German embassy in Stockholm. (See chapter six.)

Lawyer Haag visited Zurich often between November and the following March, bringing along his inseparable companion from the Baader-Meinhof Gang, Elizabeth von Dyck. He booked specific orders with the takeout service for the Stockholm hit. Apart from the usual grenades and explosives, he wanted a High Standard automatic rifle and an MP Suomi automatic. He gave "Annababi" two thousand Swiss francs to buy them on the black market, if they couldn't be stolen.[19]

On the last day of January, "Annababi" crossed over personally into Germany with these guns, delivering them to Siegfried Haag and Elizabeth von Dyck in Waldshut. Both weapons were found in the smoking ruins of the German embassy in Stockholm six weeks later.[20]

During all those months, the Swiss police had been keeping Petra Krause under discreet surveillance. They had photographed her many times in Zurich, making a meet at the Bellevue tram terminal, waiting at a phone booth for calls from von Arb or Staedeli, moving from safe-house to safe-house. Her connections were mysterious and baffling.

Wanted by the Italian police, using a false name and fake documents, she had nevertheless found hospitality for months in Zurich with Theo Pinkus, a leader of Switzerland's inflexibly pro-Moscow Communist Party. Visitors coming to see her there, in Wildbachstrasse 48, were photographed going in and out: Siegfried Haag, Elizabeth von Dyck, others from the German terrorist underground, her own Swiss accomplices. It was not easy to reconcile her staying with Pinkus with her own image (and that of her terrorist comrades) as a New Left radical whose ties with orthodox communism had been severed long since.

She had also lived on and off over the Eco-Libro Bookshop in Engelstrasse 42, later identified by an Italian court as the

Continental headquarters of a Terrorist International. The apparent successor of Feltrinelli's Zurich *centrale* (1971) and Potere Operaio's Zurich International Office (1972), the Eco-Libro circuit reportedly tied Europe's terrorist war zone from Italy, Greece, France, Spain, West Germany, and Ireland to Lebanon, Syria, Iraq, South Yemen, and Egypt. (In his formal indictment on the Aldo Moro murder case, issued January 3, 1980, Italy's Attorney General Guido Guasco stated: "Reports from the secret services indicate that subversive bands from various countries, including the Red Brigades, were in contact among themselves through a centralized office, presumably localized in the Eco Bookshop in Zurich. . . ." Through this *centrale*, "strenuous efforts were made to recuperate as much as possible for a 'Europe project' at the [high] organizational levels maturing in Italy and Ireland," he added.)

Krause also knew where to get three different forged passports for herself and an array of fake identity cards for her Swiss underlings (apparently made in Milan). Furthermore, she was good enough at her work to guide them to rare professional heights. The Swiss takeout service had just completed a record year when she was caught. In 1974 alone, her ring had stolen 192 panzermines and treadmines, 358 pistols, 123 rifles, 1,230 pounds of explosive, and a mile and a half of fuse.

Its merchandise—grenades, dynamite, mines, firearms—was stockpiled in the Continent's best terrorist safe-houses and kept turning up in suggestive places: the German embassy in Stockholm; the Baader-Meinhof Gang's hideouts in Hamburg and Frankfurt; the baggage compartment of the Catalan *Talgo* Express bound for Barcelona; the kidnappers' cove near Italy's Aqui Terme, where the wife of Red Brigades leader Renato Curcio died in a shootout with the carabinieri; a busy shopping street in downtown Milan, where a deadly panzermine was left lying in the path of oncoming cars, wrapped casually in newspaper; the Via Gradoli apartment used by the Red Brigades to mount Aldo Moro's abduction in Rome; the Roman flat where a top Red Brigades commander—Valerio Morucci—was captured, with grenades from the Swiss takeout service and the Skorpion machine pistol used to murder Moro. (Morucci had collected the grenades in Zurich himself.) [21]

The Swiss police arrested Petra Krause on March 20, 1975. She was outraged when they picked her up in Zurich's Bellevueplatz, shoulder bag swinging as she paced the crowded tram terminal, looking at her watch. "I had a date to meet a friend, when we were suddenly encircled and brutally separated by a group of men who pinioned my arms behind me, and snatched my bag," she told a reporter for *Le Nouvel Illustré* afterward. "If it had happened in Italy, and if I'd had a gun, I would have fired like a mad thing. I would have been sure it was a fascist assault. . . ." In fact, she did not have a gun, but her friend did. Arrested along with her, under the concrete canopy of Bellevueplatz, was lawyer Haag's inseparable companion, Elizabeth von Dyck. As a ranking member of the Baader-Meinhof hierarchy, she was under strict orders to carry a gun at all times. Indeed, she would die in the act of drawing one, when she was ambushed by the German police four years later.[22]

Petra Krause was held in a Zurich jail for the next twenty-eight months, without trial. She did her best to delay it, with three hunger strikes, an obstinate refusal to take fresh-air exercises, an attempted escape inviting special surveillance, and the use of legal expedients forcing repeated trial postponements, lengthening her prison stay by nearly a year.

These facts were stoically disregarded by the many Italians rallying to her defense. The indomitable committee demanding her extradition to Italy spoke only of a fine and sensitive woman with "a long history of militancy in defending political prisoners," whose experience at the mercy of her Swiss jailers was a "bloodchilling case of the violation of human rights." Her defenders were counting on the Italian courts to be far more lenient, even in the face of a ten-million-dollar arson charge; and they were right. Welcomed by a cheering crowd at Rome's airport, Petra Krause spent five days in a Naples jail and walked out a free woman. A year later, she was absolved of the charge "for lack of evidence."

She remained a heroine for most of the Italian press, for most of the last half of the decade. Lengthy reports spoke of her "slow death . . . under the psycho-physical tortures of rigorous isolation" in the Zurich jail, and the tormenting sound of a nearby "excessively noisy" hydraulic pump. Practically no Italian daily of importance mentioned the reasons for her Swiss internment. The left-Communist *Manifesto* simply spoke of "an alleged theft of munitions from a Swiss military armory." The Italian Communist Party's unofficial organ, *Paese-Sera*, referred to presumed and unconfirmed "incursions into Swiss armories." The ultra-left daily *Lotta Continua* merely mentioned that she was "accused of subversive acts which have never been proved."

Thus, very nearly until 1980, did the Italian left continue to be resolutely incurious about a case which might have shaken them out of their most comfortable convictions: that nobody who claims to hate fascism can be a terrorist; that all cops are brutes; that anybody who is against the bourgeois Establishment can't be all bad.

5

A TOURIST'S GUIDE TO THE UNDERGROUND

"Would you approve of an action by your comrades to get you out of here?" a Swiss policeman guarding Gabriele Kröcher-Tiedemann asked after her conviction for trying to murder two other Swiss policemen.

"God willing," she smiled in reply.

"And now that you know me, would you shoot me?" he continued.

"Yes," she said.

Unrepentant, unapproachable, unappeased in her rage against society, the woman described by an OPEC kidnap victim as "the most bestial" of the Carlos assault team in Vienna is condemned now to spend fifteen years in a Swiss jail. Her former husband, Norbert, who had prepared a coffin two feet wide by six feet long with air holes for his intended Swedish kidnap victim, now occupies a German prison cell barely twice that size. Both had drifted beyond an outsider's reach or understanding long before they landed behind bars. The Organization had erected its own walls around them; and anybody who wasn't in there with them was just another of the "Walking Deads," in Norbert's words.

The Kröchers, taken separately, are no more interesting than a hundred terrorists like them. They are no cleverer, no abler, no more passionately motivated, not even more coldly brutal, though Gabriele might deserve a short footnote in the last regard. Taken together, though, they are a tourist's guide to the international terrorist underground. Born around the same time and place, militating in the same clandestine group (in itself barely distinguishable from the rest), they happened, in going their separate ways, to cover the broadest of the subterranean highways linking their secret world from East to West. Gabriele's way leads straight to the Palestinians in the Middle East and to the Soviet satellite republic of South Yemen. Norbert's follows a more scenic route through Sweden, Denmark and France, Mexico, Chile and Argentina, to Cuba. From there it leads directly to another Soviet satellite, North Korea, by way of Moscow itself.

I first heard of Gabriele Kröcher-Tiedemann in Rome, in the spring of 1978. Italy was close to nervous collapse. Aldo Moro, president of the governing Christian Democratic Party and the irreplaceable key to Italian politics, was a captive of the Red Brigades. They had ambushed him in his car in broad daylight, on a busy Rome thoroughfare, gunning down his five bodyguards and eluding a monumental manhunt for the next fifty-five days. Then they finished him off with eleven bullets: "the highest possible act of humanity in this class society," they said. For speed, mobility, reconnaissance, logistics, staying power, and refinements in psychological warfare, it was a matchless performance.

Most Italians felt it couldn't be an inside job; no Italian was capable of such clockwork precision, they argued. But there was no evidence of a foreign mastermind and no reason to doubt that the Red Brigades could have done it alone. They were at the top of their trade by 1978, perfectly capable of putting a year's effort and a million dollars into an operation showing unmistakable signs of their own handiwork. Furthermore, they made such a point of being purely homegrown, and seemed so honestly outraged at suggestions to the contrary, that it began to look as if they really didn't have any foreign ties after all.

They did, though. It was someone at the Italian Interior Ministry who put me on to at least one small but hard fact—all but lost in the cascade of facts coming out in the next couple of years. Three months before Moro was kidnapped, he told me, a German woman named Kröcher-Tiedemann had been arrested in Switzerland carrying part of the ransom money from a kidnapping mounted in Austria by fellow German terrorists; another part of this ransom had been sent to the Red Brigades. "I can't give you documented proof of this," my informant added. "Why not go to Vienna and find it yourself?"

I went to Vienna, and from there to Zurich, and on to Bonn and half a dozen other European capitals, pursuing a trail that led far beyond Italian and German frontiers. The trail grew more and more familiar as I went along, tracking back first on Gabriele and then on her ex-husband, Norbert. Feltrinelli and Curiel crossed it, as well as Carlos and his Palestinian sponsors. So did the Tupamaros and the IRA Provisionals, the Red Brigades, the Polisario Front in the western Sahara, and terrorists from at least eight other nations. The Cubans and Russians came and went. Nothing I found along the way pointed to a single master plan. Certain people simply happened to show up in the right place at the right time, again and again.

The Kröchers met in Berlin when they were just turning twenty, an apparently joyless encounter. Gabriele wanted a student grant from the Berlin Land, and Norbert had the necessary residence papers. The marriage was mainly for convenience and didn't last long.

Both were born in East Germany, and neither had had a carefree childhood. Gabriele's father was an ardent Nazi, a bully and a drunk; her mother, an apparently submissive woman and an elementary-school teacher, had finally walked out on him. To the mother, Gaby was "a sweet and balanced child," who was bright in school and never any trouble. She was attractive, too, with her unusually light eyes in an elfin face and heavy blonde hair worn in bangs. While her slender, boyish body didn't change much as she grew to womanhood, her features thickened, and an air of animation gave way to alternate moods of withdrawal and defiance.

By the time she signed up for sociology at Berlin's Free

University, any early intellectual spark seemed gone. When she moved on to the huge postwar University of Bochum, a diploma mill with 25,000 students and the country's highest student suicide rate, she apparently lost interest altogether. "You couldn't have called her a distinguished scholar," a former professor of hers said to me dryly. "I wouldn't even remember her if she hadn't gotten herself caught stealing cars." Perhaps it was a sense of such helpless anonymity that made her want to steal them in the first place, he suggested. Like most of her companions in terror, at any rate, she never did finish school.

Norbert's parents were the opposite of Gabriele's, suggesting the uselessness of amateur psychiatry in these matters. His father was a committed Communist and active anti-Nazi who died before he was born. His mother, who worked as a concierge (a bit grander than an American janitor, though not much), also had strong leftist views. Indeed, she appears to have had strong views about everything. The harshly unbending ethical standards she imposed on her son were a torment to him, he said later, cutting him off from others his age and turning him inward.

Judging from the number of girls who jumped into bed with him during his few grown-up years of freedom, he overcame his childhood inhibitions. But the girls attracted by his brooding heavy features and air of interior suffering always ended up being afraid of him. Gaby's mother, who hated the sight of him, called him an alcoholic and an "unpleasant ruffian." A former accomplice of his confessed that, even in his early twenties, he "emanated an atmosphere of threat."

He became a radical anarchist while still in his teens. He was working in the Berlin post office then, as a technician in telecommunications, his first and last steady job; his first political venture was to set up a Red Cell later to hook up with the Baader-Meinhof crowd in the Red Army Fraction. That was around 1969, when Andreas Baader and Ulrike Meinhof hadn't yet joined forces to flabbergast the German bourgeoisie, when the Tupamaros of West Berlin had just started Bombing for Peace, and bands of mocking youths roamed Berlin's Kurfürstendamm with congenial posters demanding warm underwear for cops and toilets for dogs.

By 1970, Norbert had given up working for good and fell in with a student collective, Kommune I. While smoking hash and making love with the rest, he took little part in the others' ponderous self-searching. He didn't care much for talk, preferring action.

Meanwhile, Gabriele was moving fast from vague radicalism to the harder stuff through contact with the IRA Provisionals. The Provos of Northern Ireland, though not then the ultraleft Marxists they would become, were among the first in Europe to embrace the cult of indiscriminate terrorist killing; and they were just starting to fan out across the Continent in search of arms and money. West Germany's rich and restive students were longing for a new cause after the Vietnam War petered out. The IRA, cheek by jowl with the Palestinians, found the hunting very good there. Gabriele and hundreds of German students like her visited Ireland several times (just as they would take to visiting the Palestinians in the Middle East). At Bochum, she edited a German-language page of the Provos' inflammatory journal *An Phoblacht*. Sketches showing how to build and throw bombs were its outstanding feature.[1]

When Gabriele and Norbert met and married in 1971, both had gravitated toward a band of twenty or thirty Berlin youths calling themselves the June 2 Movement. Less flamboyant than the militarist and elitist Baader-Meinhof Gang, the June 2 Movement was a looser formation, slightly kitsch and tending at first to lag behind in the intent ferocity of its designs upon society. Still, it was all for the "disorganization and annihilation of the existing regime," in the best traditions of the anarchist Bakunin; and as time went by, it got to be rather good at that.

Many an engaging hash rebel had wound up in the June 2 Movement early on, including former Tupamaros of West Berlin like "Bommi the Bomber" Baumann, the jaunty courier who would drop in on Giangiacomo Feltrinelli in Milan to collect those generous checks for the German underground. But it wasn't long before Baumann's group pulled abreast of the flashier Red Army Fraction—indeed, surpassed it—in a vicious display of bloodshed and desecration. When "Bommi" himself broke away and fled to India in 1975, he was running for his life, from his comrades and the pig police alike. "The group principle is that there is no entrance fee, but quitting is impossible—the only way out is through the cemetery," he wrote later. By then, the soul of the June 2 Movement was mirrored in its leader, Ralf Reinders, who planned to bomb Jewish House in Berlin "to get rid of this thing about Jews that we've all had to have since the Nazi time." [2]

The Kröchers were no sooner married than Norbert robbed his first bank—a proletarian expropriation, he would have called it. At the time, the newlyweds were already contributing to the anarchist review *Fizz*, mostly on the art of building time bombs, and related matters. Their material was lifted right out of Havana's *Tricontinental* magazine; *The Anarchists' Cookbook*, copying blackboard diagrams from Cuba's guerrilla classrooms; and similar pedagogic material from Feltrinelli's chain of Italian bookshops.

What with sticking up several other banks, stealing cars, and pulling guns on the German police, the Kröchers saw the wisdom of moving to Sweden for a while. That was late in 1972, with their marriage already on the rocks. Their ways parted when Gaby returned to Berlin a month later.

She must have sensed that she was getting in too deep. "Several doctors have advised me to get psychiatric help, and I will," she wrote to her mother that spring. She added, however, that, for the time being, "it is necessary for me to cut off all contacts with you." The next summer, caught in the act of stealing car license plates, she ended a wild flight through the streets by shooting a policeman in the foot. ("She always did aim too low," Norbert observed in Stockholm, when somebody phoned to tell him the news.) By August 1973 she was in her first prison cell, sentenced to serve eight years. But her fellow terrorists in the June 2 Movement got her sprung in well under two. They had only to do what terrorists have always done and will always do so long as the blackmail works. That is, they snatched a hostage and held him until the German government agreed to free five terrorist prisoners, Gabriele among them.

With this particularly prominent hostage, Berlin's Christian Democratic leader Peter Lorenz, the terrorists merely had to hold out for six days. The deceptive ease of their victory—the enormity of the Federal German government's swift surrender—would release a surging terrorist force that would soon plunge the country into its gravest crisis in a quarter of a century. From the fatal day in March 1975 when Chancellor Schmidt's cabinet caved in, the Germans were caught in a remorselessly escalating tragedy. A savage assault on the German embassy in Stockholm, of unforgettably mindless and barbarous cruelty; the murders of a chief federal prosecutor, a leading banker, a judge; the kidnapping and killing of top industrialist Schleyer; the hijacking to Mogadiscio of a Lufthansa plane carrying eighty-two passengers, within minutes of death when army commandos freed them: all this and more can be traced to the illusions born of that early terrorist success. So can the blasted lives of Norbert and Gabriele Kröcher.

Freed from jail with $10,000 in pin money apiece, Gabriele and four other terrorist convicts were all put on a Lufthansa Boeing and flown straight to South Yemen, where the Palestinian Rejection Front ran (and still runs) a finishing school for urban guerrillas from every part of the world. All five, on graduating, went right back to Europe to resume their careers at a higher professional level. All are back in jail again, along with a score more who—remembering the government's nerveless surrender that first time—went right on kidnapping and killing to get them out again, this time with no luck.

Gabriele did not want to leave with the rest in 1975. A few rather dreary years in the Movement had not yet brought her up to its exacting standards. The Revolutionary Catechism, prescribed for nineteenth-century tsarist Russia by the nihilist Nechayev, had become scripture for her comrades a century later. It required a revolutionary to "stifle in himself all considerations of kinship, love, friendship, even honor . . . and know only the science of destruction." Evidently hard put to stifle all those bourgeois considerations, Gabriele, from prison, was still writing affectionate letters home. "Dear Mummy! I send you much love for your birthday on the 12th. Congratulations and all my best wishes! Alas, I don't know if this letter will reach you punctually. Please don't be angry if it's late. You know I have no influence over that. . . ." [3]

When the offer of release came, her instinct was to turn it down; in a few more months, she would be eligible for parole and free to start life over again. She discussed it with her mother for five anguished hours. "It may sound strange for a mother to want her daughter to stay in prison, but I implored her to do it," Frau Tiedemann said, and that is what Gabriele decided. But a last-minute phone call changed her mind. Telephoning long-distance from a different prison (a convenience rarely mentioned in terrorist fright-stories about German *Lagers*), another of the five due for liberation made Gabriele's position perfectly plain. The June 2 Movement was not asking but ordering her to leave with the others. It had already liquidated a backslider and class traitor named Ulrich Schmucker, who was shot to death the previous year. Gabriele was left in no doubt of the fate in store for her if she stayed behind.

"Mother, try to understand. I must go," she wrote in a farewell note. She was filmed by TV cameras walking up the gangplank of the departing plane, clutching the hand of Protestant Pastor Heinrich Albertz, looking painfully young and afraid. Albertz, the former mayor of Berlin, flying with them as hostage until their safe landing, said she was the only one of the five with an open face. "I don't think she was on board of her own free will," he added.[4]

In a Swiss courtroom three years later, an icily detached Gabriele would offer a different version of that last prison scene. "My mother tried to blackmail me by threatening suicide if I left with the others. I have never seen her again," she said.[5]

Aden was the end of Gabriele.

As the capital of South Yemen, Soviet Russia's satellite then and its military property now, Aden was and still is a peculiarly advantageous location for Russians and left-wing Palestinians both. Scores of other areas may be available for basic guerrilla courses, and I will be listing some. But Aden is not just another place for young hopefuls to learn how to use a Russian- or Czech-made Kalashnikov assault rifle, say, or the Makarov and Skorpion automatic pistols ideal for assassinations and bank heists. Safe from prying eyes and safely distant in geography from Soviet soil, the capital of South Yemen has been used for what might be called the Dirty Tricks Department in international guerrilla warfare.

The Russians, for instance, have trained special guerrilla

bands there from highly sensitive areas of direct strategic interest to Moscow. Among others, the desert tribesmen of Dhofar province have had a special camp reserved for them near Aden since 1968; until their insurrection failed in 1975, the Russians were sending them back home armed to the teeth for the conquest of little Oman, afloat on a bottomless sea of Arab oil.

At the same time, Palestinian Marxists have been using South Yemen for more than a decade to screen and groom an elite multinational terrorist force. George Habash, whose Popular Front for the Liberation of Palestine was the first to export Middle East terrorism to Western Europe, keeps his official headquarters in Beirut but his choicest guerrilla camps in Aden. So, until his reported death in 1978, did Habash's close associate Wadi Haddad, supreme strategist of the Palestinians' European terror network. It was under Haddad's gifted command that Carlos the Jackal directed a swinging mixed killer-team from his Paris headquarters in the mid-seventies, spreading death and panic from the Baltic Sea to the Mediterranean. Carlos happened to be one of the people Gabriele met in Aden.

It is impossible to say how many other luminaries she may have met. The flow in and out of the camps was endless. Hundreds of Iranians trained there, before lending their professional skills for the overthrow of the shah and the cause of Permanent Revolution in Iranian Islam. Turks, Irish Provisionals, Eritreans, South Americans of a dozen nationalities, South Moluccans who would win overnight fame in Holland by taking a whole passenger train hostage, drilled side by side with Dutch, Belgians, Spanish, Scandinavians, Swiss, Italians, Japanese.

German terrorists had been in residence from the start. The Tupamaros of West Berlin got to one or another of Habash's camps as early as 1969, just when the millionaire Italian publisher Feltrinelli was beginning to hand out money to the Germans and Habash both. All the hard-core Baader-Meinhof people started to check in to the Mideast by the next year. They were moving on to the specialized South Yemen camps by 1975.

The first eyewitness account of the camps came from Ludwina Janssen, an attractive young Dutch girl who had gone to the Habash-Haddad Camp Khayat in 1976 with fifteen comrades from Dutch Red Help. Arrested in Israel on her first mission after graduation, she promptly confessed. Apart from a number of Germans there, including Siegfried Haag and Wilfred Böse, head of the German Revolutionary Cells, she had seen members of the Provisional IRA, Iranians, Turks, various South Americans, Eritrean separatists, and Japanese. Cuban instructors played a very important role, she said.[6]

All this and more was confirmed in 1978 by Hans-Joachim Klein, a defector from the German Revolutionary Cells who had been on Carlos's OPEC team. He had actually taught in the Aden camp for eight months after the OPEC raid, training five women colleagues of Gabriele Kröcher-Tiedemann. When he joined the others in South Yemen, he said, "I found that those at the top lived like kings, and the others like dirt. The chiefs had movies, discothèques, a special restaurant and cash, and we shared their privileges. The Palestinian troops had nothing." The Revolutionary Cells, less known than the Baader-Meinhof Gang outside Germany but no less deadly within, had been on Haddad's payroll for years, with an allowance of $3,000 a month.[7]

Not many others at the camps were getting handouts, though. The majority, awash in money from bank heists and ransoms, were paying through the nose, and the Germans were in the top income bracket. Before the June 2 Movement's secret kangaroo court condemned the backslider and class traitor Ulrich Schmucker to death, he had told a Federal German court something about this.[8] By his reckoning, the June 2 Movement must have paid the Palestinians 10,000 Deutschmarks, then around $4,000, to train Gabriele Kröcher-Tiedemann; that was the going rate. Germans on the run had to shell out 3,000 DM for temporary refuge in Lebanon or Iraq; Schmucker himself, sent to shop for weapons in the Middle East, had paid 15,000 DM for small arms, as much again for explosives, and 5,000 DM each for hand grenades and machine pistols.

Still, the service was good. Returning from their Palestinian schooling, German terrorist rookies were transformed into the Prussian Junkers of the guerrilla movement. Business was sternly separated from pleasure, love from grim revolutionary duty. Hash, blues, rock music, and general horsing around were out, and martial discipline was in. "When they came back . . . with their hair cut short and false passports, they were strangers to us," wrote "Bommi" Baumann in *Come è Cominciata* (How It Began). The New Man, they gave him to understand, was born with a gun in his fist.[9]

As luck would have it, Gabriele was thrown in with a particularly glamorous crowd of Germans at the Aden camp. At least three of her compatriots were present as instructors, not trainees, sharing the guest lecturers' podium with Cuban and East German guerrilla specialists. The top celebrity, teaching explosives and close body-fighting under the game-name "Khaled," was the Heidelberg lawyer Siegfried Haag. "Authoritative, cold, calculating, intelligent," according to Ludwina Janssen, Haag had just gone underground that spring. He had just stopped being legal counselor to the first-generation Baader-Meinhof leaders, to lead the next generation himself.

By then, in fact, Siegfried Haag was twisting the strands in Germany leading to the downfall of Norbert Kröcher in Stockholm. As a result, Gabriele's former husband would beat her back to jail by nine months.

It is unlikely that Gabriele was much the wiser politically for her stay in Aden. She had to put in a grueling twelve-hour day, often ending in trips to the field hospital for treatment of wounds or bruises. There was little leisure time for talk, and even then Wadi Haddad would not permit it between different national groups except by special dispensation. Hans-Joachim Klein said later of all his months in the camp: "I don't remember having had more than one real political discussion." [10]

But Gabriele was not sent to the Middle East to talk politics. She was meant to be shaped and hardened for the exacting tasks of transnational terrorist warfare. Taught by the world's foremost specialists on the subject, that is what became of her.

Carlos was not mistaken in choosing Gabriele for his OPEC raid in Vienna, where she certainly acquitted herself better than all the rest. (Klein, "nauseated" by the "demented actions of international terrorists," called it quits soon afterward. The three Palestinians who went along did not distinguish themselves in action.) Her debut as a killer won warm praise from Carlos and later from the boss himself, Wadi Haddad, when he met with the team in Aden to review the whole operation. Only Klein saw anything wrong with her virtuoso performance. The elderly Austrian policeman she knocked off with her Makarov at OPEC headquarters was already making for the elevator—running away—when Gabriele shot him in the back of the neck, Klein said. He did not see what a gangster killing like that had to do with revolution.

Her job in Vienna well done, Gabriele flew off to Algeria with the Carlos team and its captive Arab oil ministers, flew on with them to Aden for the postmortem with Wadi Haddad, and dropped out of sight. It was exactly two years before authorities found out where she was and what she might have been up to. A few days before Christmas 1977, she was driving into Switzerland from France with a German terrorist companion when she was stopped for a routine customs check at the border town of Porrentruy. Reaching into her handbag, she got out of the car, steadied her Makarov with both hands to take aim, and fired. Two Swiss border guards were rushed to the hospital, one to be an invalid for life; Gabriele was back in jail.

Her traveling kit said a lot for the new kind of life she was leading. She was carrying false Austrian identity papers, ordnance maps of north Italy, a summary of Swiss laws, a confidential German government report on the Schleyer case, a floor plan of the Israeli embassy in Brussels, two extra guns and a flick-knife, coded documents, and $20,000 in cash.

Among the documents was a sheet headed "Rome," bearing the cryptic letters "Al. Mo."—no longer so cryptic when Aldo Moro was kidnapped in Rome three months later. The money was part of a two-million-dollar ransom collected from Austrian textile magnate Michael Palmer the previous June. That was the small hard fact I had started out to hunt down from Italy.

The Austrian police had gathered considerable evidence on the Palmer kidnapping when I got to Vienna. The operation had taken months of elaborate preparation, they told me, and it was carried out by three women in Gabriele's June 2 Movement. All three—Inge Viett, Gabriele Rollnick, Julianne Plambeck—had taken part in the original kidnapping of Christian Democratic leader Peter Lorenz in Berlin two winters before, springing Gabriele from her prison cell and sending her on that fateful flight to Aden. After the Palmer snatch, all three went on to Aden themselves (where Hans-Joachim Klein ran into them). Most of the $2 million they collected from Palmer has never been recovered. But Gabriele Kröcher-Tiedemann was in fact carrying part of it when she was arrested in Switzerland. Another part was found on two young Austrians, picked up at the Swiss border near Chiasso two weeks before Gabriele was caught. They were taking their moneybags to the Red Brigades in Milan, they confessed.[11]

The two Austrians, mere "manual laborers" in the trade, would hardly have been privy to the Red Brigades' plans. They had no idea if the hot money in their bags was simply to be recycled through Italy or was destined for the million-dollar kitty needed to catch and kill Aldo Moro. Gabriele would have known, though.

She made her last headlines in the fourteenth-century Porrentruy castle that served as the town's courthouse and the setting for her trial. Two hundred Swiss policemen mounted guard with machine guns, and helicopters circled overhead, as she came before the judge in handcuffs—a slight figure, with her hair cut short, wearing boots and jeans. "My God! How small she is! How fragile she looks!" somebody cried out in the hush. Her lawyers argued that the wounds she inflicted on the two Swiss guards proved she was not shooting to kill. Apparently, they meant that she was too good a shot to miss the heart or head unless she intended to. She must have learned to correct her old habit of aiming too low.

She did not try to explain herself politically, beyond saying that she belonged to the "World Armed Anti-Imperialist Struggle." Outside, at a safe distance from the four-tiered ranks of armed police, a group of young Swiss anarchists tried to explain things for her. Their protest, and hers, was "against the boredom and air-conditioned misery of capitalism," they said.[12]

Gabriele's part of the Kröcher trail stops there. Norbert's, which we're coming to now, is even more instructive.

6

OPERATION LEO

Operation Leo became a nonstory on or about the first of April 1977. The most remarkable gang of its kind ever assembled in Europe was about ready to move when Norbert Kröcher, caught off guard and reaching for his gun, was overpowered and arrested on a downtown street in Stockholm. If not for the bulls, or pigs, or whatever they are called in Swedish, he might have won his niche in the pantheon of legendary terrorist heroes. With fifty accomplices from nine different countries, he was surely on the path of glory.

He would have been welcome to the glory, as far as his patrons were concerned. But the plot that failed in Sweden was really theirs, not Norbert's. The moving forces behind it were thousands of miles away, in Havana and the mountainous jungles of Tucumán in Argentina. While Norbert named it Operation Leo, they thought of it as Operation Europe: the initial move in a master plan to destabilize the western half of the Continent from Scandinavia to Gibraltar.

Among the assorted foreigners on Norbert's transcontinental team were several of unusual dexterity and provenance. Their exposure to a public trial might have set alarm bells ringing around the Western world and caused acute embarrassment to Cuba and Soviet Russia. They were never exposed to public trial. Within three or four days of their capture, Sweden had bundled them out of the country and closed the case. It was not the first or last example of a nation under siege going out of its way to preserve the civilities of international diplomacy.

By the time Norbert Kröcher was arrested, his gang had robbed two banks for the funds they needed; set up five safe-houses around Stockholm; collected forty pistols, sniper rifles, machine guns, and gas masks; acquired a roomful of sophisticated electronics gear; prepared three beauty cases full of wigs, false beards, and theatrical makeup; and amassed a ton of dynamite—enough to blow up several square city blocks.[1]

Some of the dynamite was packed and primed in the pillars of Noorbro Bridge, leading to (or cutting off, if blown) the medieval Old Town, Gammla Staden, heart of the Swedish capital and its government offices.[2] A coffin with breathing holes was ready in a soundproofed cellar for Norbert's intended guest. He and his accomplices had only to pick up the required fleet of stolen cars—an easy last-minute chore.

He had thought of abducting Sweden's former Social Democratic prime minister, Olof Palme, a figure of some international standing. For reasons of biblical vengeance, he settled instead on Palme's immigration minister, Anna-Greta Leijon. She was going to be held in her coffin for a four-million-dollar ransom and the release of eight German terrorists imprisoned in their own country, not Sweden, thus putting two sovereign nations on the rack. Mrs. Leijon, a popular young politician and mother of three small children, had been warned anonymously and was "very afraid," she confessed after Norbert was safely under lock and key. He had in fact marked her for execution on her sixth day of captivity, unless his demands were met.

It was all written down. Every step Norbert had made over the previous two years—his thoughts and worries, the options he considered and discarded, the tough training he devised to form his guerrilla band, his sketches and schedules for Operation Leo, along with notes on secret basement meetings, comrades marked for isolation or liquidation, the girls he slept with and prescriptions he renewed for recurrent bouts of gonorrhea—were all neatly recorded in two hundred pages of manuscript. Known to his accomplices as the Black File, it was dedicated in Norbert's hand to "Members of the World Movement Against the Zombies." A Member was anybody opposed irrevocably to the established order anywhere. The Zombies were the Walking Dead populating the rest of society, recalled from the grave by witchcraft: us.

Norbert was only twenty-two when he fled to Sweden on the eve of 1973, his revolutionary career cut off too soon. Three or four years in a Berlin commune and the June 2 Movement had not been enough to prove his considerable organizing talents, still less appease his anger against society. There were times when he did think of getting lost, taking off with a girl and a brand-new identity to some place where he could forget and be forgotten. Then he would recall how brutal the Berlin cops used to be, or something Ulrike Meinhof had once said, and snap out of it.

During the first half of his five years in Sweden, he didn't do much besides stick up a bank, and even that was more for personal than political needs. He was a hunted man, wanted in Germany for armed robbery and possibly worse, obliged to lie low. It was easy in Sweden, where he was known and accepted as "Hardy Dohnel," a victim of police persecution at home, just another among thousands of political exiles milling about. Prime Minister Olof Palme was famous for his hospitality to such fugitives. Living in the country with generous government subsidies, during Norbert's last year there, were 400 American army deserters (only 23 from Vietnam), 4,410 Argentinians, 397 Bolivians, 492 Brazilians, 2,411 Chileans, 344 Colombians, 214 Peruvians, and 732 Uruguayans from Tupamaro land.[3]

Some were simple refugees, others not so simple. For professional terrorists in search of sanctuary, or rest and recreation, Stockholm in Norbert's day was a home away from home. A local arms Mafia catering to their needs—buying, selling, renting, and exchanging popular guerrilla weapons—did a roaring trade. Hundreds of Latin Americans installed there had stopped over in Cuba for a while and then passed through Paris, for a visit to Henri Curiel's Help and Friendship people. The Baader-Meinhof pioneers had started to slip U.S. Army deserters in from West Germany around 1969. German terrorists themselves seemed to come and go at will, as did Tupamaros, Argentinian Montoneros, and Japanese Red Army cadres.

For the Palestinians especially, Sweden was a northern Europe outpost. Anybody in the know could have told you where Black September hung out—in Stockholm's Gangsgatan—before and after its hit-team massacred eleven Israeli athletes at the 1972 Munich Olympics. The PLO's more official military arm, Fatah, sent its first three hundred young Swedes to a Fatah guerrilla camp in Algeria in 1969.[4] George Habash got a first batch of his own off to his Middle East camps at least that long ago. His PFLP also had a standing arrangement with a small band of Swedish Maoists, responsible for "hiding Palestinians between missions," one said.[5]

(The case of Jun Nishikawa, arrested and expelled from Sweden in March 1975—just when Norbert Kröcher was flexing for action there—shows how the Swedish sanctuary worked. A member of the Japanese Red Army, Nishikawa had been trained in Wadi Haddad's Aden camp, then sent to Haddad's Baghdad headquarters in Iraq to await orders. On September 7, 1974, he was flown to Vienna to rendezvous with a Palestinian from the PFLP's "liaison office" in Sweden. The liaison man sent him on to Amsterdam, where Carlos was planning his spectacular Japanese occupation of the French embassy in The Hague for September 13. Carlos sent Nishikawa in with the Japanese assault team and, when the action was over, packed the whole team off to Stockholm to be hidden out until the hunt died down. Captured by the Swedish police, Nishikawa told them all this himself.)[6]

In so congenial an atmosphere, a visitor like Norbert would have no trouble finding some Swedes to help him settle in. For their part, the Swedish authorities seemed to take no notice of the newcomer passing as "Hardy Dohnel," who had entered the country in a stolen French car with a forged French passport, did nothing to earn a living, always carried a gun, and even slept with a Walther P-.38 under his pillow. When his wife Gabriele went back to Germany, early in 1973, he set up house with a gay, fresh-faced Swedish woman journalist we will call "Karin," some years his senior, and melted into the background.[7]

But Norbert was a political animal, chafing at restraint. "I have always believed in the Armed Struggle and Permanent Revolution, in Sweden, in Germany, everywhere," he insisted in prison afterward. Struggling with his halting command of Swedish, bickering irritably with his nest-building "Karin," who dreamed of getting married and raising a family, he slowly built up an adoring circle of radical young Swedes. He was "a symbol of the persecuted of the world" for them, one said. Every now and then, he would slip back into Germany to pick up supplies (weapons, dynamite, false passports), and comrades from the Old Country would drop by to see him in Sweden. In effect he was setting up a Scandinavian branch office of the June 2 Movement, soon to hook up with the second-generation Baader-Meinhof Gang.

The first fruit of that union was a fearful attack on the German embassy in Stockholm on April 24, 1975. Norbert was not involved, as far as we know, the plans having been made by his comrades in Germany. But their calamitous defeat would bring his consuming hatred into focus.

The German embassy in Stockholm was stormed and seized barely seven weeks after Peter Lorenz was kidnapped by the June 2 Movement in Berlin and exchanged for five terrorist prisoners. Exhilarated—exalted—by Chancellor Schmidt's unconditional surrender of those five, the German terrorists now wanted freedom for another twenty-six. No thought of failure so much as crossed their minds. In Stammheim's maximum-security prison, Andreas Baader, Ulrike Meinhof, Gudrun Ensslin, Jan-Carl Raspe briskly called off a longer hunger-and-thirst strike and began limbering up with gymnastic equipment to get back in shape. In Hamburg, nine other prisoners on the freedom list packed their bags, ready to take off. "I'll be leaving today," one assured an astonished warder gaily, on the eve of the action.[8]

The assault plan had been worked out with Wadi Haddad's blessings in Aden and active help from his lieutenant in Paris, Carlos. The strategy was copied from the one Carlos had thought up and tested in Holland the previous autumn. The occupation of the French embassy there was the first such terrorist operation on the Continent, and the resulting release of three Japanese terrorists from a Paris jail had been a dazzling success.

Enormously impressed, the German terrorists went to Carlos to ask how he did it. Not only did he tell them, but he visited Stockholm personally to inspect the site. Traveling with his inseparable aide, Michel Moukarbal, he spent two days in the Swedish capital, leaving just forty-eight hours before the attack began.[9]

Directing operations from Germany was the Heidelberg lawyer Siegfried Haag, who, with police at his heels in the resulting uproar, then fled to Aden (where Gabriele Kröcher-Tiedemann met him). Haag was just taking over from the original Baader-Meinhof leaders, who were all in jail, and he was bringing several subgroups like the June 2 Movement into joint operations. He had gone to Zurich himself to pick up weapons for the Stockholm raid, from Petra Krause's takeout service. He had also handpicked the six Stockholm raiders, whose behavior was at least medically understandable. All six were members of the Heidelberg Socialist Patients' Collective—former inmates of a psychiatric ward turned terrorist for therapeutic reasons. Known in the trade as the Crazy Brigade and later described in Jillian Becker's valuable study, *Hitler's Children*, they were persuaded to Bomb for Mental Health and Kill for Inner Peace.

They stormed the Stockholm embassy at eleven in the morning and left the blazing building in stark panic around midnight. During those thirteen hours, they held the German economics attaché up at a window so as to shoot him within range of the TV cameras; put three bullets into the military attaché and dumped his dying body over the stairwell from the third-floor landing; and mined the upper floor with thirty-five pounds of dynamite, some of it packed into tins in the ambassador's refrigerator.

Faulty wiring trailing from the refrigerator caused a shattering explosion that ripped off the embassy's roof. Gigantic flames then drove captors and captives screaming into the night and devoured the mutilated corpse of a terrorist who had blown himself up by dropping a hand grenade in his fright. Another of the raiders, running straight into the arms of the police, died of burns and a fractured skull in the Stammheim prison hospital ten days later. He was Siegfried Hausner, explosives specialist of the Heidelberg Socialist Patients' Collective, whose clumsy wiring had brought the affair to its shrieking end.

It was all for nothing. The raiders had issued an ultimatum, demanding release of the twenty-six Baader-Meinhof prisoners, with $20,000 apiece and a Lufthansa Boeing to fly them away (they didn't say where); they were turned down flat. Incredulous, they repeated the message and got the same answer. Germany's Chancellor Schmidt, facing "the most serious challenge in the twenty-six-year history of our democracy," had recognized the unspeakable danger of giving in again. Sweden's Prime Minister Palme would not even consider it. While Palme was responsible for his country's decision, however, it was his immigration minister, Anna-Greta Leijon, who ordered the extradition to Germany of four surviving raiders and the mortally injured Siegfried Hausner.

So began Norbert Kröcher's mission.

"To choose the victim, to prepare the strike with circumspection, to satisfy one's implacable revenge, and then go to bed—there's nothing sweeter in this world," Stalin once said. Norbert, hungering blindly for revenge since his earliest youth, chose his victim at last and got on with it.

His obsessive purpose was to spring those four raiders, together with another four prisoners of mixed terrorist affiliations (an ecumenical custom common to terrorists everywhere). His project began to look so exciting—the combined impact on West Germany and Sweden could be so devastating, the prime time on satellite television so priceless—that the German underground gave it top priority. When lawyer Haag was caught near Hanover in the autumn of 1976, his coded documents listed Norbert's operation as "Margarine I." The abduction of Schleyer came fourth on his list, falling due only six months afterward.[10]

In Stockholm, though, Norbert kept his Swedish helpers in the dark until nearly the end. Secretive and incurably suspicious, he was reluctant to confide in a soul. As the project matured, he would jot things down in his Black File. "It is important to continue keeping my identity a secret here," he noted, and indeed he did not reveal his own name to anyone but his fourth and last Swedish girl friend. ("Karin," too clinging, by then was long gone.) It took longer still for his lesser staff to learn the name of his chosen victim.

The twenty-odd Swedes he had clustered around him were very young, operationally raw, and ideologically untutored. Immersed in revolutionary conspiracy one day, they might take off for a Greek holiday the next; they squabbled incessantly over who was sleeping with whom. Two or three had once bombed a Spanish tourist agency, and Norbert had made a few others rob a store, as much to get a hold over them as for the money. He had to do better than that. "I must find some real revolutionaries, who have fought in the Third World," he wrote to himself as 1975 wore on, and . . . there they were.[11]

A fellow German terrorist and in-between mistress of Norbert's, also a fugitive in Stockholm, knew just the sort of chap he had in mind. Along came a Mexican named Armando Carrillo, followed some weeks later by Maria, his Chilean wife; Norbert was in business.

Norbert's German girl friend had found Armando Carrillo, or he her, at Stockholm's rump Refugee Council, whose offices in Apelbergsgatan had opened only a month or so before, in November 1975. The new council contained the most intractably ultra of Sweden's ultra-left foreign guests, expelled by the parent body for egregious support of the international terrorist celebrities in their midst: the Japanese Jun Nishikawa, for instance. More than half the rump council's members would be picked up by the police when Norbert's ring was broken up. The council's general secretary soon got to be Norbert's right-hand man.

Armando Carrillo had been turned away twice from Stockholm's Arlanda airport, sent back by way of Prague to Cuba, where he came from. When he was finally admitted in January 1976 as a political refugee, he came in on an odd passport. It was a Mexican passport, authorizing travel only to Cuba, later amended to authorize passage from Cuba to Europe—one way.

The passport's bearer was Norbert's dreamboat. Armando

Carrillo belonged to MAR (Movimiento de Acción Revolucionaria), catapulted to brief world fame in 1971 when the Russians were caught in the act of trying to take over Mexico. The whole documented story has been told by John Barron in his *KGB* and is too long to repeat here.[12] What matters for our own story is that MAR was founded in Moscow, under KGB auspices, by ten Mexicans enrolled in Soviet Russia's Patrice Lumumba University for foreigners, in 1968. Its founders were then sent back to Mexico City to recruit candidates for intensive guerrilla training in North Korea. At the time, North Korea was ahead of South Yemen as Russia's favorite satellite for these things.

Fifty Mexicans in all went to North Korea, and Armando left with the first contingent. Traveling with thirteen other men and two women, he got his $500 allowance in Mexico City, proceeded to Paris and West Berlin and on to East Berlin, picked up his North Korean passport there (turning in his own), and boarded a night train for Moscow. Five days later, he was flown straight to Pyongyang.

In a mountain camp thirty-five miles from the North Korean capital, Armando was turned into a professional all-purpose guerrilla-killer, indistinguishable from the Gabriele Kröcher-Tiedemann who later came out of Aden. His grinding seventeen-hour days were spent in mastering the techniques of arson, explosives, karate, assassination, extortion, ambush, disguise, clandestine travel, recruitment, communications, and weaponry. On returning to Mexico early in 1969, he was a star performer.

His MAR group worked superbly for the next two years, under the talented supervision of the KGB Referentura at the Soviet embassy. When Mexican authorities stumbled on the conspirators, in the nick of time, Armando was among the first nineteen MAR guerrillas to be captured and jailed for robbery, murder, and attempted insurrection. (The head of the Referentura and four other Soviet diplomats were expelled from Mexico shortly afterward.)

He was freed in the usual way. On May 4, 1973, the American consul, Terrance Leonhardy, was kidnapped, to be exchanged for thirty imprisoned comrades. It was the first such abduction in Mexico, and the government didn't even think twice. Armando was flown to Havana, where he stayed put for the next two and a half years.[13]

He never did say what made him suddenly pick up and move to Sweden, where there was nothing legitimate for him to do. Nor did his wife Maria explain why, after several years' separation from her husband, she decided to leave her work in Chile's underground Communist Party and travel from Chile to Sweden by way of Portugal—a revealing itinerary, as we will see—to rejoin Armando. Both found jobs right off the bat, though, with the rump Refugee Council, and Armando at once got to work collecting passports to be forged for his Mexican friends.

The Carrillos first met Norbert over a glass of wine in Stockholm's Modern Art Museum Restaurant, and he was thrilled. "I could hardly contain my strong delight to be sitting eye-to-eye with a real freedom fighter who had been to North Korea," he wrote in one of those little notes to himself. They all tended to be wary at that first encounter. But after a few evenings of wine and guitars—Maria Carrillo played, Armando sang, "Karin" cooked—they got down to brass tacks.

Norbert outlined his plan, and the Carrillos seemed to think it was brilliant. Armando offered invaluable advice as well as expert aid: he volunteered to kill Mrs. Leijon's bodyguards, for instance, while Norbert would be the one to kill the lady herself if things came to that. They agreed on the need to rob a bank or two for the working kitty, round up dynamite and weapons, and recruit more skilled personnel. "Both of us have friends scattered around the world who will help," wrote Norbert, understating it.

Armando, in Sweden for barely six weeks, had already arranged for two other "Mexican refugees" to fly over from Cuba. Both were traveling on similar funny passports and so needed somebody to "prepare the terrain" for their arrival. Norbert sent his "Karin" off to Brussels and that helpful place in Paris to see to it. The enterprising Armando also happened to run into just the right contact in the local arms Mafia. That took care of the weapons problem.

A few more weeks and up came Armando (and his wife Maria) with yet another promising recruit. This one, an Englishman, was the very fellow who had been thrown out of Stockholm's old Refugee Council as a "disruptive element" and formed the rump group headed by himself. At twenty-three, Allan Hunter was an extremely knowledgeable revolutionary who obviously had terrific connections. He had been an anarchist in Britain, a kibbutz worker in Israel, a clerk with the British armed forces in Berlin, and he had just come from a lengthy stay in Switzerland, procuring arms for the Saharan Polisario Front.[14] (This was in 1975, when the Swiss anarchists were rushed off their feet running their takeout weapons service.)

In Stockholm, Allan Hunter ran a tight little ship within his rump Refugee Council, in close alliance with resident Palestinians, Iranians, and Chileans. He was studying Arabic in his spare time.

No sooner did the swiftly expanding gang get down to practical matters than Armando produced still another trusty Mexican comrade. This one came straight from Cuba too and was going to help Armando bring over even more Mexican comrades from the same place.[15]

Thomas Okusono Martinez was not a fellow member of Armando's in MAR. He and his brother Jaime belonged to the Armed Communist League and had their own show going in Mexico's Sinora Hills. A gang of twenty-eight Death Valley Desperados calling themselves the Campesinos, they were regarded by local authorities as "tough and extremely dangerous." When Thomas was arrested in northern Mexico in 1972, police found fifty thousand cartridges and twenty-two assorted weapons in his Monterey hotel room. It took just one day to spring him from the Monterey jail in the customary way. His Liga Comunista Armada had only to hijack a plane heading for Mexico City and demand his release. He flew off to Cuba too.

From 1972 until early 1976, both Thomas Martinez and his brother Jaime received intensive guerrilla training in a Havana camp run by the Soviet-supervised DGI, the Cuban intelligence service. Then, in April 1976, they took off for Europe together.

Thomas headed for Stockholm and Jaime for Copenhagen, just across the way in Denmark. They seemed to know exactly what they were doing.

While Thomas worked with Norbert Kröcher in Sweden, Jaime worked on an alternative project with two other German terrorists in Denmark. Jaime's ring intended to seize the Swedish embassy in Copenhagen, just as the German embassy had been seized in Stockholm the previous year. ("C" for Copenhagen came third on lawyer Haag's embassy hit-list.) But the police of Sweden and Denmark must have been swapping information: both gangs were broken up within the same month.[16]

Jaime had an impressive weapons collection when he was caught, as well as coded correspondence with the German underground. He had been in constant touch with his brother Thomas, it turned out. Not only had Thomas come over to visit in Denmark, but both Martinez brothers had been picked up by the Norwegian police in nearby Oslo, hardly a month after they reached Europe. Although they were carrying "mysterious material," indicating "regular contact" with West German terrorists, the Norwegians let them go.

In Stockholm, Thomas Martinez found a blonde Swedish girl friend and a flat at a discreet twelve miles' distance from Armando Carrillo's suburban house in Trollbacken. He used Carrillo's address for his letter drop and the rump Refugee Council to exchange secret messages. The two would meet on the sly, unknown to Norbert—on a bench for a long talk in Vasa Park or at some offbeat subway station, splitting and rejoining to avoid detection. (They were detected anyway, as they found out too late.)

Later that spring, they asked Norbert if he could use another couple of Mexican helpers. Ever obliging, Thomas Martinez made several transatlantic calls to Havana. Using the code name "Maria de los Angeles," he arranged for three other Mexicans to fly over from Cuba. When two of them reached Europe that November—traveling under the names of "Saucedo Gomez" and "Maria Nunes"—the Refugee Council's obliging Allan Hunter went to pick them up at the Brussels airport and escort them to the Swedish capital.

Not to be outdone, Norbert Kröcher came up with a professional compatriot to complete the team. Manfred Adomeit hailed from Norbert's June 2 Movement in Berlin and was also on the lam. The German police were after him for murder—that is, for his part in June 2's liquidation of "the traitor" Ulrich Schmucker, whose bullet-ridden body had been found in the Grunewald Forest by American soldiers the summer before. When police got too close, Manfred slipped into Sweden, and homed in on Norbert.

In just a few months, a ragged band of flighty Swedish kids revolving around a single experienced bandleader had acquired four Mexicans, a Chilean, an Englishman, and an extra German, all highly qualified for the matter at hand. Other aides, emerging from the rump Refugee Council, included a Colombian, a Tunisian, a South African, a Greek, and several more Germans. Another Chilean, Juan Soto Paillacar, based in Italy, had been called in as part-time consultant. Before entering Italy as a political refugee, he had stopped off in Cuba for two years of guerrilla training.[17] He was eventually arrested in 1979, as the presumed head of a Latin American band—four Chileans and four Mexicans, all seized along with him—running a terrorist training school for Italians in Rome.[18]

By January 1977, Norbert and his Latin American co-pilots were putting the finishing touches to their scheme. The Polisario Front had sent somebody to help pick out a spot in the western Sahara where a Hercules C-130 could land with the eight German terrorists to be sprung. The spot was circled on a map in Norbert's Black File. Arrival in that Saharan sanctuary was scheduled for the sixth day of Anna-Greta Leijon's stay in her coffin. The hour of takeoff from Stockholm, set for maximum TV coverage, was noted in Norbert's timetable too.

Then those flighty young Swedes of his spoiled everything. Their symbol of persecution in the world was falling dangerously low in their esteem. Norbert never told them anything, ordered them around with military arrogance, frightened them with his inquisitorial manner and threatening stare, infuriated the girls in the gang by treating them not only as sex objects but as a kind of subspecies—a surprisingly common attitude among male guerrilla heroes everywhere. Several were also shaken to the core when they finally discovered the name of Norbert's kidnappee.

Shocked by the enormity of the risk he hadn't told them they were taking, they forced a showdown in their basement hideout at the end of January. Norbert, bombarded by criticism from his own acolytes, left in a fury. "Do they think they're in some silly students' club?" he wrote indignantly in his Black File. But he added: "It is important not to demand too much of the comrades. I must remember that we are not all endowed with the same strength. To tell secret revolutionaries more than they need to know is to make them share heavy responsibilities. The fact that I don't tell them is really an act of respect...." [19]

He resolved from then on to cut some of the Swedes out altogether, have them all watched, and eliminate a couple if necessary, paying a few calls to scare the wits out of them. ("The air was thick with menace," a twenty-year-old told interrogators, of one such visit. "I'd never tell about it in court. Even if he's in jail now, I have a terrible fear of Norbert," said another.) He could still count on backing from lawyer Haag's band at home, though, and in Stockholm, he could manage perfectly well with his fellow Germans, his Mexicans, the Englishman, a Chilean or two, and lesser foreign aides from the Refugee Council, or so he figured. In reality, he was done for after that basement showdown.

It was a tip from a Swedish gunrunner, who got it from a Swedish helper of Norbert's, that led the police to close in. They were not unprepared. Norbert and his whole foreign crew had been tailed for months.

By the winter of 1977, Sweden was not such a haven for international terrorist outlaws anymore. Olof Palme was no longer prime minister. Regulations for admitting political exiles had been tightened. Insistent espionage by the Russians, East Germans, and Poles and sabotage training for Swedish Communists at special Russian and East German schools had sharpened the interest of security agents in possibly related matters. Moreover Sweden had, and has, the most advanced and computerized police force in Europe.

The rump Refugee Council had been under discreet surveillance all along. Allan Hunter had been photographed on his
mysterious visits to Switzerland and Belgium. Norbert's Mexican contingent had caught police attention from the day Armando Carrillo showed up at Arlanda Airport with his peculiar
passport. The phone calls to Havana, the arrival of his fellow
refugees, the furtive meetings with Thomas Okusono Martinez,
could hardly have passed unnoticed. By the time everybody in
the ring was rounded up, Swedish authorities had grounds to
believe that they were up against something far more disturbing than a mere German terrorist plot.

Directly after the arrests, Sweden's foreign minister summoned the Cuban ambassador for a chat about Armando Carrillo. The government was determined to avoid a show trial
with such an array of foreign villains and wanted them out of
the country at once. Why, the foreign minister wanted to know,
was Cuba stalling about taking Armando back? Who had invented his dubious passport in the first place? Why, knowing
his penal record for terrorist homicide, had Cuba sent him to
Sweden without saying a word about it to the Swedish authorities? [20]

The Cuban ambassador explained that Fidel Castro himself
had more or less invented the passport. On Castro's request to
President Echeverría, in the summer of 1975, Mexico had
agreed to amend the restricted passports of certain Mexican
exiles in Cuba—not all—for travel to some European country.
Why they should be allowed to make the trip over, but not
back, the ambassador failed to say. He didn't say how these
particular Mexicans came to be picked for European export
from Cuba either.

It was at this point in my pursuit of Norbert Kröcher's story
that I felt a shock of recognition. Then I found that, in interrogating Norbert's Latin American accomplices, the Swedish
police had accused them bluntly of acting on orders from a
Cuban-backed formation called the Junta for Revolutionary
Coordination.[21] Evidently, the Swedish security services had
felt the shock too.

Every intelligence agency in the West, Sweden's included, had been watching out for something exactly like this since early 1976—exactly when Armando Carrillo and his Mexican friends came to Stockholm and crossed Norbert Kröcher's line of vision.

What they were watching for was an elaborate project known as the Tucumán Plan.

The plan, drafted in May 1975, was uncovered by Argentinian police the following winter. The incriminating reports were were found in a safe-house of the ERP, a Trotskyite terrorist band, and dealt with a secret meeting held in Argentina's Tucumán province by the Junta for Revolutionary Coordination.[22]

The junta was formed under Cuban patronage in April 1974 by the Tupamaros of Uruguay and like-minded terrorists of Chile, Bolivia, and Argentina. Its purpose was to lead a continent-wide armed struggle for liberation in the Western hemisphere. But conditions weren't too good for an armed struggle in the Western hemisphere by the time the junta met in Tucumán. Only a month before, the Argentinian police had raided its main headquarters in La Plata, seizing several million dollars' worth of arms as well as a weapons factory, a subterranean firing range, forgery presses, and voluminous files. Now, with its installations gone in Argentina, a police state looming in that country, and a solid wall of other police states surrounding it (largely of the terrorists' own making), the junta was moving to Europe. Many of its best guerrilla fighters were sheltering there already, and formation of a Latin American Europe Brigade followed naturally.

At full strength, the brigade was supposed to be manned by 1,500 qualified Latin American terrorists. About half that number were on the ground, scattered around the Continent and the Middle East. The rest would be sent to Europe from Cuba—some chosen from among countless professionals idling in exile on the island, others freshly trained for the JCR on a four-thousand-acre estate near Guanabo.[23] Seen in that light, Castro's interest in his Mexican passport agreement, shortly after the Tucumán meeting, made sense.

The brigade was intended to do just what Armando Carrillo and his Mexican comrades intended to do in collusion with Norbert Kröcher: link up with the European terrorist movement; heighten an atmosphere of panic on the Continent by terrorist actions and kidnappings; liberate political prisoners; and build up a war chest, mostly with ransoms and bank heists.[24]

Operations were to start in 1976. The primary target countries were Germany, Italy, Great Britain, and France. Strategic planning would be done at JCR headquarters in Paris, where Henri Curiel's France, Land of Asylum would provide the service network. The brigade's privileged sanctuary would be Portugal, where the JCR held its first public press conference, in April 1975, to announce the opening of offices in Lisbon and Paris.[25]

Portugal was a practical choice. In the spring of 1975, it seemed to be falling inescapably under Communist rule. The Armed Forces Movement had been listing heavily leftward since the coup in April of the previous year; Communist leader Alvaro Cunhal, who flew over from Havana when revolution broke out, appeared to have the army in his pocket. He would have had every reason to befriend the JCR, which, at the time, was befriending him. Encamped in loose militia units on the south bank of the Tagus River were several thousand foreign defenders of Portugal's revolutionary left, including Tupamaros, Chileans, and Cubans.[26] (A good number of heavily armed Tupamaros and Chileans were arrested before they could decamp, when the Communists' grip was broken in November 1975. The Cubans reportedly moved on to join the first Cuban contingent in ex-Portuguese Angola, landing there during that same month.)

The new Latin American Europe Brigade would also have a particular friend in Soviet Ambassador Arnold Kalinin. Appointed barely three months after the Portuguese army coup, Ambassador Kalinin flew to Lisbon from Havana on August 9, 1974. Prior to that, he had been counselor of the Soviet embassy in Cuba, where, as the KGB's representative, he would certainly have been on familiar terms with the JCR.

The change in Portugal's political climate—the Communist failure there—inevitably altered the JCR's plans. It is still operating out of Paris, Rome, Stockholm, and Madrid along lines I will be following later.

For all anybody in Europe knows, the Carrillos and the

Martinez brothers may be working from its Paris office by now, with new versions of their funny passports. When last heard from, they were heading back to Cuba, the asylum they chose when Swedish authorities asked them where—outside of Sweden—they wanted to go. Everybody else of foreign nationality connected with Norbert Kröcher's ring was expelled from the country in a matter of days. The Swedes involved had a short trial and drew still shorter sentences, all but three acquitted. Norbert and his main German aide, Manfred Adomeit, were extradited to Germany within seventy-two hours.

The European press covered the story for a day or two, then dropped it.

In the summer of 1979, Norbert Kröcher and Manfred Adomeit were tried in a German court and sentenced respectively to fourteen and twelve years in prison. In the Frankenthal jail near Mannheim, they occupy cells scarcely larger than Anna-Greta Leijon's intended coffin, with narrow cracks for light. Neither has given up hopes for spreading urban guerrilla warfare and a Communist revolution.

"They will pay, the fine lords, to their last drop of blood," wrote Manfred, smuggling a note to Norbert from his cell.

"Friend! Brother! We must pull it off, if only because of our hate. . . . Did I say a word against terrorism? Forget it!" Norbert wrote back.[27]

7

THE PALESTINIANS COME TO EUROPE

Wanted! Courageous comrades to join us, a group of politically committed friends, for a tour of several months in the Middle East as war correspondents to study the

WAR OF LIBERATION

of the Palestinian refugees to reconquer their homeland. If you have tank experience, apply at once. Money is no obstacle. What matters is a comradely spirit and personal courage. Information on the Palestine Liberation Organization free on request.

The ad happened to run in the Nazi *National Zeitung* of Munich, but at the time—October 23, 1970—it might have served interchangeably for the Continent's ultra-right or ultra-left. Both were raising volunteers to fight Zionist imperialism by then and jointly sponsoring the Palestinian terrorists' fateful entry into Europe—a fact that did not seem to bother either the ultra-right or the ultra-left, or the Palestinians.

Ideology had little to do with exporting the Arab nationalists' fight to foreign soil. George Habash, who started it all, was not yet an inflexible Marxist-Leninist when he sent a commando to hijack his first plane in Rome, in 1968. He had simply

113

recognized the unlikelihood of defeating Israel by conventional warfare after the 1967 Six-Day War, Israel's third humiliating victory in nineteen years over standing Arab armies.

Shattered by that war, as all Palestinian leaders were, Habash had formed his Popular Front for the Liberation of Palestine (PFLP) three months afterward. European leftists like Feltrinelli were urging him to internationalize the conflict, "make contact with other revolutionary forces," use terrorism "to sow panic not just in the Middle East but all over the map." [1] Dr. Habash did not have to believe in everything Feltrinelli said to grasp the essential point. "We think that killing one Jew far from the field of battle is more effective than killing a hundred Jews on the field of battle, because it attracts more attention," he explained.[2]

That first tentative foreign venture of Dr. Habash's proved momentous. The El Al plane he hijacked, whose thirty-two Jewish passengers were held hostage by the Algerian government for five weeks, attracted gratifying attention. During the next year or so, his PFLP hijacked thirteen other foreign planes, the last four all at once, exploded three of those four on the ground in Jordan before a rapt worldwide television audience, and blew up a Swissair liner in flight, killing forty-seven passengers and crew. From nowhere, the Palestinians shot to the center of the planetary stage.

The rest couldn't have happened without them: the focus and sequence, the intercontinental arms traffic and training, the multinational hit-teams on satellite television, the stage sets for revolution, privileged sanctuaries, diplomatic blackmail. But not everybody might have foreseen that so soon. At the opening of the terrorist decade, the Palestinians just looked very promising to all concerned.

Later, when Habash and other Palestinian leaders were themselves swept leftward by the logic of events, radical leftists everywhere began to think they had invented what became a quintessentially revolutionary cause. Nevertheless, the radical right was there first. Europe's Black International had not only discovered the anti-Zionist cause a good quarter of a century earlier; it worked side by side with the Red International for years, using the same slogans, providing the same services, dealing with the same Palestinian agents. The curious brotherhood lasted at least until midway through the decade (when the Russians finally took over the care and maintenance of the Palestine Resistance). Some say it is with us yet.

The Black International operated out of Paris, under the name of the European New Order. It consisted of Nazis and Fascists left over from or related in spirit to Hitler's Germany, Vichy France, Franco's Spain and Salazar's Portugal, Mussolini's Italy, the Greek colonels' military junta, and their Black terrorist offshoots, hardly distinguishable in practice from the Red ones. It had a kind of homogenizing Nazi-Maoist formation too, urging open collusion with the Red International in their common interest. The two sides did have interests in common, starting with annihilation of the established democratic order. (The militant Communist Feltrinelli and Italy's Fascist Black Prince Valerio Borghese even met secretly in Switzerland to talk that over, in 1971).[3] Annihilating imperialzionism was another thing they apparently could agree on.

The first summit of the Black International on the Palestinians' behalf was held in Barcelona, on April 2, 1969.[4] General Franco, still alive and well, gave his blessings. Two representatives were there from Fatah, Yassir Arafat's military arm in the Palestine Liberation Organization. The PLO, a political umbrella group for various terrorist formations (mostly founded after the Six-Day War), was still living from hand to mouth in those days. Arafat was planning to send Fatah into Europe also, following the example of Habash, whose PFLP joined the PLO a few months later.

The Barcelona meeting dealt with several of Fatah's requests. The delegates talked about raising money, organizing efficient arms traffic, providing ex-Nazi military instructors to help the guerrillas get started, recruiting white Caucasian youths to beef up Fatah's forces in the Middle East, and "collecting elements disposed to collaborate in acts of sabotage in Europe." They also discussed a propaganda campaign, combining all-purpose slogans—"Long Live the Glorious Palestinian Fighters Against Imperialzionism!"—with anti-Semitic classics like the *Protocols of Zion* and a volume about Israel entitled *The Enemy of Man.*

There were several Black summits for the Palestinians after that. One met on March 28, 1970, in Paris, where a Belgian ex–SS officer put his Rexist Party "totally and unconditionally at the service of the Palestine Resistance." [5] Another gathered in Munich on September 16, 1972—barely ten days after the Palestinian hit-team, Black September, massacred eleven Israeli athletes at the Olympic Games in that city.[6] Six hundred delegates to this particular Nazi-Fascist gathering cheered Black September to the rafters. They also handed out leaflets in praise of the Palestinian Sirhan B. Sirhan for assassinating Robert Kennedy. "I did it for my country!" was the caption under his picture.[7]

Yet another such conference was held on March 9, 1974, at the Rome Hilton. Colonel Qaddafi of Libya, putting his oil money where his heart was in those days—in neo-Fascist pro-Palestine groups and a string of anti-Semitic bookshops—was worried about Marxist encroachment in the Palestinian movement, and he sent his prime minister, Ahmed Jalloud, to the Hilton with the usual moneybags to strengthen the Black side.[8] (By then, however, Qaddafi was also financing the Palestinian network in Paris led by Carlos, shot through with international terrorists of the deepest red. It wouldn't be long before Qaddafi himself became "objectively" leftist, in left-wing parlance.)

Meanwhile, Palestinians were leading a heady double life in Europe. The toast of the Continent's New Left and most incorrigible right, they had the best of two worlds. Feltrinelli bought shiploads of arms for them in the name of worldwide Communist revolution, while Colonel Qaddafi's neo-Fascist retainers did so for anti-Semitism's sake. The cream of the Red International hared off to the Middle East for training in Palestinian camps, while Palestinians flocked to Black International camps in the Spanish Pyrenees and northern Italy's Alto Adige (at Malga Croun).[9]

The ultra-left sponsored a huge rally for Arafat in Milan, and Italy's most flamboyant neo-Nazi, Franco Freda, held one to honor Arafat's Fatah in Padua.[10] Freda, serving a life term for terrorism now, was a boon companion of the PLO's man in Rome, a poet named Wael Zwaiter (later assassinated by Israel's secret service), who spent alternating comradely evenings with the choicest of Italy's left-wing intellectuals.[11] The Swiss anarchists' takeout service, run by the Jewish Petra Krause, whose parents died in the Nazis' gas chambers at Auschwitz, smuggled arms to the Palestinians' Paris network for Carlos, and Carlos sent couriers to pick up more at the Diplomat Club in Rome, hangout of a huge neo-Nazi gunrunning ring.[12]

The Red and the Black were nowhere more strongly entwined than in Switzerland, where the director for Black September in Europe made his home. Hassan Salameh, known in the game as "Abu Hassan," had been intensely committed to the Palestine Resistance since his father was killed by a Jewish Haganah bomb in 1948. He was the movement's most captivating personality, wildly handsome and irresistible to women, immensely rich and fond of good living, worldly, clever, charming, educated at the Sorbonne, warmly welcome in the Continent's best avant-garde drawing rooms.

To his hundreds of intimate foreign friends, Salameh was no more than a personable and cultivated political spokesman for PLO leader Yassir Arafat, who happened to be his cousin. Few knew that he was also a prime quarry of the Israeli secret service for seven years, until he was finally blown apart by a bomb in Beirut.

Even then, the international press presented him as no more than Arafat's right-hand man for Fatah's military operations. Actually, he had commanded handpicked personnel from Fatah and the PFLP both, as European director for Black September. Formed after King Hussein threw the Palestine Liberation Army out of Jordan by force of arms, in September 1970, these supersecret death squads were widely believed to be Fatah's creatures. In fact, they were the progeny of Arafat and George Habash both, formed in the newspaper offices of the PFLP's *al-Hadaf*.[13] Wadi Haddad, directing military operations for Habash, was an invaluable ally of Hassan Salameh's on the Continent. Some of Haddad's most gifted disciples were on Black September's hit-team for the Munich Olympics, though Arafat's Fatah got all the credit.

The Olympics massacre was shattering evidence of how

fragile and vulnerable a mighty state can be, under the resolute assault of a few armed men; and it was Hassan Salameh who planned the whole thing. It was Salameh, too, who arranged for Germany's ultra-left Revolutionary Cells to set things up for the Palestinian hit-team in Munich; [14] who brought the Baader-Meinhof Gang into a first joint German-Arab endeavor—an attack on a Jewish old people's home in Munich, leaving seven dead; [15] who shipped Andreas Baader off to the Middle East for early talks on broader two-way collaboration.

Salameh had no particular political bias. Black September had a lot of work to do in Europe—bombing, arson, abduction, assassination—and Salameh took help where he could find it. One of his closest collaborators was Mohammed Boudia, Wadi Haddad's top man on the Continent, who had been a Communist since the beginning of the 1950s.[16] Boudia had wide left-wing connections. In Italy, for instance, he got a couple of Red Brigades irregulars to help him set Trieste's huge oil depot ablaze; he had an ambitious project in hand with the KGB and Czechoslovakia's Communist authorities when he died prematurely, in 1973.

Inevitably, Salameh was thrown in with leftists of every sort as he traveled for his work, shuttling from Geneva to Prague and Belgrade, Rome and Milan, Paris, Madrid, London, Oslo, Stockholm. The various terrorist formations in Italy, the Irish nationalists, the Spanish Basque separatists, and Third World guerrilla exiles encamped on the Paris Left Bank were easily accessible, and available. All had been in contact with Arafat's Fatah since 1969 and Habash's PFLP since 1968, and Zurich, seat of a new Red International (which I will explain later) was a hop and skip from Salameh's Geneva villa. He was among the first Palestinians to perceive the extraordinary potential of all the European left-wing terrorist formations.

No leftist himself, however, Salameh would hardly overlook the potentialities of the racist right. Some of his best friends were in the Black International. Prominent among them was the man Salameh chose to be the Palestinians' banker in Europe: François Arnoud. Arnoud was a founder of Switzerland's neo-Nazi Party and had been a trusted banker for the German Nazis too. The documents he published after the war, autographed by Hitler, reportedly came from the renowned Martin Bormann's archives.[17]

Arnoud, well connected in Arab circles from Cairo to Tripoli and Algiers, was a pillar of strength for Fatah and Black September on the Continent. He would take care of legal counsel for their hit-men temporarily embarrassed by the Swiss authorities, cultivate valuable business contracts, advise on investment portfolios when the big money came in. And the money came in. Colonel Qaddafi, still on the Black International's side, donated his first $50 million to the PLO shortly after the Olympic Games massacre (throwing in a five-million-dollar bonus for those particular hit-men.) [18] Other Arab oil states began to contribute generously, impressed by Palestinian achievements abroad. The PLO imposed a three-to-seven-percent Liberation Tax on Palestinian wages in all Arab states, checked off at the source; a fifth of its income was allotted to European operations.

As head of the Arab Commercial Bank in Geneva, Arnoud soon became a formidable financial power. Tens of millions of dollars passed through the hands of this neo-Nazi financier for the Palestinians' use in Europe. Much of it went to the militant Communists forming the world's first multinational terrorist band in Paris at the time. All anti-imperialzionists must have looked alike to them.

Although the public knew nothing of this band's existence until Carlos the Jackal made it famous, Carlos didn't create it. Most of the groundwork was done before he inherited the Paris assignment, following the assassination of his predecessor, Mohammed Boudia. (Both Boudia and *his* predecessor, Mahmoud Hamchari, had been on Black September's Olympics hit-team and were accordingly murdered in 1973 by an Israeli secret service team calling itself the Wrath of God. Hamchari was killed by telephone, with an electronic booby trap; Boudia was blown up in his car with a trembler bomb.)

The Paris office had started out as a base for Black September, using Palestinian personnel from Fatah and the PFLP both. Its early work had more or less followed the original lines conceived by Habash: killing Jews abroad and striking at targets directly related to Israel (tourist agencies, commercial enterprises, banks). Before long, Fatah got better at this than the PFLP. Backed by Arafat's personal prestige and organizational clout, it had more money, more cadres, more friends at court and chances to make global news, in widely ranging assaults from Copenhagen to Teheran and Bangui. What this still boiled down to, though, was little more than an extension of the Arab-Israeli confrontation on the home front. These were constricting bounds.

By the time Carlos took over the Paris network from Boudia, midway through 1973, his target area was greatly expanded. When he retired, late in 1975, almost anybody could be blown up or shot down by anybody else in the name of the Palestine Resistance, anywhere in the Western world. It no longer mattered that Carlos happened to be a Venezuelan by the name of Ilich Ramirez Sanchez who hadn't even set foot on Palestinian soil until 1970. If anything, the image helped.

His maiden voyage to the Middle East was arranged in Moscow. Carlos was studying there, at the Patrice Lumumba Friendship University for foreigners. So was Mohammed Boudia, the PFLP's star performer in Europe. By 1970, Habash and Haddad were already working out a broader strategy of terrorist violence "always and everywhere." It was arranged before Carlos left Russia that he would sign up with them.[19]

He arrived in Jordan just in time to join the Palestinians in their fratricidal clash with King Hussein. Tension had been rising for months, as the Palestinian *fedayeen* entrenched in Jordan grew more thrusting and threatening to the Hashemite monarchy; the PFLP provided the final provocation with its quadruple hijacking that September. Hussein turned his Bedouin warriors loose on the Palestinians just four days after Wadi Haddad's commandos blew up three of its hijacked airliners on Jordan's Zarka airfield, alerting crack TV network teams well in advance.

The battle in Jordan was dreadful, taking thousands of lives, leaving encrusted deposits of human bitterness, convincing Palestinian leaders that only by internationalizing their war with Israel could they hope to win it.

They all moved left after that, though some went farther than others. There was much to be said for radicalizing the Palestine Resistance. It had a quelling effect on rich and conservative Arab rulers—the richer and more conservative, the more quelling—who might otherwise be tempted to sell the Palestinians short or cut their leaders off without a dime. Whereas it made sense for the poor, who represent most of Arab society. It made historic sense, in a region so overexposed to Western imperialist penetration. Most of all, it could capture the kind of worldwide sympathy that had saved the day for Vietnam, bringing victory through diplomacy where none could be had by military means.

Nevertheless, there was a distinct difference in war aims. For PLO leaders around Arafat, liquidation of the Zionist state was enough. "Peace for us means the destruction of Israel, and nothing else" was Arafat's view. Habash, however, affirmed that "our enemy is not just Israel, period." Israel was the misshapen issue of imperialism, he argued, and the imperialist monster had to be struck in its worldwide dimensions. "We must recognize that our revolution is a phase of world revolution: it is not limited to reconquering Palestine," he said. "To be honest, what we want is a war like Vietnam's. We want another Vietnam, and not just in Palestine but throughout the Arab world." [20]

Actually, what Habash wanted was one, ten, one hundred Vietnams.

The PFLP had been racing leftward since 1968; by 1970, Dr. Habash proclaimed it to be an "armed Leninist Party." He announced this in the North Korean satellite capital of Pyongyang, where the Russians' guerrilla training camps were already in full swing and where Habash himself had come to shop for weapons. "No frontier, be it political, geographic, or moral, can resist the action of the people," he told a cheering audience of four hundred delegates, gathered from the four continents to discuss revolutionary strategy. "Nobody is innocent, nobody can be neutral in the world of today." [21] ("There is no such thing as an innocent bystander" is how this theory of extended terrorist warfare was put a century earlier, by Germany's original left-wing terrorist, Johann Most.)

Habash was more explicit at a secret terrorist summit in Lebanon's Baddawi refugee camp. "Palestine has joined the European Revolution; we have forged organic links with the revolution of the whole world," he explained to the inner circle gathering around him. The IRA was there, and the Iranian National Front, the Turkish People's Liberation Army, the Japanese Red Army, the Spanish Basques' ETA, the German Red Army Fraction, the Italian Red Brigades, the Tupamaros.[22] That made at least half a dozen Vietnams right there, doubtless to the gratification of the Cuban ambassador to Lebanon, who was reportedly also present.

Dr. Habash certainly wasn't the only one training foreigners in the Middle East. As early as 1969, some two hundred of them were in camps run by Fatah as well as the PFLP (including forty-eight Britons, twenty French, eighteen Germans, and four American Black Panthers). [23] By the year of that Baddawi meeting in 1972, everybody in and out of the PLO had some such arrangement. Non-Arabs could be found in guerrilla camps strung out over the great Arab arc of Fatahland from Baghdad and Damascus to Aden, Cairo, Tripoli, Algiers.

It was not yet the colossal terrorist machine it would become midway through the seventies, when the Palestine Resistance would attain to fabulous wealth, nearly limitless armament, an impregnable diplomatic shield, and an enviable hold on the world's most valuable piece of real estate. Even so, they could offer exceptional facilities as the decade of terror opened, to outsiders with nothing like their open camps and freedom of movement.

They might or might not charge money for the services, depending on their outlook and the state of their finances. The PFLP, which scorned the dirty money of reactionary Arab oil magnates, was more inclined to extract high fees than the others. In general, though, they all expected to be repaid by foreign graduates sooner or later, in the coin of the terrorist realm—armed propaganda, as it is known in the trade.

Armed propaganda meant that a camp graduate would call public attention to Palestine as well as to his own national concerns on getting back to work. Thus, a Nicaraguan-born American would help the Palestinians' famous hijacker Leila Khaled seize an El Al airliner in London, losing his life in the episode (September 6, 1970); Turkish guerrillas returning from a Lebanese camp would kidnap and kill the Israeli consul in Istanbul—"as partial repayment to the Palestinians," so they said on May 23, 1971; a Japanese Red Army commando would shoot up Israel's Lod airport, leaving twenty-six dead (May 30, 1972).

In all three cases, the graduates came from PFLP camps. Dr. Habash was famous for driving this particular bargain, for particular reasons. Other Palestinian groups might merely be interested in public-relations assistance or backup aid from non-Arabs. But Habash was building history's first integrated multinational terrorist strike force.

His PFLP camps in Baalbek, Beirut, and Aden were small and spartan—early trainees lived mostly on beans—but thoroughly professional. The courses were advanced, the instructors expert (there were a good many Cubans and East Germans, as well as Chinese at first), the discipline exemplary under Wadi Haddad, and admission was highly selective. The candidates had not only to be cool, committed, and Marxist, but they had to come from the right places.

The list of Dr. Habash's geopolitical priorities in the seventies makes provocative reading in the eighties. He was partial to Iran (whose Islamic Revolution upset the planet-wide balance of power at the decade's end); Turkey (guarding NATO's southeastern flank and Russia's entrance to the Mediterranean through the Dardanelles); Japan (the West's industrial partner in the Orient); the desert sultanate of Oman (commanding oil-tanker passage westward from the Persian Gulf); Ethiopia (dominating a third of Africa, acquired by Russia as a Communist client-state in the mid-seventies with direct Soviet and Cuban military intervention); and terrorist bands (German, Italian, Spanish, Irish) encircling the heart of Western Europe.

There was always room in his camps for others, from any of a dozen Latin American republics and the smaller European states. They might lie dormant for years, as his Greeks did until 1980. Or they might serve mostly to deliver messages or explosives, usually the case with his Belgians, Scandinavians, and the two score or so in Dutch Red Help. Nevertheless, there was no mistaking his preferences.

The Iranians were among the first to join his camps. They came by the hundreds, perhaps by the thousands. No reliable head-count is available, but results are what matter and his Iranians got results. "The Palestinian Revolution has opened the way for many Iranian fighters to benefit from practical training in the use of arms," reported the Lebanese paper *al-Ahad* on December 19, 1971. "This first aid began in 1968, when a contingent of the Iranian revolutionary movement left Iran for training with the Resistance Movement. After their return to Iran, they began to train other members. . . . Owing to the direct influence of the armed Palestinian struggle, revolutionary groups began to study armed struggle and to carry out armed actions inside Iran." How many of them were at it—as far back as 1971, eight years before their Islamic Revolution peaked—is suggested by the arrest of seventy-five Iranians in a single group that year, all trained and supplied by the PFLP.[24]

The IRA was another early starter. The first Irish contingent reached a PFLP camp in 1968 as well, and the flow never stopped. Their close alliance was strengthened by a bilateral pact of mutual assistance in 1972.[25]

Next, Dr. Habash literally went after the Turks and Japanese.

After a 1968 start in his camps as well, Turkish guerrilla forces had terrorized their country straight into martial law by 1971. A dazzling and almost daily run of bank heists, bombings, abductions, and assassinations was cut short by a ruthless military crackdown. Massive arrests over the following year led to giant-sized public trials, with as many as 250 defendants at a time, a good number facing life sentences or execution. For some two or three years the Turkish terrorists were immobilized. Since they couldn't come to Habash, he went to them.

"The Popular Front for the Liberation of Palestine sends instructors to Turkey in order to train Turkish youth in urban guerrilla fighting, kidnappings, plane hijackings, and other matters," Leila Khaled declared to the Turkish daily *Hurryet* on May 26, 1971. "In view of the fact that it is more difficult than in the past for Turks to go and train in PFLP camps, the PFLP is instructing the Turks in the same way as it trains Ethiopians and revolutionaries from underdeveloped countries. The PFLP has trained most of the detained Turkish underground members." It was something to bear in mind ten years later, when terrorist violence in Turkey was taking the lives of nine or ten people a day.

The Japanese Red Army was in worse trouble still. At the height of its glory, in the great student uprisings of 1968 and 1969, it had three or four hundred violently revolutionary leftist followers and a hypnotic hold on the public. By 1972, a prosperous materialist society and watchful police force had cut them down to an intractable handful. Hunted house by house and street by street after a rash of armed robberies and cop killings, the Red Army's remaining leaders holed up with a woman hostage in an empty resort hotel at Karuizawa.

There followed ten days of relentless police siege. Under klieg lights, with television cameras grinding, the terrorists fired at anything that moved, while police lobbed tear gas, crashed through the roof with a steel demolition ball to pump in icy jets of water, and finally stormed the building. The cameras followed them in, to a grotesque scene.

In the midst of the siege, thirty Red Army militants had ended up in an orgy of self-purification. Half of them had sentenced the other half to death for "absence of revolutionary sincerity" and "bourgeois deformities" such as wearing earrings and fornicating and childbearing (in wedlock). The fourteen bodies recovered by police had been stripped, bound and gagged, tortured, mutilated, ritually stabbed, strangled, buried alive under floorboards, or left in the snow to die of exposure.[26] Such was the tremor of shock across the country that the Red Army's remaining soldiers cleared out of Japan bag and baggage; one girl deposited her baby on the steps of a Tokyo subway station as she went.

Dr. Habash had taken a keen interest in the Japanese terrorists since meeting nine of them in North Korea, during his 1970 visit. (Doubtless inspired by his own display, they had hijacked their way to Pyongyang from Tokyo with a Japan Air Lines plane.) He had arranged later for Leila Khaled and her husband to visit them in North Korea, talking over possible joint ventures and a Japanese "international unit" under PFLP auspices in Beirut. When the crisis came in Japan, he sent Leila there to see what she could do. The tattered remnants of the Red Army saluted her arrival by blowing up five Tokyo police stations and then took off in a body for the PFLP's camp at Baalbek. "The PFLP has undertaken to train the Japanese because it is impossible for them to undergo such training in Japan," observed the Beirut paper *al-Usbua al-Arabi*, rightly.

The Japanese paid their bill in armed propaganda at Lod airport. Three months after their self-purification rites at the hotel in Karuizawa, a suicide mission selected by Wadi Haddad left Baalbek on a circumspect journey to next-door Israel by way of Frankfurt, Paris, and Rome. Armed with Czech automatics and shrapnel grenades (delivered in Rome by Carlos, traveling as "Hector Hypodikon"),[27] the three commandos raked the crowded airport terminal with automatic fire. Twenty-six people were killed and seventy-two more wounded. Sixteen of the dead were Christian pilgrims from Puerto Rico, on a visit to the Holy Land. There was no such thing as an innocent bystander anymore, as Dr. Habash had made plain to heady applause in Pyongyang.

The singular mindlessness of the slaughter distracted attention for a while from the developing design behind it. "The Palestinians are drowning and will pull the whole world down with them," warned the *Daily Star* of Beirut. Fusako Shigenobu, pitiless woman leader of the Japanese Red Army abroad, put it another way. "The mission's purpose was to consolidate the international revolutionary alliance against the imperialists of the world," she said in the PFLP's *al-Hadaf*. Few took it in fully even so. The fact that Palestinians had sent Japanese to kill Christians and Jews alike would only fall into place when Habash and Haddad turned Carlos loose in Paris, a year later.

The times weren't right, and the Carlos network wasn't quite ready, in the spring of 1972. Hardly any of Europe's ultraleft terrorists had actually begun to kill anybody yet. (The IRA was just getting back into form, the Basques' ETA had bagged three, the Germans one, the Italians none at all). Arafat's Fatah still took up a lot of room in Europe and mopped up a lot of resources. The Black International was still competing with the Red one for Palestinian affections. Colonel Qaddafi's heart and purse were still on the Black side. And the Russians were still seemingly of two minds about Arab terrorism for export. (Though they had been arming the Palestinians in the Middle East since 1969, they did not supply weapons for Fatah's use in Europe until thirteen days after the Munich Olympics massacre, in 1972.) [28]

The great tilt came on Yom Kippur in October 1973. For once in a quarter of a century, the Arab armies caught Israel by surprise. The Egyptians penetrated deep into the Sinai with four thousand tanks, and the Syrians were massed on the Golan Heights. The Arab oil states used their oil as a weapon of war for the first time, by withholding it and nearly doubling the price. Western Europe crumpled at the hint of an oil embargo. The Russians threatened armed intervention when Israeli forces drove the Egyptians back over the Suez Canal and very nearly to Cairo. The White House forced the Israelis to withdraw. After twenty-five years of humiliation and frustration, Arabs of Arafat's leanings could believe at last in the chances of victory through diplomatic pressure.

They prepared to negotiate in Geneva; the Rejection Front was born.

The new age of diplomacy plainly required a statesmanlike posture: no more rough stuff, such as burning up a million dollars' worth of oil in Trieste or Rotterdam, or slaughtering athletes at Olympic games. Whatever the advertising value in such ventures, they did not sit well with foreign governments, as Arafat knew. (He denied for years having had anything to do with the Olympics massacre, despite undeniable proof to the contrary.) The whole proposition of exporting Palestinian terrorism thus began to look dubious in top PLO circles. Fatah's last big strike abroad was its seizure of the Saudi Arabian embassy in Sudan early in 1973, ending with the murder of three Western diplomats including the American ambassador. For Arafat, the Yom Kippur War some months later put a stop to all that: Fatah would have to pull back to its home ground, and Black September's supersecret death squads abroad would have to go.

Elegantly informal as always, Arafat's cousin Hassan Salameh let it be known in European chancellories that the Palestinians and Israelis had agreed to stop killing each other on foreign soil, confining the practice to the home front. Though Israel's secret services hotly denied agreeing to this or anything with Salameh, he was taken at his word. Henceforth, Western European governments would redouble their efforts to fail to notice Palestinian terrorists on their territory who were no longer supposed to be there.

In reality, there were more around than ever. Although Black September folded, rival Palestinian factions within it never stopped using the Continent to hunt and destroy one another, and by pulling out of Europe, Fatah simply left the field to Habash and Haddad.

Arafat really wasn't giving much away. His *fedayeen* went right on killing Jews inside Israel, and the PLO charter continued to deny Israel's legal right to exist. Nevertheless, his position implied eventual acceptance of a Zionist state in some form. Habash would have nothing to do with such "political solutions." Claiming his full doctrinal rights as a scientific Socialist, he insisted that worldwide Zionist imperialism was still the enemy, to be fought on a worldwide front without quarter. (Asked if he minded the prospect of perhaps bringing on World War III in the Middle East, he replied, "Honestly, no.") [29]

He became the leader of the Rejection Front. Half in and half out of the PLO umbrella group, it embraced fanatic Marxist revolutionaries from Ahmed Jibril to Naif Hawatmeh and Abu Nidal, all long and intimately connected with Moscow. The Arab states solidly behind them—Syria, Iraq, South Yemen, Algeria, Libya—were, or would soon become, Moscow's good friends too. Colonel Qaddafi, carried away by the Russians' attachment to the Palestinian cause, began to lose interest in the Black International. Before long he was among the Soviet Union's best customers for military equipment, parceling it out to the choicest terrorist bands of the Red International, Habash's allies. When Qaddafi also agreed to bankroll the Carlos network in Europe, it was on.

By the autumn of 1973, Habash and Haddad had a fine Old Boy network going on the Continent, and Paris was The Place. The Turkish People's Liberation Army, the Iranian National

Front, and the Japanese Red Army, all in prickly circumstances at home, were operating mostly out of the French capital. The Japanese kept their biggest cell there; the Turks and Iranians were sharing a headquarters with Carlos in a suburban villa at Villiers-sur-Marne. (That December a raid by the French internal security service, DST, uncovered quantities of weapons smuggled in from Bulgaria, explosives, a forgery factory for false documents, and a number of detailed hit-plans.)

German and Italian terrorists, the Irish, and the Spanish Basques were in and out of Paris, on call. Latin American guerrillas were long in residence (not just Tupamaros, but Colombians, Venezuelans, Chileans, Argentinians, Brazilians). Belgian, Dutch, and Scandinavian auxiliaries could be sent on scouting expeditions or deliver a few pounds of dynamite here and there. Henri Curiel was on hand with his Help and Friendship services. A close friend of Mohammed Boudia's since the 1950s, when both worked in the Algerian underground, he was a mainstay for Carlos after Boudia died.

The inner circle often met to review plans. They might have a chat at the Secretariat of International Coordination office in Zurich or drop in on one another in Frankfurt, London, Amsterdam, Brussels, Milan. At a series of clandestine meetings in Dublin, they worked out courier routes, codes, weapons procurement and exchange, frontier getaway points, safe-houses (the Japanese Red Army alone had fifty of these scattered around the Continent). At one of these meetings, the PFLP divided up a million dollars' worth of arms.[30] (The money seems to have come from a five-million-dollar ransom collected by Haddad for a hijacked Lufthansa plane, though South Yemen cut into that by demanding a percentage for "landing rights.")

The Russians were lining up logistic support. Habash had gone to Moscow in 1972 and was received quietly but well. Standing arrangements were made to smuggle arms through Eastern Europe to the Western side and smuggle terrorist fugitives heading the other way. Habash's own men went to Russia to do some graduate work in guerrilla training. (So did Arafat's, but they were deployed in a different war zone.)

There followed an amazing two years. Nobody really knew

how amazing they were at the time. Dozens of mysterious and sinister events seemed unrelated then. Carlos himself would be very nearly at the end of his career before the police were aware of his existence. Most of the forty or fifty international professionals he boasted of having trained personally would be dead or imprisoned before the links among them came to light. Not until the end of the fright decade would the target countries come to see the dimensions of the Carlos network, and its furthermost limits were barely discernible even then.

It might have been worse, had it not been for breakdowns and trivial accidents, the casual ruin of extravagant plans, intricate plots foiled by the odd policeman or faceless secret agent. Even so, the band had a good run. By the summer of 1974, Habash and Haddad would be sending someone out to meet secretly with the inner circle at Viareggio, in Tuscany, to "rejoice over the results" of their collective efforts. Their siege of the Continent, mounted from Paris, directed from Aden, and boosted with the utmost discretion from Moscow, would have a devastating impact on the Western world while it lasted, and lasting effects for years to come.

8

"CARLOS"

"When I saw the trap I was in, I pulled my revolver. It was a Russian Tokarev 7.62. I shot the three policemen in the head. There was only Michel left in the room. He came toward me with his hands over his eyes. He knew the rules of the game: a traitor is condemned to die. He stood before me, I shot into his eyes, he fell to the ground, I shot once more into his temple. I was calm. I jumped out of a third-floor window and walked away as if nothing had happened. . . . No, I am not a professional killer. It isn't easy to shoot somebody in the eyes when he's looking right at you, especially if you've killed four people in less than ten seconds as I did. . . ."

Carlos, recalling the scene that had forced his hasty exit from France in 1975, was still making up the part he liked best. The lightning draw, the stern retribution for betrayal, the gallant remorse, steely control, lithe leap from improbable heights. . . . Actually, he was rather overweight and more than a little drunk that evening, at the boozy end of a raucous surprise party in the Latin Quarter. The police, arriving without the smallest idea of who he was, were unarmed. He had excused himself to go to the bathroom, retrieved the gun he kept there, and come out firing. His closest aide, Michel Moukarbal, never had a chance to stand penitent before him, barely getting past the door when Carlos drilled him between the eyes—a professional assassin's best target, he observed in the interview. Then he slipped into the hall and over a balcony rail to some scaffolding below.

If he may have felt a twinge of remorse for Moukarbal, he expressed none for the three policemen or any of his other victims—the boy whose hand was sheared off at the wrist by a grenade he once tossed, for instance. Knocking people off did not appear to affect him much one way or another. "I can't understand why they didn't kill the ambassador," he remarked as if honestly puzzled, telling about the time his Japanese commandos took over the French embassy in Holland.

The Interview (it deserves capital letters), given in hiding to an Arab journalist for the Paris-based weekly *al-Watan al-Arabi*, was the only one Carlos ever granted.[1] Much of it was old stuff by then—December 1979. He seemed anxious to revive fading memories of his exploits, as an elderly veteran of some forgotten battle might do to impress the irreverent young. "And so, when everything looked hopeless, I was capable of reversing the situation and transforming it into total success. . . ," he went on, about the French embassy affair.

There really was no need for him to prove how good he used to be at his work. In his brief career as head of the Paris team, the rate of international terrorist attacks on the Continent rose fourfold. When he left the scene in 1975, Western Europe held the all-time worldwide record for such attacks, outdoing every other region on earth in the scale, scope, and number of its assassinations, incendiary and explosive bombings, armed assaults. Obviously he was good at his work.

The legend about Carlos contains a lot of hot air. He was not the Al Capone of the terrorist underworld, though he enjoyed newspaper fiction to that effect: "the crazier the stories about me, the less a flatfoot might care to go after me," he would say. His job in Paris was simply to carry out Wadi Haddad's orders from Aden. He was given the material and told what to do with it. He was to orchestrate a multinational strike force around the Palestine Rejection Front, show the face of international revolution, disrupt and demoralize the imperialist West. Practiced, scrupulously efficient and conscientious, he was also safely lacking in compassion; his value to his superiors lay in dependability, expertise, and a flair for showmanship. "I got that from my grandfather on my mother's side," he said.

Carlos stood for "Carlos Martinez-Torres" of Peru, when he wasn't "Cenan Clarke" of New York, "Hector Hugo Dupont" of Britain and France, "Glenn Gebart" of the United States, "Adolph Bernal" of Chile, "Hector Hypodikon," "Salem," or Ilich Ramirez Sanchez at home. Switching names, nationalities, and identities was no problem for this resourceful young professional who managed to lead a complicated triple life for the better part of a decade.

Between 1966 and 1975, Carlos was an amiable, partygoing, skirt-chasing, guitar-playing Latin in the Continent's social whirl; a senior executive in the international terrorist circuit; and an orthodox Communist operative under KGB control. Not until he gunned his way out of the Paris flat in Rue Toullier, at twenty-six, did the authorities learn about his second life, and it took still longer to find out much about the third.

Up to that sweltering summer night in Paris, he passed merely as a South American playboy having a whale of a time abroad. His father had made himself a million dollars in Venezuelan real estate, his mother was an attractive divorcée popular in London's diplomatic set, and he was a playboy.

He had more than enough money and plenty of time to indulge his idle and expensive tastes. "I like good food and good cigars," he said in The Interview. "I like to sleep in a good bed freshly made. I like to walk in good shoes. I like to play poker and blackjack. I like parties, and dances, and going to see a dramatic play from time to time. I know I'm going to be assassinated someday, so I like living to the hilt." He liked staying at Hiltons, too, and hot showers (which he took all day long), and pretty girls.

Not all the girls liked him. The fastidious Anglo-Saxons who went to Cheltenham were put off by his fleshy lips, tightly waved dark hair, and stoutish figure impeccably tailored in flannels and blazer. (Plump since childhood, he was nicknamed "El Gordo" by his schoolmates: "Fatso," in rude English.) But Latin women liked him a lot, and he often kept three or four on the string at a time.

His politics were unobtrusive, and he could hardly help his

name. His father, whose lifelong devotion to communism did not interfere with amassing a fortune, had christened all three sons after his favorite historic character, Vladimir Ilich Lenin. His firstborn was Ilich, the younger boys Vladimir and Lenin ("Vlad" and "Lenny" on the playing fields of their good British schools). The name was not necessarily a label for Ilich, though, and nobody he met socially would have thought he cared more about the Communist movement than his dilettante father did. Many could not quite believe it even when he said so himself, long after his retirement. "I would renounce everything for the Revolution. The Revolution is my supreme euphoria," he declared.

He was remarkably candid about his political past in The Interview, doubtless feeling that it no longer mattered: by late 1979, his cover was thoroughly blown. Casually, perhaps even a little contemptuously, he made fools of the objective reporters and judicious government officials who, for years, kept on keeping an open mind about his incriminating Soviet ties. He had, he said explicitly, been a pro-Moscow Communist Party activist since the age of fifteen.

"Marxism has always been my religion," he began by saying. "It was hereditary, first of all. It was in the atmosphere of our house, in my parents' blood. Later, I acquired a personal culture by traveling in Russia. . . ."

He disclosed that he had joined Venezuela's hard-line, Moscow-oriented Communist Party in 1964, something his father had always stoutly denied. (Dr. Ramirez, delighted to hear that Ilich was the famous Carlos—"My son is a general!" he exclaimed on getting the news—insisted that Ilich had never joined the Party or been supported financially by anybody but Dr. Ramirez.)

In his very first year as a Party member, Ilich revealed, he became "an active intermediary among the Party's different branches." By the next year, he was running an underground Party cell with two hundred members in Caracas and "coordinating many street demonstrations that even frightened the president of the republic." When his father sent him to London in 1966, he went on, "I founded the first student international in the labor world, with Irish and British comrades." Then, in

1968, "I went to Patrice Lumumba University in Moscow; the Communist Party of Venezuela paid my way. . . . It was at this university period of my studies that I engaged in some modest operations, of which I cannot speak in detail."

Several details he felt unable to speak of are known to Western Intelligence services by now. No sooner did he fly the coop in Paris than they started coming to light.

His name had been in the CIA's files since 1969, when a Cuban diplomat in Paris called Orlando Castro Hidalgo defected to the United States. Hidalgo had quit Cuba's intelligence service, the DGI, after the Russians took it over, and he knew quite a bit about it. His precise information on Cuba's guerrilla training camps included the then obscure name of Ilich Ramirez Sanchez.

On the way from Caracas to London, young Ilich had stopped off in Havana for a while. That was in 1966, historic year of the Tricontinental Conference in Cuba. He was among 150 Venezuelans sent to the island by his country's Communist Party, engaged at the time in an advanced stage of intensive guerrilla warfare.[2] With two years of terrorist experience under his belt, he was a promising seventeen.

At Camp Matanzas, just outside Havana, he studied urban guerrilla tactics, automatic arms, plastic explosives, sabotage, map making and map reading, photography, forgery, and disguise. His camp supervisor was KGB Colonel Viktor Simenov, soon to be installed in an office next door to the director's at DGI headquarters. His chief instructor, using the name "Antonio Dages Bouvier" on a fake Ecuadorian passport, would follow Carlos to Europe and stick with him to the end—his KGB control.[3]

From Cuba, Ilich was sent back to Venezuela on two secret missions. Neither went too well, and the second time he got his name on the police blotter. Nevertheless, his Party sponsors still thought enough of him to recommend and stake him for schooling in Moscow.

The Patrice Lumumba Friendship University is not as selective, or subversive, as the Lenin Institute, reserved for mature Communist Party leaders from Europe and elsewhere. Lumumba U. was founded by Nikita Khrushchev in 1960 to train a broader swatch of Third World "intelligentsia cadres." The university, directed and largely staffed by the KGB, has as its mission the education of "students from underdeveloped countries so they can return to their homelands to become the nucleus for pro-Soviet activities." Thousands of young radicals processed there have gone back to be such nuclei in homelands from Iran to Chile, in Angola and Mozambique, the Palestine Resistance, the entire Arab world, the whole of Latin America. It was at Patrice Lumumba—while Carlos was there—that the KGB selected ten Mexican students to work with, for what, as we mentioned in Operation Leo, became an elaborate Soviet plot to capture Mexico in 1971.

Lumumba University, with some twenty thousand students, is inevitably something of a grab bag. Not every alumnus works out, and those with a high potential yield are customarily sent on for advanced training in other Soviet institutes. Carlos himself would return secretly to Moscow in 1974, for specialized courses in political indoctrination, sabotage, weaponry, and killer karate.[4] That was another detail he left out of his glamorous life story.

During his second and final year at Lumumba, Carlos was a public disgrace. Installed with his kid brother Lenin and a handsome allowance from Dad, he let it be known that he would never join anything so dreary as the Party, still less be bound by its oppressive discipline. He threw money around, drank, slept with girls when he should have been attending lectures, hurled a bottle of ink at the Libyan embassy for turning anti-Soviet overnight (after Colonel Qaddafi seized power, late in 1969). Chided officially once or twice, he was finally sent down from the university for "hooliganism." But he was not sent out of Russia—a curious mark of indulgence toward the dissolute rowdy from Caracas. On the contrary, he stayed on in Moscow awhile, attending to those "modest operations" he mentioned a decade afterward. That took care of the never very credible story that the Russians had washed their hands of a good-for-nothing idler—recognizably an old KGB dodge.

It is not clear whether Carlos was put on to the Palestinians or they to him, at Lumumba University. Either way, that is where he met Mohammed Boudia.

An underground Communist Party leader during Algeria's war of independence in the fifties, Boudia is known to have worked with the KGB at least since 1967.[5] His control then was Yuri Kotov, a Soviet specialist in Middle Eastern affairs who became the KGB's director for Western Europe in Paris. When Boudia himself became top man in Europe for the PFLP, in 1969, he was sent to Moscow for a bit of extra professional polish. It was on his warm recommendations that Carlos signed up with George Habash and Wadi Haddad in 1970.

Before going to meet them in the Middle East, Carlos detoured to East Germany, as he would often do again. The Communist regime there was just setting up its rapid-transit system for terrorist fugitives from West Germany, a godsend for both German and Palestinian terrorists. (The Baader-Meinhof Gang maintained an emergency safe-house in East Berlin from 1970 onward—a ten-minute subway ride to safety if the cops were after them. The Palestinians, who had twenty-three bases in West Germany by 1972, used East Berlin as a natural back-door entrance and exit.) [6]

Moving on to Jordan, Carlos spent three months as a privileged guest in PFLP camps and took part in the Black September clash with Hussein's Bedouin troops. It was "a useful guerrilla experience," he noted in The Interview. Then he was assigned to work with Boudia on the Continent.

Until 1973, Carlos was mostly a sleeper in England. Next to France it was the best place for him to be. Like France, Great Britain had time-honored traditions of political asylum. London teemed with foreign guerrilla fighters, laying their plans, generally without interference from the British authorities so long as they were not laying siege to British citizens. Palestinians in particular were as free there as in Paris to carry out their internal vendettas, and to plan assaults on the Continent. (Not until 1980, when the Iranian embassy in London was occupied by Iranian dissidents did British authorities crack down with their traditional efficiency.)

When Carlos arrived in Paris, Boudia was busy creating the necessary infrastructure for Wadi Haddad's band of international impresarios; Carlos would turn up occasionally to help out, as he did for the Japanese kamikaze mission to Lod airport. In London, meanwhile, he was creating his cover as an amiable social nitwit and building an infrastructure of his own.

At the time, the United Kingdom was a hive of activity for Soviet agents abroad. In 1971, the British government expelled 105 of them at once, the biggest such cleanup on record. Since that practically emptied the Russian embassy in London, the burden of its clandestine work fell to the Cuban DGI. That made things more convenient for Carlos. It wasn't long before Antonio Dages Bouvier, his former guerrilla instructor and KGB control, flew over from Camp Matanzas, Havana, to join him.

Completing his trio was a handsome and high-born Colombian lawyer called Maria Nydia Romero de Tobon. Separated from her husband, she lived in London with her two sons, and worked at the Colombia Center. Most of her acquaintances regarded her as a charming and scatty woman of generous heart and vaguely Maoist sentiments, inclined to dismiss the Soviet Union as too bourgeois. In fact, she was in the secretariat of Colombia's pro-Moscow Communist Party, where her husband was a senior official, and she was in regular contact with the DGI through a second secretary at the Cuban embassy. (He was Angel Dalmau, indicated to Scotland Yard's Special Branch by the French DST in 1975, after the Carlos shootout.) [7]

Together, the threesome went house-hunting around London, setting up several hideaways in the West End. Nydia posed as Bouvier's wife at the real-estate agencies, though she actually shared a flat with Carlos (who shared another with a Spanish girl, found later to be storing an arsenal of weapons for him). Nydia, too, stored weapons for Carlos, along with confidential papers and passports for both men. She also took to commuting between London and Paris when Carlos replaced Boudia there, making frequent side trips to East Germany; Carlos would use her in London to relay urgent messages or put a little money aside for him. From Paris, he sent her 500 francs a month to keep on deposit for a rainy day. (The rainy day having fallen on a weekend, in Rue Toullier, Carlos could not draw on these emergency funds for his getaway.) But Nydia de Tobon was not his real banker in Britain; Bouvier was.

Here, also, a small fact buried in the archives would only fall into place after Carlos was on the run. In April 1973, Israeli forces raided the Lebanese corniche of Ramblatt-el-Blida and found themselves able for a while to listen in on messages transmitted by a Soviet KGB officer under diplomatic cover in Beirut. By chance, therefore—they were still in the dark about Carlos, like everybody else—they learned that he was drawing checks on the London bank account of a KGB agent named Antonio Dages Bouvier.[8]

Until summoned to higher duties in Paris, Carlos worked hard with Bouvier in London, preparing and researching lists of Jews and other people to be shot in the name of the Palestine Resistance. The list was up to a fanciful five hundred when it fell into Scotland Yard's hands, after Carlos fled from Paris. Heading the list was Zionist leader Joseph Edward Sief, owner of the Marks and Spencer clothing chain, followed by stars of the musical, literary, theatrical, political, and financial worlds. The violinist Yehudi Menuhin was on it, along with playwright John Osborne and former Prime Minister Edward Heath.

Diverted to other work in Paris, Carlos never got past number one on his London hit-list, and he fumbled it. The operation is described in The Inverview. "To handle an assassination correctly, you should have two pistols; one with a silencer, the other very powerful for self-defense in case of surprise. This is considered a strict minimum for success," he said. "Well, you see, I had only one old revolver a friend gave me that I hadn't even tested. I cleaned it, got into an old car, and went along to Sief's house. . . . I ordered the butler to take me to his master, who was in the bathroom. I fired three times, but only one bullet hit him, on the upper lip. Generally, I fire three bullets at the nose, which kills instantly. But this fellow was lucky. Only one bullet got him, and his teeth checked the shock. So he escaped death."

Considering the abundance of staff and weapons he could have drawn on, it is hard to explain this sloppy performance.

Perhaps he was showing off, which seems likely. But he would not slip so badly again.

The Paris network had passed to Carlos only a few months earlier, after Mohammed Boudia's death. Summoned to Aden for consultations with Wadi Haddad, he returned to Paris with an efficient adjutant, the Lebanese Michel Moukarbal; a ready-made "terror bank" of expert personnel; smoothly running organizational machinery, put in order by the late Boudia; and Colonel Qaddafi's promise to foot the bills. "My existence as a marginal revolutionary was transformed. I had become somebody effective," he said. "It was the moment when 'Carlos' was born."

What did Carlos do, exactly? A bit of everything, really, so long as it kept the international terrorist flag flying.

His vital function was to keep Wadi Haddad's Old Boys in line and give them their orders. Haddad was a stickler for a centralized command and could impose it: all of Europe's terrorist groups were coming to depend on him heavily for money and weapons, some desperately so. "It is always said that the Baader-Meinhof Gang, the June 2 Movement, and the Revolutionary Cells are totally independent. That is utterly untrue. Without Haddad, nothing works," said the German ex-terrorist Hans-Joachim Klein in 1978.[9] Klein had quit the Revolutionary Cells, not long after the 1975 OPEC raid, because he was "nauseated with the demented acts of the terrorist international." The Revolutionary Cells were practically the property of Haddad, who kept them on a monthly allowance of $3,000, Klein said. But all the others also took Haddad's word for law. (After a month's research in Rome on kidnapping the pope, for instance, the German June 2 Movement dropped it when Haddad told them to.)

Thus, many European terrorist spectaculars that seemed to originate on their native soil were in reality Carlos-supervised and Haddad-induced. Carlos himself led only a few of the big ones, radiating international solidarity in between.

He introduced diplomatic hostage-taking to the Continent, with his Japanese commandos' seizure of the French embassy in The Hague. He used that critical situation to bring the French government to a standstill for 101 hours, and then to its knees. In Paris, he speeded up its ignominious capitulation by reducing Le Drugstore on the Boulevard Saint-Germain to rubble, tossing a couple of grenades, killing two and injuring twenty, unmanning the French Establishment and half the population of Paris. He set things up for the German terrorists to imitate the Hague operation in Stockholm and tried (but failed) to do the same in Copenhagen and Berne.

He used French helpers to bomb the daylights out of three Parisian newspapers: "I got praise for that from Beirut," he said. He used Dutch and Belgians to survey international airline routes, laughing South American girls to carry booby-trapped parcels aboard planes, the Baader-Meinhof Gang to add sixty stolen U.S. Army grenades to his arsenal, passing half of them along to the Turks and Iranians in Paris.

He sent Michel Moukarbal to pick up supplies from the Swiss anarchists' takeout service in Zurich, securing (among other things) twenty-two of the devastating panzermines that were their specialty. He used the Swiss service to supply the Spanish Basques' ETA with the explosives they used to blow up Admiral Carrero-Blanco, General Franco's designated heir; and he did the same for the IRA, on the eve of a big bomb launch it was planning for London. He also tried, through Moukarbal, to talk the Swiss anarchists into bombing the Japan Air Lines office in Zurich (and got turned down).

He distributed the Curiel network's exquisitely forged passports to the needy: transient Japanese commandos, South American guerrillas-on-leave, even the South Koreans who tried to assassinate President Park in Seoul (but missed, merely killing his wife). He used Italy's Red Brigades to provide authentic stolen passports, German and Italian terrorists to rent cars for his hit-teams, assorted European palefaces to camouflage his more conspicuous Palestinian button-men. He used Turks to smuggle weapons in from Eastern Europe and Germans to relay weapons by the trunkful after delivery to Europe in some Libyan diplomat's luggage. He used a Brazilian to oversee his armory and a Greek to transport his first Soviet Strela missile into Italy.

The Strela was one of his more aggravating failures. Five Palestinians were already positioned on a balcony near Rome's Fiumicino airport, ready to blast a departing El Al plane with this portable heat-seeking missile, when police caught them on a tip from the Israelis. He never did have any luck with El Al planes, failing miserably twice with Soviet-made RPG-7 rockets at Orly airport in Paris.

He describes those occasions rather testily in The Interview. An even earlier attempt at Orly had been a washout: "A wildcat strike of El Al workers ruined everything: they stopped flying into Orly." On the next try, "we timed everything carefully. But our bazooka man hit a Yugoslav plane by mistake, and his second shot went wild. He was brave, but he cracked up. We decided to try again a week later, and I checked everything out personally at the airport. We picked a Sunday for the hit, because so many French families come to watch the jets take off on Sundays.

"We hid our weapons in the toilets, but people started to crowd in there, and we couldn't get back in to get our weapons until the plane was moving. It was 350 yards up when our bazooka man fired: too late. My men panicked when they saw police closing in. They opened fire and threw grenades [injuring twenty], grabbed six hostages [one a pregnant woman], and locked them in the toilets until they got a safe-conduct for the Middle East. I was preparing a backup action to get them away. . . ."

If not for such setbacks, which littered his path, he might have done better yet. Even so, he didn't do badly. Terrorism was getting to be a profession, a career with a future, when he left the scene. Any number of terrorist bands had learned to dig in properly, communicate through well-established subterranean channels, improve and coordinate their timing, acquire the latest Eastern bloc weapons through the Palestinians' underground railroad. Hans-Joachim Klein recalled the day he dropped in on Carlos in Paris and was shown how to handle the deadly and then novel Czech-made Skorpion, soon to become a terrorist favorite for closeup work. As the leader, if only for a brief interlude, of a "guerrilla network reaching from Europe to the Middle East, South America and the Orient. . . ," Carlos "was one of our most brilliant agents," said a PFLP spokesman when he retired.[10]

Throughout all this, the French police didn't have a clue about Carlos. But the Cubans did.

It was pure chance that led the police to 9, Rue Toullier. Michel Moukarbal had been picked up for questioning in a random way at the Beirut airport, and it happened again at the Paris end of his journey. He could hardly have informed on Carlos, since the DST's agents, following Moukarbal's trail, wandered into the Rue Toullier flat unarmed. They had just dropped in for a chat, they told the slightly tipsy Carlos, truthfully. But when they sent down to bring Moukarbal up for a tri-cornered conversation, Carlos lost his head and fired.

Police quickly learned the nature of his business from the dead Moukarbal's diaries and neatly kept expense accounts. Before long, they discovered that Carlos was keeping at least two Paris flats and four Venezuelan girls, several if not all taking turns in his bed. (One was also storing a huge cache of weapons for him under her own bed.) Three of the four had boyfriends passing as "diplomats" in the Cuban embassy. One of the girls worked there for a DGI operative who organized "international youth brigades" to harvest sugarcane in Cuba. Among the three boyfriends, all DGI agents, was the DGI's chief of mission in France, Paul Rodriguez Sainz.[11] Not only were they assiduous visitors to Rue Toullier, but they were on close working terms with Carlos himself. Indeed, he had been meeting regularly with the Cubans in Paris, London (through Nydia de Tobon), and elsewhere on the Continent. The DST was sure he had Cuban help in escaping the nationwide police dragnet when he made his getaway.

Ten days later, France expelled the three Cuban "diplomats," not as spies but as secret agents aiding and abetting terrorism. "The Carlos case, which until now constituted a striking demonstration of the unity of action among terrorist groups, has been enriched with important elements showing the assistance given to international terrorism by certain states," said the spokesman for Interior Minister Michel Poniatowski (who turned out to be on the Carlos network's lengthy French hit-list). "Developments in the case confirm the close links between terrorist networks and the espionage services of certain states. . . . It is disquieting to find that Cuban espionage agents together with those of certain East European countries are interfering in the activities of this international of violence." [12]

Poniatowski was dying to name the Soviet Union among these "certain East European states," but President Giscard d'Estaing wouldn't let him. Nevertheless, the Russians' direct collusion with Carlos was unmistakable in at least one instance.

The Schönau Castle Operation in Austria in September 1973 was not so much, as thrill-packed terrorist spectaculars go. Nobody died, nothing burned down or blew up, no ambassadors were snatched. All it took was the seizure of three frightened Jewish refugees in a second-class railway compartment to show how easily a couple of armed men could blackmail Europe. Some of the biggest smash hits in the Carlos repertoire might never have come off without it.

The operation had been planned in detail by Mohammed Boudia before Carlos took over and would have been out of the question without Russian help. Schönau Castle was a transit camp for Russian Jews emigrating to Israel. The Russians hated it as a provocative reminder of their need to knuckle under to the West on this matter. The Palestinians' feelings were self-evident. Black September had tried to infiltrate the camp earlier in 1973, under Hassan Salameh's guidance. But his six armed commandos were spotted by Israel's Mossad agents and barely got away alive. Arrested later, they confessed that they were to have telephoned to "the East"—Prague or Budapest—when the camp was full enough for a good hit.[13]

The Boudia project overcame this reconnaisance problem. The Russians, who knew how many Jews they were releasing and when, had only to indicate which train they were on, to Palestinians waiting in Czechoslovakia. Two armed Palestinians thereupon boarded the train on the Czech side of the Austrian border and walked along its corridors until they found some Jewish emigrants. By holding an aged couple and younger man at gunpoint, they had no trouble commandeering a Volkswagen Kombo at the Vienna station, moving their hostages to the city's airport. There, they just waited. Within thirteen hours, Chancellor Bruno Kreisky agreed to close down the Schönau Camp for good. Then he sent the Palestinians on their way in a Cessna plane provided by the Austrian government.

The two had arrived in Czechoslovakia from Beirut by way of Paris. They had evidently been in the country before, since their forged passports were stamped with Czech reentry visas.[14] They had also loitered around the Czech border town quite a while until the right train pulled in, carrying their Kalashnikovs and other bulky weapons loosely under their coats. Anybody who has tried crossing the borders of Soviet-occupied Czechoslovakia will get the point.

Chancellor Kreisky seemed cranky about the hullabaloo his swift compliance raised in the foreign press. "Differing views of such events are taken in countries which are at war, and those which are not," he said, presumably referring to the proxy war Russia was waging on the West, through the Palestinians, over neutral Austria's head. By the rules of terrorist warfare, however, he was not buying his way out of trouble but asking for it. His abject surrender in 1973 was taken as a cordial invitation to come again—which Carlos did, in the OPEC raid two years later.

Once Austria's soft neutrality was assured, the OPEC operation was a pushover. All the necessary inside information could be had from Colonel Qaddafi. It was his idea, after all, as Hans-Joachim Klein conceded obliquely after the event (adding that the inside dope "proved 100% correct"); the Libyan oil minister was right in there at the meeting with all those other oil ministers. Carlos, after sheltering further along the North African coast in Algeria following the Paris fiasco, had moved to Libya. He had six months to check things out with Qaddafi's men, ship his weapons to the Continent through the diplomatic pouch, and round up his Aden-trained teammates.

He descended on Vienna just before Christmas 1975, with Hans-Joachim Klein, Gabriele Kröcher-Tiedemann, two Lebanese, and a Palestinian. A backup crew from the German Revolutionary Cells consigned the weapons and withdrew to stand by in an outlying town forty miles away. Carlos stayed at the Hilton and went shopping (he bought a beret). They took a streetcar to the OPEC building on the appointed day, swinging their Adidas bags crammed with guns and grenades. The guard at the door said a cheery good morning, and they went upstairs knowing the conferees had no protection to speak of; killing three inattentive security guards was more a matter of psychology than necessity. "We needed an exemplary precedent," Carlos told Klein, after putting seven bullets into his victim's head and chest. (Klein himself got a severe dressing-down from Wadi Haddad afterward for having failed to kill anybody.)

The Austrian government laid on a Boeing for them as expected, and off they went, waving to cameramen, with eleven hostages representing four-fifths of the world's petroleum reserves. The satellite TV coverage could not have been better. People from Lapland to Patagonia had been advised of the Palestinian desire to annihilate Israel. They had also seen convincing evidence of an icily efficient and seemingly impregnable revolutionary terrorist international at work.

Carlos retired soon afterward, just in time. The summer would bring supreme humiliation to Wadi Haddad at Entebbe. Haddad was on hand in person when his mixed German-Palestinian team touched down in Uganda with their captive French Airbus in July 1976. Directing operations at his side was the false Ecuadorian with the KGB bank account, Antonio Dages Bouvier.[15] Together, they watched their hijackers separate 78 Jewish hostages from the remaining 168 passengers, just as the SS used to do it at Buchenwald. *"Schnell! Schnell!"* shrieked the German woman terrorist waving her gun, herding off her prisoners still marked with the tattooed numbers of Hitler's concentration camps.

By a supreme stroke of luck, Haddad and Bouvier both managed to slip away, after the Israelis' lightning rescue mission. But all the hijackers died, save one. Among the dead was team leader Wilfred Böse, head of Germany's Revolutionary Cells. Carlos would have missed him in Paris, where Böse had called in regularly for assignments after giving the Palestinians a hand with the Olympic Games massacre. Carlos would not be going back to Paris, however.

He was sighted all over the place, after OPEC: in the beachside villa Colonel Qaddafi gave him in Libya, in Aden,

Beirut and Baghdad, London, Bonn. He was supposed to be in Montevideo, waiting to assassinate Chilean dictator Pinochet on an official visit to Uruguay, and in Montreal, for the Olympic Games there. The Ayatollah Khomeini announced solemnly that he had sent Carlos to Mexico to assassinate the former shah of Iran and the rest of the royal family. The press said he was leading Colombia's M-19 guerrillas when they took fourteen ambassadors hostage at a diplomatic reception in Bogotá. The CIA and its West German counterpart, the BND, said he was in Belgrade for an international terrorist summit, and that at least was true.

West German and Yugoslav agents were both present when Carlos landed in Belgrade on a commercial flight from Algiers, on September 6, 1976, with five accomplices, including two Germans. The CIA had forewarned Yugoslav authorities of his arrival. Far from consigning Carlos to the West, though, the Yugoslavs whisked him off to a secluded VIP lounge and into town. Four days later, he took off for Iraq unmolested.[16]

Wherever he went, he never came back.

Some say he quit while he was ahead. That is how Hans-Joachim Klein told it in 1978, upon announcing his own retirement to the German weekly *Der Spiegel*. Having traveled "down shit road" as far as OPEC, Klein said, Carlos retired discreetly lest somebody should see to his forcible removal. In effect, he had sold out. As chief of the OPEC hit-team, Carlos was supposed to have "suppressed" Saudi Arabia's Sheikh Yamani and Iranian oil minister Amusegar, Klein declared. "He was instructed to take care of it after we got out of Vienna; otherwise we might not have been let out at all. . . . But when we reached a certain Arab country [Algeria], Carlos made a deal. They must have given him a mountain of money [$5 million is the going estimate]. Then he told us he was calling the whole thing off: the operation was going to end without killing Yamani and Amusegar."

Knowing the code very well—"a traitor is condemned to die" was his own explanation for shooting his aide Moukarbal between the eyes—he had taken elaborate precautions to cover his retreat. He wrote a formal letter of resignation in triplicate, Klein said, sending copies to Europe and Aden, using Wilfred Böse as his courier. In short, "Carlos told Haddad not to get any funny ideas, and Haddad said, 'OK, go your way.' "

Where did he go? Russia, Klein thought.

"He used to talk about his stay in Russia all the time. I even got to know the subtle difference between Beluga and Malassol caviar. . . . He always hoped to go back to Moscow. He would say that they expelled him from the university, but not from the country," Klein recalled.

"Whatever would Carlos do in Moscow?" asked *Der Spiegel*.

"He would live there, seeing that he's being hunted everywhere else," Klein replied.

Actually, Carlos was not being hunted all that hard. Midway through the fright decade, to which he had made such a signal contribution, no Western government was eager to put anybody connected with the Palestine Resistance behind bars. Some had gone to extraordinary lengths to avoid it, as we shall see. If Carlos dropped out of sight forever, in 1976, it was probably because he had become an embarrassment and a liability to his own side.

Wadi Haddad and George Habash had other reasons beyond his possible OPEC sellout to be furious with Carlos. Michel Moukarbal was a highly valued operative, whose death was not so easily justified. The Paris network had fallen apart after that whole trigger-happy performance by Carlos in Rue Toullier. Laborious efforts were needed to regroup Haddad's personnel in Europe and restore the circuit to working order. Indeed, it never recovered. Haddad himself could pull off only one more big multinational coup—the Lufthansa hijack to Mogadiscio, in October 1977—before dying of cancer in an East German clinic a few months later.

A still likelier version is that Carlos was simply recalled to Russia as a blown agent with a swelled head. Sheikh Yamani, who talked with him for hours while in captivity, felt that Carlos had "started out doing everything on Moscow's orders, but then began to exceed them." Yamani did not believe he was a "convinced communist" or even that he cared particularly about the Palestine Resistance. "Carlos doesn't really believe in the Palestinian cause, except as a way of spreading international revolution," [17] Yamani said. Doubtless, he meant the Maoist Permanent Revolution, favored by the New Left to the Kremlin's chagrin.

But there was nothing so newfangled about Carlos. In The Interview, at the end of the seventies, he was still talking pretty much like the orthodox Communist of the sixties. "We are not going to take part in the dispute between the two Communist superpowers," he said flatly. "The only war that counts is the one between socialism and capitalism."

The Palestinians had their uses in that war, he explained, because the homeland they hankered after happened to float on a boundless bed of oil. Thanks to the Palestine Resistance, therefore, "we have the possibility of blowing up all the oil-fields in the Arabian Gulf, from Kuwait to Oman, in Saudi Arabia and Khuzestan, maybe even in Venezuela. Petroleum is the weapon that can inflict the mortal wound on American imperialism. . . ."

Boris Ponomariev, directing the Kremlin's international Communist affairs, could hardly ask for more.

9

THE LONGEST WAR: THE PROVISIONAL IRA

No sooner did Billy Kelly take a few drinks than he would forget himself. Once he poked a U.S. Senator in the ribs and muttered, "Any hardware?" At another meeting, he complained that the Catholic Church had made a lot of trouble for Ireland. "Excuse me, did I hear you say something against the Catholic Church?" asked an agitated Irish-American lady. "Fuck off," he snarled, and was hurriedly summoned home.

Billy Kelly had been among the first to pot a Protestant in Belfast and doubtless suffered from battle fatigue. Indeed, he began his American fund-raising tour in 1971 by missing his plane to New York after a hard night's drinking. Though "in many ways a representative freedom-fighter of the Irish Republican Army," wrote Maria McGuire in her book about life among the Provos,[1] he certainly blew it in the States.

Like everybody sent over to extract arms and money from Irish-Americans, she explained, Kelly "had been carefully briefed as to how the audience should be played." He was instructed "to make copious references to the martyrs of 1915 and 1920–1922—the period most of the audience would be living in." (Ireland won its independence from Britain in 1922, except for the six predominantly Protestant northern counties.) "Anti-

British sentiment, recalling . . . the potato famine and the Black and Tans, could be profitably exploited. By no means should anything be said against the Catholic Church. And all reference to socialism should be strictly avoided. Tell them by all means that the Ireland we were fighting for would be free and united. But say nothing about just what form the new free and united Ireland would take."

Thus were fifteen million Irish-Americans conned into bankrolling the Provisional IRA's war. They thought it was an open and aboveboard war to free the Irish north from Britain and merge it with the free Irish south. In fact, it was and is a war against north and south both—the "colonial north" and the "quisling south"—fought to "destabilize capitalism in the whole of Ireland," and in Great Britain as well, and in all Western Europe besides. The Provos have said as much, in so many words, to their friends. ("We must educate the workers to destabilize capitalism in the whole of Ireland through armed struggle, creating an irremediable conflict between the needs of local capitalism and international imperialism, and those of the popular masses," they confided to *ControInformazione*, the house organ of Italy's Red Brigades.) [2]

The bombing and murder have dragged on for more than ten years: 2,500 dead, 12,000 hurt or crippled, 800 kneecapped for backsliding or informing, a quarter of a million pounds of explosives strewing wreckage and death around the Six Counties and the British Isles—"Britain's Vietnam," Senator Edward Kennedy has unblushingly called it—the longest, dirtiest, and most dishonest terrorist war of the fright decade.

It could have been worse still, for it was the IRA's hope to extend the war to the United Kingdom itself. Its repeated efforts to do so were contained by one of the most skilled police performances in Western Europe, along with the exemplary cooperation of the British public, who refused to be intimidated.

There used to be a time when nine-tenths of the Provo's weapons and most of their funds came from the United States, but not anymore. Fund-raising is done at home nowadays, through protection rackets, brothels and massage parlors, drug-running (four IRA men were caught in 1979 with $2.3 million worth of marijuana hidden in a truckload of bananas),[3] and bank stickups (preferably in Dublin, where police are unarmed). And the incoming hardware is largely Soviet-made.

The first Russian helicopters and RPG-7 rocket launchers were in the Provisionals' hands as early as 1972.[4] Bazookas, mortars, hand grenades, carbines followed soon after. Kalashnikov assault rifles are gradually replacing the once indispensable American Armalite, which has killed more British soldiers than any other weapon in Ulster. Whatever else the Provos need along that line may be had for the asking now from the Libyans, or Palestinians, or Russians (who supply the others anyway). All three were starting to arm and train the Provos even as Billy Kelly took off for New York.

The Russians in particular might have seemed then to be backing the wrong horse. In those early days, the Provisionals were widely regarded as roughnecked political boors, without a radical thought in their heads. To all appearances, they had simply risen in wrath to defend an unarmed and exasperated Catholic minority against a bullying and overbearing Protestant majority. If anybody was radiating Marxist-Leninist doctrine at the time—pretty strong pro-Moscow stuff, at that—it was the Official IRA of ancient glory. The Provisionals had actually split away in 1969 because they considered the Officials "a bunch of Communists," as well as cowards who wouldn't fight. ("IRA = I Ran Away," jeered Belfast's embattled Catholics in graffiti on the city's walls.)

The Officials, having long since opted for a "political solution," had given up the armed struggle in 1962. So far gone were they by 1968 that they even sold off their arsenal, to a "Free Welsh Army"—the vanguard of the Welsh Nationalist movement—whose dozen-odd hopefuls were promptly arrested in Wales.

When the shooting war started in 1969, the Protestants had all the guns. The Catholic Provisionals hadn't a decent firearm among them. At most, there were a few moldering weapons left over from the IRA's storied battle for Irish freedom half a century before. (Maria McGuire recalled "a wizened old man who came into Kevin Street and produced various parts of a rusty

Thompson machine-gun out of a brown paper parcel. " 'Tis a present from the boys in Cork,' he announced.")

Even when weapons began to come in from across the Atlantic, they arrived three or four at a time, packed into the false bottom of a suitcase. The Spanish Basques from ETA were a blessing in 1971, when they showed up with fifty revolvers to swap for lessons in handling explosives.[5] To get off the ground, the Provisionals' Army Council desperately needed a whopping shipment of good, modern arms. Once again, as so often happened while the worldwide terrorist battalions were forming up, Somebody Out There got the message. In the autumn of 1971, the Provisionals were given to understand that four and a half tons of good, modern arms made in Czechoslovakia were (or could be) theirs.

Maria McGuire, who went on that purchasing mission with the Provisionals' David O'Connell, said nobody at headquarters knew how it came about. A man they'd never heard of, using an all-purpose name, just dropped in one day to say the arms were available. Led by their mysterious "Mr. Freeman," they crossed over to the Continent, wandering from Paris to Berne to Amsterdam while the connection was made. O'Connell "was sure he was being followed by the Czech and Soviet secret police," McGuire wrote. Then he made contact with Omnipol, an arms factory in Prague run by the Czech security service and tightly controlled by the KGB since the 1968 Soviet invasion. "He came back with a glossy Omnipol catalogue, profusely illustrated, and the arms were very, very good," she went on. O'Connell thereupon ordered four and a half tons of bazookas, rocket launchers, hand grenades, guns and ammunition, filling 166 crates.

Air-freighted to Amsterdam to be smuggled on from there, the shipment was intercepted by police at Schiphol airport. With Interpol in hot pursuit, the Provisionals' hunted pair raced for cover in Dublin. "It should have been no problem getting back," they were told by the Provisionals' Belfast commander, Joe Cahill, once safely home. "You had only to fly from Prague to Havana, and then on to Shannon," he said, describing a standing arrangement for colleagues everywhere in their position.[6]

The Provos were shattered by the loss of their first big

arms consignment, but there would always be more where that came from.

By 1971, the IRA was getting to be a focus for worldwide armed revolution second only to the Palestinians. Northern Ireland offered stimulating prospects in that regard. To foment civil war in the Six Counties was to put colossal strains on the United Kingdom, interlocked with the entire Western structure of trade, industry, banking, and military alliances. Outwardly a religious and nationalist confrontation, it would in reality be an assault on vital organs of the Multinational Imperialist State. And it looked like a pushover.

The Six Counties were a living reminder of past imperial errors and sins. A million Protestants and half a million Catholics were forever at each others' throats. Catholic rage and rebellion went back three centuries to Oliver Cromwell, Lord Protector of Presbyterian England, Scotland, and Ireland, and two centuries before him to the archcolonizer, King James I of Scotland. Protestant arrogance had not diminished noticeably since Scots and Britons had settled there by the thousands under James's protection. Overlords of Northern Ireland since partition in 1922, the Protestants held the power in the Stormont (Ulster parliament), showing little disposition to share it. The Catholics, mostly workers and wretchedly poor, mocked for their papish beliefs, frozen out of jobs, housing, and public life, were pushed around like plebes.

The headlong collision in 1969 hardly came as a surprise, but the strength of Catholic fury did. Protestant extremists, the first to start cracking heads, were startled by the Catholics' enraged response. The radical Catholic students who had started it all with their civil rights march—Bernadette Devlin and her People's Democracy group at the University of Belfast—snapped to attention. So did the IRA, ravaged as it was by age and neglect. So did others abroad who take a natural interest in these things.

With riot following upon murderous riot, both wings of the IRA were soon in fighting formation. They were welcomed into the international terrorist set with open arms.

The first IRA contingents were off for Jordanian guerrilla camps that very year.[7] Invited by both the PLO and PFLP, they were soon drawn into the intimate circle around George Habash, on the lookout for just their sort of people. Two years later, in October 1971, they were guests of honor in Florence at the historic conference that launched Europe's Red International.

Assembled by Feltrinelli and *Potere Operaio*, meeting under the unsuspecting Jesuits' roof at the Stensen Institute, delegates from fourteen countries decided to coordinate international terrorist plans—an "unprecedented and dangerous development" noted by British and Irish government authorities at the time, ignored by the world's press for the next eight years.[8] An international division of labor was agreed upon, with Northern Ireland serving as a "terrorist laboratory."

The oldest guerrilla army in existence—it went back to before World War I—had a lot to teach newcomers. A full day of the conference was given over to the Official IRA's Seamus Costello, who analyzed the Irish experience and illustrated the tactics of sabotage and guerrilla warfare. For a European tenderfoot, at the start of the seventies, it was an eye-opener.

Arrangements were made for the IRA to take in foreign trainees, in exchange for an assured supply of guns. Plans were made to smuggle the weapons across the Continent in heavy trailer-trucks. The IRA Officials' Malachy McGurran was assigned to a working committee to oversee the gunrunning operation.

Whether by chance or not really, Czechoslovakia's first shipment of weapons to Northern Ireland was on the way to Schiphol airport just two weeks later.

Curiously, the weapons were meant for the *Provisional* IRA, an apparent eccentricity on the Russians' part. Why not the Officials? More than mere Marxists, the Officials were paleolithic Stalinists: they had endorsed the Soviet invasion of Czechoslovakia and openly demanded a "National Liberation Front for an Irish Socialist Republic allied with the Soviet Union." Furthermore, they had been coming closer to Moscow every day since the outbreak of hostilities in Ulster.

Until then, the Kremlin couldn't really be bothered. The

IRA had been a joke in Moscow since the early twenties, when its emissaries came to beg for help during the Irish Troubles and were turned down as braggarts and buffoons. But the Russians faced about briskly after assessing the riotous Belfast scene. Before long, the Soviet Central Committee was sending representatives from Boris Ponomariev's department to confer with the Official IRA. Victor Louis, most celebrated and freewheeling of KGB agents, visited the Officials more or less openly several times. The KGB set up channels of regular contact, through the British and Irish Communist Parties. Three KGB agents settled into Dublin to keep in touch: Tass correspondent Yuri Ustimenko, *Pravda*'s Yuri Yasnev, and the Soviet Intourist's N. V. Glavatsky. (A fourth, Dublin's Tass correspondent Vladimir Kozov, was identified in 1975 as a KGB agent from Department V, responsible for assassinations and sabotage.) By using the British Communist Party in London for liaison, the KGB also brought in the Cuban DGI. Drawn up under KGB supervision, the DGI's operational plans for 1972 stipulated that "Cuba would train the IRA in terror and guerrilla-warfare tactics," as defectors revealed later.[9]

It seems unlikely that many Officials made it to Havana after all. Committed to an orthodox Marxist "political solution," they had never cared much for infantile leftist hotheads. "Small groups handling gelignite without discernment" were a menace, they said. In the spring of 1972, with Northern Ireland skidding toward civil war, they declared a unilateral cease-fire and dropped out of the terrorist game.

That suited the Russians. The very intimacy of their relations made it awkward to give the Officials direct military aid: open connivance with terrorism is not a customary feature of Soviet diplomacy. They went right on helping the Official IRA politically, their virtue saved. (A spokesman for the Officials admitted in 1974 that "all relevant propaganda" printed for their "Anti-Imperialist Festival" in Dublin and Belfast had been done "through the good offices of Soviet representatives in Ireland.")[10] For a military buildup, meanwhile, the truculent and loudly anti-Communist Provisional IRA offered Moscow an ideal alternative.

Few outsiders realized then that the Provos were being swiftly "politicized" too. It was uphill work with their Billy Kellys, who would never be heavy Marxist thinkers. And it had to be done on the quiet, to spare Irish-American feelings. Irish freedom fighters touring the United States for guns and cash did not go around calling the free Republic of Ireland "a fascist state designed for privileged capitalist sycophants," as they did at home. Nor, on profitable junkets to the Bronx or Brooklyn, did they mention their "total commitment to revolution across the board and from top to bottom." [11] In reality, though, the Provisional IRA would be well to the left of the Official wing before the decade was out.

It had, after all, grown out of a militant confrontation pressed by rather heavily politicized people. Bernadette Devlin, the Irish Torch who roused the world to the Catholics' plight in Ulster, had joined the Trotskyite IV International in 1969. So had her partner in founding People's Democracy at Belfast University, Michael Farell. Neither could be accused of narrow nationalist views or revisionism.

For Bernadette Devlin, the struggle in Northern Ireland was "an integral part of the international working-class movement"; therefore it was necessary "to take part in international combat, not only in the framework of the struggle for our country's liberty, but in establishing relations with international organizations." For Michael Farell, "Victory in the north means not just defeat of the [Protestant] Loyalists and the unity of Ireland, but also the collapse of the government in the south and an anti-imperialist revolution in that country. And a revolution in Ireland could have incalculable consequences in disturbing the United Kingdom and, considering the crisis of Western capitalism, in all Europe." In this sense, he added, Northern Ireland had "the most important of revolutionary movements and student revolts in the world." [12]

A lot of people setting up the world's Armed Parties agreed with him. (Italy's Red Brigades would later call the IRA an "unrenounceable point of reference for generalized guerrilla warfare on the European Continent.") A number of prominent IRA men did too. Seamus Costello, the Officials' assistant chief of staff, would lead his own group out in 1974 to form the Irish

Republican Socialist Party and its military arm, INLA, the Irish National Liberation Army—a terrorist band of unrivaled ferocity, even by the Provisionals' own standards, fighting alongside them with inflexibly revolutionary war aims. It would not be long before the Provisionals themselves were committed to "demolish the Quisling Regime in the Free State of Ireland and the colonial regime in the Northern war zone": that is, the south and north both.[13]

In this they were heartily encouraged, as they started out on the road to civil war, by the political sophisticates they kept meeting abroad. By the end of 1972, they had met just about everybody. In the course of that remarkably busy year, charismatic leaders of the Trotskyite IV International practically commuted from Paris, Brussels, and London. Palestinians, Tupamaros, ulta-left Germans, Italians from Potere Operaio and Lotta Continua, Swiss anarchists, French Gauchistes and separatist Bretons, Spanish Basque nationalists and Marxist urban guerrillas, beat a path to their door. And they themselves went visiting.

From Provisional headquarters in Belfast that year, Sean O'Bradaigh set out to tour the Continent in search of more substantial support. Ultra-left fan clubs sprouted in his wake, straight across Europe. He was an especially big hit with West Germany's Baader-Meinhof Gang and June 2 Movement. (Gabriele Kröcher-Tiedemann started out on her terrorist career as a recruit of his, at the University of Bochum.) The Germans became the IRA's next-best friends after the Spanish Basques, and Irish-German underground traffic picked up smartly. In fact, two-way trade in arms, hideouts, and targets improved all around between Northern Ireland and the Continent. The top brass in Belfast was pleased. "The Irish Republican Movement has shown that it is not just insular and inward-looking. It is spreading its wings worldwide," reported the Provisionals' journal *An Phoblacht*, welcoming O'Bradaigh home.

Meanwhile, the Palestinians were advancing their claim of friendship. In May 1972, George Habash and Wadi Haddad brought the Provisionals into their inner circle at the Baddawi terrorist summit in Lebanon. Two months later, in Paris, Habash's Palestinian Front signed a formal "Declaration of Support" for the Provisional IRA, signed in turn by armed bands of twelve other nationalities.[14] Fifty Provos were thereupon selected for advanced guerrilla courses in Lebanon, after which the Provisional IRA never looked back.

Before long, there would be a steady flow of IRA men to South Yemen, getting crack training in Wadi Haddad's camps under Cuban and East German instructors, as Ludwina Janssen and others have since reported. The whole familiar German crowd had checked in by 1975—lawyer Siegfried Haag, Gabriele Kröcher-Tiedemann, her four fellow terrorists released in exchange for the kidnapped Peter Lorenz in Berlin, her OPEC teammate Hans-Joachim Klein, not to speak of Carlos himself. Irish-German friendship was renewed on the shooting range, in field practice, in Haddad's private movie house at camp, where a privileged few could watch Western films after a hard day's drill. Twelve fraternal bombings of the British army on the Rhine would follow soon.

The Palestinian connection began to pay off at once. Starting in 1972, the Habash-Haddad front held a series of secret meetings in Dublin, putting together the multinational terrorist team soon to take off under Carlos. When a million dollars' worth of weapons were divided up among them, the Provisionals got the lion's share.[15] In another year or so, Carlos himself would be taking the trouble to procure explosives from the Swiss anarchists' takeout service for the Provos. While they had already learned to manufacture their own (from farm fertilizer), it was always welcome.

Colonel Qaddafi of Libya spotted them that same year. Though still on the Black International's side in 1972, he was enough of a go-getter to overcome his anti-Red prejudice when the occasion warranted. "We support the revolutionaries of Ireland who oppose Britain and are motivated by nationalism and religion," announced his Libyan radio that summer. "The Libyan Arab Republic has stood by the revolutionaries of Ireland. . . . There are arms and there is support for the revolutionaries of Ireland. . . ." So there were.

Even as Qaddafi spoke, the Provisionals were sending a man out to establish a bridgehead in Tripoli. A Donegal schoolteacher, Eddie O'Donnell stayed on as Qaddafi's personal adviser throughout the decade.[16] A year later, the Provisionals' former Belfast commander, Joe Cahill, appeared in the Libyan capital to negotiate a sumptuous shipment of 250 Kalashnikov rifles and other weapons, supplied to Qaddafi by the Russians. The S.S. *Claudia*, carrying five tons of the very best in Soviet-bloc hardware—and Joe Cahill—was steaming toward the coast of Ireland when it was seized by the Irish navy, on March 29, 1973.[17] A British agent had sneaked an electronic tracking device aboard, to Qaddafi's chagrin.

The ship's West German owner, Gunther Leinhauser, admitted to the press afterward that he had gone to Tripoli personally "to fix the deal with Joe Cahill." He got the impression then that Qaddafi would really have liked to provide weapons for both sides killing each other off in Northern Ireland. "For a while," he said, "Qaddafi toyed with the idea of giving weapons to Ulster's Protestant Militia too. He thinks anything that keeps the fires of revolution going is worth doing."

In fact, Qaddafi did invite the paramilitary Ulster Defense Association (UDA)—the Protestants' version of the IRA—to Libya shortly afterward. He thought that they also "might qualify for support as anti-imperialists opposing the British," reported the *Belfast Telegraph*. But nothing came of it.

He had chipped in $2.3 million for the Provisionals' cause by then and clearly thought it was worth every cent. When an IRA bomb wrecked London's Olympia Exhibition Hall in 1976, the Libyan paper *al-Fajr al-Jadid* rejoiced: "These bombs which are convulsing Britain and breaking its spirit are the bombs of the Libyan people. We have sent them to Irish revolutionaries so that the British will pay the price for their past deeds."

From Belfast, grateful Irish revolutionaries paid homage to the Libyan philsopher-king. Qaddafi's Green Book of thoughts on the Islamic Revolution "would have a familiar ring to Irish Republicans," said *An Phoblacht*. "Like all great political thoughts, Qaddafi's message relates to a much wider canvas than the desert societies of North Africa and Arabia," it added without flinching.[18]

Once, further on in the decade, the colonel thought he detected signs of human frailty among his Irish disciples. They were no longer revolutionary enough to deserve his military aid, he said, and he was going to cut it off. But nothing came of that either. Irish Provisionals went right on training in Libyan guerrilla camps, as they had been doing since 1976 and were still seen to be doing in 1980—at Tokra, northeast of Benghazi, where Cuban instructors offered the world's most advanced courses in sabotage; at Sebha, deep in the desert south of Tripoli; at Camp Az Zauiah "for Europeans," boning up on sabotage, weaponry, explosives, and psychological warfare with fellow warriors from Italy, West Germany, Spanish Basqueland, Turkey, Greece, French Corsica and Brittany. (See chapter fourteen.)

The subsidies went right on flowing, too. By the late seventies, Qaddaffi was giving the Provos $5 million a year; or so we are told by Peter McMullen, hiding out in America since they sentenced him to death for welching on an assignment.[19]

The flow of arms from one or another Arab source never stopped for long, either. The S.S. *Claudia* was a setback, of course, and there would be others. In November 1977, the S.S. *Towerstream* was seized off Antwerp with half a million dollars' worth of Palestinian weapons. Loaded in Lebanon and sailing by way of Cyprus, the *Towerstream* carried 29 Kalashnikovs, 29 submachine guns, 29 machine pistols, 7 rocket launchers, 56 rockets, 108 grenades, 428 pounds of TNT, and 400 pounds of plastic explosives. All were from the Soviet bloc. The Provos' Sean McCollum got ten years for that.

Still, no amount of policing could keep weapons out of Northern Ireland. By the mid-seventies, the entire international terrorist network was covering for the Provos. "Terrorist groups in all the world are now organizing deliveries of arms and explosives to the IRA," was the story leaked to the press by British intelligence.[20] More than seven thousand weapons and nearly a million rounds of ammunition were confiscated in the Six Counties alone between 1970 and 1978. That did not count shipments from the Irish Republic, south of an unsealable three-hundred-mile border. Nor did it take into account the weapons and ammunition smuggled into London for the IRA's use in terrorizing the British at home.

It is impossible to say how much of this got to Northern

Ireland through the good offices of Soviet representatives or terrorist formations using them as *fournisseurs*. The Irish-American contribution undoubtedly accounted for much of it, especially early on. But the size of shipments that were stopped suggests how much must have gotten through from elsewhere.

One of the routes originated directly in Prague. The Czech secret police would ship SRS automatics and RPG antitank rocket launchers to East Germany, for relay to West Germany. From there, willing hands in the underground shifted them to Versailles, on the outskirts of Paris, for storage. When there was enough for a shipload, the weapons were trucked into Brittany, loaded on French fishing boats in the Breton port of Quimper, or Benodet, and smuggled across the English and Irish channels.

A more elaborate route, published in detail by the London *Daily Mirror*, was supervised in Canada by Jean Materot of the Marxist Quebec Liberation Front. Weapons from Czechoslovakia and East Germany were delivered to Syria and Libya, transshipped across the Atlantic to Montreal, and shipped back again to the French port of Le Havre. Then on to Quimper, and by French fishing boat to Cork, and by Irish fishing boat to some remote beach for unloading. Breton separatists could see to this at each end. Forced to flee France because of their wartime collaboration with the Nazis, many had taken up permanent residence in Ireland.[21]

It isn't as if all this monumental investment of time, money, and effort has brought freedom closer for the Catholics of Northern Ireland or anybody else. Those who might have thought so dropped out of the IRA long ago.

There is nothing inventive about the pattern of violence in Ulster. The more professional it has grown, the more predictable it has been. The Italians' phrase for it is "*Tanto peggio, tanto meglio*," meaning, the worse, the better. The principle is at least as old as a Russian secret society called Zemlya i Volya (Land of Freedom), which assassinated Tsar Alexander II on March 13, 1881—the very day he signed a decree establishing the first thing resembling a constitution in Imperial Russia. His assassins believed reform was the death of revolution. The more the masses suffered, the more likely they would be to rise up against their tormentors, the reasoning went. Optimum suffering—political, economic, social, religious, ethnic—was the ideal condition to be achieved, or sustained, as the case might be.

The entire fright decade bore this imprint. Carlos Marighella built his strategy of terror around it in the *Mini-Manual for Urban Guerrillas*. The Tupamaros of Uruguay followed his counsel to the letter, in their purposeful course toward "intensified repression," "unbearable persecution," and "transformation of a political situation into a military one." Their associates abroad seemed to envy their success. "It is necessary to provoke the latent fascism in society. We must force the exposure of the fascist in the police for all to see; and then the people will turn to us for leadership," said Ulrike Meinhof at the height of her reign as queen of West Germany's radical chic.[22] "The pigs will stumble around in the dark, until they are forced to transform the political situation into a military one," said her partner Andreas Baader, showing how well he knew his Marighella.

Norbert Kröcher, mustering the biggest international terrorist crew of the decade for Operation Leo in Stockholm, noted the need to "transform the political situation into a military one" (in his Black File). Spanish Basques in ETA, threatened with democracy after Franco died, still followed the same line they had established since claiming a "major achievement" for having chivied Franco into "committing a thousand wrongs and atrocities."[23] The Turkish People's Liberation Army spoke of sparking enough revolutionary violence so that "reactionary elements in the Turkish armed forces . . . would have to intervene," as the armed forces had already done twice in twenty years.[24]

Giangiacomo Feltrinelli said it in 1968: "The guerrilla's task is to outrage [the state] in every way . . . and so reveal its harsh, repressive, reactionary essence."[25] His fellow guerrilla Renato Curcio, founder of Italy's Red Brigades, plainly knew his Marighella too. "Faced with working-class terror, the bourgeoisie by now has an obligatory course: to reestablish control by intensified repression and progressive militarization of the state," he wrote in an early self-interview.[26]

The IRA has said it more eloquently, by acting it out year

after year since August 15, 1969. That was the day British troops moved in to break the siege of Londonderry's Bogside, transforming a political situation into a military one.

Though it was Protestant mob violence that brought British troops into Northern Ireland, it was largely the Provisional IRA that kept them there for the next decade or more. Pinned down by terrifying civil disorder, galled into predictable acts of repression, balked methodically whenever a settlement seemed near, a peace-keeping force that longed to go home was made to look like a permanent army of occupation, defending the last outpost of a ruined colonial empire.

Perhaps it could all have been avoided if British troops had defended an unarmed Catholic minority from the start, as they were supposed to do. Bogside Catholics had cheered their arrival on that assumption. More than a year would pass before the first British soldier was shot by a Catholic sniper in Belfast; another went by before Catholic trust was thoroughly shaken. That happened on January 30, 1972—Bloody Sunday—when, after siding repeatedly with homicidal Protestant vigilantes, British paratroopers shot thirteen Catholics dead in a Londonderry civil rights demonstration.

Yet it was in just those months that Ulster's Provisional IRA became suspect. Four hundred and fifty-three people had died of Catholic-Protestant violence by then. Both the Provisional IRA and Protestant UDA were arming fast. Provo bombings had quadrupled during the previous year. Very nearly everybody concerned grew desperately anxious to stop the ineluctable slide toward civil war. The British government suspended the Protestant-dominated Stormont and introduced direct rule from London, hoping to get peace talks going. Responsible Protestant leaders offered their first real concessions. The Official IRA declared its unilateral cease-fire "because of the growing danger of sectarian conflict." The Provisionals' own Army Council opened negotiations to suspend hostilities.

After prudently jacking up their bomb hits to four a day, "to strengthen their bargaining position," the Provisionals agreed to a truce on June 22, 1972. The 102nd British soldier to die in Ulster was shot dead two minutes before the truce went into effect.

Six people died the next day, in crossfire between Provisional and British troops, including a girl of thirteen and a Catholic priest giving extreme unction to a dying fifteen-year-old boy. Twelve more British soldiers were killed the next week. A hundred-pound IRA bomb wrecked Skipper Street in downtown Belfast, killing nine. Twenty IRA bombs went off within a single hour in Belfast just afterward, killing eleven and injuring a hundred and thirty; Bloody Friday, this one was called. That took care of that truce.

"And now the poverty of thought within the Belfast [Provisional] Command was revealed," wrote Maria McGuire, who walked out on them then. "All along they had believed that by terrorizing the civilian population you increased their desire for peace and blackmailed the British Government into negotiating. But now it seemed that Belfast could not deviate from its course. . . . All the Provisionals knew was to bomb. . . ."

The year of that first broken truce was the year the IRA Provisionals got locked fast into the international terrorist circuit. It was from the midsummer of 1972 onward that massive terrorist aid began to flow in from all over the world: from Habash's Marxist Palestinian Front and hard-lining Arab states of the Middle East, from Libya, from Eastern Europe and Russia. A worldwide Soviet-sponsored campaign "against British repression in Ireland" suddenly materialized, piloted by the hoariest of Soviet-front groups: the International Union of Students (with headquarters in Prague), the World Federation of Democratic Youth, the World Federation of Trade Unions, the World Peace Council (which declared an "International Day of Solidarity" for the IRA that summer). The Provisionals started to use Soviet rockets against British tanks in November.

What followed over the rest of the decade brought Ireland closer than any country in the West to the kind of conflict that Marxist revolutionaries call a civil war of long duration. There was no such thing as a political solution, if the Provos could help it: no way to end it on their terms, no way to alter their terms, and not much hope of their ever calling it off so long as they had a bountiful international terrorist confraternity to fall back on.

A million Protestants of Northern Ireland could not be incorporated into the southern Irish Republic against their unanimous will. Half a million Catholics could not be left alone with the Protestants without iron guarantees for their physical safety, social welfare, and political equity in the Six Counties. Some sort of federated union between two autonomous Irish republics might be worked out, but only by mutual consent. Britain could not withdraw its troops unless and until all three conditions were met. The Provos would never allow that to happen, while they had the means to obstruct it.

The first test came in the first half of 1973, when the British government introduced power-sharing in a new Northern Ireland assembly elected by proportional representation. The Provisionals used 48,000 pounds of explosives to kill it off. "We see no future in power-sharing," as they observed some years later.[28]

In the last half of 1973, laborious negotiations got under way for some elementary form of confederation between north and south. The Provos accordingly tripled their bombing rate and stepped up ambushes, assassinations, cross-border raids, and rocket assaults on British army camps in Ulster. In London, they dropped fire bombs at Harrod's, Liberty's in Regent Street, and the Stock Exchange. Obliging as always, Ulster's Protestant terrorists quickened their own pace to keep up.

At the year's end, Britain and the Irish Republic agreed tentatively on a joint North-South Council of Ireland complete with a consultative assembly and secretariat: a first stab at federation, known as the Sunningdale Agreement. Neither the Protestant diehards nor the Provos cared for it. This time the Provos observed their own cease-fire for exactly three weeks; it was the last time. "There is absolutely no question of another cease-fire or truce," they declared.[29]

Guerrilla warfare raged for the next six years. Many things changed for the better meanwhile. The worst of Protestant terrorism in Ulster was brought under restraint by vigorous British police action. The worst of the Catholics' original grievances were remedied, by laws guaranteeing minority representation in Ulster's government, fair electoral practices, fair housing practices, fair employment practices. Billions of dollars of foreign capital were invested in the Six Counties through elaborate governmental efforts, creating several thousand new jobs for the multitudinous Catholic unemployed. Sickening war-weariness brought Catholics and Protestants together in a growing movement for peace.

Faced with the threat of a peaceful settlement, the IRA did what like-minded guerrillas always do in such cases. They took the advice of Carlos Marighella, as laid down in his handy *Mini-Manual.* "Rejecting the so-called 'political solution,' the urban guerrilla must become more aggressive and violent . . . heightening the disastrous situation in which the government must act."

The curve of IRA violence shot up. Terrifying fireballs of plastic explosives hurtled through packed Irish pubs, leaving charred bodies in their wake. A thousand-pound car bomb—enough to destroy several square city blocks—was found primed on a busy street. A fire bomb was smuggled into Belfast hidden under a baby in a pram, wheeled by two teen-age girls. Bodies of dead British soldiers were booby-trapped to explode at the touch. Railroad tracks were mined. The Royal Victoria Hospital in Belfast became a "legitimate target" because of British soldiers on the grounds, the Provos said. Thirty-five incendiary bombs went off in twenty-five commercial shops within forty-eight hours. An IRA bomb exploded in La Mon House Hotel with seven hundred people inside, including sixty children.

Intermittently, the Provos took their war abroad and into Britain itself, planting bombs in the London Underground at rush hour, on crowded Oxford Street, in the shopping centers of seven British cities during Christmas week, at a huge oil dump that they evidently hoped would set all London ablaze. Fire bombs, letter bombs, snipers' bullets, took out British soldiers in the German Rhineland and British diplomats in Holland, Belgium, Washington. The superterrorist INLA made a smashing appearance in London at the Provos' side, with an ultrasophisticated car bomb that killed prominent Tory leader Airey Neave in the basement garage of the House of Commons.

All that effort seemed on the verge of going to waste in the summer of 1979. The best proposition yet for a federated Ireland was looming. Known as the Fitzgerald Plan, it seemed to be favored by both the government and opposition parties in the Irish Republic, Ulster's moderate Protestants and Catholics, the British government, and the Irish-American Establishment headed by the Kennedy family clan. The Provisional IRA's response to that intolerable threat was to blow up Lord Mountbatten on his fishing boat in Donegal Bay, with fifty pounds of gelignite.

The seventy-nine-year-old hero of World War II had had nothing to do with politics since serving as Britain's last Viceroy to India a quarter of a century before. There, he had presided over the liberation of the second largest nation on earth from colonial rule. But the Provos were nothing if not candid about their reasons for doing him in. The Fitzgerald Plan was "unacceptable," they said flatly, a week after his death. Their spokesman was Ruairi O'Bradaigh, IRA man of thirty years' standing and president of their lawful political arm, the Provisional Sinn Fein. "We do not want a confederation of the South with the North. Nor do we want an independent Ulster. We want a general dismantling of the existing Establishments in the Irish Republic and Ulster both," he declared.[30]

What, then, did the Provisional IRA have in mind for its own version of a free and united Ireland? Enough to raise the hair on the heads of nine Irishmen out of ten, on either side of the Atlantic. "We want a Democratic Socialist Republic," replied O'Bradaigh: something "Third World-ish," a bit like "Allende's Chile" flavored with thoughts from Colonel Qaddafi's Green Book, "similar to communism but not exactly like it," "Marxist in analysis" if not necessarily in practice, designed to "nationalize industries, control the means of production and distribution, and take over agriculture under state-run cooperatives," emphatically "not German social democracy" and not quite a dictatorship of the proletariat either, but almost. The Stalinist model of democratic centralism was not desirable, he explained. "But we could not risk having parties around who want to bring colonialism back. There would have to be a reckoning with them." [31]

If that sounded ominously like one-party rule of an all too familiar sort, he did not appear to mind. "We would have to see," replied this veteran freedom fighter to the reporter who asked the question. "Who knows what will happen when power is in the hands of the people?"

It wouldn't have to be *all* the people. "A revolutionary movement does not depend on a popular mandate as a basis for action. Its mandate comes from the justice and correctness of its cause," said a Provo leader in Dublin, speaking for a revolutionary movement that has yet to poll more than five percent of the Irish vote, north or south.[32]

Meanwhile, as the Provos keep saying, the war must go on. "We are not prepared even to discuss any watering down of our demands," they declared in *An Phoblacht*. There could be no future either in a "restructured" parliament and bill of rights for the north or in the "fascist" free state to the south, "whose legitimacy we will certainly never accept." Lest a small doubt remain, they stated flatly: "Both the Quisling regime in the Free State and the colonial regime in the Northern war zone have failed to produce a lasting solution. The war will continue until these structures are demolished." [33]

They are still peddling it to the broader public as a war of national, ethnic, and religious liberation, a wonderfully profitable way of putting it. The war they are really fighting, though, is hardly distinguishable from the one waged by Armed Parties everywhere—by the Red Brigades in Italy, say. For all their outraged denials, especially before an Irish-American audience, they were refreshingly frank about this in the Red Brigades' own *ControInformazione* toward the decades's end.[34]

The "nationalist factor" had won "vast popular support . . . for our armed struggle to destabilize capitalism in Ireland," said the Provos' spokesman. But for all the distinct edge that gave them over ordinary terrorist formations, "it absolutely does not diminish the legitimacy" of urban guerrilla bands like the Red Brigades, the German Red Army Fraction [Baader-Meinhof] and the Spanish GRAPO. "We recognize their motivation, based on social injustice," he declared. "Our cooperation with international groups is certainly not based on narrow national considerations, but on the common struggle against colonial and imperialist domination," he went on. "The tactical advantages of cooperating with other groups in Europe have been made abundantly clear by certain operations against

British forces on the Continent in the past twelve months."

He was speaking of a dozen-odd bomb attacks on British troops in Germany: the start of the Provisional IRA's extended war beyond the boundaries of the United Kingdom, the hoped-for beginning of "generalized guerrilla warfare on the Continent," an expression of the "maximum possible operative collaboration with the IRA" that the Red Brigades set such store by, mounted with help from the German, Dutch, Belgian, French, Spanish, and Italian undergrounds.[35]

Their collaboration could hardly be questioned since several confessed to it. (A Dutch Red Helper admitted to having helped the IRA assassinate a British diplomat in Holland because "the IRA asked us to." A repentant leader of the Red Brigades revealed, in 1980, that Italian terrorists had recently divided up a huge consignment of Palestinian arms "with the IRA and ETA." [36] "We have concrete proof of ties between the IRA and other European terrorist organizations," said the Irish Republic's minister of interior at the close of the seventies. "The Terrorist Multinational exists," he added without any ifs, ands, or buts.[37]

The Provos couldn't possibly manage without that network anymore. The days are long gone when they could have any help for the asking from their Catholic countrymen or pass as noble freedom fighters in the Bogside. "In the small West Tyrone town of Castle Derg [bombed out by the IRA], twelve families have lost most or all of their belongings," said the Roman Catholic bishop of Londonderry late in 1978. "Fifty-eight people were left homeless, including a family of ten, and the refugees ranged from a ninety-six-year-old man to a six-month-old child. . . . Perpetrators of these bombings are guilty of cowardly and totally immoral actions against defenseless, harmless people. . . . The Catholic community, like the whole community here in the North, is sick and tired of the Provisional IRA." [38]

It is doubtful whether the Provisional IRA took much notice. The Provos may like, but do not really require, to be loved. They never did need more than a few hundred professional guerrillas to hold down a British army thirty or forty times their size—a standard equation in modern guerrilla warfare. Northern Ireland has a huge pool of unemployed and disaffected youths, brutalized by a decade of war. Catholics who hate what the Provos are doing can be savaged into helping them do it all the same. Most of their recruits in 1980 were adolescents of fifteen or sixteen, a good many of them girls, frightened into it by the appalling results that could come of refusing.

The Provisional IRA no longer relies merely on a Black and Decker drill to kneecap those it wants to keep in line—though a special orthopedic hospital has been set up in Belfast to deal with its crippled victims. It has gone on from the electric drill to a block of concrete, dropped from a considerable height onto an offender's outstretched arms.

This is not mindless violence. For a civil war in perpetuity, some of the best minds in the business recommend it.

10

TERROR IN BASQUELAND

In the Spanish Basque village of Beasáin, in the late hours of January 5,
1979, a young rural policeman named
Antonio Ramirez Gallardo and his
girl friend, Hortensia Gonzales, were
shot dead as they got into their car
after an evening in a discothèque.
Deaths like these were running to
three or four a week in Spain around
then, theirs differing from the rest
only in an odd detail. The man's life-
less body had slumped across the
steering wheel, pressing on the horn.
For twenty minutes, until an ambulance came, his
horn wailed through the quiet streets. Dozens of people stood
looking on, but not a soul went near him.

To say they were afraid is not to single them out for judgment. Of course they were afraid. The purpose of terrorism is to
terrorize, as Lenin said. The terrorists of Beasáin, trained in the
world's best guerrilla camps since 1964, knew all about that.

There was nothing personal in shooting this particular policeman, still less his girl. He happened to be wearing the right
uniform. Nobody loves a cop, and few cops are less beloved
than those in the late Generalissimo Franco's Guardia Civil. If
none had been around, though, the gunmen could have gone
for some politician or editor instead. What mattered was not so
much the identity of their corpse as its impact on their audience. Faceless assassins seemingly able to strike at will, suddenly, swiftly, repeatedly, anywhere, anytime, can usually be

172

counted on to stir an anguished dread. "Kill One, Frighten Ten Thousand" is an elementary premise of guerrilla warfare. "Punish One, Frighten One Hundred" was Lenin's way of putting it.

The Beasáin story would be too commonplace to tell here if not for the date. General Franco was dead and gone in January 1979, and Spain was free. Yet more people were dying at terrorist's hands in the country's fourth year of freedom than in forty years of suffocating dictatorship—in freedom's name, and in Basqueland.

Nobody could beat the Basques for their freedom fighters' credentials. They were the magnificent *gudaris*, pride and strength of the Loyalist Army in the Spanish Civil War of 1936-39, with its million dead and haunting claims on the world's conscience. From then until the end of Franco's reign, they were everybody's heroes. They were surely mine, since the first time—the first of many times—that I slipped across the French border to meet secretly with the Basque Resistance in San Sebastián. The idea that Basque patriots might someday obstruct and betray the democratic order they were fighting for was unthinkable then. It is a wrench to think so now, but there it is.

The story I heard from old Basque friends, in the weeks I spent among them at the end of the seventies, bore a striking resemblance to Northern Ireland's. Here, too, was a long-persecuted ethnic minority, valiantly defended at first only to be used and defrauded later, for an occult cause that could bring nothing but misery. "The terrorists are trading on our sentiments today, reminding us of how stupendous they used to be when Franco was on our backs," said a Basque journalist I've known for years. "They *say* they're killing for the sake of Basque nationhood, but their whole purpose has changed. They're really doing it to destablilize the Spanish state—to hit the police, the army, judges, institutions, for the same reasons the Baader-Meinhof Gang does, or the Italian Red Brigades." Or the Provisional IRA, he might have added.

They were indeed stupendous under Franco. The civil war's worst horrors were reserved for the Basques in the dreadful bombing of Guernica, historic meeting place of what they have considered their own ethnic nation since the Middle Ages. But nothing Franco did could break their resistance, throughout the war and after it.

The celebrated trial of Burgos in 1970 was a monument to the Basques' defiance. Sixteen young members of their nationalist underground ETA (Euzkadi Ta Askatasuna, Freedom for the Basque Homeland) were accused of attempting to subvert the Franco regime by armed violence. Nine were condemned to death, the remaining seven to a sum of 519 years in jail. Few cases in our time have aroused such an international outcry.

They were accused of multiple crimes against the Fascist state, from illicit meetings and demonstrations to bank robberies, bombings, and sabotage, but of only three murders. In all those years of grim resistance, the Basque nationalists had taken just five other lives. They did not take the next until December 20, 1973, when the long nightmare was nearly over, and that added immeasurably to their fame.

The assassination of Admiral Luis Carrero Blanco, Franco's premier and chosen political heir, was a stunning piece of workmanship. Terrorists everywhere have been trying to copy it ever since. A split-second error in timing saved NATO's retiring supreme allied commander, General Alexander Haig, from an identical ambush on a Belgium highway in 1979. Pure luck, soon afterward, saved two hundred sleeping men in a Barcelona Guardia Civil barracks from getting blown to bits the same way.

ETA itself had trouble proving it could have done the job all alone. Four Etarras who claimed the credit held a press conference in the south of France, wearing black hoods with slits for eyes, to convince incredulous reporters that they were capable of such expert extermination work without help, say, from their old buddies in the IRA, if not the KGB. The real commando team wrote a full-length book about it, entitled *Operation Ogro* (for ogre).

They described a year of patient preparation: lengthy exploratory visits to Madrid, suitable safe-houses, months of watching the victim's every move. They told about hauling two hundred pounds of dynamite to the capital in the trunk of a stolen car (failing to mention the dynamite's provenance, from the IRA, which had it from Carlos, who got it from the Swiss anarchists' takeout service.) [1] They spoke of laborious weeks in a basement flat, tunneling under a busy downtown street and storing the rubble neatly in plastic garbage bags; block-long outdoor electrical wiring, done in full view of passing Madrileños, to detonate the explosive from a distance; a double-parked dummy car packed with more explosives at the target point, just over a city gas main; a sentry positioned to signal at exactly the right moment. They got it so right that the admiral's heavy Dodge Dart flew up over the roof of a five-story building to land on a second-floor balcony of the inner courtyard.

The ETA commandos had toyed with the idea of assassinating Henry Kissinger too, if only "as an act of solidarity with the Palestinians," they said.[2] They thought better of it, though he was passing through town just a day sooner, not only because police were too thick on the ground for his visit but because Carrero Blanco alone made such a perfect hit. He was the only man with the political and military clout to assure the continuity of Franco's rule. "We know that when you kill the head of any system, somebody else is substituted. But the damage has been done," one said later. The damage proved irreparable, and Franco's dictatorship was buried with him.

Many Spaniards are still grateful to the once heroic young Etarras for that. The Basques in particular have been understandably reluctant to disown them. "I could never bring myself to inform on them: not now, not ever, not for any amount of money. It just isn't something I could do after all these years. No matter how they've gone wrong, they're still our sons," said a Basque woman who fought Franco all her life.

Nevertheless, from the day Franco died on November 19, 1975, ETA has done its implacable best to destroy the democratic government replacing him.

It is no spurious democracy. The Spanish people were enchanted with their liberation. (In Barcelona's Iberian Airlines terminal, the girl checking my ticket pulled out a bottle of champagne and waved it wildly when the dictator's death was announced. "I've been saving this for three years!" she cried, and a roomful of passengers cheered.) Their passage to constitutional liberty was remarkably quick and sure—miraculously so, after nearly half a century without it. The new system wasn't perfect, but what system is? Considering the punishment it has taken from Basqueland's freedom fighters, the wonder is that it has survived at all.

Less than a week after Franco's death, and twenty-four hours before King Juan Carlos was to grant a promised amnesty for political prisoners—749 of them Basque—the Etarras were on the kill. Their victim was the mayor of a small town in Guipúzcoa, "executed" as "an oppressor of the people," they declared. Their next two victims were an inspector of city buses and a taxi driver, neither in a position to oppress anybody.[3]

The taxi driver was murdered in Guipúzcoa on the very day when the Spanish embassy in Paris was issuing new passports at long last to 848 refugees from the defunct Franco regime: all but 9 were Basques, and 608 had some association with ETA. "The Revolutionary Basque Socialist Organization of National Liberation, ETA, continues its campaign," it announced, explaining why the unknown taxi driver had to go. "NO to collaboration with the Spanish State! All collaborators will be executed!"[4]

That happened on the first of March, 1976, when the Spanish state had been in democratic hands for three months. Within another month, four more Spaniards were killed, four wounded, and two kidnapped to raise money. One, a Basque businessman—and loyal Basque nationalist—was found with his brains blown out, after his ETA kidnappers turned down an offered one-million-dollar ransom payment as "negligible." (They had demanded $3 million.) By the end of the year, ETA had killed 19 people, a higher score in one year than in the previous forty, and the police had arrested 290 Etarras for terrorist activity, seizing a ton of explosives, half a mile's length of explosive fuse, four hundred detonators, thirty-nine shotguns, twenty-six pistols, and eight machine guns.[5]

In 1977, the kill rate rose to 30, up fifty percent. Among the victims was a kidnapped industrialist "executed" for failing to pay a demanded ransom of $16 million. In 1978, ETA announced "a permanent offensive against the forces of public order," and its kill rate doubled to 66. In 1979, the rate doubled once more to 130, leveling out then to an average two or three a week. "We have transformed traditional and romantic Basque nationalism into progressive and revolutionary nationalism. We have introduced armed struggle in workers' combat. And we have revealed the Basque cause to the world," said a leader of ETA-Militar, (the ETA-Milis), a radical-left faction of the parent group, to the respected journalist José Maria Portell in the spring of 1978—all this with no more than fifty or sixty hardcore activists, he added.[6]

Portell might well question the splendor of the achievement. For much of the previous year, he had been an informal go-between in discreet negotiations with ETA for a general amnesty and lasting truce: the equivalent of that first truce agreed to and broken irretrievably in Northern Ireland by the Provisional IRA. The Spanish government had approached Portell for this, with ETA's approval. The talks went unexpectedly well for a while, whereupon the ETA-Milis abruptly broke them off. "In regard to the basic proposal for an agreement . . . I must inform you that all my efforts to contact the political organization in question have been fruitless," wrote their negotiator "Peixoto" to Portell in April 1977. That May, the Milis launched a "Month of Urban Guerrilla Warfare" with the same clinical savagery applied by the IRA Provos in similar circumstances on their Bloody Friday. It was, said Portell, "the most bloody, anarchic, uncontrolled, ferocious, and threatening month in the last five hundred months of life in the Basque country." [7]

In June, ETA-Militar announced formally that the truce, never really on, was off for good. Spain's first free elections in forty years were coming up in just two weeks.

The following winter, Portell tried to revive the truce talks through the columns of his paper, *Hoja del Lunes*. Early one morning, as he was leaving his home in Portugalete for the office, the ETA-Milis killed him. He was "usurping his function"; from a mere go-between, he had tried to become "a protagonist," they said.

The Basque Etarras were not alone in the terrorist field by

then. Once Franco was gone—with his special military tribunals, *somarisimo* trials, firing squads, and secret police—all sorts of terrorist formations came out to breathe the winey air. They were largely Marxist-Leninist groups closely resembling the Baader-Meinhof Gang and Italy's Red Brigades. The deadliest was a "Reconstituted Communist Party" called GRAPO, born while Franco lay on his deathbed. It got started by mowing down four policemen in Madrid, going on to assassinate another thirty policemen and ranking army officers in the next four years. A list of three thousand more candidates was found on its leaders when they were caught in 1979. Their high point that year was the bombing of Madrid's crowded Café California on a Saturday afternoon at teatime, killing eight customers and injuring forty-two in a scene of indescribable panic.

Whatever these terrorist revolutionaries had in mind for their countrymen, it wasn't a sturdy democratic order. Democracy made them nervous. Like fellow terrorists of similar conviction everywhere, they were *"tanto peggio, tanto meglio"* cultists who had long believed in the advantages of a repellent right-wing dictatorship to incite a popular armed uprising. From their point of view, Spain was better off when it was worse off.

ETA had followed that line from the start, far back in Franco's day. Its main reason for assassinating Admiral Carrero Blanco, it said in *Operation Ogro*, was to "break the rhythm of evolution of the Spanish state [toward more liberal rule], forcing it into an abrupt leap to the right." The Fascist state having collapsed on them instead, the Etarras set out methodically to get it back.

Every move to consolidate the country's new political machinery brought a punctual spurt in the Etarras' kill rate—around polling days for a constituent assembly, a representative constitution, a renovated parliament, renewed city councils, a statute of autonomy for Basqueland, a regional Basque government.

For ETA, the Statute of Basque Autonomy was something like the Sunningdale Agreement and Fitzgerald Plan would be for the Provisional IRA, rolled up into one. During negotiations for that historic agreement, in the summer of 1979, the

Etarras accordingly warned millions of foreign tourists to go home, machine-gunned the Paris-Madrid express, set packed hotels ablaze in Majorca and Saragossa, bombed Madrid's airport and railway stations (eight dead, over a hundred hurt), and took to killing once a day, every day. Evidently, they were racing to put democracy out of business before the opposite happened.

The Statute of Guernica, as it was suitably known, should by rights have been the end of ETA. It had not only conceded the Basques' right to speak and study in their own language, fly their own flag, run their own schools and courts, and collect and invest their own tax revenues after paying a fair share to Madrid; it even gave them their own police force, which was more than they got the last time (from a short-lived republican government in 1936, before Franco took it all away again). In fact, they got nearly everything they might ask for short of outright secession, which most of them didn't really want.

Apart from a few exceedingly bright-eyed youths, I met nobody in the Basque region on the eve of the referendum who actually wanted to secede from Spain. Even those voting against the Statute of Guernica did so mostly to pressure the Spanish government into behaving itself once autonomy became a reality. And only four percent of the Basques did vote against it, for all the ETA-Milis' chilling fright campaign.

Nevertheless, another third of them stayed away from the polls. If some were merely indifferent, others were afraid, or incurably suspicious of Madrid, or reluctant to turn their backs altogether on the fighting Basque patriots of olden days. The Etarras weren't finished yet. There was a lot that a few dozen practiced professional terrorists could still do, by playing on Basqueland's ancestral passions and millennial dreams.

The volcanic force erupting every so often from the world's ethnic minorities continues to amaze people who don't belong to one. Irishmen, Welshmen, Cornishmen and Scots, Flamands and Walloons, Bretons and Corsicans, Sardinians, Armenians, Macedonians, Eritreans, Ibos, Serbs, Croats, Beluchis, Kurds, might take on governments and states ten or a hundred times their size, for generations on end, risking lives, money, property, economic ruin, political calamity, and international war to assert their identity. Fighting against improbable odds, they can always use a helping hand, and helping hands can use them.

A good many of these ethnic minorities were charter members of the international terrorist confraternity, surprised and pleased to find weapons, training, money, and shelter thrust upon them. Most have been manipulated and exploited, by right- or left-wing extremists, calculating politicians, and foreign agents who couldn't care less about their ethnic identity.

The Basques are among the sadder examples. An ancient and much put-upon people, mysterious in their prehistoric origins and even physically unlike other Europeans, implanted in a strategic fold of the Continent between France and the Iberian Peninsula, they have inevitably attracted a certain kind of foreign attention. Among those taking a warm and generous interest in their nationalist cause since the early sixties have been the Chinese under Mao, the Albanians, the Trotskyite IV International, the Cuban DGI, the Russian KGB, Colonel Qaddafi of Libya, the Palestinians, and everybody else who counts in the ultra-left terrorist underground from the IRA to the Tupamaros, the Swiss anarchists, the Algerians, the Baader-Meinhof Gang, the Red Brigades and the whole terrorist complex in Italy. It is hard to believe they were all moved by honest sentiment, even for the Basques.

They are surely an attractive and gallant people, and their landscape is distractingly beautiful. Lying high above the Atlantic on the black-green sculpted foothills of the Pyrenees, it is unlike other landscapes: luxuriant, secretive, strangely patterned in an etherized pastoral stillness. The fact that it is gashed with hideous industrial scars—its biggest city, Bilbao, is Spain's Pittsburgh—suggests something of the population's cultural stress. If the Basques are in love with their past, they are also very much a part of the technological industrial present.

Centuries of folklore don't necessarily make them simple, barefoot peasants. Their steel mills, mines, and shipyards are on a level with the giants of Western Europe. They are, or were, as rich on average as the citizens of wealthy Benelux in the Common Market. They used to have the highest personal incomes in Spain—forty percent higher, in Bilbao and the surrounding province of Guipúzcoa—until terrorism flared and capital fled, after Franco died.

Factory after factory closed down after 1975, as hundreds of industrialists—impeccable Basque patriots, most of them—picked up and ran to escape ETA's fund-raising methods: abductions, killings, beatings, a bank robbery a day, a steep "Revolutionary Tax" extracted on threat of death and payable monthly into ETA's Swiss bank accounts.[8] ("What's keeping me here?" a plump and jaunty Basque businessman asked me over a steaming dish of *zupa de marrascas* in San Sebastián. "My brother's wife and child were held at gunpoint until he cleaned out his bank balance for ETA, and he's gone. My uncle got sick of paying through the nose month after month, so *he's* gone. *I'm* sick of paying through the nose; and what's more, I have no intention of forcing my five kids to learn a faked history in school or speak a dead language that doesn't even have a written alphabet. So you can assume that the next time you come, *I'll* be gone.")

Thus, in the few years since ETA moved on from romantic nationalism to the armed revolutionary kind, has the Basque province of Guipúzcoa dropped from first place to fifteenth in the scale of national Spanish incomes.[9]

There are only about two million Basques in all, of whom some two hundred thousand live in France. The Spanish Basques barely exceed a million and a half, in a national population of thirty-seven million; and even in their four traditional provinces of Alava, Vizcaya, Guipúzcoa, and Navarra, they are matched if not outnumbered by immigrant workers from poorer parts of Spain. (Since these immigrants now make up the mass of Basqueland's proletariat, the Etarras' claim that this was how their region was "colonized by Spain" would seem to be twisting history's tail.)

Their memories go back to the stirring days when valorous Basque warriors drove off Visigoths, Franks, Normans, Moors, and cut the rear guard of Charlemagne's army to shreds (at Roncesvalles, in A.D. 778). But they were never an independent nation. The closest they got was a set of treasured *fueros* at the close of the Middle Ages: self-governing powers over trade, taxation, and military service, granted by Ferdinand II of Aragon.

They certainly *feel* Basque still, especially when they are picked on. General Franco, who picked on them unbearably in his Castilian arrogance, might as well have sat on a hive of hornets. Nevertheless they are not always obsessed by "the absurd racial virginity" of their Basquetude, as Miguel Unamuno puts it. Unamuno, their best-known writer, considers himself a Spaniard, as do many or most Basque intellectuals. There is very little in the way of a written Basque culture. The language, unrelated to any other, is spoken by perhaps one Basque in twenty. Even the idea of a separate Basque state did not come up until 1894.

It is no longer the seductive idea it became under Franco. Young ETA recruits of fifteen or sixteen—too young to have fought in the true Resistance—may dream of an independent Basqueland as a sylvan retreat, miraculously free of noxious effluents while abounding in modern consumer goods, safe from piratical capitalists, predatory neighbors, and immutable economic laws. Few older Basques have such innocent illusions. Their own separatist dreams had to do with bolting for freedom from a despotic ruler, who made a point of persecuting Basques on top of everything else. Those were the days, for the Milis. Never has Basque nationalism been so inflamed, before or since.

There was no mistaking ETA-Militar's purpose as autonomy drew near in 1979. "They want the prisons overflowing with Basques again, screams from the torture chambers, the martyr's stigmata. They want Spanish tanks in the streets of Bilbao," Manuel Azcarate of the Spanish Communist Party told me in Madrid. They wanted to "block peaceful co-existence, foment mutual distrust, and provoke a military coup d'état," said the Basque National Council representing all the region's political parties.[10] They wanted to "Ulsterize Basqueland," said the Milis themselves, referring to the wonders done by Ulster's Provisional IRA to keep peace forever out of Northern Ireland.

In the manner of the IRA Provos, they have done their level best to goad a constitutional government into losing its head and behaving like a police state.

The fact that the Basques and everybody else in Spain got stuck with their last police state for forty years does not appear

(*Wide World Photos*)

Giangiacomo Feltrinelli, Milan, 1967. *(Wide World Photos)*

The body of Feltrinelli next to dynamited power pylon near Milan, 1972.
(Wide World Photos)

Petra Krause, escorted by Swiss police at Rome airport, 1977.
(Wide World Photos)

Two photos of Gabriele Kröcher-Tiedemann
(United Press International Photo)

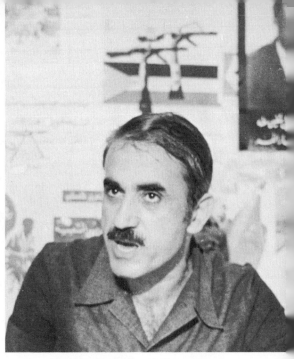

Norbert Kröcher.
(Wide World Photos)

George Habash, 1973.
(United Press International Photo)

Munich, 1972, Olympic Village room where Israeli hostages were held. Bloodstains and bullet holes mark the place where the Israeli weightlifter Moshe Romano was killed. *(Wide World Photos)*

Tripoli Arab Nations Summit Conference, 1977. Left to right: Yassir Arafat, Ahmed Jibril, George Habash. *(Wide World Photos)*

Colonel Muammar Qaddafi (center, in uniform) visits Moscow in 1976 in a "constructive and friendly atmosphere," as reported by Tass. *(United Press International Photo)*

**Carlos at the time of
The Interview in
al-Watan al-Arabi.
(Wide World Photos)

Seamus Costello.
(Wide World Photos)

**London, 1979. Car outside Parliament shattered by bomb blast that
killed the Conservative M.P. Airey Neave.**
(United Press International Photo)

Rome, March 16, 1978. Site of Aldo Moro's kidnapping. The black limousine at right is the car in which Moro was riding and the white car at left was his escort's. In the foreground are the body of a policeman killed in the ambush and, near the body, a pistol used by policemen. *(United Press International Photo)*

Rome, May 9, 1978. Car containing the body of Aldo Moro.
(United Press International Photo)

A photograph brought into the United States by an Iranian shows American hostages reading mail in the United States embassy in Teheran, 1980. *(United Press International Photo)*

to bother the Milis. Nor does the fact that what finally delivered Spain from its dictator was not a Communist revolution but a biological solution. (The same argument holds true for Hitler's Germany and Mussolini's Italy, delivered respectively from ten and twenty years of fascism by a world war, not a popular armed uprising.)

So far, the Etarras have been wrong in assuming that the Spanish army, having taken the country over once, could be incited to do so again. At best, or worst, their violence has provoked a response in kind from roaming gangs of right-wing terrorists, themselves every inch as vicious as the Etarra killers. But if the army itself hasn't moved, yet, the Milis still seem to think that, with suitable provocation, it will.

Their strategy was formulated at ETA-Militar's seventh *asamblea* in September 1976, Year One of the post-Franco era.[11] It presumed that an army so long conditioned by Franco would take a dim view of freely elected governments. Since the Basques had rasped on military nerves for years, ETA could reasonably hope to stir a murderous lust for revenge in army circles by killing officers and policemen monthly, weekly, or daily if necessary. Reprisals were bound to follow (and did), with indiscriminate arrests, torture, and a familiar posture of outraged Spanish authority. The banked fires of Basque nationalism had to leap into life again (and did). More killings, more reprisals, more anger in Basqueland, more killings, more reprisals, more anger, more killings . . . "Action, Reaction, Action," the Milis call it. The Provos of Northern Ireland know all about that.

A nearly identical strategy had worked splendidly more than a decade earlier, in the palmier days of Spain's martial rule. "We have achieved one of our major objectives: to oblige the enemy to commit a thousand wrongs and atrocities," said ETA's official program in 1964, when it had already harried Franco into filling his prisons with Basques. "Most of his victims are innocent. Meanwhile, the people, more or less passive until now, become indignant against the colonial tyrant and, in reaction, come over entirely to our side. We could not have hoped for a better result." [12]

They might have lifted the paragraph word for word from

Marighella's *Mini-Manual*, which they apparently went on to learn by heart. By the time Franco died, they were in fact following Marighella's counsel to the letter, for the last stage in revolution but one—the stage of dismantling a democratic government and exposing the "farce" of free elections, just as the Tupamaros of Uruguay and the Provos of Northern Ireland had done (within a few months of each other, in 1972–73).

Marighella's text on the subject was explicit. "Completely rejecting this election farce and the 'so-called political solution,'" it ran, "the urban guerrilla must become more aggressive and violent, resorting without letup to sabotage, terrorism, expropriations, assaults, kidnappings, and executions, heightening the disastrous situation in which the government must act. . . ."

But the Brazilian guerrilla leader had published his classic *Mini-Manual* in 1969, whereas that early official program of ETA's came out five years before. Not only had the Basque guerrillas studied at the same school as Marighella; they got there ahead of him.

The first batch of Basque Etarras was shipped to Cuba in 1964.[13] The Russians had just decided then to increase their investment in terrorism abroad by a thousand percent. The Tricontinental Conference in Havana, reflecting the Kremlin's new policy, was still two years away. So was the Guerrilla International born of the conference, not to mention the honeycomb of training camps set up around Havana under the supervision of KGB Colonel Vadim Kotchergine.

The Guines camp, not far from the Cuban capital, was taking only a few select trainees when the Etarras got in. Its curriculum, limited to kidnapping, subversion, and sabotage techniques, was rudimentary by standards soon to be attained there and elsewhere.

The young Basques who made it to the Guines camp in those days knew little of Marxism, or of Lenin on the National Question. They had barely moved on from romantic nationalism to vaguely humanist socialism. Not until 1970—the opening of the fright decade—did ETA declare itself a Marxist-Leninist movement, committed to the dictatorship of the proletariat.[14] Its commitment to democratic centralism—telltale mark of "real socialism" in the Soviet bloc—came along three years later. But the hard-lining paleo-Communist influence at the inner core of ETA-Militar, exactly like the Italian Red Brigades' and Provisional IRA's, did not grow clear until the decade was nearly over.

There is no following ETA's doctrinal wrangles over the years. Factions kept splitting off like amoebas, toward the Trotskyites, the conventional Spanish Communist Party, an array of Maoist formations, free-style New Leftism. Whatever their differences, though, they all made a beeline for the international terrorist circuit.

Few Armed Parties have left such distinct tracks through this subterranean maze. From Cuba in 1964, the Etarras fanned out to train with the Tupamaros in Uruguay and like-minded Montoneros in next-door Argentina. Then they moved on to Algeria, with like-minded guerrillas from everywhere. A model for the world's armed revolutionary left after its long war of liberation, Algeria led the radical Arab bloc in the Third World, listing heavily toward Moscow. Its guerrilla camps were flung wide open starting in 1968, to American Black Panthers, German and Italian ultra-leftists, the IRA, ETA, Palestinians without end. Cuban instructors were there from the early seventies, and so was at least one from the KGB when the Etarras came along.

The Basque reporter who told me this in Bilbao was among the most reliable I know and had been at ETA's side all through the Franco years. It was the KGB instructor in Algiers who brought ETA and the Provisional IRA together in 1971, he said. They were natural allies, and the timing was right. Moscow was just beginning to take a proprietary interest in the Provos, with the four-and-a-half-ton arms shipment from Prague that year. Both of these armed bands had prime nationalist and ethnic sentiments to build on and excellent targets to strike at; and both were already moving toward radical no-surrender positions in guerrilla warfare. In fact, they did become the most inseparable of partners in the European underground.

Maria McGuire, writing of her lively year with the Provos, described the initial meeting in Ireland, in 1971, between the Etarras and Sean MacStiofain, the Provisional IRA's commander-in-chief. "They had come to offer us [fifty] revolvers in return for training in the use of explosives . . . struggling with words like 'detonator' and 'gelignite,' " she wrote. They were bright pupils, as Admiral Carrero Blanco would discover.

The partnership was tied up tight in 1972. That January, the two groups met at the Spanish Center in London to talk logistics.[15] There, ETA's "Iñaki" (José Ignacio Bustamante Otaduy) arranged to send Etarras in groups of four to IRA training centers in Dublin and Ulster. (The centers had already been agreed on in Florence, when the Red International's founding fathers met under the auspices of Feltrinelli and Potere Operaio. ETA was present, of course, taking in every word of Seamus Costello's day-long presentation of the IRA's history and customs.) By the end of 1972, a formal pact of mutual assistance had sealed the bonds between ETA and the Provisional IRA.[16] Eventually, ETA sent a permanent representative to Ireland to keep in touch. (He was a former priest named Elias Jauregui.)

Like the Provos, the Etarras too got locked into the international terrorist circuit that year. Before it was out, they had signed a formal declaration of alliance with the Tupamaros, the separatist Kurds, and Fatah, military arm of the Palestine Liberation Organization.[17] They had also attended the Habash-Haddad terrorist summit in Baddawi, and they were present at those planning sessions in Dublin where the multinational Carlos team was set up.

New horizons opened in 1973. Carlos was installed in Paris, the Red International's Zurich office was open for business, and The Organization in Italy was doing its best to create "multiplying mechanisms" for revolution on the Continent. Secret correspondence, discovered by the Italian courts much later, revealed The Organization's special interest in "ethnic minorities . . . such as the Basques, the Bretons, and the Irish," along with plans for "an international conference to launch the theme of insurrection in Europe." [18]

The conference was held in Dublin late that year, with the slogan "For a Revolutionary Western Europe." Sure enough, ETA was there, as were the IRA, the French Corsican Liberation Front (separatist and Marxist), the French Breton Liberation Front (separatist and Marxist), the Quebec Liberation

Front (separatist and Marxist), and the French Red Brigades (a pale copy of their Italian counterpart). A worldwide terrorist summit in Dublin the next January included them all, together with the usual Palestinians, Italians, Germans, et al.[19]

By 1974, the Etarras were hooked into the Trotskyite IV International and Maoist China both. A wing of ETA went over to the Trotskyites in a body, while others joined the World Front for the Liberation of Oppressed Peoples, with headquarters in Brussels. The Front, Trotskyite by birth, became the voice of Peking in Europe as well. Before long, its Brussels office was a humming distribution center for weapons and money, arriving circumspectly from the Orient through Libya and Algeria. A branch route for the arms traffic passed through Albania and Austria.

In 1975, Franco's death spurred ETA-Militar to action. At a secret *asamblea* in the south of France just a month after his funeral, the Milis voted to face the new political challenge—democracy in Spain—with intensified terrorist training.[20] Algeria was offering graduate courses in the field, and 143 Milis were selected to go there for a doctorate in guerrilla warfare.

They were sent off from Basqueland in batches of thirty the following spring, by train, plane, and Mediterranean steamer, by way of Paris, Nice, Geneva, Brussels, Rome. Their destination was the police school in Souma, twenty-five miles from the Algerian capital, where they were stripped of their passports, confined to a three-story building behind high walls, enjoined to "absolute obedience," and forbidden to talk to anybody but their Algerian and Cuban instructors.

For three arduous months, they slogged away at map reading and map making, target practice, grenade launching, weapon maintenance, logistics, shortwave transmission, explosives, judo, karate, and open-field commando exercises.[21]

That autumn, Libya and Algeria got together to put the scheme on a regular footing. Carlos had left his Paris network in a shambles upon fleeing France, and nobody had yet replaced him. A return to something like normality threatened Western Europe. In November 1976, therefore, Colonel Qaddafi of Libya and Colonel Boumedienne of Algeria agreed secretly on a joint aid program for Europe's armed underground.

Libya took special responsibility for the inseparable IRA and ETA, while Algeria (with Libyan financing) adopted the Bretons and Corsicans. Training was shifted to the Blida military camp southwest of Algiers and to the "Europeans' " Camp Az Zaouiah in Benina, near Benghazi, Libya.[22] Within a year, the rate of terrorist attacks doubled in Ulster, in Spanish Basqueland, in French Brittany, and Corsica.[23]

By 1977, the ETA-Milis had a couple of hundred finely honed and superbly armed *pistoleros*, who could knock off a cop in San Sebastián and slip over the border to safety in southern France (or "northern Basqueland") within half an hour. France, hospitable as always to "political exiles," let them be. French recruits in their earliest teens could be trained right there in the south of France, or in Algeria and Libya, then given a gun and told to shoot anything in uniform. The machinery for killing practically ran itself, and no political force inside Spain still had the power to turn it on or off.

That was when "it became unmistakably clear to us that nothing we said, or did, or promised could bring the ETA-Milis to the peace table," a left-wing Socialist Basque leader explained to me. "They were in the international groove for good; local political solutions simply didn't interest them." What did interest them was no longer simple Basque separatism but Continent-wide insurrection—on the Western side of the Continent, that is.

For ten days that summer, the Milis mingled in Spain with a mixed terrorist bag, ethnic and urban (IRA Provos, Bretons, Corsicans, Welshmen, the German Baader-Meinhof Gang, Revolutionary Cells and June 2 Movement, the small French ultra-left NAPAP, Italy's Red Brigades, and The Organization's Front Line.)[24] Hosted by GRAPO, they were coordinating strategy and beefing up logistical services. The sensational kidnapping and murder of German industrialist Hanns-Martin Schleyer (whose body was found in France) came just a few weeks later.

Much the same group assembled in Frankfurt in October 1978, as "viewers" at a West German "anti-Fascist" conference.[25] Practically the whole bunch then went on to Yugoslavia, meeting in Belgrade with Palestinians from Habash's

PFLP (and a KGB "viewer," according to Western intelligence sources).[26] "In a secret meeting in Yugoslavia early in October 1978, participants included the Palestine Resistance, South and Central American guerrillas, and representatives of the Red Brigades to discuss the strategy and program of international revolution," wrote Italy's Attorney General Guido Guasco in December 1979. Meanwhile, the Milis had met, on the side, with the Italian Red Brigades and IRA Provos, in Portugal.[27]

Since these things take time, it was a while before outsiders got a tantalizing glimpse of what they had in mind.

There was a preview of sorts in the autumn of 1978, when the IRA Provisionals took their war to the Continent; hard work must have gone into getting the European network ship-shape for that. But a much more intriguing clue came to light in the spring of 1980, when four Italian terrorists were caught napping on the French Riviera. They were living in style, dressed in the costliest of natty sportswear, drinking champagne with smoked salmon tidbits, waiting for repairs to be done to their eighty-thousand-dollar cabin cruiser, the *Marie-Christine*. Three of the four were notorious Red Brigades fugitives, high on the Italian police wanted list for kidnapping and murder. The fourth had a record for peddling drugs.[28]

The cash they were spreading around actually belonged to a miners' pension fund in northern France. It was part of a four-million-dollar haul they had made, with the help of Spanish Basques and French terrorists in a mixed holdup team. Eighteen of their teammates, including three Spanish Basques, were arrested around the same time in Paris. A nineteenth, picked up the next day, was an Italian woman terrorist from The Organization's Front Line, assigned to work in the French capital. Among the items found in her flat were 1,320 pounds of dynamite, five machine guns, and eight automatics. Her co-workers on the Riviera had stashed away a thousand blank Italian identity cards.[29]

A few days' interrogation made it plain that here was another Carlos network in the making. Italy's Red Brigades and Front Line, having come a long way since Carlos's day, were passing on their expertise to others in an organically knit multinational hit-team. The French had merged two or three sluggish outfits like their own Red Brigades and NAPAP into a feisty band called Direct Action, learning fast. The mainstays of the band were Italian, French, Spanish, and Irish. (The German terrorists were too heavily infiltrated by police in 1980 to be trustworthy.) The four-million-dollar stickup was to furnish the front money. It had already paid for the *Marie-Christine*, planned as their fast getaway vehicle and floating headquarters.[30]

This was one the Russians couldn't dodge: they had to know about it. Whatever the KGB's lines to the Italian, Irish, and French terrorist undergrounds, its line to the ETA-Milis was a matter of record. For once, the KGB had been caught in the act of meeting directly with, and providing weapons for, a major terrorist band in Europe.

Two KGB agents were expelled from Spain largely for that reason in February 1980—only a few weeks before those spectacular arrests in France. One was Oleg Suranov, manager of the Soviet airline Aeroflot in Madrid, who was put on a plane for Warsaw. The other was a first secretary of the Soviet embassy, Anatoli Krassilinikov, who was bundled off to Moscow. Their expulsion brought to six the number of Soviet agents thrown out of Spain in the three years since the two countries had established diplomatic relations.[31]

The Soviet embassy in Madrid opened its doors in February 1977, with a staff of 130 people. Spain's democratic order was barely a year old, and vulnerable. Terrorism was simmering in Madrid and boiling in Basqueland, where autonomy was still far away. The ETA-Milis (which had split off recently from the ETA Politico-Milis) rejected any "political solution" and opted for unconditional guerrilla warfare. The Milis had just lost their invaluable Chinese patrons. Mao Tse-tung had died the previous autumn, the Gang of Four was in jail, and the whole Red Chinese support apparatus for Maoist guerrilla formations throughout the world was collapsing. The vacuum was irresistibly inviting in Spain, and the Russians filled it.

ETA-Militar changed visibly that year. (Whether by chance or otherwise, so did the Provisional IRA, at the same time and in the same way.) Its structure was tightened and modernized, its personnel changed and improved, its war aims broadened to

Continental dimensions. Nothing leaked to the press about a possible KGB hand in this, beyond news of the first Soviet agent's expulsion from Madrid—a month after the Soviet Union's embassy opened there. Then, on July 14, 1978, the Spanish intelligence service actually witnessed a meeting in Saint-Jean-de-Luz, in southern France. The KGB agent was *Izvestia* correspondent Vitali Kovich. ETA-Militar's man was Eugenio Echeveste Arizgura, "Anchon," a member of its top directorate.[32]

There had been plenty of gossip about the KGB's penetration of ETA-Militar before that. I myself had been told the same story, by two well-informed Basque journalists, about four Basques who quit ETA to join the orthodox Spanish Communist Party in exile, in 1971, and were promptly sent to Cuba. The four did not resurface in Spain until 1976, after Franco died and ETA-Militar had been formed. One of my informants ran into the most brilliant of them, "Makaven," in Saint-Jean-de-Luz on his return. "It was amazing to see how much he must have learned in Havana. I was impressed," he told me. Shortly after that casual encounter, "Makaven" went straight into the Milis' supreme strategic command.

Still, "Anchon's" assignation with the KGB was not gossip, but fact. The story made front-page headlines in Spain that autumn, stinging the Russians to a reply. A note in Tass stiffly rejected the report as "fantasy," and the Soviet Union thereupon solemnly condemned ETA-Militar's "extremist terrorist methods." That was in February 1979. A consignment of three hundred Soviet-bloc assault guns and fifteen bazookas reached the ETA-Milis exactly a month later (on March 20, 1979).

By then, the Russians themselves had confirmed their hold on ETA-Militar, if only obliquely. When the Spanish foreign minister visited Moscow that same February, his Soviet hosts offered a straight swap: if Spain would promise not to join NATO, Russia would promise to help Spain fight ETA. If not, not.[33] The uses of terrorism to Soviet diplomacy have rarely been made so plain.

Much the same proposition was put in reverse to the PLO's Yassir Arafat when he visited Madrid that year. If the Palestinians promised to stop helping ETA, the Spanish government would promise to recognize the PLO.[34] The British had made a similar proposal, in relation to the Provisional IRA, but Arafat was hardly the man to ask in either case. The source of heavy Palestinian aid for ETA and the IRA both was not Arafat, but George Habash, who did not share Arafat's diplomatic fancies. The last thing Habash had wanted since the fright decade began was a political solution for any ongoing terrorist conflict, in or out of the Middle East.

It was no secret to the Basques by the decade's end that their honest ethnic feelings were being put to disingenuous use. They themselves told me nearly everything I've written about them here. Yet the Etarras' fiction of political purity persists. The younger the Basques I came across, the more they wanted to believe it. But none was so serene in his certainty as the Catholic priest of sixty-odd who has presided over their privileged sanctuary in southern France for many years.

I had saved Père Lazarbal for last on my visit to northern Spain in 1979, driving over the border from San Sebastián to meet him. "Monsieur le Curé," as he is known in the farthest corners of Basqueland north and south, received me in a freezing little study of his modest parish house in Socoa. He had been in the job too long to have false hopes about the foreign press. His manner was affable, but the clear, vivid blue eyes behind half-moon glasses, under a beret one feels he must wear to bed, were watchful.

He could see the enemy had been at me. If there was one thing I could be sure of, he started out, it was that ETA had absolutely no connection with any foreign groups, still less any foreign *terrorist* groups. "We are not terrorists. We are liberators," he explained. Another thing I must realize is that they weren't Marxists, whatever they said. "I do find the younger Etarras more radicalized, but their Marxism is skin-deep; they are always patriots first," he went on. They weren't trying to frighten anybody by using violence but were simply defending themselves. "If you don't defend yourself, you're crushed!"

And after all, they were at war. "This Basque country of ours is under foreign occupation, just as France was under the Germans. This is a war too, like World War II. Well, then, in any war, do you kill or don't you? War is like that," he said.

All life was like that, he went on. "All, all is a struggle, for animals or vegetables, beasts or men. If you don't fight, you're destroyed. The weakest go down. That is a law of nature and of Christianity. So which side are you on?"

He must have decided I was on the wrong side, because he gave me up. I shouldn't be fooled by false pacifists or milksops meekly submitting to a "false marriage" between Basqueland and Spain, was his parting advice. "We Basques have an old saying: 'It is better to be the butcher than the calf,' " said this Man of God as he showed me out.

11

THE ISHUTIN SOLUTION

When I last saw Carlo Fioroni, late in 1978, he was alone in his steel cage in a Milan courtroom, on trial for the kidnapping and murder of his best friend. His co-defendants, all ex-convicts, all to be found guilty, were in a separate cage and shunned him. In prison later, where he was serving his twenty-seven-year sentence, his former revolutionary comrades shunned him too. Kept under special guard, he took his fresh air alone and ate alone, his meals prepared by a police inspector for him alone. The fact that he was still alive by 1980 seemed surprising even so. There probably wasn't a man in Italy whose death was so earnestly desired by the terrorist underground.

Fioroni not only knew—he embodied—the secrets of a subterranean high command whose brilliant planning brought Italy very nearly to full-scale guerrilla war in less than a decade. He was in it from the start: in the mother cell whose proliferating offspring were responsible, by the decade's end, for a terrorist attack somewhere in the country once every three hours and four minutes. Not only did he know and embody these secrets, he talked.

His confession, from prison late in 1979, stripped away ten years of sanctimonious deceit. It revealed an artfully concealed alliance of terrorist killers and the virtuous intellectual gurus providing them with thick protective cover. It disclosed the squalid partnership of both with the criminal underworld:

deals for kidnapping and armed robbery, splitting the take fifty-fifty; hired professional assassins from the Mafia and French Foreign Legion; gangster killings to shut the mouths of witnesses. It traced an unbroken line from the beginning to the end of the seventies, starting with a search for primitive arms and funds, ending with a fortune on deposit in Swiss banks and an arsenal extending to Soviet weapons like the SAM-7 Strela missile—the heat-seeking missile guided infallibly by an infrared eye to disintegrate a plane in flight.

The picture Fioroni provided was the first to come from the interior of a modern Armed Party anywhere, and Italy's Armed Party represented the highest state of the art among them. Nowhere else had a handful of students from the 1968 generation worked so diligently and long or gotten so close to turning a transient mutiny into a civil war of long duration. No others had made such adroit use of their country's every fault and merit: its political dilapidation and generous democratic impulses, its haunting memories of fascism and rich vein of radical-left traditions, the widening gulf between its governing class and people—the *pays politique* and *pays réel.* There was no question here of manipulating ethnic or religious passions for cover, as in Spain or Ireland. This was straightforward strategic planning for extended Communist guerrilla warfare, well advanced when Fioroni spoke out.

His confession confirmed what a few harassed Italian magistrates had been telling an incredulous public for months. Behind the seemingly spontaneous growth of terrorism in Italy was an elaborately contrived apparatus, operating at two levels and penetrating deep into Italian society. A political arm for mass insurrectional propaganda worked out in the open, through a sprawl of apparently formless Autonomous Collectives on the far but legitimate left. A secretly interlocked military arm worked underground, through an acronymic wilderness of large and small terrorist bands: Br (Red Brigades), Pl (Front Line), NAP (Armed Proletarian Nucleus), RP (Proletarian Patrols), PFR, UCC, FCC, and a couple of hundred more. Presiding at the top were widely admired academic luminaries and popular stars of the great 1968 upheaval. They called it all The Organization.

There is no mistaking where the idea came from. The original model was invented in tsarist Russia a century ago. A Moscow revolutionary named Nicholas Ishutin thought it up in January 1866. Its open political arm did the pedestrian work of insurrectional agitation and propaganda (in schools, libraries, provincial intellectual retreats, social clubs). Its secret arm was devoted to assassination, armed robbery, blackmail, and so on, introducing terrorists and common criminals both to the radical Russian scene for the first time. Ishutin called his outfit The Organization too. The name he gave its secret terrorist arm was Hell.[1]

Ishutin died in Siberia, hopelessly insane, a dim figure in the folklore of the Bolshevik Revolution that took another five decades to mature. He did get the Revolution started in Russia, though. That is evidently what The Organization had in mind for Italy, with what it called "the civil war of long duration."

Carlo Fioroni was there when it began. A language teacher in a northern Italian high school, he was twenty-six when he was drawn into the tumultuous student happenings of 1968. Even now, he looks young and self-effacing enough to be called *"Il Professorino"* (The Little Professor). Short, meager in frame, slope-shouldered and stooped, he has the pinched face of a precocious child and the inner pallor of a self-scourging penitent. The crime he is serving time for was an act of insanity, in his words. "We were wrong about everything, everything! Come back before it's too late!" he appealed from the court-room, to former comrades who evidently missed his point.

Like so many others, Fioroni started out in radical politics with Potere Operaio (Workers' Power), known as Potop. A self-defined "revolutionary Communist organization" at the outer-most rim of legality, Potop was the furthest left of all the formations to the left of the Italian Communist Party, and it was a magnet for a rebellious student generation demanding Everything, Now. At its peak in 1969, it had about five thousand members. Only one in five held the "red card" of an acti-vist, and probably no more than one in those five—two hundred in all—had the makings of an intrepid Bolshevik conspirator. If not exactly representative of a whole generation, they were, as we have seen, just what Giangiacomo Feltrinelli was looking for. The mother cell of Italian terrorism grew out of their revo-lutionary ardor and his money and connections.

Giangi Feltrinelli was the only man in Italy rich enough to underwrite Potop's mountainous debts. On the closest of terms with its leaders, he could also borrow from its ranks to help shape his own underground GAP, Italy's first left-wing armed terrorist band. In 1971, when The Organization was just taking secret form within Potop, Carlo Fioroni was seconded to Feltrinelli. "Do your best; he can be useful" were Fioroni's instructions.[2]

The *Professorino*'s first brush with the law came just a few months later, when he was caught with false identity papers provided by his millionaire patron. He had a letter in his pocket at the time addressed to "Osvaldo," Feltrinelli's still unknown game-name. Had the police grasped the letter's import, they might have deflected the national calamity that Italian terrorism has become. But they filed it and forgot it for the next eight years, and turned Fioroni loose.

The letter was a dead giveaway of The Organization's extravagant military plans. Feltrinelli, as "Osvaldo," had written to an unknown "Saetta" in the autumn of 1971, proposing a joint high command in the north for an underground Army of National Liberation. "Saetta" was in fact Franco Piperno, one of Potop's most forceful and fiery national leaders at the time, who had asked the *Professorino* to deliver his answer by hand. His letter, dated November 10, 1971, confirmed an agreement in principle "on the broad lines of a program arranged on two levels, which I consider serious and above all, urgent." He proposed a "dialectic relationship" between Potop and Feltrinelli's armed terrorists in the underground GAP, leading toward "an operative unity of command in Milan." His own people must not be utilized simply as "technicians," he specified, lest they should merely "be asked to become killers, and not revolutionary leaders." He closed with a tribute to "Osvaldo," as "one of the few revolutionaries who have taken the right road . . . the sole, correct course toward revolution."[3] (Feltrinelli died soon afterward, taking his secrets to the grave. The identity of "Saetta," and the text of his letter, remained a mystery until Fioroni spoke out in 1979.)

Released by the police that first time—January 1972—Fioroni was picked up and released again a few weeks later, after the worst street riots to hit Milan since the days of Mussolini's Fascist *squadristi* half a century before. Feltrinelli himself was in the heart of the mob, throwing cobblestones at the windows of the *Corriere della Sera*, magisterial voice of the Establishment. Fioroni was rounded up when police raided the Feltrinelli safe-house where—amid a profusion of Molotov cocktails, explosives, custom-made steel clubs, and walkie-talkies—the plans had been made to orchestrate the riots.

Feltrinelli's mutilated body was found barely seventy-two hours later, after the bomb he was setting had blown up in his hands, and the *Professorino* was back in custody once more. This time he was sure he would land in jail, since he had personally insured the Volkswagen Camper abandoned at the scene. Instead, an avuncular magistrate let him go. "They tell me at police headquarters that you are a flaming revolutionary, but don't worry," the magistrate said with a benevolence outstanding even in those years of Italy's resolute self-deception. "Your story holds water, so you can go. You won't run away, will you?" The *Professorino* went underground that night.

Three years passed before Fioroni surfaced. In May 1975 the Swiss police caught him recycling $100,000 of hot money. (His co-worker Petra Krause had been arrested in Zurich in March. She claimed afterward that it was Fioroni who borrowed her car for the ten-million-dollar arson attack on the ITT plant in Milan, and Fioroni confirmed it.) The bills found on the *Professorino* at the time of his arrest were part of a ransom running to nearly ten times as much. They had been paid out earlier that May by a wealthy Milanese family, for an abducted son who never came back.

The victim was Carlo Saronio, a promising young engineer who was the *Professorino*'s closest friend. It was Saronio who hid the fugitive in his family's exclusive home after Feltrinelli died, who gave him $1,000 and got him across the Swiss border to safety, who later sent a sympathetic priest to escort him back to Milan. Then, in mid-April 1975, the twenty-six-year-old engineer went out to dinner, and vanished.

Carlo Fioroni's arrest a few weeks later led to the roundup of half a dozen others in the kidnap ring. They were all thugs with chromatic criminal careers. One belonged to the notorious Vallanzasca Band, adept at every kind of felony and closely identified with Black Fascist terrorists. Another, known as "*Cic-ciobello*," Pretty Fat Boy, was a repeater in and out of the jug. "How come I kicked in a million lire [around $1,500] for a speedboat after the snatch? Because I go out to steal, not to slave in a factory; spending a million lire doesn't bother me," he told the court. Even the "politicized" crook who headed the ring, Carlo Casirati, admitted that he had taken off for Venezuela with the $200,000 of ransom money he was asked to launder, after throwing a glorious farewell party. "Fioroni asked me—me, Your Honor, an escaped convict!—to get the money changed," he exclaimed in wonder to the judge.

Casirati, who didn't feel up to such a big job alone, had brought in a true expert named Giustino de Vuono. A Mafia boss and professional contract killer, de Vuono had the unusual distinction of having been thrown out of the French Foreign Legion for excessive violence. Dreaded even by his fellow gangsters for his calloused cruelty, he was accused later of having helped the Red Brigades kill Aldo Moro. (The police haven't caught him yet, as I write, but they did turn up his signed receipt for a sixty-thousand-dollar payoff after the Saronio kidnapping. It was found in a Red Brigades hideout.) [4]

The story pieced together at the trial was that Saronio was kidnapped upon leaving his dinner party and suffocated by an accidental overdose of chloroform. The gang then buried him in a suburban patch of wasteland, and demanded an eight-million-dollar ransom. (They settled for a down payment of $800,000.) Police found his skeleton fours years after its burial, when Casirati consented in prison to give them a crude map. A tin of white pepper had been placed near the skull to put dogs off the scent.)

In court, Carlo Fioroni took the blame for everything. "As a Communist, I accuse myself of organizing the abduction," he told the judge. He did it to raise money "for the effective logistic defense of the Armed Movement," he said. This was pretty exotic stuff for the Italian public at the time. Even as late as the autumn of 1978, when Fioroni was testifying, the ordinary Italian had not the foggiest notion of the Armed Movement and its money-raising customs. The only Armed Movement they knew about consisted of groups like the openly terrorist Red Brigades; they assumed that was what Fioroni meant. But he hinted at something incomparably more labyrinthine.

"When I say 'The Armed Movement,' I mean the *entire Armed Area*," he wrote in an imaginary letter to his murdered friend Saronio (which he passed on to the press). "Because 'They'—even 'They,' the Red Brigades—lean on the Party when they need this and that, or a place to rest when their nerves are shot." [5]

Which Party? What Armed Area? The *Professorino* didn't say. But he implied that the dead victim had known all about it. In fact, he suggested that Saronio had collaborated in getting himself kidnapped, not consciously but "objectively." He described the two of them, in that grotesque letter, sitting in a sunny garden of the Saronio family's country villa, talking the whole thing over. "We'd discussed it. . . . You wouldn't have had the courage to break the umbilical cord [extort a fortune from his own parents, that is]. But you would have contributed objectively to an operation you weren't prepared for subjectively. . . . One day, I would have told you the truth, and you would have understood."

Beyond that, Fioroni would say nothing in court about the "atrocious enigma" of Saronio's death. Yet he clearly longed to say more. No punishment could be worse than the heavy guilt he carried inside for "having betrayed a friend I loved," he said to the judge. He spoke of the "collective delirium" that made the betrayal possible, the pervasive "fascination for clandestinity and the armed struggle" when the crime took place in 1975. "We lived in a dimension in which the most demented pronóuncements could be taken for doctrine, common criminals could be accepted as a revolutionary force, a fight for our fellow men could become a fight against our fellow men. . . ." He hoped somebody out there was listening, he concluded.

Though not on speaking terms with the *Professorino*, who had turned them in, the thugs on trial confirmed his veiled allusions. The neo-Fascist chap confessed that "the ultra-left politicals" who sponsored the kidnapping had also invited him to lift a few Renaissance paintings worth a million dollars.[6] Casirati, "the honest thief," swore he had been present at a "political meeting" where Saronio was selected as a money-raising target. Indeed, said Casirati, he had belonged to

Fioroni's own group for more than a year before the snatch, assigned to convert more crooks for just such work. It was no miserable little *gruppetto*, either, but a whopping big *gruppone*. If the court really wanted to get at the truth, "other people would be sitting here among the accused whose names would raise the roof!" he declared. "Then you wouldn't have to believe that paranoiac, frustrated liar of a Fioroni," added the honest thief, who had been confined to a mental institution three times.[7]

The other people's names did not remain hidden much longer. The roof was going up already when the *Professorino* made his tremendous confession.

The truth about Saronio came rushing out with everything else, unveiling a conspiratorial underworld of Dostoevskian sweep. The rich young engineer Saronio had been a militant Communist too, in the *Professorino*'s own secret group near the topmost level of The Organization. Several of The Organization's attractive and congenial leaders had invited him to dinner on the appointed night, sending him out into the hands of his abductors.[8] When the matter of raising money came up, Saronio himself had suggested two still richer kidnap candidates who lived right next door. To his superiors in The Organization, however, their own well-heeled comrade seemed a safer bet. They never told him so, and if they hoped he would get around to understanding it subjectively, their arrangements ruled that out objectively. In the deal they made to get him kidnapped, the professional bandits were going to collect nine-tenths of the expected eight-million-dollar ransom. Once Saronio had seen the villainous faces of his captors—"*Cicciobello*," say, or Foreign Legionnaire de Vuono—they would never have let him go alive, not with over $7 million at stake.

Shortly after Saronio disappeared, another militant young Communist, Alceste Campanile, was shot through the back of the head—a classic revolutionary execution. The radical left promptly blamed his death on the Fascist right. But his father fought desperately to prove that Alceste was murdered by "Red Fascists," his own comrades, because he knew too much about the Saronio case. As it turned out, Alceste had in fact seen some of the ransom notes and, guessing the rest, had been silenced.[9]

Deaths like these, chillingly reminiscent of the Mafia, were not uncommon. Yet another militant Communist had been found decapitated on a railroad track; a girl from the same movement had been shot through the heart in an empty field near Rome; a young man in the group had been taken for a ride by his comrades in Milan. All were accepted as suicides, by a public altogether unaware of the shadowy Organization behind them.

The anguish of this knowledge was almost certainly what made Carlo Fioroni talk at last. He felt morally obliged to expose "those who are no longer 'misguided comrades' but political delinquents," he said.

His confession made him the Joe Valachi of Italy's revolutionary underground. He supplied names (150 for a start), places, dates, many soon verified and others only too plausible as the pieces fell into place. Public shock was all the greater because so much of what he said had been known all along. Key figures in The Organization had been arrested and released time and again. Telltale evidence gathered in hundreds of trials and interrogations lay around everywhere in official archives. The Organization itself had announced its intentions at every step of the way, in publications on sale in any left-wing bookshop.

"Widespread public disbelief, a perverse cultural habit of showing more comprehension for the violent than for the victims of violence, the fear of using a punitive judiciary to strike at the citizen's inviolable rights and the fundamental values of democratic life—all this made for a weak and uncertain response," wrote Judge Achille Gallucci, directing the court's investigation in Rome. "The blueprint for subversion grew under everyone's eyes, feeding . . . on the tolerance of the system it was undermining." [10]

The Red Brigades were just the tip of the iceberg. They had hogged the headlines for years, with their quartets of spruce and smiling young men and women, firing their Skorpions and Kalashnikovs into the knees, hearts, faces, heads, and backs of lawyers, judges, journalists, politicians, factory managers, shop foremen, and policemen, all but the last unarmed. But it is no trick nowadays to kill a man and melt away, once you get the hang of it.

What matters is the before and after: money, weapons, drill, documents, reconnaissance, deep security, safe havens at home and abroad, popular tolerance, political collusion. No terrorist underground can survive long without a massive flanking movement to help out with this. The German terrorists couldn't last out the decade for the lack of one. The Italians had a whole Second Society to count on.

They called it the Autonomous Area. It was big enough to take care of them all—the Red Brigades, the equally murderous Front Line, the Armed Proletarian Nucleus, the two hundred fly-by-night armed bands changing names weekly to convey the impression of an inexorably advancing guerrilla army.

Nothing like it could exist anywhere else, not only because Italy has been relentlessly misgoverned for thirty years—so have a lot of other countries—but because no other country has anything comparable to the political territory vacated by the West's largest Communist Party. The Party had been growing steadily since World War II, when, after twenty years of fascism, Italy had gone on to thirty years of democratic but sclerotic governments, falling once a year with depressing regularity. The country's swift postwar transformation from a predominantly agricultural to a highly industrialized society had created raw social scars, enormous economic deformities, and Western Europe's most radical working class.

Though the Communist Party was largely responsible for radicalizing the workers, it could not lead them to revolution; Stalin had put a stop to that at Yalta. Inevitably, Party leaders moved instead toward government partnership, a proposition known since 1973 as the "historic compromise." The policy was alluring to the middle class—thirty-four percent of the electorate voted Communist in 1976—but the Party's rank and file was not at ease. An estimated one of every three Party members had never renounced violent Marxist revolution in their hearts. (They were called "the Afghans" in 1980, for their pigheaded endorsement of the Russians' invasion of Afghanistan, condemned by their own Party leaders.) In effect, that made their Party open-ended leftward.

For Marxists already far out on the left, the chances of

"recuperating" this leviathan Communist force for revolution opened dazzling prospects. The Red Brigades frankly considered destruction of Italy's Christian Democratic regime as merely "an intermediate objective," a "necessary premise" for the Communist Party's "historic turn"—or return—to its classic revolutionary role.[11] The real Enemy, for the Brigades, was not the Christian Democrats but Communist Party Secretary Enrico Berlinguer and his "Berlingueriani," selling out the working class in their pursuit of ministerial portfolios.*

Every advance in the Party's purposeful march toward the government thus enlarged the empty space to its left, skillfully turned into a vast privileged sanctuary for Italy's terrorist forces.

The subtle brain behind this operation, said Carlo Fioroni, was a celebrated political science professor in Padua. Antonio Negri, "Toni" to his thousands of reverent followers, had risen

---

* This is the primary clue to the Red Brigades' strategy in the Aldo Moro case. With his unique influence over the Christian Democratic Party he headed, Moro was the only politician capable of carrying his ruling party into its first formal government partnership with the Italian Communist Party—by now the "Berlinguerian" Party—since 1948. After two months of exquisitely intricate negotiations early in 1978, the Christian Democrats did form a government with official Communist backing. It was to appear before Parliament for a vote of confidence on the very morning in March when Moro was abducted. He was on his way to the Chamber of Deputies for this debate when Red Brigade commandos ambushed his car on a busy Roman thoroughfare, gunned down his five bodyguards, and dragged him off in a van that swiftly melted into the traffic. Despite a frantic nationwide manhunt, the Brigades' hideout was never found. Fifty-five days later, they left Moro's bullet-ridden body in the back of a stolen car, halfway between the headquarters of the Communist and Christian Democratic parties. The message could hardly have been clearer. Moro, architect of the grand new Catholic-Communist alliance, had paid the price for thus diverting the Italian Communist Party from its classic revolutionary course. The Grand Alliance won its vote of confidence on that turbulent day in March but was unmistakably doomed—it barely lasted out the year. In this historic sense, the Red Brigades' judicious choice of victim and timing certainly brought them a victory of epic proportions.

to Continental fame as the headman in a seemingly headless body of collectives calling themselves Organized Autonomy, Workers' Autonomy, Armed Autonomy, Armed Workers' Autonomy, or just Autonomy; he was in jail already on some twenty-seven charges having to do with armed subversion. His arrest on April 7, 1979, with twenty collaborators, had sent shockwaves through the New Left of all Europe.

Accused of subversion along with him were some of the biggest names in the generation of 1968: Franco Piperno ("Saetta"), Oreste Scalzone, Luciano Ferrari-Bravo. All had been revolutionary Marxists since their teens and leaders of the now extinct Potere Operaio, but none was known to have picked up a gun. Cultivated, ardent, implacably committed to the destruction of capitalism, they were all attractive and intelligent spokesmen of the New Left. Toni Negri—gaunt, electrically intense, almost stammering in his high nervous voice to keep up with the excited speed of his thoughts—was the one they all deferred to.

At the time of his arrest, Negri was an anti-institutional institution at the University of Padua and, in Paris, as guest lecturer at the Sorbonne. His many academic works, written in "a kind of impenetrable intellectual shorthand" according to the British left-wing historian Eric Hobsbawn, were the height of fashion in Europe's radical circles. His book *Marx Beyond Marx*, his lectures on the "Gundrisse" of Karl Marx, his theories on Communism as "nonwork and subjective-collective-proletarian planning to suppress exploitation" were treasured texts in his admiring circle. Where his friend and benefactor Giangi Feltrinelli had longed to be the Castro of Europe, Toni Negri plainly saw himself as its Lenin.

He made no secret of his belief in armed insurrection, the more violent the better. "Violence is the auroral, immediate, vigorous affirmation of the necessity for communism," he wrote in *Marx Beyond Marx*. "A live animal, ferocious with its enemies, savage in its considerations of itself and its passions— that's how we like to foresee the constitution of a communist dictatorship," he wrote in 1978, in his *Dominion and Sabotage*.[12]

He didn't deny himself the pleasure of saying he was a

terrorist either, until his arrest. Privately, he made no bones about it. ("Maybe that is why I can be a terrorist," he wrote in a letter later confiscated.) [13] Publicly, he would allude to it in more elliptical prose, with something like sexual excitement. "Nothing better reveals the enormous historic positivity of the workers' self-valorization than this role of the sniper, the saboteur, the deviant, the criminal that I find myself living," he wrote in *Dominion and Sabotage*. "Whenever I pull on my *passamontagna* [a knitted face-mask worn by terrorists and mountain climbers], I feel the heat of the proletariat. Nor does the eventual risk offend me: it fills me with a feverish emotion, as if I were waiting for a lover. . . ." [14]

But these were just expressions of opinion, he asserted, surely no crime in one of the freest countries of the West. Was this renowned intellectual figure being prosecuted for his opinions? Was he merely a thinker and dreamer, or a doer? Carlo Fioroni, in at the birth of The Organization, said he was both. If only in exquisitely textured, sometimes indecipherable, phrases, Toni Negri had often implied as much himself.

The case is still in court as I write, necessarily limiting conclusions of guilt or innocence. What follows here is material largely drawn from the documented charges made against him and a 350-page volume published by the April 7 Committee in his defense.

The Organization was born in a back room in Rome on September 26, 1971. Out front, raucous delegates to a Potop congress shouted their ritual imprecations against capitalist imperialism. But Potere Operaio, whose membership had never exceeded half of one percent of the Italian student population, was on the skids. Italy was still sinking under its social and political afflictions, worsening if anything since the 1968 student uprising. But after two or three years of *contestazione*, more and more contesters were either opting for conventional left-wing parties or dropping out of politics. While Potop's rowdy rank and file let off steam, therefore, cooler heads went behind closed doors to ponder the Ishutin Solution.

Few delegates had ever heard of Ishutin and his Organization, still fewer of his particular Hell; no majority could have been mustered among them for the latter, even in Potop. But the delegates were not told about Hell and its terrorist devils. They were simply asked to establish Potere Operaio as "the party of insurrection," mainly engaged in agitation and propaganda. Someday, came the word from the back room, it would go on to become "the Armed Party"—"as intrinsic a consequence as Jesus Christ to the Father, and the Holy Ghost to both," explained Toni Negri. Nevertheless, "the thematic of militarizing the movement," though "absolutely fundamental to its credibility," would have to wait until the masses were ready, Negri said.[15]

Ready or not, though, the masses were getting a shove. The inner circle around Toni Negri at the Potop congress—Piperno, Scalzone, several others among those arrested eight years later, and Carlo Fioroni himself—had decided that "militarization" had to start at once. "Violence will be imposed upon us, and it's best that we start now to prepare our response," said one of the future defendants (Mario Dalmaviva). "The problem of militarization must be resolved here and now," said another (Emilio Vesce, future editor of the Red Brigades' *ControInformazione).*[16] "Expropriation is not enough, comrades. We pronounce ourselves for militarization and the seizure of power," said Piperno. "The themes of expropriation . . . and militarization are absolutely conjoined," said Negri himself.[17] It was all recorded on tape.

What actually happened at the Potop congress is suggested in a Red Brigades' self-interview made a few weeks after the congress ended (confiscated in a safe-house of theirs in 1979). "The transformation of the political vanguard into the *political-military* [italics mine] vanguard has in fact begun," the document said. "In practice, we can now realize the unity of revolutionary forces, the armed proletarian organization." [18]

Without a word to the congress's delegates, Potop's inner circle had in fact set up a secret military arm. Franco Piperno, as "Saetta," wrote to Feltrinelli two months later, confirming their agreement for a joint underground military command in the north. The first military commander of Potop's Illegal Works Department, as it was called, was Valerio Morucci, who went on to become Rome column commander for the Red Brigades. (He was arrested in 1979, with the Skorpion that killed Moro.) After changing names several times, the Illegal Works Department ended up as the deadly Front Line in 1976.[19]

Potere Operaio didn't last long. As the vision of Hell grew increasingly vivid, the better half of its remaining members backed away. It dissolved itself in 1973.

By then, The Organization had a new political arm in the emerging Autonomous Collectives and a secret array of terrorist cadets. None of these fledgling terrorist bands came to much as yet nor did the Red Brigades themselves. No Italian had even been kneecapped, and Italy's first political murder was a good year ahead. Evidently, Italian workers were not ready for violent insurrection. As Negri put it, the Autonomists would have to supply "traction" for the masses.

Autonomy's Marxist program of agitation and propaganda had been drafted secretly even before Potop folded. It combined irreproachable workers' demands—housing, jobs, higher wages, lower household utility bills—with ravishingly reckless proposals for "zero work," absenteeism, industrial sabotage, "beating up political adversaries," "destabilizing the schools," "aggravating street demonstrations" by sending in "public-order squads" armed with P .38s, and "proletarian expropriations" (as in supermarket holdups). The whole list, eventually carried out to the letter, was found by the police in 1972.[20] That was filed and forgotten too.

What with glamorous New Left thinkers, learned seminars, trendy international conferences, counterculture bookshops, and a chain of private broadcasting stations, a program like that could pick up a lot of traction. Thousands of Italian radicals (perhaps as many as 200,000) were drawn into an Autonomous Area where they could practice "proletarian illegality" just enough to intimidate the state but not enough to be criminalized and outlawed—so they thought.

Actually, they were getting criminalized step by step, coaxed along from innocent acceptance to guilty compliance as terrorist formations raised their sights.

What could be wrong, in 1971 or 1972, with a little arson here and a bomb or two there? Who could blame the fellows who went on to a quickie snatch of a factory manager, draping a sign around his neck that read BITE AND RUN—PUNISH ONE, INSTRUCT A HUNDRED!? Was it so bad, then, to kidnap a company executive and publish his photograph with a pistol held to his head?

Before the masses knew it, they were in traction, as the same fellows went on to capturing and interrogating "People's Prisoners," to killing an Establishment judge, to kneecapping an unaccommodating editor, to abducting and murdering Italy's leading statesman, to "shooting into the heap" at miscellaneous targets, to martial assault in full drill, taking 110 hostages in an institute for managers, and machine-gunning ten in a row.

This last happened to be a Front Line operation, while the Red Brigades had handled the Moro affair. There was a difference in strategy. The elite, militarist Red Brigades operated independently of the masses, whereas Front Line's terrorism was supposed to derive from, and reflect, the proletarian will. Negri, speaking after his arrest of his "profound, ample, reasoned rejection of armed struggle in any form," [21] nevertheless did distinguish between the two.

While strongly critical of the Red Brigades on occasion, he had never criticized Front Line. (When seven armed workers from Front Line were arrested, for instance, Workers' Autonomy defended them hotly as "comrades fallen into the enemy's hands.") [22] "What must be fought in the terrorists' position is certainly not the use of violence," Negri declared. "The aspect of terrorism to be fought is the programmatic will which does not establish an organic relation between the subjectivity of workers' power and the subjectivism of the use of violence" was his characteristic way of expressing it.[23]

For all their differences, the Red Brigades' Renato Curcio and Autonomy's Toni Negri met secretly several times to discuss stages in the escalation of violence. (Fioroni was present, and several other witnesses confirmed it.) [24] The last meeting Fioroni knew about was in the summer of 1974, when the two leaders discussed an expected leap to armed insurrection by autumn.[25] (This was when Petra Krause and Sergio Spazzali obtained forty-two devastating panzermines from the Swiss takeout service for their left-wing Italian comrades.)

The outcomes of such talks were reported faithfully in the

Red Brigades' *ControInformazione*, godfathered by Negri himself, and Autonomy's *Rosso*.[26]

The underlying strategy was mapped out in dozens of secret documents, stashed away by Negri and his associates, confiscated in 1979. Many were written or annotated in Negri's own hand, defining his ultimate intention "to destroy democracy and build a dictatorship of the proletariat," by "articulating the program of Autonomy towards an irreversible deepening and enormous extension of the civil war." [27]

The strategy was a huge success. In the congenial atmosphere of an Autonomous Area contiguous to the terrorists' own, a Red Brigade or Front Line gunman could easily be presented as an honest if occasionally misguided revolutionary comrade. (Autonomy's *Rosso* summed up "congenial" terrorist acts until 1977 as attacks on carabinieri, judges, and Christian Democratic or neo-Fascist MSI [Italian Social Movement] headquarters, popular expropriations, and beatings of university professors—all parts of the "coagulant of the movement's subjective energy," including the "heroic battle of avant-garde comrades in the Red Brigades." [28] Killing off the captive Aldo Moro was misguided, on the other hand.)

Seven or eight years of this not only assured a title of legitimacy to the Italian terrorists, it established their claim to the Mafia rule of *omertà*: a conspiracy of silence. Practically all the nation's intellectuals and any number of upright citizens became the terrorists' involuntary accomplices. Civilized and socialist-minded people do not betray an honest comrade, however misguided.

The Organization's secret military arm could thus shoot up in luxuriant hothouse growth. Carlo Fioroni, with Feltrinelli until the latter's death early in 1972, and then Potop's underground military commander for the Italian north, could watch it all happening from the earliest days: the days when Feltrinelli didn't yet have a safe-house to call his own, when his GAP gave the Red Brigades their first hundred pounds of dynamite, and Potop's Illegal Works Department had to send Fioroni himself begging to Renato Curcio for a couple of guns. They were years of fantastic but hardly spontaneous growth.

The Organization's first momentous move was to hook into the international circuit. Feltrinelli, who knew everybody and could foot the bills, was just getting the circuit going on the Continent around 1971. His own Zurich *centrale* was succeeded by Potop's "International Office" there, which became a Secretariat for International Coordination.[29] From its headquarters in the Eco-Libro Bookshop, the secretariat ran a Europe Project to promote the Ishutin Solution on a Continental scale: "to organize . . . both faces of armed violence, the violence of the masses on the one hand and . . . red terror on the other," in Negri's words.[30] A branch line also ran to the Middle East, where twenty-four multinational terrorists were arrested in 1978, trying to break up the first Cairo round of Egyptian-Israeli peace talks.[31]

By the time the Italian courts caught up with all this, The Organization was "in close and permanent contact" with the German Baader-Meinhof Gang, the IRA, the Spanish Basques' ETA, the French ultra-left underground, all the Palestinian terrorist formations, and the exiled Tupamaros.[32] All these and four or five other armed groups (including the Black Panthers) held their first summit in Florence, in October 1971. Toni Negri was the keynote speaker at this Feltrinelli-Potop gathering in the Jesuits' Stensen Institute.[33] Seamus Costello of the IRA took up the delegates' first day, discussing urban guerrilla tactics and sabotage. The next was spent on weapons supply and liaison arrangements. Recurrent summits, regularly denied by host-country governments, were held all over the map thereafter, from Beirut and Tripoli to Dublin and Belgrade.

The international circuit was not, or not merely, an expression of romantic revolutionary indulgence. It was an elementary necessity. All of Europe's armed groups needed somewhere to hide in a hurry, for one thing. The Italians kept open house for fugitives from all over the Continent, Germany especially, and the courtesy was returned. Feltrinelli did the same with his villa in Prague, as did Henri Curiel, who reserved two hideouts specially for the Italians in Paris. The Organization maintained fully stocked logistic bases for Italians abroad in Switzerland, Germany, and France (where, by 1978, Toni Negri was thinking of setting up a Hot Red Line telephone service).[34] The Palestinians could claim shelter from any of the Europeans in the circuit and vice versa.

The circuit was also indispensable for weapons, especially when everybody was starting from scratch. The Swiss anarchists' takeout service was invaluable in those early years, particularly once Petra Krause took it in hand. The *Professorino* himself was sent up to Zurich for some of the hot merchandise. The national commander of Potop's Illegal Works Department, Valerio Morucci, went too.[35] Roberto Mander, who helped to get the Swiss service going in 1971, became a frequent caller on behalf of his Autonomous Collective in Rome.[36] They all kept getting arrested, and released.

Meanwhile, nobody seemed to be looking as The Organization went about learning to use its weapons. Strangers came; Italians went. Feltrinelli brought in German instructors for his GAP boot camps in the Piedmont mountains. Autonomy's occult armed bands brought in Palestinian-trained instructors for their own camps, scattered around the Italian north and southern Switzerland. Toni Negri sent a personal emissary to Lebanon to negotiate accommodations for his trainees in the Middle East, as Feltrinelli had done before him.[37] A hundred Italians trained in one or another Palestinian camp in the 1971–72 season and about a thousand flocked to Lebanon in 1975 for the Battle of Tal-el-Zatar.[38]

A substantial number also trained in Czechoslovakia, though nobody could be sure of that until the decade was out.

Throughout those critical ten years, Italian authorities had carefully overlooked nagging rumors about the transfer of Soviet expertise to an Italian terrorist nucleus. Two or three Red Brigades leaders were known to have spent time in Prague, as Feltrinelli had. But the aristocratic Red Brigades were particularly haughty in rejecting the notion that any foreigner could ever have had anything to teach them. Just once, long ago, Renato Curcio had mentioned carelessly (to a People's Prisoner he was interrogating) that "some of us learned our guerrilla tactics abroad."

Just where they had gone abroad was eventually established by General Jan Sejna, for one. The former secretary-general of Czechoslovakia's Defense Ministry and military counselor to the Communist Central Committee, who had defected to the United States in 1968, gave a first-hand account of Soviet training facilities in Czechoslovakia to an American writer in January 1980.[39] Starting in 1964, he said, the KGB ran a school for terrorists in Karlovy Vary, while GRU provided more intensive paramilitary training at the Doupov parachutist camp near Prague. Trainees came from "all over Europe and the Third World," he said. He provided his own handwritten list of twelve Italians who had attended, apart from Feltrinelli himself. Among the names were four of the Red Brigades' ten original founders, two widely known leaders in Autonomy, and one of the three top leaders of the 1968 national student uprising.[40] In a later interview, General Sejna added that Toni Negri had attended a special leadership course in Czechoslovakia in 1966–67.[41]

That alone should have gotten the Italian terrorist underground off to a good start. But there was more. Again in 1980, a repentant Red Brigader of topmost rank also decided to talk. Arrested that spring, Patrizio Peci had been the Red Brigades' Turin column commander and a member of their high strategic command. His sensational confession put even Carlo Fioroni's in the shade, providing information that would land four hundred Italian terrorists behind bars, decimate the Red Brigades, and virtually wipe out Front Line.

Peci covered a lot of ground, in a confession running to four full-length, closely printed newspaper pages. One thing he said was that Red Brigaders had "continued to go to Czechoslovakia for training all through the seventies." They had also received quantities of Czech weapons, he added: pistols, machine guns, grenades, shipped from Prague by way of Hungary and Austria.[42]

That single blow might have been enough to send an ordinary Italian reeling. On top of it came still more spectacular disclosures of the whole Italian underground's entangling international alliances. By the late seventies, Peci said, "All the arms reaching the Italians, of whatever make or provenance, save those taken from policemen and carabinieri, were coming from a single distribution center stocked by Palestinian formations." [43]

He described two leisurely yachting trips made to the Middle East by the Red Brigades' Rome column commander, Mario Moretti, to shop for arms. Without even landing in Lebanon, Moretti took on large weapons consignments at sea, in the summers of 1977 and 1979. The first time, he brought back the Skorpion used to kill Moro six months afterward. Returning from the second trip, he offloaded in Mestre, the industrial port of Venice, and parceled out the weapons—grenades, explosives, heavy "Energa" antitank mines, machine guns, SAM-7 Strela missiles—to various terrorist formations in Italy and to the IRA, the Spanish Basques, and various German terrorist formations.[44]

The arms, unmistakably coming from George Habash's PFLP, were also unmistakably reaching not just The Organization's occult military arm but its open political arm in Autonomy. Shortly after midnight, on November 8, 1979, one of Autonomy's noisiest leaders in Rome, Daniele Pifano, was caught traveling with two Strela missiles in the quiet Adriatic resort town of Ortona. The missiles, nailed tightly into a chest, were hidden under the floormat of a Peugeot station wagon driven by one of his two Roman companions. They claimed to have found the box somewhere along the *autostrada* and thought the Strelas were telescopes.

It turned out, though, that one of them was carrying the phone number of the PFLP's agent in Italy: a Jordanian with a South Yemeni passport, Saleh Abu Anseh, who was also rushing toward the scene. The captain of the cargo ship *Sidon*, flying the Panamanian flag but a well-known Mediterranean gunrunner for the Palestinians, had happened to call the same PFLP agent from the port of Ortona that night. The *Sidon* pulled out of port at first light, and vanished. The Jordanian-South Yemeni Saleh Abu Anseh went to jail with Pifano and the others. The PFLP, outraged, wrote a formal letter to the Italian government and the Chieti court trying Pifano demanding everybody's immediate release on "moral grounds." They were just giving the Palestinians a helping hand, the letter said.[45]

(Pifano too claimed later that he had merely been helping his Palestinian comrades. A hundred "disgusting lies" had been invented about the Strelas, he said; they were "exclusively defensive arms," used by popular liberation movements like the Vietnamese, the Angolans, the Eritreans, the Palestinians.[46] He did not mention the Strelas used by Joshua Nkomo's Rhodesian Patriotic Front to shoot down two Rhodesian passenger planes in flight, in 1978, killing all passengers. "If it was a missile, it was our chaps" were Nkomo's memorable words to a *Washington Post* reporter on that occasion.[47])

The cumulative effect of all these revelations on the Italian public was shattering. On top of everything else came Fioroni's devastating disclosures of The Organization's underworld connections.

The Organization had pressing money problems even with Feltrinelli alive. Rich as he was, the grand financier of the Italian revolution insisted that good revolutionaries had to pay their own way (as Stalin had in his youth, by robbing banks in Georgia). His own GAP set the example, with Italy's first terrorist kidnapping for money in 1971. In enlisting convicts and drug addicts for that job, he set a lasting precedent. "For the cause, anything goes!" he had decreed.[48]

The question, Negri reportedly confided to Fioroni, was how to set up an "informal" structure with "Mafia productivity" to bring the money in. How else, if not with the Mafia itself? A fifty-fifty split with crooks became standard practice. Increasingly versatile terrorists and convicts between them stole priceless paintings; held up banks; robbed factory payrolls at gunpoint; operated a Kidnapping, Inc., service to abduct wealthy businessmen; and even kidnapped a champion racehorse. (As the horse was getting too old to race, his owners never paid the $300,000 ransom.) [49]

The Mafia's Calabria branch, the 'Ndrangheta, practically bought into The Organization. Home clan of Foreign Legionnaire de Vuono, the 'Ndrangheta was on intimate terms with all concerned. It got its split from the Red Brigades' $2.5 million ransom (paid to redeem the millionaire shipbuilder Angelo Costa), which was intended to finance the Moro operation.[50] It had a lucrative deal going with Unity of Communist Combat

(UCC), a terrorist unit specializing in armed robbery for all the other terrorist units. (Together, the UCC and 'Ndrangheta pulled off a picaresque raid on the sporting Club Méditerranée on the Calabrian coast, netting upward of $2 million in cash and jewels, and a bonus of three hundred foreign passports.)

Toward the end of the seventies, The Organization's own Front Line and the 'Ndrangheta were chummy enough to hold a joint chieftains' meeting for an overview, at the deluxe Calabrian summer resort of Tropea.[51] (They sent picture postcards.)

At the decade's close, The Organization had reached the last stage but one. It was awash in financial liquidity. Its arsenals were crammed with the latest modern weapons. It had an impregnable fortress at Toni Negri's University of Padua, where professors unacceptable to Autonomy were beaten with bicycle chains, spit at, shot at, burned or bombed out, and howled down. Elsewhere in the country, it had strong political fortifications in most big cities, manned by thousands of truculent Autonomists who had the Establishment buffaloed.

The exponential curve of violent civic disorder was rising steeply. "Zero work" and industrial sabotage were spreading through the big northern factories, especially at Fiat, where proletarian justice had taken the lives of three company executives and kneecapped nineteen others. The schools were splendidly destabilized. "Dispersed terrorism" was spreading to the provinces, running the nationwide assassination score up to 116 in seven years. Despite setbacks—more than 500 ultra-left terrorists were in jail before the big police crackdown, after which the figure doubled—there were 2,750 terrorist assaults in Italy in 1979, claimed by 215 "leftist" groups. The Red Brigades, Front Line, Organized Proletarian Communists, Armed Proletarian Squads, and other usual fly-by-nights were still going strong; Workers' Autonomy bands were beginning to boast openly of having joined them.

From 1977 on, The Organization's open political arm began noticeably to merge with its submerged, occult one. Autonomous bands went underground, joining one of the fly-by-nights or Front Line.[52] The Red Brigades' growing estrangement from the Autonomous masses did not prevent their operative collaboration with Front Line (and vice versa). The two bands were swapping information, weapons, hideouts, strategic plans, and personnel, revealed in dozens of repentant terrorists' confessions by 1980.

It was just about time to bring up The Organization's submerged bottom, join its political and military branches, come out in the open with the Armed Party, and get on with the irreversible civil war.

Then Toni Negri and twenty other leaders of Autonomy were arrested. Scorching documents were published. Yet another twenty Autonomists were arrested. Superwitnesses broke a ten-year law of silence; Fioroni was only the first, followed by others of high and low rank, in the openly terrorist Red Brigades and Front Line and the still legitimate ranks of Autonomy. Thirty-three members of Autonomy in Padua went on trial, not for the crime of ideas but on seventy specific charges of armed violence, thefts, arson, planned incitement to mob riot. Three made full confessions; the others drew sentences up to seven years. For the first time a band of Autonomists were condemned by a court not only on precise criminal counts but for organized subversion.[53]

Italian terrorism did not thereupon come to a magical end, but its involuntary accomplices were pulled up short. Like the great auk of ancient legend, they began to fly backward to see where they had been.

They had been close to destroying Italian democracy. "I had the impression that the moment of final confrontation was near," said the Padua judge, Guido Calogero, who gathered the evidence leading to the Autonomy arrests. "Toward the end, Organized Workers' Autonomy abandoned its open mass struggle. Public demonstrations diminished noticeably, while violent nocturnal assaults mounted: shootings, Molotov cocktails, fires, Nights of Flame. New recruits were showing up more frequently in actions both of the Red Brigades and Front Line . . . an evident symptom of accelerated military practice. It seemed to me that we were facing one of the last possibilities for the democratic state to react against the terrorist offensives, that a tragic moment was approaching for the community—insurrection and civil war." [54]

It would not have been for an ennobling proletarian cause. There was no chance in Italy of a genuinely popular uprising. Italian workers, though the most militant in Europe, were not ground under the heel of an autocratic tsar; the working class was not about to storm the Winter Palace. "The last of the socialist revolutionaries are mistaking Italy of the 1980s for Russia of 1917," wrote a group of Red Brigade defectors toward the last—whereupon they were threatened by the Brigades' imprisoned leaders with "a good dose of lead." [55]

At most, The Organization could have hoped to reach a level of uncontainable guerrilla warfare, forcing the democratic government to behave like a police state. In Italy, as in Germany, Spain, Ireland, Turkey, and everywhere else since the Tupamaros set their first shining example in Uruguay, the ultra-left terrorists were dead on course for a right-wing dictatorship.

They may manage it still. Any angry young Italian can get to be a terrorist these days if he wants to. He has plenty of bands to choose from now, up-to-date, well stocked, and running regular beginners' courses, and he still has plenty to be angry about. The one thing he may no longer have is assurance of continuing popular acceptance and protection, as a "misguided comrade."

Nothing counted as much as that, in the long frightening decade of terrorist ascendancy in Italy. The country's eternally immobile governing class was naturally a help, as was a Communist Party alternately preaching "permanent conflictuality" in the factories and redemption through the historic compromise. But the secret of the terrorists' success lay in the decent, well-meaning citizens forming a protective Second Society around them.

"Listen! First we'll start unrest!" says the satanic Peter Verkhovensky in Dostoevski's *The Possessed*, written more than a century ago. "Do you know that, even now, we are terribly strong? We have people other than those who cut throats, set places on fire, go in for classical assassinations, and go around biting people. . . . I have them all at hand already. We have the teacher who makes the children entrusted to his care laugh at their God and at their families; we have the lawyer defending the well-educated murderer because he has reached a higher stage of development than his victims; the schoolboys who, to experience a strong sensation, kill a peasant, are also with us; the juries who acquit criminals are all working for us; the prosecutor torn by his anguished fear of not being liberal enough does us a service. Ah, we have so many high government officials with us, and so many literary figures who don't even know it themselves!"

12

TURKEY:
THE ANARCHY

"Violence is as Turkish as apple pie,"
said the American embassy counselor
in Ankara, reviewing the scene for
me—Turkish apple pie, it would be
kind to think he meant. The Turks do
have a violent streak. Their menfolk
often pack a gun as a badge of virility
and use it to defend their honor, or
settle a score, or merely celebrate a
happy event. Kurds fire their Kalashnikovs into the air at country wed-
dings. Marks of the same sheer
exuberance pepper the ceilings of the
Istanbul Hilton.

None of this has much to do with the ungovernable violence rampant in Turkey by the late seventies. "Crimes of
honor are obligatory in my country. But until the terror, we
Turks had never heard of premeditated murder," a leading
journalist in the capital told me. By "the terror," she meant
nine or ten premeditated murders a day, every day, 250 dead in
1977, 1,000 in 1978, 1,500 in 1979, 2,000 in the first half of
1980—the world's worst case of raging terrorist warfare.

But the world has just begun to notice. Until the military
coup of 1980, Turkey rarely rated more than a few paragraphs
on the inside pages of Western newspapers. Yet it was Islam's
last free society: a democratic island of forty-five million souls
in an Islamic sea of seven hundred million, the sole remaining
Moslem state to have authentic elections and multiple parties.
It is a strategic landmass of enormous importance, straddling
the Dardanelles at the eastern entrance to the Mediterranean.

With Western Europe's largest land army, it is indispensable to its NATO allies for the defense of southern Europe and the eastern Mediterranean. It has been coveted by Russia since the first tsars dreamed their first imperial dreams. It has been slated for political demolition since 1968, and doubly so since 1979, when neighboring Iran fell to Ayatollah Khomeini. At Khomeini's side in Teheran, within days of his victory, a leader of the Palestine Liberation Organization announced publicly that Turkey would be "next." [1] It may very well go next, though you would never know it from reading the Western press.

I have spent considerable time in Turkey on and off and once even drove across it from end to endless end. But nothing prepared me for the shock of my visit late in 1978. The *Turkish Daily News*, which I took up to my hotel room on arriving, carried a daily box score on the killings: five dead that night, six the next, eleven the third—young, old, men, women, right, left. On Mondays, the *News* would run a full-page weekly roundup on "The Anarchy," like this:

Nov. 6 Monday
Two die in the eastern province of Kars in rightist-leftist clashes.

Ali Akçam, wounded in coffee-house shooting in Adana, dies at hospital.

Two bodies recovered, one a woman, in Tarsus forests of Toros mountains.

Nov. 7 Tuesday
Mehmet Kalkan shot to death by unidentified persons in suburban Aktepe of Ankara. A girl, Elvan Güneş, who stabbed and wounded Yuksel Karagoz in the Sentepe district today, caught by police.

Three wounded in Istanbul when unidentified people opened fire on people waiting at a bus stop in Kakirköy region.

Eleven persons wounded in various anarchic incidents in Adana, Elbistan, Afyon, and Kayseri.

Five drunken policemen [rightist-inclined] demonstrated in front of prime minister's residence.

Nov. 8 Wednesday
Body found in Üsküdar, Istanbul. Two die in clashes in Adiyaman and Üsküdar. Five wounded in the incidents.

Nationalist Movement Party [rightist] local office bombed in Istanbul.

Nov. 9 Thursday
Erdoğan Gökbulut, Republican People's Party official [Socialist] shot and seriously wounded in Malatya.

Duran Caliminli died in Gaziantep, when gunmen opened fire while he was walking on street with father. Father seriously wounded.

Nov. 10 Friday
No important anarchic incidents were reported today.

Nov. 11 Saturday
Anarchy takes three lives today. Three armed persons killed owner of café in Eskişehir. The owner was strangled. In Istanbul, Sadettin Kazan died when gunman opened fire from a car. Four persons wounded in Istanbul. Student in Adana dies of gunshot wounds in hospital. . . .

"The Anarchy" seemed insanely shapeless, creeping into the interstices of Turkish life from every side. Masked gunmen might burst into a café, ask, "Are you rightist or leftist?," and mow down half the customers. Or, they might not ask, and mow them all down. A gunman might step up to the ground-floor window of a private flat and drill anybody sitting there watching television. Whole city neighborhoods were "liberated" by rightists or leftists, to be entered at mortal risk. Children having to cross hostile territory to get to school were escorted by police. ("What if you see a letter lying on the street?" a teacher asked her third grade class. "Don't touch! Could be bomb!" was the reply in chorus.)

Entire cities formed up sides, becoming closed citadels: Erzerum, near Turkey's border with Iran, was rightist; Kars, on the Russian border, was leftist. No one dared to journey from one to the other. Traveling on a bus through the countryside was a drama; just walking down a city street could become one, with machine-gun fire suddenly crackling across the road.

Rightist and leftist gunmen might shoot it out in a high-school classroom. ("Lie down on the floor and don't move," a teacher advised her class on such an occasion.) Policemen checked I.D. cards and searched for weapons at university gates and often sat in lecture halls to keep rightists and leftists physically separated. Student hostels, offering the only cheap lodgings for indigent youths from the provinces, were a nightmare of beatings, stabbings, and inquisitorial interrogations.

Armed bank robberies ran to about twenty a day, half of them "people's expropriations." Journalists, professors, tradesmen, high-school kids, might be found with their throats cut or bound tightly with wire, strangled, stabbed, mutilated, tortured, shot to death, and laid on railroad tracks. The victims seemed to be chosen at random. ("No, my wife and I haven't been threatened, because we don't take sides in politics," said an Istanbul professor I was visiting, whereupon the phone rang and a voice told his young schoolteacher wife: "All right, you bitch, you're dead.")

Killers under eighteen were in heavy use because Turkish law does not allow the death penalty for killers under eighteen. The prisons were full of them: 1,052 rightists and 778 leftists were in jail on terrorist charges when I was there, most of them below the legal age. Few seemed to have given much thought to ideology. "I am a rightist and I am opposed to leftists and Communists," a seventeen-year-old prisoner told Emel Anil of the Associated Press. "But I really don't know what rightist or leftist means. All I know is that my family ran away from the cruelty of communism [in Russian Turkestan] and Communists are bad." [2] Hundreds of such prisoners, asked why they were willing to kill and be killed for their cause, answered simply, "Because I'm anti-Communist" or "Because I'm anti-Fascist."

"What are fascism and communism?" the daily *Millyet* asked elementary-school children. "Curse words!" they replied.

I was not in the country to see the worst. A month after I left, "The Anarchy" reached its demented peak in the southeastern town of Karahmanmaras. It started during Christmas week of

1978, with a bomb in a right-wing theater, followed by the assassination of two left-wing schoolteachers, followed in turn by a mob of howling rightist-leftist rioters at the funeral. From that came "a week-long rampage of sectarian killing, raping, and looting which left 111 dead, several thousand injured, and hundreds of buildings reduced to smoking rubble," reported the Associated Press. The dead had been clubbed, shot in the stomach, set afire with gasoline-soaked rags, hacked to pieces with machetes.[3]

More than a thousand townspeople were arrested, leading to what is surely the century's most singular trial. Herded into a sunbaked arena in the provincial capital of Adana that summer were 807 defendants from the right and left both—men, women, children, policemen, teachers, students, artisans, farmers, a garbage collector, a judge, a Sunni Moslem imam, and two deaf mutes. The state prosecutor demanded the death sentence for 330 of them.[4] (Eight were condemned to death in August 1980.)

After Karahmanmaras, a left-leaning Republican Party government imposed martial law, largely blaming it on the right. Brought down by election reverses, the Republicans were replaced by a right-leaning Justice Party government, which retained the martial law and blamed the left. Both seemed to have a good case.

It was impossible by then to know who was behind "The Anarchy." No single strategic command could still be directing it. Terror was running amok. There were no solemn communiqués, explicit demands, ponderous Resolutions on Strategic Direction; nor did the choice of victims suggest any special effort to strike at the heart of the state, in the manner of Italy's Red Brigades. Policemen, army officers, judges, politicians were no more popular targets than anybody else. Those who were killing each other off seemed to have much the same background. They were mostly poor (though rightists tended to be poorer than leftists), jobless (youth unemployment ran to forty or fifty percent), and socially dislocated by Turkey's great exodus from the countryside to the cities in the sixties. All seemed caught in a closed circle, with rightists killing leftists who killed rightists who killed leftists to avenge their dead.

Leftists were also killing other leftists, vying for place among their multi-Marxist competitors. There were at least twenty-five Marxist revolutionary bands in Turkey when I was there, if not thirty-five or forty-five. Wherever I went, somebody would thrust yet another incomprehensible acronymic chart at me, tracing the lineage of assorted Stalinist, Leninist, Maoist, Trotskyite, and anarchist underground formations. A desperately lonely Albanian-inspired one was on especially murderous terms with its former Maoist allies. The Maoists themselves hated the pro-Soviet Marxists deeply enough to open fire at a May Day rally in 1977, killing thirty-four and wounding a hundred.[5] (One Maoist faction blamed another in that case, calling themselves respectively People's Way and Proletarian Revolutionary Brightness.)

The rightists had a clearer profile. It belonged to Colonel Arpaslan Turkeş, whose Nazi-style paramilitary Idealists were also known as the "Gray Wolves" and howled when their Leader came before them. The colonel was nothing if not plainspoken. "If anybody calls me a Fascist, I'll tear his mouth apart," he would say.[6] His followers did not haggle over ideology. Superpatriotism, "Turkishism," and anti-communism were enough for them.

The truth about these opposite extremes was unusually hard to get at, because there was so little middle to Turkish politics. One side's Good Guys were the other side's Bad Guys, as the two major parties took turns at governing the country. No sooner would one replace the other than it would suppress or leak selected secret-service reports; grant amnesty to the terrorists in jail and imprison a batch from the other side; purge the opposition's forces in the schools, the media, the ministries (especially the Interior Ministry). Editors caught in the political crossfire were gunned down. Current events were rewritten in the classroom, depending on which teachers' union and student cabal might have it in hand. Even the police had their rightist and leftist unions, the Pol-Bir and Pol-Der. To be "fair," they had to be sent out in pairs (one of each) when terrorist arrests were made. "Our police force is sick," admitted Republican premier Bulent Ecevit, before going under for perhaps the last time.

During Ecevit's year and ten months in office, the terrorist kill rate had more than quintupled (from less than one to over five a day). A decent and civilized left-wing democrat, he had started out in January 1978 believing that the right was at the bottom of all the nation's troubles. He was a much-chastened man when he stepped down.

There was no separating the Fascist right from the revolutionary Communist left in Turkey's spreading terror. Both were in it up to their necks, with the same sinister intent, and had been egging each other on for a good ten years. There wasn't much doubt about who started it, either. The left did.

More precisely, the Russians did. For invaluable clues in this case we are indebted to a defector from the KGB named Viktor Sakharov, whose documented story is told in John Barron's *KGB*.[7] A bright young man with five years of Arabic studies, Sakharov was sent to Yemen in 1967 to be broken in. He went on to Kuwait in 1968, as a full-fledged KGB agent. The KGB *rezident* there, who specialized in Turkish affairs, spoke no Arabic. Neither did the man from GRU, handling Russian military intelligence. A translator from the KGB Center was long overdue, causing a huge backlog in communications. Sakharov, asked to help out, had access to a fabulous store of information.

He was operating at the heart of the KGB's VIII Department, embracing the Arab states, Afghanistan, Iran, Yugoslavia, Albania, Greece, and Turkey. Agents' reports crossed his desk from all over the area. (They were actually written in invisible ink.) Accordingly, he was able to learn in detail about three major Soviet operations in his zone. They were:

1. to sabotage Saudi Arabia's oilfields and, if possible, dislodge its pro-Western monarchy;
2. to build terrorist cells in the Arab oil sheikhdoms around Kuwait and the Persian Gulf, notably Qatar, Bahrain, and Oman, offering scholarships and guerrilla training in the Soviet Union; and
3. to mount a "brutal campaign of urban terrorism, kidnapping, and assassination against Turkey."[8]

The going wasn't too easy in the sheikhdoms, whose rulers were deeply suspicious and extremely well informed. Still, eighty tribesmen did get off to Moscow from Qatar alone while Sakharov was around, to his knowledge. Oman's Dhofar tribesmen also began to shape up around then, for the ten-year siege to come. (The special camp reserved for them near Aden, in South Yemen, was set up in 1968.) The earliest Palestinian guerrillas got started then as well. But of the three major projects, Turkey's was the most advanced by far.

As NATO's farthest outpost in the Middle East, facing the Russians across the Black Sea and guarding the Dardanelles, Turkey was a very special Russian target. The Russians had come close to neutralizing if not annexing it just after World War II, when they were stopped short by the Truman Doctrine. They were in a better position to try again after 1960, when nearly half a century of rocklike Turkish stability came to an end.

Kemal Ataturk's extraordinary revolution had swept the Turks from a closed and medieval Islamic society to a Europeanized nation with parliamentary government by then. But Ataturk, though still revered, was dead; his political legacy had been squandered by a recklessly spendthrift and venal regime; and a patriotic army took over briefly in 1960 to set things straight. The army promised to restore civilian rule and, miraculously, kept its word. (Colonel Turkeş, bent on tough military rule even then, was sent off as ambassador to India to be kept out of mischief.) Though the democratic order was restored, however, the system was weakened at the core and never recovered its strength.

The convulsive change for the worse may be measured by the fact that not a single Turkish life was lost when the army took over in 1960. Indeed, the last straw for army leaders that year had been the death of two students—two—in demonstrations against a wildly corrupt and inefficient government. There would be no further political bloodshed until 1969, by which time the Russians had put in quite a lot of work.

Sakharov, who defected from his KGB post in Kuwait midway through 1971, had ample evidence of Russian penetration starting in the early sixties. It began when the KGB in Ankara recruited a few promising young Turks for training in Russia.

Back home, the freshly groomed Turkish agents recruited more radicals into a nascent terrorist movement. These were shipped secretly to Syria for guerrilla training. Ostensibly, they were going into Palestinian camps there. Actually, the arrangements were made for them by two KGB agents working out of the Soviet embassy in Damascus: Vadim A. Shatrov and the usual embassy "chauffeur" Nikolai Chernenkov.

From Syria, Turkey's terrorist cadets inevitably spilled over into other Palestinian camps from Lebanon and Jordan to South Yemen, to be taken in hand by George Habash and Wadi Haddad. University students in Ankara and Istanbul "would just disappear for three or four months and then just show up again," as an Ankara professor told me. By 1970, a group had already been caught in the act of mounting a terrorist hit, as they returned from training by way of Diyarbakir in eastern Turkey—on a straight line as the crow flies from Baghdad, Wadi Haddad's headquarters in Iraq. Year after year after that, Turkish graduates of Palestinian camps—Russian-supervised or the Habash-Haddad Front's—would be picked up as they made their way back home: in batches of ten or twelve, by boat or car, loaded down with Soviet-bloc weapons.[9]

Meanwhile, the KGB's Disinformation Department (Department A of the First Chief Directorate) was setting the scene for a high-priority campaign against the American-NATO presence in Turkey. Between 1966 and 1970, the Disinformation Department carried off three spectacularly successful forgery operations. One was a widely circulated book purportedly written by a Turkish senator, "proving" an American plot to undermine "progressive" Turkish politicians and strengthen right-wingers. Another document "proved" American interference to beef up rightist forces in the Turkish army. A third "proved" an American conspiracy with the ruling right-wing military junta in Greece to take over the half-Turkish island of Cyprus by military coup, annex it to Greece, and tack it on to NATO. This last was passed on to the Turkish Foreign Ministry as urgent intelligence information—by Soviet Ambassador Vasili Federovitch Grubyakov, a veteran KGB officer—with sensational results.

The combined effect might have led any red-blooded young

Turk to vow that Turkey would be "the graveyard of American imperialism," just as many a young Turk did. Few realize to this day that all three "documents" were egregious fakes.[10]

The anti-American riots breaking out on Turkish campuses in 1968 looked natural enough. Who wasn't rioting against the United States in 1968? The appearance of an inflammatory Marxist student organization called Dev Genç in 1969 looked natural too. Turkish students were bound to feel the pull of revolution, in a society wrenched from its rural and traditionalist Islamic moorings; struggling to pull abreast of industrial Europe; stricken with inflation, unemployment, corruption, and wretched shantytown slums. Yet the leap in a single year— from setting fire to the American ambassador's car on a campus in 1968 to a ready-made, professional underground terrorist apparatus by 1969—was a dead giveaway.

It wasn't long before Dev Genç showed unmistakable signs of prefabrication in structure, strategy, methods, slogans, litany, logistics. "A subtle change in the catchwords of students' public statements, meetings, boycotts, was observed during the late '60s, particularly since 1968. . . . Instead of merely deploring the situation in moderate terms, demands were voiced loudly and insistently and sometimes expressed by violent deeds," noted a widely respected scholar of Turkish affairs. Catchwords changed no less while in foreign affairs "the emphasis shifted from Cyprus to anti-imperialism, anti-Americanism, neutralism, foreign capital and the Vietnam War." [11]

Dev Genç's classic two-tiered form alone became a textbook model for the decade's urban guerrilla movements. (The Organization in Italy, the Provisional IRA, and ETA-Militar all followed suit a couple of years later.) An open political arm handled revolutionary propaganda, demanding a Leninist regime in place of parliamentary democracy.[12] An underground military arm got going right on schedule, with a "brutal campaign of urban terrorism, kidnapping and assassination against Turkey." [13]

The campaign was not a response to Fascist provocation; there was none to speak of in 1969. While Colonel Turkeş did set up his first youth camps around then, he was attracting a mere handful of Wolf Cubs, and he could barely muster the popular support to get a single deputy into parliament.[14] If his party was up to sixteen deputies by 1977, he had a lot to thank the terrorist left for. When he did turn his own right-wing terrorists loose in the early seventies, he could claim with reason to be responding to Communist provocation.

While Turkey had long since outlawed its official Communist Party, Dev Genç was the next best thing. An undeviating Marxist-Leninist movement, it was implacably hostile to NATO, unfailingly friendly to Russia, and devastatingly good at its job of destabilizing the NATO state closest to Russia's frontiers.

Several armed clandestine groups sheltered under the Dev Genç umbrella. The biggest, from then to now, was the Turkish People's Liberation Army (TPLA). Headed by an Istanbul law student named Denis Gezmis, the TPLA led the field in armed bank robberies, bloody clashes on campus, orchestrated mob violence, cop-strafings, bombings of public buildings and kidnappings (of NATO servicemen and an occasional Israeli diplomat). Its purpose was to force a right-wing military takeover, which it very nearly did within just two years. (It was during those same two years that the Tupamaros did the same thing in Uruguay, on the other side of the planet.)

Martial law was in fact imposed, on the insistence of Turkey's armed forces, in 1971 and continued until 1973. Civil liberties were suspended. Intellectuals were massively intimidated. Five thousand leftists were arrested, many on the flimsiest of charges. For a multitude of Turks hoping to straighten the country out by lawful political means, those were hard, black times. (In July 1980, the pro-Moscow Communist Dev-Sol, or Revolutionary Left, assassinated former premier Nihat Erim as "punishment" for his brief period in office in 1971. A moderate and widely respected Social Democrat, he was considered the only statesman who might have restored law and order at the time of his death.) [15]

The TPLA's own ranks were decimated. Two hundred and thirty of its members and helpers were put behind bars. Denis Gezmis was taken after a shootout with police, in one of several dozen terrorist safe-houses the authorities found—basements and garrets transformed into bunkers, stocked with fake documents and sophisticated electronics equipment from Eastern Europe, crammed with Kalashnikovs, revolvers, and grenades, largely Soviet-made. By April 11, 1973, the police had seized 4,457 guns and 4,646,220 rounds of ammunition.[16]

Wanted for a long list of capital crimes, Gezmis was tried and hanged. His nearest in rank, Mahir Cayan, died in a nine-hour shootout soon afterward. A fanatic Marxist, Cayan was also a psychopathic killer who, "as partial payment to the Palestinians," had kidnapped the Israeli consul in Istanbul, bound his hands behind him, and shot him in the back of the head. Jailed for that, he tunneled his way to freedom, kidnapped three NATO technicians, and held them hostage in a safe-house near the Black Sea. When police caught up with him and his gang of eleven accomplices, he shot all three hostages two hours before a bullet got him. "The road to revolution is enlightened and reddened with the blood of every guerrilla who fell here," he had scribbled on a crumpled piece of cardboard before dying.[17]

Between them, Cayan and Gezmis thus became legendary martyrs for the Turkish ultra-left. Dozens of young Turks are killed regularly in riots on the anniversary of their deaths.

They had guessed wrong about Turkey's armed forces. The nation's military leaders would not have tolerated a *right-wing* military takeover in 1971, any more than they would have done in 1960, or would be prepared to do in 1980. Nor were there any officers in sight who seemed tempted to have a go at it. If anything, the threat came from the opposite direction. Fifty-seven *leftist* army officers were expelled for plotting a takeover, when martial law was imposed.[18] Having helped to arm Marxist terrorists in the TPLA, they had intended to say they were responding to right-wing provocation.

Proof of the army's honorable intentions came in 1973, when martial law was lifted and national elections were held. A left-wing government headed by Bulent Ecevit was voted into power, under the army's benevolent eye. It lasted eight months—just long enough to invade Cyprus and grant amnesty to all five thousand leftists imprisoned under martial law. The innocent among them went back about their business. So did the professional terrorists.

The Turkish People's Liberation Army and its smaller associates dug deeper underground, built up enormous new arsenals of Soviet-bloc weapons (forty thousand guns were seized by police over the next four years), and tightened its ties with the Habash-Haddad Palestinian Front. By then, the TPLA was in Habash's innermost circle. A large contingent was installed in Paris for overseas operations, headed by Cayan's wife Gülten, sharing headquarters with Carlos in a suburban villa outside Paris.[19] (The French police rounded up their cell leaders midway through 1973, before they saw much action.)

The Palestinians had also worked assiduously inside Turkey under martial law to build up terrorist cadres. As Leila Khaled proudly announced to *Hurryet* on May 26, 1971, the Popular Front for the Liberation of Palestine was "sending instructors to Turkey in order to train Turkish youth in urban guerrilla fighting, kidnappings, plane hijackings, and other matters . . . in view of the fact that it is more difficult than in the past for Turks to go and train in PFLP camps abroad." The PFLP "has trained most of the detained Turkish underground members," she added.

The TPLA had not renounced its original strategic aim, and never would. It was to "rouse the peasant masses . . . and strike at local feudal elements, establishing revolutionary rule in some areas." Then, *"reactionary elements in the Turkish armed forces, together with foreign troops supporting imperialism, would have to intervene jointly.* [Italics mine.] A popular war would start. . . . The Enemy in rural areas would be repulsed into the sea, while urban guerrilla warfare would clean up the towns." [20] With luck, that should put Turkey right up there among the top ten of the world's potential one, ten, one hundred Vietnams.

That was still the TPLA's purpose in 1978, when I was last in Turkey. "The uncontrollable terrorist left is leading inexorably to military intervention," I was told by Professor Mumtaz Söysal, once the radical left's top intellectual guru. "I'm telling you this with a broken heart," said another dedicated Socialist professor. "We of the left would like to see purposeful acts. But the terrorists believe in forcing a military government, thus proving that the Turkish Republic has been Fascist since its inception and must be overthrown."

By then, it looked unnervingly like a self-fulfilling prophecy. Colonel Turkeş had seized his golden chance, in the first purposeful wave of left-wing terror. His Gray Wolves were out in force by the time martial law was lifted in 1973, doing more than their bit to get it reimposed five years later. Once the right-left spiral of violence was set in irreversible motion, the colonel's Nazi-style Nationalist Action Party surged ahead. By 1974, a right-leaning Justice Party government under Süleyman Demirel took in Turkeş, as vice-premier. He lost no time in packing the schools, media, police, and ministries with his own followers.

The terrorist left naturally retaliated. The two-way kill rate rose ineluctably. Right-wing military officers supplied weapons to right-wing killers, while the Soviet Union accelerated shipments to the leftists. Huge consignments of Soviet-bloc arms were smuggled in from Bulgaria, trucked overland or shipped by sea. On June 3, 1977, Turkish security forces stopped the Greek cargo vessel *Vasoula* in the Bosporus, coming from Varna, Bulgaria. She was carrying *sixty-seven tons* of armament. Some was going to the Greek leftist underground in Cyprus, where Greeks and Turks lived in a chronic state of war. But a good part was earmarked for the left-wing underground in Turkey.[21] The Turkish government's protests to Bulgaria got no further than such protests usually get.

The vicious circle of right-left violence was producing a corpse a day when Bulent Ecevit got back into office in 1978 (and a corpse an hour by the spring of 1980). Since the Marxist wing of his Republican Party was open-ended toward the terrorist left, however, he kept looking the other way. As if in a grotesque parody of a Mack Sennett comedy, out went Colonel Turkeş's Bad Guys and in came the Marxist Good Guys, recapturing the state machinery. Once again the schools, the media, the police, the ministries, were staffed by people who had eyes only for the threat from the right. "Obviously, there are some factions of the left as well who desire to overthrow the regime by armed struggle and prefer a Fascist regime to the existing government," said Ecevit's cultural affairs minister Ahmet Taner Kislali in the summer of 1978. "But these groups were pushed into this by the terror perpetuated by the right. . . ." [22]

While Premier Ecevit tried toward the end to correct his course, it was much too late. "The Anarchy" score was up to five corpses a day, and half the country was under martial law, when he was voted out of office in the autumn of 1979. Both extremes had swelled to frightening proportions. The extreme right used Ecevit's forbearance toward left-wing terror to "prove" that Turkey was going Communist, and so justify its own terror. The extreme left, far from behaving better under his indulgent rule, simply grew bolder. So did the Russians, who could see Turkey slipping off its tenuous perch at the outermost edge of NATO. So did the Palestinians, who had only to seize the Egyptian embassy in Ankara for a few days to establish their triumphant ascendancy.

Ecevit's government not only surrendered at once in that siege, agreeing to formal recognition of the Palestine Liberation Organization; his interior minister actually embraced and kissed the Palestinian terrorists as they came out of the building.[23] It was a curiously ingenuous display, in a country whose terrorist left had been groomed by the Palestinians for a decade to overthrow its democratic government—a government publicly marked for slaughter by the Palestinians themselves.

Volumes might be read into that short ominous phrase pronounced by the Palestine Liberation Organization's spokesman in Teheran when Iran had fallen to Ayatollah Khomeini. "Turkey will be next," he said. Next what?

He was talking about Turkey under Bulent Ecevit, whose left-of-center government bore a growing resemblance to the late Salvador Allende's in Chile.[24] The Ecevit government was cold to NATO, ill at ease with the United States, distrustful of "Western financial imperialism." (The Gnomes of Zurich and the International Monetary Fund were its new demons, urging stern austerity to check an eighty-percent inflation rate.) Ecevit's New Defense Concept was based on the assumption that the Soviet Union was no longer a serious threat to Turkey.

He had made open advances to the Kremlin and allowed Soviet warships to call in at a Turkish port for the first time in forty years (provoking outraged Maoists into a three-day riot). He had turned to Colonel Qaddafi of Libya for rescue from a yawning multi-billion-dollar deficit. And his government was on cordial terms with the Palestinians themselves. Where was Turkey supposed to go "next"?

It could hardly go the way of Iran. Turkey had no despotic shah to be overthrown, no fabulous oil wealth to redivide, nothing comparable to the religious sentiment behind Iran's Islamic Revolution. Turkish Moslems had been living with Kemal Ataturk's Westernizing revolution for well over half a century. They had also been living fairly peaceably with each other, though three out of four were Sunni Moslems, and the rest Shi-ites of the same sect dominating Iran. If the minority Shi-ites were more inclined toward the left and the Sunni majority toward the right, there had been no serious friction between them until the previous year—deliberately incited by the terrorists on both sides. Nor did the Turkish electorate tend to vote along religious lines. The only party making a main point of its Islamic faith polled barely sixteen percent of the national vote.

Yet the Palestinians were certainly planning a massive assault on Turkey. Ecevit could not help but notice a steady infiltration of heavily armed Palestinian guerrillas, hooking up with the Turkish underground and fanning out toward the eastern regions bordering on Iran. "There are foreign elements who want to start a movement in Turkey similar to that in Iran," he said, tactfully not naming names.[25] What the foreign elements wanted to start was inflammable religious and ethnic warfare in the remote eastern provinces, orchestrated with urban violence. There were damning documents to prove it at NATO headquarters in Brussels when I stopped by in the spring of 1979.

But far more incriminating evidence would come from the Habash Front itself. On April 8, 1980, the Front sponsored a press conference in a catacomblike hideout deep inside the ancient Casbah of Sidon, Lebanon. A dozen men and two women muffled in black hoods with slits for eyes were presented as "Armenian guerrillas and Kurdish insurgents in Turkey" who had "joined hands in a common struggle against the Turkish government" (the conservative Süleyman Demirel's again, by now). Ringed by Palestinian gunmen armed with Kalashnikovs, they announced their intention of "mounting military operations against the Turkish authorities until the regime falls and Armenian and Kurdish aspirations are fulfilled." They claimed to speak for an "Armenian Secret Army of Liberation" and a "Kurdistan Workers' Party"; emphasized their links with Marxist Palestinian formations; and "had only praise for the Soviet Union, blaming the United States for what they described as provoking the Soviet intervention in Afghanistan," reported *The New York Times*.[26]

It was the first anybody had ever heard of a Kurdish "insurgency" in Turkey. Till then, no "Armenian Secret Army of Liberation" had ever raised its head on Turkish soil either.

The Secret Army had indeed been heard from in Europe, where it specialized in the double bomb—one timed to go off several minutes after another on a busy street, to catch the crowd drawn by the first explosion. But none of Europe's Armenian communities knew a thing about the bomb throwers. Nor was there a sign of their Palestinian connections until the Palestinians were obliging enough to provide it.

True to form, Habash had been training his Armenian wards in Lebanon and South Yemen for years, along with his Kurds. But he'd had trouble placing both. Turkey's seven or eight million Kurds are fully integrated, generally regarded as loyal citizens, mercifully free of the ethnic grievances eating at fellow Kurds across the borders in Iraq and Iran. Until a Kurdish separatist movement could be invented in Turkey, Habash's Kurds simply operated with all the other Marxist guerrillas in the TPLA. Known as the Kawa group, they had close working ties with the Soviet-backed Kurdish separatists in Iraq and Iran and with Iran's pro-Soviet Tudeh Communist Party. (Judging from the Kawa Bookshop not far from Istanbul's central police headquarters, they were Tudeh's mouthpiece in Turkey.)

The Armenians had more of a liberation problem. There is an Armenian Soviet Socialist Republic, which the Soviet Union has been trying to enlarge southwestward into Turkey since

1920, but Habash's Armenians showed no interest in going back there (still less in making trouble for the government in charge). The part they were after was the Turkish part, which ceased to exist as a geographical entity after World War I. A dreadful massacre did drive 1,750,000 Armenians out at the time, dispersing them to the four winds. By 1980, however, they had long since settled down elsewhere. Not for sixty years after their dispersion had a single shot been fired to re-create their homeland. Nor has a single Armenian community anywhere in the world condoned the Secret Army's no-longer-so-secret terrorist war.

The sheer malice of wishing such extra afflictions on the sadly afflicted Turkish nation was more than unforgivable. It was peculiarly sinister, since the interests served by Dr. Habash and his Popular Front for the Liberation of Palestine could not be mistaken in this case.

On July 27, 1980, the Ankara correspondent for the *Sunday Times* (London) reported bluntly that the Turkish government "believed that some of the Marxist organizations [engaged in the escalating violence] were receiving money and training from the Russians." In the eastern region of Kars, a Kurdish heartland bordering on the Soviet Union's Armenian Republic—and Iran—"extreme left-wing groups" presumably receiving such Russian benefits were so dominant that no one could penetrate their territory without their permission, added the *Times* correspondent. The incitement of Kurdish separatists in this volatile region, by left-wing groups clearly on the Russians' payroll, was common knowledge in Turkey by then.

What, then, did the Russians themselves have in mind for Turkey "next"?

They must have been banking on a military takeover. It was certainly too late for anything else. By the summer of 1980, indeed, the Turkish armed forces did take over—though hardly in a manner living up to Soviet expectations.

It would have been plausible to expect a military coup by either extreme, on the right or left. The one—on the right—would have stirred vibrant, worldwide protest, legitimizing a guerrilla army of Turkish Freedom Fighters under Soviet patronage. The other—on the left—might well have ended in a

Turkish Soviet Socialist Republic resembling, say, Russian Armenia's or Afghanistan's. Neither military solution would have been likely to do the Turks much good. Either would have greatly speeded the runaway destabilization of the Western world.

The Turkish armed forces rejected both. Once again in 1980, as in 1960 and 1971, they intervened to rescue, rather than replace, the nation's democratic order. They went about it by arresting right-wing and left-wing terrorists alike, along with top political leaders favoring one or the other. The nationwide terrorist kill-rate thereupon plunged: from one an hour to two or three a week. Life began to look almost normal.

It was not really normal, and peace did not come cheap. Some ten thousand Turks were imprisoned, and all constitutional liberties were suspended. In almost any other country, that would doubtless have meant what it seemed to mean. But Turkey's army is not like other armies, Uruguay's or Chile's, for instance, or Spain's in the 1930s, or Greece's in the 1960s. Twice before in the last twenty years, Turkish military leaders have kept their promise to restore civilian rule. They have said they are going to do so again, and, for all the fury of a frustrated terrorist underground, many or most Turks appear to believe them.

13

THE MAGNETIC POLES (I): CUBA

In the summer of 1968, the Soviet Union forced Fidel Castro into a secret agreement whereby Cuba surrendered sovereign control over its foreign policy to the Kremlin and consigned its intelligence service—the Dirección General de Inteligencia (DGI)—to the KGB.[1]

That same summer, the Soviet Communist Party's Central Committee decided, on the KGB's urging, to reverse its old policy of avoiding Palestinian entanglements. Arab Communists, meeting secretly in Moscow in July, were instructed to infiltrate, spy upon, and gain ascendancy over the Palestine Resistance. Meanwhile, the Soviet Union itself undertook to train and arm the Palestinians.[2]

In two moves, within as many months, the Russians had connected with what would soon become the two magnetic poles of worldwide terrorism. So began their left-handed war on the West.

Few of the terrorist bands mentioned in this book can be shown to have had direct links with the Soviet Union; but not one could have gotten started or kept going without help from Havana, or the Palestine Resistance, or both. They probably didn't realize at first that this would hook them into a closed circuit necessarily passing through Moscow. Nevertheless, what they didn't know in 1970 was an open book by 1980. The terrorists were telling it themselves, in courtroom testimony, omnibus confessions, eyewitness reports, interviews, press releases, published memoirs.

Those doing the talking were largely second- or third-generation terrorists in the Palestinian orbit: the retired German terrorist Hans-Joachim Klein, Patrizio Peci of the Italian Red Brigades' high strategic command, Muhammed Abu Kassem, or "Hader," who trained for *Fatah* in a Russian "friendship camp" near the Black Sea. (See chapter sixteen.) But the pioneers who paved the way for them had a Cuban matrix, going further back by a good ten years.

Castro had always wanted to export his revolution. No sooner did he come to power in January 1959 than he sent his first expeditionary force to Panama, where it flopped. He tried again three times that year, in Nicaragua, Haiti, and the Dominican Republic, and sent a full battalion of Cuban "medics" to help liberate Algeria. Barely two years later, he had already bagged the future leader of Africa's first successful Marxist coup, in Zanzibar.

Few knew, when "Field Marshal" John Okello seized this small island off the East African coast in January 1964, that he had just spent three years in Havana training for the job.[3] Looking back, one feels that his supreme confidence and studied brutality should have given him away. A giant of a man who never stirred without two guns stuck in his belt, Okello was a walking fright-story. (Traveling with him from Dar es Salaam in a chartered Cessna plane, around coup-time, I was too frozen with fear to open my mouth.)

His coup was faultless. It took just a few hours for his six hundred men—many of them Cuban-trained—to overthrow the Arab sultanate and proclaim a Communist "people's republic." Thousands of nonblack Zanzibaris, Arab and Indian, were slaughtered with deliberate savagery in the next few days, and thousands more fled in terror. A sliver of clove-scented land, with a population of under 300,000, thereupon became an operative base for penetrating the African mainland from Tanganyika to the Congo—where Castro's former field commander, Ché Guevara, soon turned up to train still more guerrilla warriors.

Okello appeared to be mostly Red China's idea at the time, which need not have embarrassed Castro. Reluctant to choose sides in the Sino-Russian dispute, Castro did not break with Peking until 1966, when his party paper *Granma* attacked Red Chinese "subversion." (The Chinese recalled their ambassador soon after and did not send one back for another four years.)

Apart from obliging the Chinese Communists in Zanzibar, however, Castro was pursuing his own dreams of a Cuban presence in Africa. Long before the Russians asked him to, and to their evident irritation, he had set out to Cubanize the black continent's liberation movements. As early as 1961, the year John Okello showed up in Havana, Castro sent a shipload of Cuban weapons to the West African coast. Offloading at Casablanca, it took on a return cargo of guerrilla trainees from Ghana, Nigeria, Mali, the Congo, South Africa, Kenya, Tanganyika, Spanish Equatorial Guinea, and Zanzibar itself.[4]

From then on, his country would keep turning out professional guerrilla fighters for just about every new African state. Here and there, he helped set up a few little "Marxist" protectorates, less interested in what they did than in the Cuban presence they assured. The most noteworthy was the former Spanish colony, Equatorial Guinea, whose political fields were tilled assiduously by black Cuban visitors from 1962 until 1969—when Spain withdrew, consigning the tiny ex-colony to the National Miracle and Devil-God Francisco Macias Nguema.[5] Surrounded and shielded by Cuban janissaries for the next ten years—three or four hundred Cuban "counselors" were at his side till the end—Nguema murdered 50,000 of his 350,000 subjects (many with his own hands), drove another 100,000 into exile, paid himself a state salary of $5 million a year, and turned his once prosperous ministate into a derelict noncountry in the name of scientific socialism. He was drinking a glass of human blood a day by 1979, when he was overthrown and executed. (This is not the stuff of legend but a factual eyewitness account by David Lamb of the *Los Angeles Times*.)[6]

Meanwhile, Castro was training the advance guard of the coming European fright decade—Palestinians, Italians, Germans, French, Spanish Basques—and forming guerrilla nuclei in practically every Western hemisphere state south of the

American border. As far back as 1962, his camps were taking in 1,500 Latin American guerrillas a year.[7]

How much of this was pure Castroism is hard to say. There was indeed a time when Castro was pushing an evidently homegrown revolutionary product abroad. He had announced in 1961 that he had "always been a Marxist-Leninist and will be one till the day I die." [8] But he was apparently trying not to be a Stalinist. The Cuban revolution did look like an original Third World model, strongly appealing to other states in Cuba's position and offering a comradely hand to one and all. "Any revolutionary movement anywhere in the world can count on Cuba's unconditional support," he told the opening session of the 1966 Tricontinental Conference in Havana.

By then, however, Castro was no longer in a position to make such an offer without conditions. The Tricontinental was Russia's proposition, not his. Colonel Kotchergine of the KGB would soon be supervising a new honeycomb of training camps around Havana for Russian-approved candidates from Europe, Africa, and Asia. The newly organized Cuban Communist Party (1965) was shot through with Moscow-line Communists— starting with Fidel's brother Raúl, a favorite in the Kremlin— and Soviet agents. Such freedom as Castro still had in 1966 would be gone for good by 1968.

The Russians brought him to heel by cutting off shipments of oil, raw materials, agricultural machinery, and industrial supplies.[9] The economy ground to a halt. The secret agreement that followed, midway through 1968, was hardly secret for long; Cuban defectors saw to that.

For their part, the Russians promised to underwrite the entire Cuban economy. The terms were generous enough to make a nation of seven or eight million people helplessly reliant on Soviet handouts. By 1978, *Time* reported, Russia was giving Cuba $6 million a day in straight subsidies and loans; selling Cuba 190,000 barrels of petroleum a day at half the world price; buying 3.5 million tons of Cuban sugar a year at four times the world price; and equipping all of Cuba's armed forces at Soviet expense.[10] As a Western diplomat observed, Castro was in hock to his eyeballs.

In return, Castro agreed "to accept the historic role of Communist Parties in world revolution," meaning the pro-Moscow kind. More precisely, he promised "not to discredit these parties publicly, or make public pronouncements against the USSR." [11] He started by endorsing the Soviet invasion of Czechoslovakia that August—if only with clenched teeth, said the press reports—and kept his word forever after.

As part of the bargain, Castro also accepted five thousand Russian advisers (ten thousand, ten years later), posted in various economic sectors, the armed forces, and the DGI. Soviet Colonel Viktor Simenov of the KGB was given an office adjoining the director's own at DGI headquarters in Havana. Twenty-five DGI agents a year (later fifty) would be selected with his approval for training in Moscow. (Ten percent of these were regularly recruited into the KGB.) All the DGI's operational decisions, and its annual budget, had to be cleared through Colonel Simenov. From then on, Cuba would be the only Soviet satellite state whose intelligence service was directly subsidized by Russia "for extending its range of activities abroad." [12]

Anything Cuba did in aid of worldwide terrorism after that would have to be done with the Russians' knowledge and consent, under their close supervision if not at their express command.

Among the DGI defectors explaining how the arrangement worked was Orlando Castro Hidalgo, who testified at length before a United States Senate committee. Hidalgo had quit his cover-job in Cuba's Paris embassy in 1969, simultaneously leaving the Cuban Communist Party, which, as a DGI agent, he had been obliged to join. Shortly before he defected, he said, the DGI sent a confidential circular to all its missions overseas, saying: "We are now working for our associates, and will be taking on some of their jobs." His chief of mission, Armando Lopez Orta, put it more succinctly: "We are closer to the Soviets now," he said.[13]

Hidalgo's duties in Paris at the time were "mainly to support revolutionary activities in Latin American and African countries." Candidates for training would fly over to Paris at Castro's expense, and Hidalgo would then "provide lodging, money, messages from Havana, and visas to Czechoslovakia" to camouflage the trail of guerrilla trainees on their way to Cuba. (Once, he had to hare off to Prague himself with the forged passport some trainee left behind.) He also had to screen young Europeans signing up for Castro's "summer camps" after the stormy Paris May of 1968—two thousand from France itself, another six thousand from elsewhere in Europe.[14] Before they were allowed to leave for Cuba, they had to pass a final screening "by a high-ranking DGI officer named Adalberto Quintana, sent to Paris specially from Havana," Hidalgo said.

The same meticulous selection went into recruiting 2,500 young Americans in the Venceremos Brigades, which appeared the next year. A smashing success for the DGI (and KGB), the Brigades visited Cuba in ten contingents between 1969 and 1977. There, under Colonel Simenov's fatherly eye, they learned how to mount a truly effective campaign to destabilize the United States. The pace was set by the U.S. Weathermen, whose Bernardine Dohrn and Peter Clapp were invited to Havana midway through 1969 to meet a delegation from North Vietnam and the Viet Cong.[15] Chicago's "days of rage," devoted to "bringing the war home," followed within weeks of their return to U.S. soil. (The art of rioting was passed on to thousands of other American students through do-it-yourself publications like *The Anarchists' Cookbook*. Drive a large nail through a plank if no other lethal weapon is handy, advised this swinging manual, whose contents were copied word for word from lectures in Cuba's guerrilla classrooms.) [16]

Many youths making that early pilgrimage to Cuba must have thought they were following in Ché Guevara's footsteps, but they weren't. The Russians and Castro both had discarded Guevara's theory of spontaneous bushfire revolution in 1967, when Guevara himself was discarded (with the reported help of the sexy Soviet agent "Tania").[17] There was nothing spontaneous about armed revolution in the seventies. It became a matter of machine-turned, computer-calculated urban guerrilla warfare.

Furthermore, its strategic focus came more distinctly into line with the Soviet Union's geopolitical designs. Latin America very nearly dropped out of sight for a decade. (It came into view again only when conditions positively thrust revolution on

Nicaragua's Sandinistas, trained in Havana since the start of the sixties, and their counterparts in three or four neighboring states under ruthless right-wing dictatorship.) Africa hotted up. The prime target area became Western Europe and the Middle East: from Ireland, Spain, Germany, and Italy to the Arab oil states, Turkey, and Iran. Castro's services were adjusted accordingly.

His guerrilla camps at home went on catering to capacity crowds. Palestinians in particular began to check in several hundred at a time, as they would go on doing throughout the decade; both Yassir Arafat and George Habash paid stately visits to Havana to discuss these ongoing arrangements.[18] Before long, however, Cuban instructors in guerrilla warfare began to go abroad, fanning out over the great Arab arc sheltering the Palestine Resistance. Their migration began at a portentous moment for the Palestinians: just after the 1973 October War in the Middle East, when the most intransigent hard-liners, implacable opponents of a negotiated peace with Israel, formed the Palestine Rejection Front.

Barely two months after that war, in December 1973, forty Cuban experts in terrorist warfare arrived secretly in South Yemen. With them was an East German specialist in the field named Hans Fiedler, who had been in Cuba since 1971. Landing in Aden, they were at once whisked upcountry to a Palestinian guerrilla camp run by Naif Hawatmeh.[19] Second in importance only to Habash and Haddad in the Rejection Front, Hawatmeh had been an orthodox Communist all his political life.

South Yemen was not yet a full-fledged Soviet people's republic. The Russians did not complete its satellization until June 26, 1978, when Aden was shelled by Soviet naval forces and severely bombed by Cuban-piloted Soviet aircraft.[20] With the execution of President Salem Rubaya Ali, the country was more or less openly annexed as a Russian colony then. Nevertheless, the Russians had been in residence for a good decade before and had enough clout in the early seventies to make this patch of Arabian wilderness a wonderfully safe terrorist haven.

Sealed off from prying eyes by the KGB and East German secret police, it became the heart of the Palestinian Rejection Front's training network.

Everybody who was anybody in planetary terrorism passed through South Yemen sooner or later, for training or shelter or both. That was true of the whole German underground, from the second-generation Baader-Meinhof Gang to the June 2 Movement to the Revolutionary Cells (as we are told by Hans-Joachim Klein). Ludwina Janssen of Dutch Red Help had also seen the Germans there, among others. The others, according to her own and several more eyewitness accounts, included Japanese, Turks and Iranians, Armenians and Kurds, Italians, French, Irish, Dutch, Belgians, South Moluccans, the Polisario Sahraouis and—at least until 1976, when 280 of them were still in a special camp at Hauf—the Dhofar tribesmen of oil-rich Oman.[21] All received advanced instruction in guerrilla warfare from Cubans and East Germans.

When Colonel Qaddafi went into the guerrilla training business for the Palestinians' sake (and his own), the Cubans moved in on Colonel Qaddafi. The first reliable account of Libya's camp network reports that Cuban instructors were teaching Spanish Basques there.[22] That was in 1976, just when a democratic regime was struggling to take hold in Spain, and the Basque hard-liners in ETA-Militar were taken under Qaddafi's wing. Some 150 Cuban guerrilla instructors were installed in Libya by 1980.[23]

By that time, another two hundred Cubans were installed in Algeria, to train Sahraoui guerrillas from the Polisario Front.[24]

Meanwhile, yet another platoon of Cuban instructors moved in on Syria. Some were detailed to the Syrian army, others to guerrilla training camps. The first of these were spotted in 1976: according to former U.S. Defense Secretary Melvin Laird, they were training Japanese, German, and Iranian terrorists as well as Arabs.[25] Then came a massive infiltration of southern Lebanon by the Rejection Front, staking out a military enclave on the eve of Lebanon's appalling civil war. Two years later, with the Rejection Front firmly entrenched, a Cuban team turned up at the port of Tyre.

The *Journal de Genève*, a usually reliable newspaper, describes that mission in a lengthy account datelined Lebanon.

After landing in Tyre at the end of March 1978, the Swiss paper said, "the first team of Cuban instructors settled in the outskirts of Beaufort Castle, an old fortress dating back to the Crusades," discreetly accessible by sea.[26]

> Two months afterward, a second team arrived, of Cuban instructors, engineers, and experts in setting up military bases and installing missile-launching ramps. All the equipment arrived in Tyre aboard Soviet freighters: SAM missiles, artillery, transceivers. . . .
>
> At the end of an intensive eight-month training period, the first group of terrorists was reportedly ready to embark for the Persian Gulf countries, carrying false passports, false work permits, and possessing perfect knowledge of the accents, ways, and customs of these countries. These terrorists have been trained in street and desert fighting, in attacking people and buildings, in regular demolition operations, and in sabotaging oil installations. Preceding these revolutionaries, large quantities of arms were routed to the Persian Gulf countries through intermediaries traveling that route, who carried the component parts.

This *Journal de Genève* report was dated January 20–21, 1979. The shah of Iran, policing the Persian Gulf since British forces pulled out east of Suez, was swept from his throne that same month, in an irresistible revolutionary tide.

The uses of Cuban expertise abroad, starting in the mid-seventies, grew clearer when plans for the Latin American Europe Brigade were discovered by Argentinian police around that time. As we have seen, the top-secret Tucumán Plan, drafted under DGI-KGB supervision, involved the transfer in a body of the Cuban-sponsored Junta for Revolutionary Coordination, the JCR, to Western Europe. Its four main guerrilla bands—Uruguay's Tupamaros and like-minded groups from Argentina, Bolivia, and Chile, all forced into exile with the advent of right-wing military regimes—were to work out of headquarters in Lisbon and Paris, for an orchestrated assault on the Continent. Castro had set up special camps for them, on a four-thousand acre estate near Guanabo, providing intensive three-month courses in explosives, sabotage, weaponry, and urban guerrilla tactics.[27]

Something of the stealth and interlocking interests involved in this preparatory program may be gathered from the itinerary of the Argentinian heading the JCR, Espinoza Barahona, after graduating from the Guanabo camp. Barahona left Cuba on December 16, 1975, bound ultimately for Argentina, where he planned to oversee the JCR's move to Europe. From Havana he flew straight to Moscow, using a fake Costa Rican passport in the name of "Guillermo Arce Roldán." After an overnight stay, he flew to Prague on Cuban Airlines, switched airlines for a flight to Zurich, paid cash for a different airline's flight to Paris, and switched again to Air France for the last leg of his journey to Buenos Aires. His fake Costa Rican passport was found in the JCR's safe-house there, along with all the other documents revealing the details of the Tucumán Plan.[28]

The Tucumán Plan never quite got off the ground. One early sally failed in Stockholm, when police broke up Norbert Kröcher's Operation Leo. Prospects in Rome were darkened when police dislodged and expelled a good-sized band of Argentinian Montoneros during the nationwide search for Aldo Moro, in the spring of 1978. Henri Curiel's indispensable service network was exposed and fell apart in Paris. Above all, an expected takeover by Portugal's inflexibly Stalinist Communist Party was unexpectedly thwarted. Without the assurance of a privileged sanctuary in Portugal, an operation of such Continental magnitude was out.

There is another and bigger side to the Cuban story abroad, of course. Russia's deal with Fidel Castro in 1968 applied to his armed forces as well as his intelligence service. Starting in the mid-seventies, he would be sending Cuban troops halfway around the planet on the Kremlin's behalf. Between forty and fifty thousand of them were deployed around Africa and the Arabian peninsula by 1980.[29]

Twenty-odd thousand were in Angola alone, fighting insurgents in the south and generally shoring up a semi-Soviet satellite established when Portugal's revolutionary army junta freed this strategic colony. Seventeen thousand were on active service in Ethiopia, the first wholly Sovietized black African state. To help install Colonel Mengistu's Marxist-Leninist regime, the Russians had airlifted ten thousand Cubans from Angola to Ethiopia, fifteen thousand Cubans directly to Ethiopia, and ten thousand Cubans from Cuba to Angola, keeping Castro's military forces at home up to strength. According to London's Institute for the Study of Conflict, the Soviet airlift required about five thousand flights within seven months, or some twenty-four flights a day.[30]

The airlift also worked the other way, rushing Cuban troops from Ethiopia to South Yemen in the cover of night, the following winter. Cuban troops were needed to help the Russians not only in consolidating their hold on South Yemen but in trying to force North Yemen into the Soviet orbit.* During the abortive border war late in 1978, the number of Cuban troops in South Yemen rose from 700 to 1,700 (reportedly rising to 6,000 or 7,000 by 1980). Sources at NATO headquarters in Brussels claim that bodies of Cuban soldiers were found on North Yemen soil while the fighting was on.[31]

The days had surely passed when the Kremlin was riding herd on Fidel Castro for his reckless exploits abroad. Cuban expeditionary forces in Africa, criticized in Moscow as "adventurism" in the sixties, became "acts of international proletarian solidarity" in the seventies. The Cuban army became a priceless asset to the Kremlin, free to go where the Russians could not, fighting the Soviet Union's imperial wars. Its Third World cachet—nonaligned, at that—was an elegant touch.

Still, there were limits to the Cubans' usefulness in the big theater of terrorist operations. They were too far away, too easily detected, too openly compromised by Russia. The Palestinians in the Resistance movement were better off on all these counts. And they were much, much richer, especially once Colonel Muammar Qaddafi came along.

---

* North Yemen is better known as Yemen and officially known as the Yemen Arab Republic. The Soviet satellite South Yemen, the former Aden Protectorate, is now officially named the People's Democratic Republic of Yemen.

14

QADDAFI, THE DADDY WARBUCKS OF TERRORISM

Colonel Muammar Qaddafi, born in a desert nomad's tent and reared on the Koran, was a devout and austere young Moslem officer when he overthrew a senile king in 1969. Not long afterward, though, he came into an income of a billion dollars a month when Libya struck oil. Money talked.

He soon made his name as a big spender, especially in the arms department. From items like the French Mirage fighter plane and West German Leopard tank, he went on to make the biggest deal of our time with the Soviet Union: a twelve-billion-dollar order for tanks, planes, artillery, missile systems—six hundred dollars' worth for every man, woman, and child in Libya, six thousands dollars' worth apiece for the Libyan army's 22,000 troops. He was in the market for nuclear weapons too. Having set out to shop for an atom bomb as early as 1970—in Peking, when he met Mao Tse-tung—he appeared to be in sight of one by 1980. In the spring of that year, defectors from a team of atomic scientists told the BBC that they had been working on an atom bomb in Chasma, Pakistan, with $100 million put up by Colonel Qaddafi. Pakistan would make it but Qaddafi would own it, they said, predicting its completion by 1981.[1]

What with his armament, cash, ambition, and mystic exaltation, all apparently in bottomless supply, he made other names for himself as he went along. Egypt's President Sadat called him "a vicious criminal, 100 percent sick and possessed of a demon." Sudan's President Numeiry said he had "a split personality—both evil." The PLO itself called him "a madman." Deranged or not, however, he became the Daddy Warbucks of international terrorism.

He did not seem to care whether the terrorism was Black or Red, though his preference might shift as time went by. At the start of the seventies, he was practically all Black. The head of his early Italy-Libya Association, afloat on Libyan money—and eventually outlawed as a Black terrorist front—was Claudio Mutti, one of Italy's star Nazi-Maoist terrorists, jailed in 1980 for his alleged role in the Bologna railroad station bombing.[2] Mutti's close associate Mario Tuti, now serving a life sentence for terrorist killings, had picked up a hundred-thousand-lire payoff from the Libyan embassy in Rome just before gunning down two policemen in 1975.[3] Mutti claimed to have been inspired by Qaddafi's brand of "Islamic socialism." Tuti's inspirational heroes were Hitler, Mussolini, Qaddafi, and Mao Tse-tung, he said. Among others fighting Zionism on Qaddafi's payroll in those days was the fascist Avanguardia Nazionale, whose posters spoke for themselves. "We are with you, heroic Arab-Palestinian People, and not with the Dirty, Fat Jews!" ran one.[4]

It was from the Black International's side that Qaddafi made his first investment in Palestinian terror abroad, providing the funds, arms, and training for the Olympic Games massacre in 1972. He was still on that side in 1973 when, enraged by the leftward drift of the Palestine Resistance, he cut off the PLO's yearly allowance of $40 million "until the movement modified its leftist stance."[5] Nevertheless he restored the subsidy that summer, after a week's intensive talks with Palestinian leaders in Tripoli. That was when he undertook to bankroll the Carlos network in Paris, starting his own slide down the slippery leftward slope.

Almost anybody claiming to be a revolutionary could put the bite on Qaddafi after that, and did. "Apart from helping Palestinian groups, the Libyans have provided money, training and in some cases arms for virtually every group in the world with revolutionary credentials," said U.S. Undersecretary of State David Newsom, a former ambassador to Tripoli, in 1980.[6] The list ran from Nicaragua's Sandinistas, Argentina's Montoneros, and Uruguay's Tupamaros to the IRA Provisionals, Spanish Basques, French Bretons and Corsicans, Sardinian and Sicilian separatists, Turks, Iranians, Japanese, and Moslem insurgents in Thailand, Indonesia, Malaysia, and the Philippines, to name just some. (Qaddafian Libyans, ready to take revenge on "disloyal" compatriots in London, Paris, and Rome were naturally provided for also.)

He was said to have a slush fund of $580 million for his terrorist works, in 1976. The estimate, made by his former minister of planning, Omar el-Meheishi, is probably on the low side by now. Naturally, he devoted a good part of the money to the Palestinian cause, dividing his favors between Arafat's Fatah and the more radical Rejection Front. He was especially prodigal on the radicals' behalf in Lebanon's two-year civil war, endowing them with no less than $100 million and the greater part of their arms supply.[7] He also spent handsome sums on efforts to unseat "conservative" Arab rulers. He had a standing offer of $1 million for anybody able and willing to murder Anwar Sadat, and he must have blown six or seven times that much on a rocambolesque mission to overthrow Tunisia's President Habib Bourguiba.

His Tunisian venture, in January 1980, ended in the first public trial of Qaddafi-ism ever held, revealing its deep roots in Mediterranean and planetary terrorism. Of the sixty-odd raiders he sent in to seize the Tunisian mining town of Gafsa, forty-two lived long enough to testify before a high security court. (They were executed afterward.) Dozens of foreign reporters flocked to the trial. Several, fascinated by what came out in the courtroom, went on to Libya for a look around on their own. For once, some of the darker patches came to light on the mysterious "Planet Libya," as the clandestine paper *Sawt Lybia* called it.

The raid on Gafsa began at 2:00 A.M. on a Sunday morning, when Qaddafi's heavily armed and trained commandos crossed over from Algeria into the southern Tunisian desert. A million dollars' worth of weapons were already stockpiled in town for them, left behind when they fled in disarray. They took Gafsa utterly by surprise and held it for a day, waiting for all Tunisia to rise up in a popular insurrection. Qaddafi had assured them that it would, but it didn't. The survivors told their story later in copious detail.

Their commander, Ahmed Mergheni, had been in Tunisia's underground opposition for fifteen years, mostly hiding out in Libya. Once before, in 1972, Qaddafi's men had sent him back over the Tunisian border to blow up the American embassy and the Jewish synagogue in Tunis, but he was caught and jailed. Released four years later, he made his way back to Libya, where he was sent to the Tinduf guerrilla camp; it was used mostly for the Sahraoui guerrillas of Polisario then. Eventually, he was singled out by an "Arab exterior liaison bureau" in Tripoli to mount the Gafsa operation.

Given a working fund of $5 million, he was sent to Lebanon in search of Tunisians already training there with George Habash's PFLP and Naif Hawatmeh's Democratic Front. In all, Mergheni picked up twenty-eight Tunisians in the Palestinian camps, including a specialist in handling SAM-7 missiles.[8] Issued with false passports by the Libyan embassy in Beirut, they flew to Rome and on to Algiers. Later they met up with the rest of the team, coming straight from Libyan camps. The rendezvous was made somewhere along the "Qaddafi Trail": the desert track traveled by Qaddafi's weekly caravans of trucks, loaded with Kalashnikovs, Makarovs, RPG-7 bazookas, and SAM-7s for the Polisario Front fighting Morocco in the western Sahara.

Logistical supplies were lavish. Apart from the huge cache of arms in Gafsa itself, the Libyans had thoughtfully scattered weapon reserves around Tunisia's main cities: Tunis, Sfax, Kairouan, Bizerte. Lest the commandos still run short—should the populace rise to a man, say—they were told about extra weapons caches available in Europe, stored there for terrorist use. Stored where? The judges preferred to hear the answer behind closed doors, but it was relayed by defense lawyers to waiting correspondents. Sicily and Corsica, they said.[9]

All the captured raiders spoke of seeing other foreigners in

Libyan camps, by the hundreds or thousands. Their political commissar, Ezzedin Sharif, obligingly filled the court in on nationalities and place-names. Several European reporters went on to Libya over the next few months to check this out, as did a three-man team from the African review *Jeune Afrique*. Here is a composite picture provided by the Tunisian commandos and foreign journalists (as published in Italy's *La Stampa, Il Giornale Nuovo, Panorama,* and *L'Europeo,* as well as *Le Nouvel Observateur* and *Jeune Afrique).*[10] There were anywhere from ten to twenty thousand foreigners in the camps. About two thousand were Egyptians, confined to a special camp at el-Beida near Tobruk; their instructors were chiefly Russians from the Tobruk base, where units of the Soviet Mediterranean fleet often called in. (The Tobruk camp alone could accommodate five thousand trainees.)[11] The Sudanese were in another special camp at Maaten Biskara, along with guerrilla trainees from Chad. Here the instructors were Cuban as well as Russian; a nearby military landing strip had been used to airlift Cuban troops to Ethiopia in 1978.

The Tunisians themselves were concentrated at Bab Aziza, mainly with Syrian and Palestinian instructors. They were taught to handle not just the familiar Kalashnikovs, RPG bazookas, and SAM-7s, but the deadly Chilka, which fires four radar-guided twenty-three millimeter cannons. They were lectured daily on learning not to fear death. "Your cause is noble," they were assured incessantly.

Altogether, the Africans among them came to about seven thousand. On September 1, 1979, the whole African contingent came out on parade in Benghazi, where they were observed by a *Jeune Afrique* reporter. "You would have to see this army to understand its importance for Libyan leaders," he wrote.[12] "Seven thousand black men went goose-stepping past a hysterical crowd, under the gaze of Qaddafi, his eyes full of malice. Some drove tanks, others carried bazookas. . . ."

This was Qaddafi's famous "foreign legion," designed "to destabilize Africa south of the Sahara and create a vast Libyan Empire," according to Senegal's President Leopold Senghor. Marching along in that parade, indeed, were the would-be future conquerors of Mali, Nigeria, Mauritania, the Cameroons,

Tunisia, Egypt, the Sudan, Benin, Niger, Chad, Senegal, the Ivory Coast, and Polisario's chosen land of Sahraoui. (Children of the Polisario guerrillas age nine to eighteen were kept in guarded Libyan "hostels," until they reached fighting age.) "Here are the Liberators of the Third World!" blared the loud-speakers, as they went tramping by.

Quite a few Liberators seemed to be missing. There were none in sight from the Central African realm of Emperor Bokassa, for instance. (Two hundred Libyan soldiers were in his army when he was dethroned in 1979, and six thousand Kalashnikovs were found in his palace.) [13] Nor were there any from Uganda, where Idi Amin was defended by both Palestinian and Libyan troops before he took desperate flight. (Qaddafi had sent 2,500 soldiers to help out when Amin made his last stand in 1979, and at least one company of armed Palestinians gave themselves up to the Sudanese afterward.) [14]

Not one of Qaddafi's ten or twenty thousand foreign guerrilla trainees came from a Communist state in Eastern Europe or newer Soviet client states and satellites in the Third World. None seemed interested in liberating even Islamic Afghanistan, forced into the Soviet orbit by a military coup in 1978 and nailed down there by a Soviet occupation army at the end of 1979. On the other hand, a great many seemed interested in liberating the free societies of Western Europe.

For a Third World operation, the whole thing showed a pronounced First World bulge. Qaddafi's camps teemed with Europeans. Among those seen at first hand were Irishmen, Germans, Spanish Basques, French Bretons and Corsicans, Italians, Greeks, Turks. Most were clustered in three camps, at Sirte, Sebha, and Az Zaouiah. But eligible candidates went on to the more exclusive Raz Hilal camp near Tokra, for the world's most advanced courses in sabotage, under Cuban and East German instructors. They could also learn to be frogmen there, for underwater warfare. Whether a coincidence or not, the IRA used frogmen to blow up Lord Mountbatten on his fishing boat.

All guerrilla trainees from abroad were checked in and out of the Libyan capital by computer. The reception center, in the Palace of the People, was run by the Arab Liaison Bureau, run in turn by the Libyan secret service (trained in turn by the East German secret police). A golden handshake after graduation included false passports, pocket money for the trip home, and a weapon or two. For Europeans, it also included the address of Libyan backup committees in Rome, Brussels, and Frankfurt.

The Europeans, especially if on the run, could count on Qaddafi for lavish hospitality. Big shots like Carlos got handsome seaside villas, complete with staff, car, and chauffeur. Hans-Joachim Klein, wounded hero of the Carlos raid on OPEC, wrote that on getting back to Libya he was "toasted at dinner with the foreign minister, traveled in the president's private jet, dined with the head of the secret service, and was assigned a bodyguard," along with a house.[15] Smaller fry in the European underground got housed in a block of Tripoli flats whose whereabouts went the rounds of the Continent. (P.O. Box 4115, tel. 41184.) Wadi Haddad's Europe-based staff often came down to Tripoli to meet with him and the chief of Libyan intelligence, Lieutenant Colonel Mustapha el-Kharubi. If they were upper-echelon, they put up at the Tripoli Hilton.

What was in it for Qaddafi?

Western countries helplessly dependent on Libyan oil liked to think he was after nothing more than the liberation of Palestine. His views on the subject were admittedly intemperate. He insisted that all Jews who had settled there since 1948 should go back where they came from, and he was apparently trying to pick them off one at a time. "Kill as many Jews as you can" were his instructions to a Palestinian team he once sent off to shoot up the airport at Istanbul.

Even so, most European governments were inclined to make allowances for terrorists in the Palestine Resistance on "moral grounds"—the standard phrase used by their courts in deference to the undeniably passionate feelings of Palestinian nationalists. In Qaddafi's case, the allowances they were evidently prepared to make proved egregious.

I still remember vividly the day in December 1973 when the late Aldo Moro, then foreign minister, appeared before the Italian Parliament to deny an appalling charge against Colonel Qaddafi that happened to be true. On the seventeenth of that month, a Palestinian hit-team had attacked a Pan American plane at Rome's Fiumicino airport with incendiary bombs, burning thirty-one trapped passengers to death. Designed to block the imminent opening of Israeli-Palestinian peace talks in Geneva, the hit had absolutely nothing to do with the charred passengers in the plane, or with Italy for that matter. It was probably the most atrocious terrorist act of the seventies in Europe.

On investigating, the Italian Ministry of the Interior found that the hit-men had acquired their air tickets in Tripoli and were carrying weapons, fire bombs, grenades, and money provided by Libya. The interior minister's report concluded —rightly, it turned out—that Libya was responsible for this mindless tragedy. I was sitting in the press section when Moro addressed the Chamber of Deputies on the anguishing issue. He was happy to accept Qaddafi's vigorous denial of the charges, he said.

Only three months before, a tip from the Israeli Mossad had led Italian police to discover two SAM-7 heat-seeking missiles mounted on an Ostia balcony, positioned to shoot down an El Al plane taking off from Fiumicino. The SAM-7 was a top-secret weapon then, unknown to NATO experts (who examined these samples with considerable interest). The two missiles had been provided by Colonel Qaddafi and transported to Rome by a Greek courier, on instructions from Carlos in Paris.[16] Of the five Palestinians on that hit-team, two were allowed to escape more or less legally, on a court order granting them provisional liberty. The other three were flown back to Libya in an Italian military plane.[17]

The Italian government was behaving no differently from its European allies at the time. Throughout the decade, nearly all Western governments chose to consider ugly episodes like these as spillovers of an Arab-Israeli conflict that was essentially none of their business. Live-and-let-live understandings were reached with Colonel Qaddafi and Palestinian leaders in the Middle East, by France, West Germany, Great Britain, and Italy, in effect assuring immunity for Palestinian hit-men. (A survey by the Israel Information Center in the mid-seventies showed that of 204 Palestinians arrested for terrorist acts outside the Middle East between 1968 and 1975, only three were in jail by 1975.) [18]

Moro himself would one day describe the bargain he made.

In regard to terrorist acts on Italian soil, he wrote, "Liberty (with expatriation) was conceded to Palestinians, to avoid grave risks of reprisals. Not once, but many times, detained Palestinians were released by various mechanisms. The principle was accepted. . . . The necessity of straining formal legality was recognized. . . ." He went on to reveal that an Italian secret-service agent, Colonel Stefano Giovannone, was actually sent to negotiate the terms in Lebanon—where he stays on to this day.[19]

Moro was a captive of the Red Brigades when he wrote this in a letter to fellow Christian Democratic leaders. He was trying desperately to show that the government, having strained legality for the Palestinians, could do as much for him, buying his life back by releasing convicted Red Brigades prisoners.

One might argue the merits of such bargains even if the Palestinians alone were concerned. But what if Europe itself was the target, for reasons having little if anything to do with Palestine? Supposing Colonel Qaddafi, for one, had something altogether different in mind?

The suspicion that he might, or did, flared in Italy in the summer of 1980. The bomb killing eighty-four people in Bologna's railway station that August 2—the most dreadful terrorist assault on the Continent since World War II—bore all the marks of right-wing Black terrorism, reviving after five or six dormant years just when Red terrorism seemed on the decline. Only a master in handling explosives could have done it. Who could have trained him, and where?

The Italians may never find the answer. They may not even discover whether the bomb was in fact Black, or Red, or both. Either way, though, some thought they could see Colonel Qaddafi's sinister hand.

On the very morning of the Bologna tragedy, just a few hours before it happened, Italy's most authoritative daily had reached the newsstands with an arresting front-page story. Three leaders of Libya's underground democratic opposition had talked for hours, in an unnamed European city, with reporters from the London *Daily Mirror* and the *Corriere della Sera* of Milan. Both papers plainly knew and accepted them as responsible men. They spoke of Libya as a "terrorist state, a base of conspiracy against the region's security and stability, a country that has become one vast deposit of arms, a place where terrorists and mercenaries of the entire world are concentrated. In Cufra, Gadames, Sinauen and many other camps, commandos are being trained. . . ."

Not only were there Italians in the camps, they said. "There are Italian Red Brigadists and Black Brigadists getting military training, shoulder to shoulder in the camps, learning to kill and handle arms. Qaddafi makes no distinction between the extreme right and extreme left. He uses these youths to reach one of his objectives—the destabilization of the Mediterranean area."

"Destabilization" was the operative word. The Palestinian cause would have to be stretched pretty far to embrace it.

It seemed plain all along that Colonel Qaddafi was motivated by more than a single-minded concern for Palestinian liberation. Among other things, he also had a problem of scope. There are vexing limitations to ruling a country with only 2.5 million people in it. "Libya has a great chief and small population, unlike Egypt, which has a great population and no chief," he once told Tunisian President Bourguiba. No neighbor of Libya's has therefore been safe from his efforts to enlarge his realm—by way of Tunisia itself, Egypt, Sudan, Algeria, Niger, Chad. (All these efforts failed, except for the thirty thousand square miles of uranium-rich territory he took from Chad.)

Combined with such expensive ambition was a messianic sense of mission, though just what kind was less than clear. The fundamentalist Islamic part seemed clear enough, with Qaddafi evidently casting himself as the Ayatollah Khomeini of Africa and the Mediterranean. If anything, however, he was still more virulently anticolonialist and anti-Western on his "socialist" revolutionary side: the "objectively progressive" side, in radical parlance.

His Green Book on Islamic Revolution might give pause to more subjective progressives. A jumble of Koranic edicts, paternal aphorisms, and sweeping equalitarian pronouncements, it proposed the abolition of property, money, interest, and government, all of which he continued to embody as Libya's absolute billionaire ruler. "In need, freedom is latent" was a thought of his in the Green Book. "To demand equality for the Female is to stain her beauty and detract from her femininity; education leading to work unsuitable to her nature is unjust and cruel" was another of his "basic rules for freedom." His sole concession to the emancipation of women was their right to own a home because "they menstruate, conceive, and care for children." [20] It was hardly the language of Ché Guevara or Mao Tse-tung.

The language that counted, nevertheless, was in the petrodollars he could spread around. With the country he owned and the dreams he dreamed, here was a man who might indeed destabilize much of Africa, and the Middle East, and a good part of Europe besides—the soft underbelly of Europe, as Italy's leading commentators (and *Le Monde* in Paris) noted pointedly after the Bologna bomb.

Here, also, was a man who might be used in turn.

He was a delightful surprise to Soviet leaders. Premier Kosygin rushed to Libya in person to sign the twelve-billion-dollar arms contract Qaddafi asked for in 1976. The Russians were laughing all the way to the bank, a Western diplomat observed.

The ink was scarcely dry on the contract when deliveries began. Russian and Cuban cargo vessels were soon to be seen in Libyan ports, unloading tons of weapons day and night.[21] The material was incomparably superior to the obsolete junk so often dumped on Russia's Third World customers. Some items hadn't yet been given to the Warsaw Pact armies, let alone to older and valued Arab clients of Russia's such as Syria and Iraq.

Among other things, Colonel Qaddafi got 2,800 modern Soviet tanks; 7,000 other armored vehicles; several hundred MIG 23, MIG 25, and MIG 27 fighters and bombers and Tupolev-B23 long-range supersonic bombers; twenty-five missile-launching naval craft; surface-to-air missiles; and even the dreaded Scud, a highly sophisticated ground-to-ground missile with a 190-mile range.[22]

That was a lot of equipment for an army of 22,000 mostly illiterate troops (though the figure had doubled by 1980). But twelve thousand Soviet military advisers came with the deal.

They alone would control the MIG 25s (the MIG 25U Foxbat C), to be flown solely by Russian pilots. Two squadrons of MIG 21s based in Banbah would be piloted by over a hundred North Koreans.[23] Only Russians would be permitted to operate the missile systems. Three hundred Czech technicians were flown in for tank maintenance. Nine airstrips were built to accommodate the giant Soviet Antonovs transporting personnel and spare parts.[24] Should the need arise, the Antonovs could fly in enough Soviet pilots and crews to man an impressive air force in a matter of days.

A thousand Libyan soldiers a year were to be trained in Russia and three thousand more in Bulgaria, most pliant of Soviet satellites. Soviet military advisers were stationed permanently in Tripoli, Benghazi, Tobruk, and on the former U.S. airbase at Wheelus Field. The arrangements not only gave Russia a strong enough hold on Libya to turn its petroleum on or off for the West at will. But as Egypt's President Sadat observed, the Russians "were assured of a presence on the southern coast of the Mediterranean for the next fifty years." [25]

The mystic of the Libyan desert didn't seem to mind. On the contrary, he appeared to be drawn irresistibly toward the archenemy of Islam. "Marxism is closer to Moslems than Christianity and Judaism," he told *The New York Times* in 1978. "It is the Christians and Jews who commit genocide. It is the atheists who call for peace and the cause of liberty." [26] The next year he announced that he had it in mind "to join the Warsaw Pact and let the world go to hell." There were some, he said, "who officially suggest" not only that "the progressive Arab states" should join the Soviet military bloc but that "missiles with nuclear warheads should be placed in North Africa and the Arabian Peninsula to defy America's hostile policy toward the Arab nation." [27] ("How do you feel about Soviet gulags?" *Newsweek*'s Arnaud de Borchgrave asked him on that occasion. "What's a gulag?" was his reply.)

By then, Colonel Qaddafi had ceased to criticize the atheistic demons in the Kremlin—his sole reproach was that the Russians still allowed Jews to emigrate to Israel, reported Flora Lewis in *The New York Times*—while his missionary role abroad took on an unmistakable cast. He began to cultivate

Puerto Rico's separatist terrorists, paying their way to the Continent for a taste of underground high life. He homed in with his moneybags on Iran and Oman, high on the Russians' hit-list, and then on Polisario's staked-out area of the Sahara (after Oman's Dhofar insurrection was put down). He convened all of Western Europe's ultra-left groups for a conference in Malta, along with the underground left of Iran, Chile, Oman, and Puerto Rico—an intriguing choice.[28] He organized a remarkable conference in Benghazi for a "unified plan of struggle against fascism and imperialism in America." He might have been taking over from Fidel Castro at the Benghazi Conference in 1979, judging from his guest list: Sandinistas from Nicaragua, exiled Tupamaros from Uruguay, wandering Montoneros from Argentina, Marxist guerrilla bands from Chile, Costa Rica, Bolivia, Mexico, Brazil.[29]

His practical purpose at the meeting was to revive Castro's sagging Latin American Junta for Revolutionary Coordination and its Europe Brigade. Delegates came from the JCR's branch offices in Paris, Rome, Stockholm, and Madrid. What they talked about, mostly, was "how to increase the Latin American exiles' participation in international terror operations in Western Europe and the Middle East," said the London *Economist Foreign Report.*

Later that year, he co-sponsored an international gathering for the PLO in Portugal with the World Peace Council, well known—presumably even to Qaddafi, by 1979—as an instrument of the KGB. Seven hundred and fifty delegates came to Lisbon from everywhere, the majority from the Soviet bloc, at Qaddafi's expense. (It cost him $1.5 million.) Their purpose was to express solidarity with the Palestinian Rejection Front. While they were at it, they also expressed solidarity with "the socialist countries, particularly the Soviet Union." Then they expressed solidarity with "the forces of peace and liberation . . . in Afghanistan." Finally, they expressed solidarity with "the people's struggle in Africa, Asia, *Europe, and the American Continent.* [Italics are mine.]" [30]

Just which people's struggle they had in mind was not left in doubt. The delegates roundly condemned "the imperialist and reactionary conspiracies hatched against the Democratic

Republic of Yemen" (Russia's South Yemen). Then they condemned "reactionary attempts to disrupt peace efforts" (such as
their own). They went on to condemn "the increasing military
buildup in the Mediterranean to strengthen NATO's southern
flank," failing to mention the buildup of the Soviet navy in the
same area. Finally, they condemned NATO's determination—
odious to the Kremlin—to install Cruise and Pershing missiles
in Western Europe, counterbalancing Soviet Russia's otherwise
overpowering SS 20s. The last in particular gave the game
away: it was the single most vital issue of Soviet propaganda
and diplomacy in 1980.

There was nothing surprising, then, in Colonel Qaddafi's
expression of his own solidarity with the Russians late that December, when they sent 100,000 troops to occupy Afghanistan.
Among states representing seven hundred million Moslems at a
conference of protest, only Libya, South Yemen, Syria, and the
Palestine Liberation Organization refused to condemn the Soviet invasion.[31]

It came as no surprise, either, when Qaddafi finally made
the choice he did of Palestinian leaders to lead the way into
Fright Decade II. The contest for his patronage was fierce after
Wadi Haddad died, and it grew savage as Egypt and Israel
began to apply the terms of their Camp David agreement. To
speak of a peaceful settlement with Israel was to be banished
from Qaddafi's realm: Arafat's wing of the PLO and Fatah
were driven out of Tripoli, their offices closed and representatives expelled. Qaddafi was putting all his money on the Rejection Front—and not just on George Habash.

Always a favorite, Habash was more or less commuting to
Tripoli by now. But two other intractable Palestinian Rejec-
tionists were singled out for Qaddafi's princely favors. One was
Naif Hawatmeh, the orthodox pro-Soviet Communist who ad-
vocated a future Palestine "in an Arab confederation like
Czechoslovakia's." [32] The other was a man known to every
Western intelligence service for his long-standing and intimate
connections with the KGB: Ahmed Jibril.

15

THE MAGNETIC POLES (II): THE PALESTINE RESISTANCE

Ahmed Jibril is not a famous figure. His band of Arab *fedayeen*, the PFLP-General Command, is among the smaller armed groups in the Middle East. His work abroad has often attracted notice, but rarely in his name. He is the sole leader in the Palestinian movement known to have had direct relations with the KGB since the early 1960s. His record since 1968—that endlessly interesting year—is a logbook of Soviet Russia's progress in applying its decision to infiltrate, spy upon, and gain ascendancy over the Palestine Resistance.

The Palestinians were peculiarly vulnerable to such intrusion. The passionate intensity of their nationalist feeling was bound to grow, in decades of isolation and frustration. Israel, created by a unanimous U.N. vote, started out with strong diplomatic protection. The Israelis had easily fought off invading Arab armies the day they got their state in 1948 and inflicted further smarting defeats in 1956 and 1967. Never noticeably flexible about Arab refugees and newly occupied lands, their government policy on these issues grew more provocative year by year. (It seemed particularly so under Premier Begin, whose Irgun terrorists had once blown up the King David Hotel in Jerusalem, killing a hundred people, to gain Israel's independence.)

Arab rulers themselves were heartily disinclined to get entangled in the political, financial, and military thickets of Palestinian Liberation. The rich ones, with the oil, were afraid of mounting Palestinian radicalism, with reason. Even when these rulers were talked, or cowed, into putting up a lot of money, they could not provide the necessary hardware and expertise for large-scale guerrilla warfare—the "military solution." Only the Russians could.

Upon doing so after a long and cautious look around, the Russians would obviously need somebody like Ahmed Jibril.

He has always operated under deep cover, and I cannot in his case provide all the usual documented footnotes. A good deal of my information about him came from intelligence sources in Israel and Western Europe. Whatever part I've used here was told to me by more than one such source, and much of it by three or four. Nobody I met in Western intelligence circles doubted that Jibril was bent: "the Kremlin's man," they said.

He was a captain in the Syrian army when he pulled together some twenty fellow officers in 1958 to form what became the Palestinian Liberation Front. His first irregular contacts with the KGB began around 1964, when his group began its commando raids into Israel over the Syrian and Lebanese borders. He had directed ninety-five of these raids before the June War of 1967, distinguished for his cold efficiency even then.

He became a professional when the Soviet Communist Party decided on its new Palestine course the next summer. Starting soon afterward, Jibril made four lengthy visits to Russia, for special training in guerrilla warfare and political subversion. His men were among the first thirty Palestinians recruited for Russian training as "controlled agents" in 1972.[1] His second-in-command, Abu Bakr, completed an intensive Russian training course on the eve of the 1973 October War, returning to take charge of Jibril's Ayn Saheb camp in Syria.

Outside of Syria, Jibril maintained his own operative base in Moscow, a logistics and communications center in East Berlin, and a luxury flat in Sofia. The capital of Eastern Europe's most intractably Stalinist state, Sofia was warmly hospitable to Jibril's band. The agent he kept stationed there, Akram Halabi, was on excellent terms with the Bulgarian secret police.

Unnoticed by the outside world, Sofia provided invaluable

facilities to the whole Palestine Resistance. It was in Sofia, for instance, that the late Hassam Salameh met with Black September leaders to perfect plans for the Olympic Games massacre. (Unflappable as always, Soviet Foreign Minister Gromyko assured the U.N. Assembly directly after the event that it was "impossible to condone acts of terrorism by certain Palestinian elements leading to the tragic events in Munich." While he spoke—reports the veteran Middle East observer John Laffin in *Fedayeen*—a Soviet cargo plane landed in Damacus with a consignment of machine guns, mortars, and light weapons to supply Fatah's main arsenal at Al Hama, about four miles from the Syrian capital.) [2]

Thanks in considerable part to Jibril's own group, Sofia was indispensable for building a solid Palestinian terrorist infrastructure in Western Europe. Under Akram Halabi's supervision, a warehouse was set up in the city for weapons originally shipped from the Soviet bloc to Lebanon, Syria, Iraq, and Libya, and reshipped to Bulgaria for transit: explosives, grenades, rifles, pistols, bazookas, SAM-7 missiles. By the winter of 1977, these arms were moving westward in weekly caravans, loading up at the Sofia warehouse, and making stopovers in Romania, Czechoslovakia, Poland, and East Germany.[3]

Stolen cars from Western Europe were driven over for the purpose, refitted in East European garages to conceal weapons, then driven out again after loading, with advance notice to Communist border guards. Three such cars were intercepted in West Germany in 1978, and huge depots of the smuggled weapons were amassed around Paris, Marseilles, Milan, Turin, Bologna, Perugia.

It was also from Sofia that Jibril himself sent the first of his more inventive terrorist devices in 1972: a booby-trapped letter bomb addressed to the Israeli stand at the Hanover Fair. His group sent some sixty-five of these missives over the next year or so, to Israeli legations or prominent Zionist leaders in Paris, Geneva, Montreal, Vienna, London, Washington, Ottawa, Brussels, Kinshasa, Buenos Aires, and Pnompenh.[4]

Another of his imaginative booby traps, also prepared in Sofia, was inserted in transistor radios or cassettes. These were usually given to pretty girls who had no idea that they were taking bombs aboard their El Al planes, rigged to explode in flight. A Dutch girl boarding a plane for Tel Aviv from Rome was found with one in 1971, a Peruvian girl with another the next month, two English girls with yet another in 1972.[5] These last, Ruth Watkin and Audrey Waldron, had been entertained for a weekend in Rome by a couple of ardent Arab students from Perugia, who promised to join them later in Tel Aviv. Their bomb did explode in midair, failing miraculously to disintegrate the aircraft and passengers. The two Arab boyfriends, quickly arrested, were soon released on a court order and spirited out of Rome. (The carabinieri captain who drove them as far as Aquila on an icy January night became sadly famous later: he was Antonio Varisco, assassinated by the Red Brigades in 1980.)[6]

Jibril's KGB control at first was Alexander Victorovich Morozov, a longtime expert in Palestinian affairs. Working out of the Soviet embassy in Beirut, Morozov led an "action team" of KGB and GRU diplomats stationed in Jordan, Syria, and Lebanon. He was responsible for secret contacts with all Palestinian formations and for Soviet-bloc arms deliveries.

Later, Morozov was replaced by a new military attaché at the Soviet embassy, Yuri Ivanovitch Starchinov, who took over as Jibril's control. As the "action team's" leader, Starchinov got his orders directly from the Soviet ambassador to Lebanon, Sarvor Alimzchanovitch Azimov, considered the heart and soul of all Russian relations with the Palestinian *fedayeen.*

It was Morozov, meeting regularly with Ahmed Jibril in Beirut and Damascus, who spotted his special qualities and sent him on to Moscow for grooming. What impressed the KGB was not only that Jibril was a crack terrorist operator, he was also a politically faceless military figure, unlikely to be fingered as a Soviet agent, who could get along with the Palestinians' competing factions and set an example in getting on with their war.

Infighting was the Palestinians' plague. The field was littered with shards of split-away groups, often too busy fighting each other to have much time for Israel. Usually under the wing of rival Arab governments—Syria, Iraq, Libya—they killed each other off by the hundreds in periodic power feuds, on home ground or in Europe. (Not even the Bologna railway station bomb in 1980 could compare, for devastation, to the one that blew up a nine-story Beirut office building in the summer of 1978. Whether directed against the PLO, with offices there, or the Rejection Front meeting below, it killed eighty-six *fedayeen* of both persuasions.)

Jibril himself had broken away from George Habash, the dominant figure on the left, only a year after joining him. The two had stayed together in the PFLP just long enough to export the Palestinians' war to Europe, in 1968. Both were Marxist revolutionaries, who saw Israel as part of a larger anti-imperialist struggle: "a means to an end, not an end in itself." But Jibril didn't care for political crusades. Habash was talking too much and fighting too little, in his opinion. His own PFLP-GC, free of doctrinal encumbrances, confined itself to "a new school of struggle based on the highest degree of revolutionary violence." He showed what he meant in 1970 by firing a rocket at an Israeli school bus, killing nine children.[7] Action speaks louder than words.

Until 1973, Jibril did little more than establish his credentials as the most ferocious of *fedayeen* fighters. He ran a tight little paramilitary camp at Ayn Saheb and took regular deliveries of his Soviet-bloc equipment: machine guns, Katyusha rockets, night-sight field glasses, electronic range finders, and so on, shipped from Poland and off-loaded in the Syrian port of Latakia. Then came the October War, splitting Palestinian ranks for and against a negotiated settlement with Israel; Jibril's vital mission for the Soviet Union began.

The Russians were implanted in the Middle East almost wholly because of bitter Arab rancor against Israel, their only hold on an otherwise alien Moslem people. They stood to lose their whole stake there if peace were allowed to come. The last thing they wanted was a negotiated settlement. Jibril's mission for the KGB was thus to neutralize the Palestinian "rightists" interested in peace by diplomacy and ensure an ongoing military confrontation.

Jibril would have had no trouble taking on an assignment he entirely agreed with. He became the Russians' secret channel of communications, and bagman, working closely with other Rejection Front leaders: Habash, the orthodox Communist Naif Hawatmeh, Abu Nidal of Black June. Together they put relentless pressures on Arafat's forces within the PLO and especially inside Arafat's own military arm, Fatah. Little by little over the next six or seven years, they boxed him in.

Arafat was in an extraordinarily tricky position. Fatah was by far the largest of the Palestinian guerrilla forces; in the late seventies it had 8,000 or 9,000 regular fighters, compared to Habash's 700, Jibril's 250, Hawatmeh's 500. Like the others, however, Fatah was helplessly reliant on the Soviet Union for military equipment and training. It had no place else to turn.

Far from denying continued military aid to Arafat, the Russians kept plying him with more. He was showered with diplomatic courtesies on his visits to Moscow after the October War and invited to open a PLO office there the following year—a major concession. The cream of the cream of the Soviet hierarchy received him: Brezhnev, Kosygin, Gromyko, Suslov, Boris Ponomariev. The chiefs of staff of the Soviet armed forces joined in for top-level meetings with him in the summer of 1978, on the eve of the Camp David peace meeting, to consider—and grant—his demands for heavier artillery and more advanced weapons, such as antitank missiles.[8] He had to have that to retain his authority in the restive Palestinian movement. He also had to use his formidable military machine from time to time for the same reason. Like the Rejection Front, the Russians were boxing him in.

In the course of the decade, Arafat's every military want was seen to. "Well, there's no secret about that," said his PLO observer at the U.N. to a TV team in 1979. "Our boys go to the Soviet Union. They go to the Socialist countries. They go for their training, their education. Oh yes, we're getting our direct consignments to the PLO—machine guns, RPGs, explosives, and all that. . . ."[9]

There was indeed no secret about it anymore. Proof abounded in 1979 that the Soviet Union had trained, educated, and equipped every component of the Palestine Resistance from Arafat's Fatah to Habash's PFLP (Popular Front), Hawatmeh's PDFLP (Popular Democratic Front), Jibril's PFLP-GC (Popular Front–General Command). Russian military hardware and expertise had in fact furnished the officers' corp, tactics, and superb modern armament for all the Palestinians' combined forces, the most formidable professional guerrilla army on earth.

The outside world didn't know the half of it until it had been done. Shipments of Soviet-bloc weapons to the Palestinians had been shrouded in secrecy at first, transferred at sea in the early days from Soviet cargo vessels to anonymous carriers. Only in 1978 did the arms begin to arrive directly and more or less openly. For a while then, during heavy fighting with the Israelis in southern Lebanon, seven or eight Soviet-bloc ships a day were unloading in Syrian and Lebanese ports, and five or six Soviet Antonov transports a day were landing in Damascus. (On a single day that winter, a correspondent for *Die Welt* saw seven cargo ships in Sidon unloading cases of armament under heavy guard. Four ships flew the Soviet flag, two the Libyan, one the Bulgarian.) [10]

Protected smuggling routes for arms and personnel, from the Middle East to Eastern Europe and on to Western Europe, were not uncovered until nearly the end of the decade. Neither was the Soviet Union's military training program for Palestinians. The first public word of that came at an Israeli press conference on March 15, 1978, where Premier Begin displayed a graduation certificate presented to a member of Ahmed Jibril's band from a Soviet school for military staff officers. In July 1979, Israel's former chief of intelligence, General Shlomo Gazit, stated that about a thousand Arab terrorists had been "trained in fifty different Soviet-bloc military schools, some forty in the Soviet Union itself." [11]

The terrorist trainees would start with an orientation seminar in Beirut, led by Fatah's Abu Khaled Hussein. He would lecture them on how to behave "in a proper military manner" at Soviet training centers, and he gave "indoctrination lectures" to create a common political denominator and neutralize ideological differences among Palestinians of rival bands.

Then they would go off in batches of fifty, with doctored passports, traveling to Moscow by Aeroflot a few at a time. The PLO's Moscow representative would meet them at the airport, give them a quick sightseeing tour, and hand them over to the

Russians for shipment, say, to Sanprobal, near Simferopol on the Black Sea. There they would stay for the next six months.

Their working day began at 5:00 A.M. with gymnastics and morning parade. There followed two hours a day of political studies: films on the Russian Revolution; Russian mortality rates in World Wars I and II; The Achievements of the Russian Revolution; Agriculture and Industry in the Soviet Union; Principles of Socialism and Communism; The Life and Theories of Lenin, Marx, Engels, and Stalin; Russian Ties to the Third World; The Struggle Against Imperialism; Zionist Ties to Imperialism; Expansionist Israel; Egypt's Betrayal (at Camp David); the Reactionary Nature of North Yemen and Saudi Arabia; the Soviet contribution to Palestinian Liberation; and Russian language courses.[12]

After that came three hours a day of practical studies: in incendiary charges and detonators; exploding metals; the art of mining munitions dumps, bridges, vehicles, and personnel; the rudiments of chemical and biological warfare; commando field and escape tactics; urban guerrilla tactics; marksmanship and camouflage; the use and maintenance of Soviet RPG-7 rockets and shoulder-borne Strela missiles.

At the end, every trainee was mustered out with a certificate of graduation and a book on Lenin.

There were recurrent problems in the camps, having to do with hard drinking, hard-currency smuggling, God (Soviet lectures on atheism did not go down too well), mastering the Russian language, and a surfeit of political indoctrination. That did not deter the Russians from recruiting methodically for the KGB, bringing in Moslem KGB officers from Soviet Kazakhstan especially for the purpose.

Camps like these offered fifty-four courses for Palestinians—among other foreigners—in 1977, inside Russia and throughout Eastern Europe. Thirty-five such courses were given that year within Soviet borders, on the eastern coast of the Caspian Sea near Baco and on the Crimean peninsula near Simferopol. Eight were in East Germany, around Plauen, Karl-Marx-Stadt, and Dresden near the Czechoslovak border, in Schmirblitz, Babelsberg, Klein Machnow, and in the North Schwerin region—this last an international terrorist center. Four more were in Bulgaria, in the Rodof and Pirin mountains and on the Black Sea at Varna (the biggest of all). Four others were in Czechoslovakia and three in Poland.[13]

Returning from Russia, the graduates were quick to apply their new skills. Several dozen were caught and imprisoned in Israel and have described their Soviet training experience in detail. One, confirming much of what I've reported here, agreed to talk with Herbert Krosney of the Canadian Broadcasting Corporation in 1979.[14] He was Muhammed Abu Kassem, known as "Hader," who had spent six months in a Russian "Friendship Camp" near the Black Sea.

"Hader" told about his first Fatah raid after getting back home—on an Israeli coastal highway, killing thirty-seven drivers and pedestrians at random. It was called the "Sabbath Massacre." While "Hader" got away that time, he was captured on another raid that would otherwise have taken several thousand lives.

In late September 1978, "Hader" had boarded the Greek tramp steamer S.S. *Demetrios* with a crew of seven *fedayeen*. He was first mate, and his captain had also been trained in Russia. The *Demetrios*, bought and fitted out by Fatah in Latakia, sailed into the Gulf of Aqaba on the Rosh Hashanah weekend (Jewish New Year), heading for the packed beach at Eilat. Mounted with forty-two Katyusha rockets, and *four tons* of dynamite, the *Demetrios* was to approach the Israeli coast just off a huge oil dump on Eilat's outskirts. The crew would then set the oil ablaze with their rockets, set the ship's automatic pilot to head straight for the crowded beach, and make their getaway to Jordan on a rubber raft. The dynamite was supposed to explode just as the *Demetrios* ran aground. The Israeli navy intercepted it.[15]

The whole episode had been planned to coincide with the opening of Egyptian-Israeli talks in Washington leading to the Camp David agreement. Had it come off, it would certainly have been a spectacular warning about the perils of peace.

The plan was Fatah's, not the Rejection Front's, suggesting how close the two had come since the October War divided them. Arafat had indeed made satisfying diplomatic strides abroad in the intervening five years: he now had PLO offices in a hundred countries, and subsidies of $100 million a year from Arab governments. Meanwhile, however, his opponents in the Rejection Front had taken giant steps at home.

Much had happened in those few years to harden the Palestine Resistance against a negotiated peace. Habash and Haddad had turned their multinational hit-team loose on Europe, playing to a planetary audience on satellite television. The Palestinian cause had been taken up by the worldwide radical left, replacing the spent cause of Vietnam. Israel's diplomatic position had been reversed, with many of its former foreign friends and practically the entire Third World switching sides. The hard-lining Premier Begin had come to power in Israel, greatly aggravating Israel's isolation. Above all, the Palestinians' armed revolutionary-terrorist forces had doubled in numbers,[16] and grown beyond imagining in professional and logistic strength.

It was from 1973 onward that Cuban and East German instructors were installed in South Yemen, toning up the teaching quality at Rejection Front camps. Colonel Qaddafi had opened his own proliferating camps, again with the Cubans' aid. The Russians had taken in a thousand-odd raw *fedayeen* recruits, turning them into professional guerrilla fighters and officers. And Russia had supplied this army with fabulous quantities of modern military equipment.

All these factors, and the last in particular, added enormously to the pressure for an ongoing confrontation with Israel: the "military solution." The last in particular had also added enormously to the Soviet Union's hold on all Palestinian leaders, Arafat included.

The Kremlin could always count on Ahmed Jibril, of course, and on Naif Hawatmeh. Both had gained greatly in stature as the Rejection Front gained popular ground. Jibril, with his own camp in South Yemen, had become the commanding figure there in Palestinian affairs. After Wadi Haddad's death, he became Colonel Qaddafi's favorite as well, enjoying the Libyan leader's "full confidence" and most princely patronage.[17] By 1980, he had standing enough to call a press conference announcing that he had received "heavy long-range missiles" from the Russians, capable of penetrating "well inside Israel." [18]

George Habash, never unfriendly to the Soviet Union from the start, had wound up more or less in the same political position as Naif Hawatmeh. By 1980, an Iraqi government anxious to break its own irksome ties with Russia had closed down the PFLP office in its capital, because of the latter's compromising Russian connections. Habash and his entire staff of thirty-two were given twenty-four hours to leave the country.[19]

Arafat's own position was all but untenable by then. No Marxist himself, still less a natural and supportive ally of imperial Russia, he was forced increasingly into assuming that role. In effect, he was never free to pursue peace through diplomacy. That is, he was not able to pursue it beyond the bounds acceptable to Soviet Russia.

Little by little, the bounds contracted. In time, the PLO was responding to Moscow's every whim in foreign policy, as predictably as South Yemen or Bulgaria. Freedom fighters in name, PLO leaders refused to condemn Vietnam, a ward of Russia's, for invading Cambodia, a ward of China's. But they did condemn China "unconditionally" for invading Vietnam that same year.[20] Only a year later, the PLO warmly *commended* Russia for invading Afghanistan—nobody's ward, alas. "The USSR has given disinterested and altruistic aid to Afghanistan ... against reaction and for independence," said Arafat's "foreign minister," Faruk Khaddumi, who happened suitably to be in Bulgaria at the time.[21] The Russians were only going to stay there "temporarily" anyway, added Arafat in person to Iran's Ayatollah Khomeini. Charged by the Kremlin to break the news of the invasion gently to the irascible and unpredictable Imam, that was how he put it.[22]

Barely three months earlier, the PLO had come out solidly for the Russians, in their urgent efforts to block deployment of NATO's Cruise and Pershing missiles in Western Europe.

By the summer of 1980, forces like Ahmed Jibril's had gained sufficient ascendancy over the Palestine Resistance to check Arafat at the threshold of a diplomatic triumph. The nine countries of Western Europe's Common Market were preparing to recognize the PLO at their forthcoming conference in Venice and to favor Middle East peace negotiations more or less on Arafat's terms. On the eve of the Venice meeting, Arafat was taken political captive by his own Fatah. Meeting in Damascus, for its first congress since 1971, Fatah called bluntly for Israel's physical annihilation by armed force: "the liquidation of the Zionist entity politically, culturally, and militarily." [23]

Arafat, who had used those very words in an interview with Italy's Oriana Fallaci nearly a decade earlier, fought the resolution hotly in Damascus; he claimed later that it was never adopted by a full majority at the congress but simply leaked to the press through a Rejection Front ruse.[24] If so, the trick's success simply underlined his growing impotence. In any event, the damage was done. Shaken by Fatah's stand, Europe's Nine in Venice came forth with a diluted and anodyne statement blasting Arafat's high hopes. The danger of peace in the Middle East had been warded off for quite a while.

Throughout the momentous decade, the Russians had made a fastidious point of having nothing to do with the Palestinians' shady friends abroad. The Soviet Union was simply making a fraternal contribution to the liberation of Palestine. What the Palestinians chose to do with whatever they got was their own business.

Western governments went along with that fiction for ten years. Their capacity for discretion was phenomenal.

In at least one major sector, what the Palestinians were doing was certainly Russia's business, transacted in its own satellite state of South Yemen, with the active participation of Cubans and East Germans under its direct control. The eyewitness evidence had been accumulating for years. It was crowned in the spring of 1980, when the Dutch police arrested four Spanish Etarras in Amsterdam, returning to Basqueland from South Yemen. Their confessions made front-page headlines all over the Continent.[25]

Thirteen had been sent from Spain in their batch, by ETA-Militar. Foregathering in Brussels, they were given false passports, 2,500 French francs, and an air ticket to Aden. There, they were met by Habash's PFLP representatives and spent a fortnight in a suburban villa. Then they were escorted to camp by PFLP men and *two South Yemenis from the state militia*, who got them safely past the usual police state's roadblocks. South Yemeni militiamen could not escort a foreign terrorist anywhere without the KGB's permission.

The camp consisted of eight large buildings on a mountaintop, heavily guarded and sealed off by barbed wire. From sunrise to sunset for the next four months, the Etarras practiced with Kalashnikovs and other weapons, did their field drill, and spent several hours a day getting indoctrinated in "the principles of international revolutionary solidarity," they said. The camp, vacated before their arrival, still bore traces of previous occupants from Europe and Japan.

Whoever else had been there from Europe, the Italians had been among them. Habash's second-in-command, Bassam Abu Sharif, assured an Italian weekly, after the Spanish Basque story broke, that "the PFLP has taken an assortment of Italian comrades and other nationalities into our camps" (at Hauf, Mukalla, and Al-Gheida). He had no idea "whether, by chance, some Italian comrades from our camps went on to join the Red Brigades." [26] He should have known, though. Bassam Abu Sharif himself headed the PFLP's liaison committee with the Italian Red Brigades—as the Italian secret service told a court in Rome confidentially in August 1978. The report, numbered 050714, was turned over in 1980 to a parliamentary commission investigating Aldo Moro's death. [27]

The Red Brigades' Patrizio Peci, formerly of their high strategic command, had linked the PFLP more directly to the Moro tragedy in his marathon confession. Describing two yachting trips to the Middle East to pick up Palestinian weapons, he had revealed that the Czech-made Skorpion used to murder Moro was consigned to the Brigades' Rome column commander, Mario Moretti, six months before Moro was kidnapped. It seems worth repeating, in this context, that Moretti's second large consignment of Palestinian weapons—machine guns, heavy Energa antitank mines, grenades, SAM-7 Strela missiles—was shared with the IRA Provisionals, the Basque Etarras, and the German terrorist underground after Moretti landed in Venice.

Peci did not specify the Palestinian source delivering these weapons, but it spoke for itself. When Rome's Autonomy leader Daniele Pifano was picked up in 1979, traveling with two Strela missiles, he told the court that he was simply doing George Habash a favor: the PFLP had asked him to transport these missiles for its use, he said, and the PFLP actually went public to back him up. In a formal letter to the Italian court, Habash's spokesman claimed that the Italian government knew all about the Strelas, as well it might. Colonel Stefano Giovannone, in the Middle East since Foreign Minister Aldo Moro had sent him off on just such a mission in 1973, was bound to have heard about it. Not only did the PFLP feel that Daniele Pifano ought to be let off on "moral grounds" for having merely made a "fraternal gesture," said Bassam Abu Sharif to *Panorama*: the Strelas were the property of George Habash, and he wanted them back.[28]

There is hardly much need to belabor the point. Every fresh piece of evidence coming to light toward the close of the terror decade strengthened the indictment against the Soviet Union. The triangle formed in 1968 left it free for the whole of that coming decade to practice the diplomacy of détente with its right hand, professing ignorance of what its left hand was doing. Little by little, the Cuban pole of attraction merged with the Arab *fedayeen*'s. The Palestine Resistance was used, knowingly or otherwise, from Beirut and Damascus to Baghdad, Tripoli, and Algiers. The Russians donated weapons, know-how, diplomatic cover, and strategic real estate to the Palestinians; the Palestinians passed all the benefits on to an international terrorist underground busily dismantling Western society at dozens of pressure points around the globe. This too was a form of repayment in "armed propaganda" for services rendered.

It was a do-it-yourself scheme for global terrorist warfare, complete with kit and instructions.

Not a single Western government has confronted the Soviet Union with the incriminating evidence, as this is written. None has even dared to face the Palestinians with it. Both continue to thrive on their illicit gains.

Crime pays.

16

THE BENEFICIARY

Crime pays if the fix is in, and it was. Western governments knew, but wouldn't talk.

"The KGB is engineering international terrorism. The facts can be proven, documented, and are well known to the international Western intelligence community," said Dr. Hans Josef Horchem, of West Germany's antiterrorist Office for the Defense of the Constitution, in the summer of 1979.[1]

"Who conducts the worldwide terrorist orchestra?" an Italian reporter asked William Colby, former head of the CIA that same summer.

"Nobody, directly," he replied.

"And who provides the instruments?" the reporter inquired.

"For the Italians, Moscow and Prague," was his answer.[2]

Both men could speak with authority; Dr. Horchem in particular is considered one of the West's best informed intelligence analysts. But neither was speaking for his government. No Western government has gone so far to indict the Soviet Union. Some have gone pretty far to avoid doing so.

Only a year before Colby made his flat statement connecting Italian terrorists to Moscow and Prague, the CIA had declared that Italy's Red Brigades had no foreign ties at all. That was its official reason for declining an Italian request to help in the fifty-five-day hunt for Aldo Moro, when the Red Brigades held him prisoner. The head of the State Department's Office to Combat Terrorism wholly agreed with the CIA about that when I called on him. The CIA refused to discuss it when I asked. Plainly, this was White House policy—all were simply following Presidential orders.

I was often baffled by responses like these in Washington and other Western capitals. The official flight from reality seemed unaccountable, especially in Bonn and Rome. Respectively the "strongest and weakest links in the Western democratic chain," to quote the Red Brigades, West Germany and Italy had plainly been singled out as front-line states by the terrorists and the Kremlin both. In neither of these countries did the evidence of Soviet complicity depend merely on connections two or three times removed. The KGB was involved directly, in tandem with the security services of Russia's East European satellites.

The KGB's role was not a matter of guesswork, but documented fact. Unusually useful evidence had turned up by chance in 1975, when Belgian police summoned to a routine car crash found incriminating documents in one of the cars. The papers revealed the existence of a KGB *centrale* in Vienna, working to "enliven" terrorist formations in Italy, Germany, Belgium, Holland, and France. A dozen European newspapers carried the story of the Russian in charge: a high-ranking KGB officer named Alexander Benyaminov, employed in Vienna by the U.N.'s International Atomic Energy Agency.[3]

East Germany's role in this program was no matter of speculation either. It had been running a full life-support system for the West German terrorist underground since 1970, when the Baader-Meinhof Gang's first safe-house was set up in East Berlin.[4] Apart from instant sanctuary, it furnished false documents, money, paramilitary training, protected entrance and exit routes, and a kind of safety-deposit system for the Gang's stored weapons. *Die Welt*, quoting French security services, reported that when five West German women terrorists were arrested in Paris in July 1980 their decoded notes revealed that "the network has or used to have a large depot containing pistols, machine guns, and hand grenades in East Germany."

In addition, the Communist Party of East Berlin had been

donating a million Deutschmarks a year to the PLO headquarters there since 1972—the year of the Olympic Games massacre, when the PLO's Black September death squads were operating not just in Munich but all over Western Europe.[5] The same Communist Party had also shelled out subsidies for years to Ulrike Meinhof and her husband, Klaus Rainer Röhl, for their radical review, *Konkret.*

Ulrike Meinhof herself had joined the Party, on her husband's urging, as far back as 1957. Even after quitting, in 1965, the couple would still cross over into East Berlin once a month to pick up the Party's allowance: a million Deutschmarks in all, financing the intellectual guru's guide to the terrorist scene. (Röhl told the whole story in his book, *Five Fingers Do Not Make a Fist.*)

The West German government lodged no formal protests. If anything, it was paternally protective about East Germany and Soviet Russia both. When I was last in Bonn, in 1979, government spokesmen seemed discreetly dismayed that I should raise the question. The problem, if there ever was one, had ceased to exist, I was assured by Dr. Gerhard von Löwenich, director for public security in the Federal Interior Ministry. Satellite states famous as terrorist sanctuaries had evidently decided to go straight. "South Yemen has declared that it has no terrorists. Maybe it is convinced that harboring such people is not in its interest," he told me for a start, though some of his country's most wanted terrorist fugitives were hiding out in South Yemen at the time. (One was Sieglinde Hofmann, among the five women arrested in 1980 in Paris.) [6]

"We think it is most important to build cooperation with *all* countries willing to cooperate with us in the terrorist field, such as Libya, the PLO, and Eastern Europe," he went on. "We have no evidence that the Russians exert an influence on the Palestinians one way or another. We realize that the Russians have special relations with some Palestinians, and some Palestinians have some connections with some German terrorists. But we do not have any evidence of a relationship between the two." I wondered if he could mean it. He seemed to.

The Italian Establishment's reaction to such questions was more like acute distress. No governing class has done more than Italy's to preserve the illusion that it alone is to blame for the terrorist torments inflicted upon it. Proof to the contrary has not only been brushed aside, but firmly suppressed. No Italian government for more than a decade has been willing to discuss the contribution made by Russia and its subaltern state, Czechoslovakia, to the birth, rearing, and maintenance of the Italian terrorist movement.

Regularly, throughout the terror decade, accredited Czechoslovak "diplomats" were thrown out of the country as secret agents, without a word to the press. Nineteen of them were expelled between 1975 and 1978 alone, when terrorism peaked in Italy.[7] But something on that order had been happening all along. Twenty-nine Czechs were expelled in 1968, the year of Italy's great student insurrection. Another twenty or so were supposed to have gone in 1972, after Feltrinelli died, but, oddly, didn't. The head of Italy's secret service then, General Vito Miceli, had presented the list to Premier Giulio Andreotti, saying that the SID had gathered strong evidence of their relations—and the KGB's—with Feltrinelli and extreme-left subversive groups around him.[8] Premier Andreotti unaccountably let the matter drop. (In 1974, he admitted to Parliament that Czechoslovakia had indeed trained young Italians in 1968.[9] In 1980, though, he declared that "never, during my term in office as premier, did I have any knowledge of precise facts proving any international connection with Italian terrorism.") [10]

Yet precise facts were not lacking. Police had kept track of Feltrinelli's twenty-two visits to Prague before his death (the entry visas were stamped in a false passport of his, found after his death),[11] and at least three founding members of the Red Brigades were known to have made lengthy visits there in the early seventies. (One, Fabrizio Pelli, had actually worked for Radio Prague's Italian-language broadcasts.) The prefect of Milan, Libero Mazza, had reported to Rome in 1970 that Italians "in alarming numbers" were going to Czechoslovakia for guerrilla training.[12] His report was buried and his reputation ruined. (He was held up in the left-wing press as a horrible example of unregenerate reaction, or worse.)

Yet time bore him out. By 1978, the Western intelligence community plainly knew enough about the matter to make a powerful case. Citing these sources in a story from Washington, Richard Burt of *The New York Times* wrote of that intelligence community's "longstanding suspicions" and "strongly suggestive evidence" of "Czechoslovakia's ties to West European terrorists over the last decade." His sources had referred particularly to "an old link" between Czechoslovakia and the Italian Red Brigades, "whose members are said to have visited Karlovy Vary, the Czechoslovak resort, which has a center that houses the facilities of Radio Prague and an international Communist journal, *Problems of Peace and Socialism*, published in fifteen languages." Among facilities provided at Karlovy Vary, according to congressional aides, were the production of false documents and "various forms of terrorist training." The Brigades' by now world-renowned founder, Renato Curcio, had been trained at Karlovy Vary, Burt's sources said.[13]

The New York Times story was amply confirmed in 1980 by General Jan Sejna. As I have said earlier, Sejna's personal knowledge went only as far as 1968, when he fled Czechoslovakia a jump ahead of the invading Soviet army. But he had been thoughtful enough to take his archives along. I was in Prague at the time and recall the panic this spread in high Party circles there. Debriefed at length in Washington, he had been questioned only about military matters regarding the Soviet and Warsaw Pact armies; terrorism was not a Western worry in 1968, and nobody even asked him about it. Nor did that occur to anyone, after he retired to private life in the States, for the next twelve years.

In 1980, however, the American historian Michael Ledeen did ask him about it, and he dug out his notes. The KGB and GRU had set up their training camps under his own Czech army's formal auspices, in 1964, "for many Europeans . . . and terrorists of the whole world," Sejna said. He had brought along a list of names, identifying Feltrinelli and twelve other Italians, who—even if the KGB and GRU had stopped right there—would have formed an elite Italian leadership for the decade to come.

Once the Soviet occupation forces were settled in Prague, the terrorist traffic from Italy to Czechoslovakia speeded up, as Prefect Mazza reported in 1970. It continued at a steady clip throughout the decade, as Patrizio Peci of the Red Brigades' High Strategic Command informed a still incredulous Italian public in 1980. That particular item in Peci's sensational hundred-page confession appeared in a few paragraphs, in two or three papers, and dropped out of sight.[14] Even General Sejna's story was dismissed with an embarrassed shrug, on a nation-wide television broadcast, by the otherwise upright and admirable Premier Francesco Cossiga.

Why?

I don't know why.

No single motive could explain the iron restraint shown by Italy, West Germany, and all other threatened Western governments in the face of inexorably accumulating evidence. Several obvious motives come to mind. Italy, whose Communist Party was the largest outside the Soviet orbit, had at least that good excuse for holding still. The Germans, with twenty million fellow Germans on the eastern side of the Berlin Wall, had another. Both, and all their democratic allies, also had compelling reasons of state to avoid a showdown with the Soviet Union, possibly endangering the greatest achievement of the century: peaceful co-existence and civilized communion between the Communist and capitalist worlds. All were certainly appalled at the thought of tangling with Arab rulers, whose complicity was vital to the Soviet enterprise and whose oil was vital to the West.

These are stock answers, however, and they seem too pat. Western intelligence services may have had pieces of the puzzle in hand for years without matching them up. Not every intelligence service tells everything it knows to its opposite numbers. Some must have found it hard to believe that the Kremlin would take such enormous risks. Or the facts coming to their attention may simply have failed to make sense. The Soviet design took years to complete and still longer to be clearly discernible. Those who may in fact have suspected so reckless a Soviet plot might have wanted to wait for irrefutable proof—of a kind they were unlikely to get and did not really need.

It was never part of the Soviet design to create and watch over native terrorist movements, still less attempt to direct their day-to-day activities. The phantom mastermind coordinating worldwide terror from some subterranean map room is a comic-book concept. The whole point of the plan was to let the other fellow do it, contributing to Continental terror by proxy. Ordinarily, a KGB agent wouldn't come within a mile of such fellows if he could help it. Catching the odd KGB man with an Irish Provo, say, or a Spanish Etarra was just their rotten luck; in a way it was almost irrelevant.

The incriminating evidence in this case does not depend on spotting a KGB agent here and there, or finding coded documents in a wrecked car, or thinking to ask General Sejna the right questions after a considerable lapse of time, or even prying classified secrets out of Britain's MI 6, or Germany's BND, or the CIA. These things help, but a great deal of the information in this book has been available to anyone who is interested, much of it sworn to in court. The case rests on evidence that everyone can see, long since exposed to the light of day.

It can be put in a few simple declarative sentences.

Most terrorist bands started out after 1968 without experience, skills, money, weapons, or international connections. They reached their high level of performance over the following decade thanks largely to guerrilla training, guidance, weapons, sanctuary, and the right introductions provided by Cuba or the Palestine Resistance.

Cuba's armed forces and intelligence services have been in bond to the Soviet Union since 1968. Its training camps around Havana were under constant KGB supervision, and its instructors working abroad were subject to KGB discipline.

The Palestine Resistance has been wholly armed by the Soviet Union since 1968. At least one in every ten of its guerrilla fighters and officers has been trained inside the Soviet Union or its East European satellites (not to mention North Korea, where some twenty-five hundred guerrillas worldwide were trained in the early days). The others were either trained in Cuba or had the benefit of expert Cuban instruction in *fedayeen* camps from Algeria and Libya to Syria, Lebanon, and South Yemen.

All the Palestinian guerrilla formations, but the Rejection Front especially, thereupon passed on their acquired military skills and weapons to virtually the entire international terrorist set. The Rejection Front's key base of operations was in South Yemen, impenetrable to unauthorized visitors, accessible only with the Russians' permission. There, the Rejection Front was free to mount its own multinational terrorist hits abroad and provide training and shelter for the most lethal terrorist bands in the world.

In effect, the Soviet Union had simply laid a loaded gun on the table, leaving others to get on with it.

Why would the Russians do that? Well, why not?

There was no getting at the Kremlin without getting past its perimeter defenses. Cuba and the Palestine Resistance were the Russians' guarantors. Both had better revolutionary credentials than Soviet Russia's for the 1968 generation and more magnetic appeal for the Third World, European socialists, romantic radicals everywhere. Both, therefore, were in a far better position than the Kremlin to perpetuate the dangerous illusion that the terrorists were authentic leftists.

They behaved more like calculating rightists. They were intent on right-wing "military solutions" practically everywhere and detested free trade unions, a free press, free elections, every kind of social reform, left-leaning governments, and left-wing eggheads from professors and journalists to lawyers and judges: their favorite shooting targets. (Upon killing Italy's widely admired Socialist judge Emilio Alessandrini, Front Line "accused" him of "having contributed to restore the state's democratic and progressive credibility.")

Nevertheless, genuine leftists took them at their word. They were accepted as consecrated Marxist revolutionaries, a mirror of the nation's guilt, attempting to redress the wrongs of the disinherited by whatever mistaken means, "misguided comrades." To attack them on political grounds was thus to attack the entire left, and Marxism, and socialism, and worldwide liberation movements—a daunting prospect for any democratic society, and a forbidding one for some.

Most of Europe's target states lived on the support or sufferance of the left, democratic and otherwise. Mutual antipathy did not prevent the two kinds from reaching expedient agreements. Roughly half the French voters were ready, in 1978, to endorse a popular front formed by a pro-Western Socialist

Party and a paleo-Stalinist Communist Party (until the Communists broke that up). West Germany's ruling Social Democratic Party had to live with its extreme-left wing, open-ended eastward. The British Labour Party was sinking under the weight of its far-left wing, beaming its rancor westward. About one in every three Italians voted regularly for the Communist Party; nearly one in two voted for parties insisting on a government partnership with the Communists (until 1980).

If the Soviet Union's image was battered in these left-wing circles (the Communists' included), it still passed as a Socialist state. To accuse the Kremlin alone of a demonic conspiracy against the West would have been bad enough in these circumstances—striking an all too familiar chill in progressive hearts, conjuring up the grisly shade of Senator Joe McCarthy. To incriminate the Cubans, though—and worse, the Palestinians—would have been wildly reckless.

Therefore, the West did not do so. Such political considerations were almost certainly paramount for government leaders under siege who—understandably and regrettably—wouldn't talk. Had the Western intelligence community passed on something of what it knew to the public, the most intractable of hard-core terrorists might have been exposed for the uses they were being put to, stripped of their revolutionary pretensions, isolated and contained long ago. By deliberately withholding the information, Western governments preserved the terrorists' title to legitimacy—their license to kill.

The risks were negligible for the Russians. It was soon clear that no Western chancellory was going to revive the Cold War over this issue. It was also fairly clear that Russia itself would be safe from the spreading terrorist contagion. None of the Continent's swinging terrorist bands showed an inclination to strike at the Soviet Union. (When a neophyte in the German underground proposed kidnapping a Soviet diplomat to "create chaos" in the West German government, the Baader-Meinhof Gang dismissed him as a lunatic.) [15] Ethnic and religious problems had been dealt with effectively, and ferociously, in the Soviet Union for upwards of sixty years. And its political problems of dissent were altogether different from the West's. Ultra-left theories of revolution in Paris or Bonn were meaningless in the "real" Socialist states, which already had a dictatorship of the proletariat. What Soviet dissenters were after was more freedom, not less.

The anti-Soviet bias in some Western terrorist circles didn't really bother Soviet leaders either. They did not expect the terrorists to build a solid power base anywhere, still less to seize power. They did not anticipate imminent revolutions in West Germany, Northern Ireland, Spain, Italy, even Turkey (perhaps). The terrorists' primary value to the Kremlin lay in their resolute efforts to weaken and demoralize, confuse, humiliate, frighten, paralyze, and if possible dismantle the West's democratic societies.

The Italian government held at bay for fifty-five days in its futile search for Aldo Moro; the West German Government caught in an identical trap after the abduction of Hanns-Martin Schleyer; sixteen thousand British troops pitted against a few hundred armed rebels in Ireland for well over a decade; three or four dead policemen a week under Spain's fragile new democratic order; the great strategic landmass of Turkey lying prostrate, ungoverned and ungovernable, a terminal case; the United States, mightiest power on earth, helpless to liberate American citizens held hostage halfway across the planet for months or years—all were possible in the climate of terror generated by the end of the seventies. All contributed to the merciless exposure of Western impotence. All affected the West's defenses against Soviet expansion: the cohesion of NATO, protecting Western Europe and the Mediterranean; the credibility of the United States, protecting oil supplies and routes from the Persian Gulf. It was enough, and more than enough.

The unrelenting siege of free Western societies could pay off in a hundred ways, even if revolution never came. Should it come at all, anywhere, it would come in its own time, under suitable auspices. The Russians' own revolution took half a century to mature. It, too, began with the merciless exposure of government impotence. The long-forgotten Nicholas Ishutin got it started in Moscow in 1866, with his subterranean Hell: The Organization's secret terrorist arm, through which a handful of intellectuals, madmen, and criminal thugs used dynamite, theft, and murder to undermine the tsar's godlike authority. Not until that authority was destroyed irrevocably was it possible to have an October Revolution.

Few of our latter-day terrorist formations have had theorists with the historic intellect to grasp and apply this lesson, though some did. The Italians did. The Organization got further in their country in ten years than Ishutin ever did, a hundred years before. No doubt the Russians saw to that, when they selected their first Italian wards for the pilgrimage to Prague.

There are those who still insist that the Soviet Union has shown open aversion to terrorism since the October Revolution, and so it has. Not only have Soviet Communist leaders disavowed their own responsibility, many times over, they have accused the West of using this vile instrument to destabilize itself. "All these terrorist actions are supposed to be Red, but according to me they are only Black," said Juri Jukov of the Supreme Soviet and the Control Commission of the Soviet Communist Party after a visit to Rome in 1980. "I don't see anything progressive about them. Behind them are all the reactionary forces trying to destroy law and order. We Russians maintain that the political struggle is a struggle of ideas, not armed violence. It's odd that all the armed violence is happening in the West. Fortunately for the East, the terrorist phenomenon does not exist there, inasmuch as our political situation is more healthy." [16]

He was quite honest, in a way. Soviet leaders have never cared for a certain kind of terrorism, the kind that altogether evades the Party's control. "Fear like the plague the unruly guerrilla spirit, the arbitrary actions of isolated detachments and disobedience to central authority, for it spells doom," Lenin once warned.

But Lenin assuredly did not renounce the terrorist weapon, under proper control, in the pursuit of revolution. Neither did anybody else in the Soviet Party leadership, before or since. The Bolsheviks made savage use of the Red Terror to consolidate their power in the aftermath of the October Revolution. Their successors were bound to employ it in their perennial pursuit of worldwide revolution under Soviet auspices. The fact that it is indeed a worldwide pursuit, détente or no détente, has been stated (too often to need to be emphasized here) by Stalin, Khrushchev, Kosygin, Brezhnev, Suslov, and Boris Ponomariev, among others. "The struggle between the two world systems will continue until the complete and final victory of communism on a world scale," observed *Pravda* for perhaps the hundredth time, midway through the seventies, after a decade or two of peaceful co-existence.

Any terrorist calling himself a Marxist revolutionary is familiar with Lenin's views on the usefulness of terrorism in this connection. His writings on the subject in a single year—1905— have been gathered into handy pamphlet form for consultation.

"The revolutionary army is needed because great historical issues can be resolved only by force, and in modern struggle the organization of force means military organization," Lenin started out by saying. "Guerrilla warfare and mass terror . . . will undoubtedly help the masses to learn the correct tactics of an uprising." The "organization of insurrection" requires more than the Party's conventional combat forces. "What interests us is the *armed* struggle," he emphasized. "It is conducted by single individuals and small groups, partly belonging to revolutionary organizations and partly not. . . ."

"Let five or ten people make the rounds of hundreds of workers' and students' study circles," he advised the Combat Committee of Saint Petersburg, a good ten years before the masses stormed the tsar's Winter Palace. "The propagandists must supply each group with brief and simple recipes for making bombs, give them an elementary explanation, and then leave it all to them. Squads must at once begin military training. . . . Some may at once undertake to kill a spy, or blow up a police station, others to raid a bank. . . . The essential thing is to learn from actual practice. Have no fear of these trial attacks. They may, of course, degenerate into extremes. But that is the evil of the morrow. . . ."

The main thing was "learning to fight," and "contempt for death," he counseled; and he went on to say: "When I see Social Democrats proudly and smugly declaring, 'We are not anarchists, thieves, robbers, we are superior to all this, we reject guerrilla warfare'—I ask myself: Do these people realize what they are saying?"

EPILOGUE

Belatedly—though surely better late than never—the mounting evidence of terrorism's international connections brought something like an Anti-Terrorist International into being. The Schleyer and Moro cases goaded Europe especially into pooling its defenses. "Far from bringing Europe to its knees, these two cases strengthened our collective will to resist," I was told by a French Ministry of Justice official. From the day Aldo Moro was abducted, on March 16, 1978, an impressive counter-terrorist network of police and security services began taking shape on the Continent. It included the nine Common Market countries, and Spain, Austria, and Switzerland.

Their ministers met periodically, as Austria's Interior Minister Edwin Lancs explained to me, "to get a direct and fast exchange of information, coordinate strategy, install personal contact among our police forces, harmonize police equipment and radio wavelengths, set up computerized Europe-wide data banks in many fields such as car markings, license plates, hot money, and movements across frontiers."

They shared knowledge and experience, including access to ten million items of information in West Germany's Wiesbaden computers: on the life histories, travels, dental work, blood types, hair, fingerprints, reading habits, and musical preferences of known terrorists all over the world. Country-by-country units were trained in the fabulous commando techniques of West Germany's Leatherheads (the GSG9); Britain's legendary SAS; the French Gendarmerie's Intervention Group (GIGN), which was sent to Mecca on the personal plea of Saudi Arabia's

King Khaled, to free the mosque from three hundred heavily armed and skillfully entrenched terrorist raiders.

With this came tough antiterrorist laws, in Germany, France, Italy, Spain, Britain. They were tough but constitutional laws, approved by large parliamentary majorities, occasionally treading close to the borderline of civil liberties but rarely spilling over. If anything, they still gave terrorist fugitives surprising freedom of movement across national borders. (The ancient right of political asylum would have been denied to terrorists under the 1977 Strasbourg Convention, but it has still to be ratified by a majority of the eighteen signatory states.) Thus, the terrorists had failed in their prime objective: democracy did not abdicate in Europe.

In Italy, where the danger had seemed greatest, nearly a thousand left-wing terrorists were in prison by the summer of 1980; more than half had been rounded up the previous winter and spring. An impenetrable mystery throughout the decade, their legendary discipline had suddenly cracked. Whether they would recover or not in time, they were certainly suffering from massive shock—brought on partly by long-overdue actions of the police and state they despised, but also by interior collapse.

Being a terrorist might have its exhilarating moments, but it was mostly a life of corroding anxiety and dismal drudgery. To live underground anywhere, year after year, was "hell," wrote Hans-Joachim Klein of his own experience in Germany's Revolutionary Cells. "Code, decode, memorize a new code, get the addresses in your head and burn the written notes, learn a text by heart, backtrack for hours before keeping an apointment. . . . Eighty percent of your time in clandestinity is spent on security. It's crazy. . . . The longer you do it, the more you sink into the shit. . . ."

"Bommi" Baumann, the first to get out of the German underground and live to write about it, said: "Having a pistol in your belt gives you a feeling of superiority at the beginning. Even the greatest weakling feels stronger than Muhammad Ali. All you have to be able to do is crook your finger. Any idiot can do that. It has a fascination to which many succumb." Later, though, the nervous strain and fatigue set in. "An operation was always a relief. The real stress came from life in the group. You were always sitting around with the same people in the same flat, with the same personal problems that were never solved. Many of us, for instance, agreed that . . . everyone should have it off with everyone else. But not every comrade liked that, and neither did every girl, and that was enough to cause tension. . . ." The tension was often intolerable, he added. "Once, we came to blows about where to go for breakfast. . . ."

In Baumann's day, however, his June 2 Movement had nothing like the Italian Red Brigades' rigid military structure. Patrizio Peci, for all his high rank in their strategic command, was working like a navvy when the carabinieri caught up with him. In the months they had tailed him, he'd been putting in a grueling eighteen-hour day, following potential victims, snapping photographs, dodging detection (he thought) by doubling back on his tracks to make a meet. All the other "regulars" had to hit the streets day after day, gathering painstaking information for their hit-lists. (The Red Brigades' five main columns kept neatly classified files of about three thousand selected targets each.) After the outdoor work came hours of boning up on electronics, chemistry, and weaponry textbooks. (Guerrilla manuals were for beginners only. Science-fiction, thrillers, *Playboy*, and comic strips were for late-night reading.)

Housekeeping was an endless, watchful drill. The Red Brigades' book of rules, *Standards of Security and Work-Style*, went into laborious detail. Every hideout had to be chosen carefully, after lengthy reconnaissance, "in a proletarian quarter." The building's owner must not be in residence or show meddlesome personality traits. The apartment must be "modest, clean, orderly, and complete with the necessary furnishings. . . . It must appear from the outside to be decorous, with curtains, lamps at the entrance, nameplates, plants on the balcony." Special safety locks and armor-plated doors must be installed.[1]

"Regulars" were required to "dress decorously, shave regularly, keep their hair suitably cut." All had to "develop a recognizable false identity," dress the part, and keep the right hours. To pass as a Fiat worker, say, meant going off to work when a worker would and staying out rain or shine until the hour he would get back for supper. Women Brigaders were expected to play the role of housewives, on duty whenever their menfolk got home from a mission (which they might have shared). They were strictly forbidden to shop in the neighborhood, patronize local restaurants and bars, keep neighbors awake nights with noisy radios and typewriters. The tools of their trade—official seals and stamps, forged papers, files, weapons—were supposed to be kept packed in suitcases near the door, ready for a fast getaway. (Toward the end, their laxity on this point went far to give the game away.)

Rent, gas, and light had to be paid on the nail and the smallest expenses accounted for. In Via Gradoli, the Rome safe-house used to mount Aldo Moro's abduction, police found itemized expense accounts listing 3,000 lire (4 dollars) for gasoline to do a time-test on the *autostrada*, and 6,000 lire for marking-pens. Other shopping lists in the flat ran to twenty or thirty thousand dollars' worth of supplies. One specified: "Four military gas masks, one bullet-proof vest, eight briefcases, thirty-nine trench coats, sixteen men's belts, thirty flashlights, five antennae, twenty-four police sirens, two machine guns and ammunition. . . ." [2]

The wear and tear was evidently hard on all of them. Everybody took the ritual month of August off for a vacation. (Renato Curcio postponed an appointment with an infiltrator who would eventually cause his capture, because he was planning to get away for the traditional August Ferragosto holiday.) Some needed extra rest cures, in the mountains of the Val d'Aosta or on a beach in Calabria. Several got hooked on heroin, an incredible security risk for themselves and their comrades. One wrote a full-length autobiography to relieve his boredom and mental anguish, sending it off to a Milan publisher without his name and address. A top killer-fugitive in Front Line, Roberto Sandalo, simply gave himself up midway through 1980, saying: "I didn't feel like going back to earn my bread with The Firm. It was a liberation to let myself be taken. Let them arrest me, and be done with it." [3]

They had money worries, of a peculiar kind. What with rent, food, clothing, personal weapons, and pocket money (around 250,000 lire a month, Peci said), every "regular" on the Red Brigades' payroll cost about $15,000 a year. With an estimated five hundred or so living underground, the Brigades needed something like $8 million a year for normal running expenses. Italian inflation kept raising the figure by around twenty percent a year. Then there were the costs of jet travel; elegant and extravagant weapons (a SAM-7 missile might cost anything from $25,000 to $50,000); yachts like the $80,000 *Marie-Christine*, seized in drydock on the French Côte d'Azur; Mario Moretti's sailing vessel for picking up Middle Eastern weapons in bulk; the prohibitive cost of keeping up with the latest electronics equipment.

In 1980, police discovered two particularly important Red Brigade safe-houses around Venice. One, apparently its information command center, had an elaborate microfilm library, storing a full set of the Brigades' archives going back to 1971 (strategic resolutions, kneecappings and assassinations, communiqués, leaflets). Another, plainly its communications command center, contained powerful police-type radio transmitters, digital testers, impulse generators, oscillographs, a videotelex for sending safe messages to all columns in the field, and a complete closed-circuit television network. The *Corriere della Sera* estimated the cost of this apparatus at about a quarter of a million dollars.

The very extravagance of this terrorist infrastructure helped to bring on something like a collective nervous breakdown. Raising perhaps $10 million a year for the Red Brigades, and another several million for Front Line, was a continuing drain on The Organization's human resources. This was no elementary matter of "people's expropriations" in supermarkets. It meant professional grand larceny, from bank heists and payroll robberies to kidnappings for multimillion-dollar ransoms (run at a "multinational level" to collect the payoffs abroad, Peci said), and that meant a working partnership with the Mafia and others in the criminal underworld. Half the take went to an organization with lofty revolutionary pretensions, robbing in order to kill; the other half went to common crooks who habitually killed in order to rob. The moral distinction, never very strong, tended to fade away in the terrorists' own minds as time went by. Sooner or later, some were bound to ask themselves what this luxury-model killing-machine of theirs was really for.

They were a long while coming around to the question, but then they crumpled with amazing speed. For ten years, Italian authorities could extract nothing more from captured terrorists than the single phrase "I am a political prisoner," much as a conventional army officer would give his name, rank, and serial number. When Carlo Fioroni recanted in prison, he was reviled by former comrades as a renegade, compulsive liar, psychopath, and paid police informer. Yet in just another three months, Patrizio Peci was telling the judge whatever he knew—or so he said—about the deepest secrets of the Red Brigades' High Strategic Command. Within a few more weeks, at least seven other top-ranking Italian terrorists made lengthy confessions. Scores more from the lower echelons were giving away names, addresses, dates, and game plans of their most sensational killings, starting with Aldo Moro's. Their information led to the discovery of safe-houses by the dozen and hundreds of arrests: 120 from the Red Brigades, 130 from Front Line, 50 from Revolutionary Action between that January and May.[4]

Sinister threats could not stop them. "Let it be clear to this louse [Peci] that he will walk in terror of his shadow, that anyone who comes near him, in or out of jail, whether father or mother, sister or brother, will be wiped out, that their trail will drip with blood," warned the Red Brigades' *ControInformazione*.[5] The threat was real enough—three prisoners were killed by cellmates during those months—but the spell of conspiratorial silence was broken. From behind prison walls, young men with a long career of murder behind them and a life sentence ahead called on those still at large to lay down their arms.

"Comrades, it's finished!" wrote Fabrizio Giai, Front Line's former column commander for the Piedmont, in a formal call for surrender signed by a dozen-odd of his imprisoned comrades. "We must have the humility and political courage to recognize our errors and vices. . . . We have been unpardonably blind. . . . We have undervalued our own moral, cultural, and material disintegration . . ."[6]

Why did they break? One obvious reason was a new Italian government decree, halving prison sentences for terrorists collaborating with the law. Some, too, were overcome by nervous exhaustion and the corroding depression of clandestine life. "I want to get married and have children, and play with dogs," one said. Others no longer had the stomach for the carnage. "They ordered me to kneecap somebody, an office manager I didn't even know, and I refused. They forced me to do it. I begged his pardon before I fired. Two hours later, I quit Front Line," Roberto Sandalo explained.[7]

For many like him, the strategy of terror had been worse than a failure. It had not only failed to strike a mortal blow at the heart of the state, still less rouse the proletariat to revolution. It had reinforced the police; confused, divided, and demoralized the nation's entire left; and threatened the working class with a grave loss of freedom. "I realized that we were working to force the state into becoming ever more repressive," Peci said. "I wanted to do what little I could to stop this massacre, because we were going beyond every conceivable political strategy, toward madness. . . . I realized that I was wrong about everything, that hundreds of us who thought of ourselves as Communists and were seeking for change had made an enormous mistake," Sandalo added.[8]

Repentant Germans had been saying much the same for years. "You begin by giving up your humanity, and end by renouncing your political ideals. The relation between your objective and the means used to reach it becomes insane," observed Hans-Joachim Klein. "We refuse to justify the murder of unarmed civilians, massacres, kidnappings, as a form of anti-imperialist struggle. Acts like these are crimes against the revolution," wrote Horst Mahler from prison, only a few years after presiding over the birth of the Baader-Meinhof Gang.

Nevertheless there was a difference between the two terrorist formations that, between them, had brought urban guerrilla warfare to such dizzying heights in Europe.

The West German Establishment was solid, prosperous, efficient, orderly, and had no Communist Party to speak of on its left. Its terrorist underground was a voice of the radical chic in Berlin, Hamburg, Frankfurt, fighting "consumer terror": a privileged economy suffering from a glut of material goods, the ultimate badge of opulence. Ulrike Meinhof and her successors had never built a large Hinterland, drawing strength from the workers they claimed to represent. They depended on intellectual cover within the Establishment itself, playing war games.

The Continent's most competent police force, using Europe's most advanced computerized data banks, were bound to catch up with them. By 1980, all but a score on the wanted list were behind bars. The June 2 Movement had pronounced its own formal dissolution. Not a single flashy terrorist hit had been made since Schleyer's abduction three years before. Those at large were still trying, with a new and bloodchilling professionalism that showed what a few months or years in a South Yemen training camp could do. When Sieglinde Hofmann and four other German women terrorists were arrested in Paris in 1980—having come there straight from South Yemen—police found a "pharaoh's tomb" of high-level technical terrorist equipment in their hideout: a quarter of a ton of murderously explosive sodium chlorate, complex incandescent mantles for detonation; transmitters and receivers, adapted from a model-airplane set, for remote-control detonation; an eight-meter-long twin cable for connecting the detonation device, bomb, and release mechanism; an intricate control panel to open and close the ignition circuit at a distance of a mile or two; a small and mobile multiple-rocket launcher known as "Stalin's Organ," whose forty-two deadly little explosive missiles could be launched simultaneously from the roof of a Volkswagen bus.

Though still capable of hair-raising exploits, the German terrorists' isolation in their own society was complete. But Italy, with its calamitous social, political, and economic problems, was still vulnerable. Whatever the decimation in terrorist ranks, brilliant young Marxists could still labor in richly fertile fields to the Communist Party's left, as they had done from the mid-sixties onward. Their formidable Hinterland had spread wide into the universities, the northern factories, the media, the conventional political parties. Their big mistake was trying to force the pace, an enormous but not necessarily fatal blunder.

An antiterrorist expert in the Italian intelligence services summed it up for me this way. "They were doing fine in the mid-seventies, when their terrorist structure was small and compact," he said. "Their cells of four or five each were tightly sealed and impermeable to infiltration. Even if an agent could get into one, he couldn't learn a thing about any other. They didn't depend so much on outside protection, or mass support, because they could provide their own perfect security cover. They could have gone on forever.

"But they were in a hurry. They grew too fast and took on too many people they couldn't know enough about. New cells would spring up and compete with others to show how good they were. The new kids who got the guns might have been anything—emotional cripples, drug addicts, spies, crazies. They blew their own security that way, and the wilder their hits grew, the more suspicious the workers got. Don't forget that Italians have more than race memories of violence and tyranny going back thousands of years. They have living memories of fascism and the Nazi occupation. Italian workers didn't have to be told what this kind of deliberately indiscriminate killing meant. They'd been through it; they could smell it."

In Italy, predictably, the hard-liners were far from giving up. Where weaker brothers showed genuine remorse, the hard-liners' reaction to "military defeat" in 1980 was shocked surprise. Intoxicated by their own ideological reasoning, those who had thought out the whole terrorist strategy could not believe that a state so decrepit and corrupt—so very nearly inexistent—might not only survive their assault but fight back.

They spoke of the state's "intelligent and refined design" in dismantling the intricate terrorist structure. Front Line's Fabrizio Giai himself referred to the state's unexpectedly firm "determination to annihilate the humanity of hundreds of Communist prisoners and put the needs-desires of the proletarian struggle for Communism on trial." [9] In calling on his comrades to lay down arms, he was in effect calling for no more than a tactical retreat. One had only to pick up the latest copy of the Red Brigades' *ControInformazione*, on sale that summer at any Roman newsstand for 3,000 lire, to grasp the ferocity of their own determination to regroup and go on.

From their maximum-security prisons in Italy, the Red Bri-

gades' classic leaders—Renato Curcio, Alberto Franceschini—
issued fresh directives for the New Course. *ControInformazione*
opened with an outraged attack on "the inquisitorial process"
in Europe, from Torquemada and the Spanish Inquisition to
Great Britain's unforgivably efficient Anti-Terrorist Squad.
"The religion of power requires new rituals," said the lead editorial. The state demands that "every penitent must be led before his Inquisitor, receive absolution on his knees, and thus be
liberated from excommunication. . . . The repentant bow their
heads in silence. . . . The symbolic burning of the stakes takes
the place of stinking burned flesh. . . ." [10]

In Italy itself, despite the government's "grave repressive
attacks . . . the Communist Revolution goes on," the Brigades'
review continued. "As militant Communists, we will know how
to count on our own forces, which are our real strength." No
doubt this meant a return to those small, watertight terrorist
cells that could go on forever. Henceforth, however, the Red
Brigades and allied formations would try harder to establish a
bridgehead with the working class, especially in the giant industrial complexes producing cars, electronics, computers—the
economic heart of the state. The aim was to "unite the masses
in a unitary strategic design of building Red Power."

Meanwhile, the underground would press on throughout
Europe for "the passage to an anti-imperialist civil war of long
duration." The shift in pressure points was unmistakable, and
revealing. For *ControInformazione*, by the summer of 1980, the
Germans were a write-off: it dismissed Horst Mahler's "ap-
proximative and irritatingly moralistic language" in a few cutting phrases. On the other hand, the IRA Provisionals, the
Spanish Basque Etarras, and the Marxist Mujeddin of Iran
were very much "in."

This issue devoted thirteen closely printed pages to the Iranian Mujeddin, pitted against "what is now a reactionary Islamic regime," under the title "From the People's Revolt to the
Class Struggle." The Etarras came next, in a glowing tribute.
"Under Franco, ETA was merely the embryo of a movement,
still torn between uncertain Marxist-Leninist characteristics
and a national liberation front. . . . Today we know that ETA is
a military organization, cultivating the subjective conscience of

the masses for irreversible objectives. . . ." [11] (As if to confirm its intentions, ETA stole *seven tons* of explosives in northern Spain during those weeks.)

The Enemy hadn't changed at all. It was still the West, and only the West. Never before, indeed, had the Red Brigades shown such frank acceptance of the Soviet Union's own posture in that context. "IS THE SOVIET FLEET IN THE MEDITERRANEAN TRULY A THREAT?" asked *ControInformazione* in a big black headline. "No," was its answer. Were the Soviet Union's "so-called" Euromissiles—the SS 20s with their multiple atomic warheads—really a "concrete and immediate danger to Europe"? No, they were not. As always, observed the Red Brigades' house organ, the imperialist West was "waving the specter of the Russian menace" to "restore American hegemony in the strategic camp."

How drearily familiar it sounded.

Thus did the aristocrats of terror in Europe open Fright Decade II. Together with their international allies, encircling the globe, they had ended the previous decade as they began it. Not a terrorist shot had been fired for freedom within the Soviet orbit: not for the Czechs, overrun by invading Warsaw Pact armies in 1968; not for Ethiopians massacred in the thousands by a Marxist military junta, fortified by Russian and Cuban officers; not for Cambodians facing genocide with the advance of a Vietnamese army under Soviet patronage; not for occupied Afghanistan; certainly not for the most gallant freedom fighters of our time—the dissidents inside the Soviet Union, who continued in all those years to risk their own lives for freedom without firing a shot of any kind.

Soon after Soviet authorities sent the Nobel Prize physicist Andrei Sakharov into forced exile in Gorki, early in 1980, he told a *Washington Post* reporter how he felt about the worsening terrorist phenomenon.[12] "Among the problems which trouble me is the irrationality of international terrorism," he said. "No matter how high the aims predicated by terrorists (and often there are no such justifications), their activities are always criminal, always destructive, throwing humankind back to a time of lawlessness and chaos, provoking (perhaps with the help of the secret services of foreign governments) internal and international complications, contradicting the goals of peace and progress.

"I unreservedly condemn the terror of the 'Red Brigades,' the Basque and Irish nationalists, the Palestinian, Jewish and Ukrainian extremists, the Moslem Brotherhood, the Armenian 'avengers of the genocide of 1915,' and all other terrorists. I hope that people all over the world will understand the deadly nature of terrorism whatever its goals and will deprive them of any kind of support, even the most passive, and surround them with a wall of condemnation."

NOTES
AND
SOURCES

1 1968, WHEN IT BEGAN

1. Ché Guevara wrote this in a message to the Tricontinental Conference in Havana in 1966. It was cited in the house organ of Italy's Red Brigades, *ControInformazione*, in July 1978.
2. The blood drinker was one of four Black September assassins who shot the premier on the steps of Cairo's Sheraton Hotel November 28, 1971. All four were released from prison in January 1973.
3. David Milbank, "Diagnosis and Prognosis—A Research Study on Terrorism," in the CIA Annual Report of April 1976.
4. Ponomariev is cited in John Barron, *KGB*, p. 257, and Brian Crozier, *Strategy of Survival*, p. 43.
5. Sejna's testimony was given in an interview with Michael Ledeen, editor of the *Washington Quarterly Review* (Georgetown Institute for Strategic Studies), and was published in *Il Giornale Nuovo* (Milan), January 1, 1980, May 22, 1980, and September 18, 1980.
6. Stefan Possony and Francis Bouchey, *International Terrorism—The Communist Connection*, p. 47 (Dr. Possony, of California's Hoover Institute for the Study of War and Peace, is a meticulous scholar); also Jean-Pierre Vigier in *Le Monde* (Paris), October 27, 1967.
7. *Paris-Match*, November 4, 1977. These developments were kept under constant scrutiny by the intelligence services of France, West Germany, and Italy in particular.
8. *Annual of Power and Conflict*, 1977–78, notes that these *fedayeen* were in a special guard empowered to kill anybody plotting against Amin. It was called the "Clearance Squad."
9. Described in David Boulton, *The Making of Tania: The Patty Hearst Story*, pp. 8–40.
10. Described in the *Annual of Power and Conflict*, 1972–73, pp. 42–44.
11. Ernst Halpern, *Terrorism in Latin America*, p. 16.
12. *Annual of Power and Conflict*, 1972–73, p. 42.

13. Possony and Bouchey, *International Terrorism*, p. 55. Also Juan Carlos Blawed, ed., *Fundamentación de la Posición Uruguaya* (Montevideo, 1975).
14. Carlos Marighella's *Mini-Manual for Urban Guerrillas* may be bought in almost any left-wing bookstore in Europe. I found my own copy a few blocks from home and paid 500 lire (60 cents) for it. *Encounter*, in its July 1972 issue, described Marighella's background.

2 FELTRINELLI, THE PATRON
1. *L'Espresso* (Rome), April 9, 1972.
2. Quoted in Claire Sterling, "Italy: The Feltrinelli Case," *Atlantic Monthly*, July 1972, p. 12.
3. *Potere Operaio*, March 26, 1972, special issue on Feltrinelli's death, and Sterling, "Italy: The Feltrinelli Case," p. 16.
4. *Potere Operaio*, March 26, 1972.
5. *Encounter*, July 1972.
6. *Potere Operaio*, March 26, 1972.
7. *Il Borghese*, April 23, 1978, published a photocopy of an Interior Ministry classified telegram sent by radio to all local police stations and frontier guards, coded, numbered 41199, and dated October 18, 1950. The telegram was drafted by the Ufficio Affari Riservati, at that time the civil security branch of the police.
8. *CRITICON*, September–October 1977, pp. 243–46. Cited in Stefan Possony and Francis Bouchey, *International Terrorism— The Communist Connection*. The Feltrinelli guesthouse was described by Augusto Viel, a fugitive terrorist under Feltrinelli's protection, whom Feltrinelli accompanied to Prague in May 1971, to be hidden in the villa for five months. Viel, presently in jail as a member of Italy's Red Brigades, testified in court to the goings and comings of others in his position at the Prague villa. Feltrinelli used a false passport, no. 58624437, to drive Viel into Czechoslovakia.
9. For a fuller account of Sejna's story, as published in *Il Giornale Nuovo* (Milan), September 18, 1980, and told to me by Michael Ledeen, see chapters eleven and sixteen.
10. The list of Italians trained in these camps is provided in chapter eleven, note 40.
11. Secchia's belief that he was poisoned is noted in his *La Resistenza Accusa*. "Pietro Secchia died July 7, 1973, through the after-effects of a poisoning he suffered the previous year upon returning from a voyage to Chile," said the publisher's note on the back cover of the book.

12. Reported by Judge Guido Viola, who was responsible for investigating the death, in the text of his formal indictment, or *requisitoria*, published in full in *La Criminalizzazione della Lotta di Classe*, pp. 125–26. Judge Viola named Giorgio Semeria and Bruna Anselmi of the Red Brigades as having made the Swiss trip. The documents they brought back were found by police in the Brigades' Via Delfino safe-house in Milan. (Semeria was imprisoned with the other classic Red Brigades leaders soon after Feltrinelli's death. Bruna Anselmi, a fake name, vanished.)

13. General Vito Miceli, director of the SID in 1972, reported this to the Chamber of Deputies, May 19, 1978.

14. In Romano Cantore, Carlo Rosella, and Chiara Valentini, *Dall'Interne della Guerriglia*, p. 52. Feltrinelli's book contract was proposed in 1965, and Castro finally told Feltrinelli to forget it in 1967.

15. The "Paint Your Policeman" advice is cited by the Socialist publicist Carlo Ripa di Meana in his introduction (p. 32) to *L'Affare Feltrinelli*, written by a group of Socialist journalists in the Stampa Club.

16. *Feltrinelli, il Guerrigliero Impotente*, p. 81.

17. Ibid., p. 69.

18. The Socialist journalist Giorgio Bocca cites this phrase in his *Il Terrorismo Italiano 1970–80*, p. 29. See also *L'Affare Feltrinelli*, p. 128, and Possony and Bouchey, *International Terrorism*, p. 143.

19. Viola, in *La Criminalizzazione*, p. 134.

20. Possony and Bouchey, *International Terrorism*, p. 143. Feltrinelli's advice to Habash is cited in *I Dossier di Settembre Nero* by the respected *Corriere della Sera* Middle East correspondent Vittorio Lojacono (p. 146).

21. Dutschke to Valerio Riva, one-time editorial collaborator of Feltrinelli, reported by Riva in *L'Europeo*, January 10, 1980.

22. Klaus Rainer Röhl, *Fünf Finger sind keine Faust* (Five Fingers Don't Make a Fist), pp. 282–94.

23. *Potere Operaio*, March 26, 1972.

24. Interview, *La Repubblica* (Rome), April 8, 1979.

25. The Colt Cobra had been purchased by Feltrinelli in his own name, in Milan (Viola, in *Il Criminalizzazione*, p. 66).

26. *Potere Operaio*, March 26, 1972.

27. Interview, *La Repubblica*, April 8, 1979.

28. Interview with Riva, *L'Europeo*, January 10, 1980.

29. Suzanne Labin, *La Violence Politique*, p. 130.

30. The Pasquale story was told at length after his death by *Il Giornale Nuovo*, February 16, 1978; also cited in Andrea Jarach, *Ter-*

rorismo Internazionale, an unusually well researched and documented work (p. 93).

31. Viola, in *Il Criminalizzazione*, pp. 76–85.
32. Baumann's visits to Feltrinelli are described in Jillian Becker, *Hitler's Children*, p. 294.
33. Feltrinelli's Sardinian safari is described in *Corriere della Sera* (Milan), April 4, 1972, and *La Repubblica*, February 13, 1979. Throughout Feltrinelli's campaign to "politicize" and radicalize Mesina, the Sardinian bandit was being referred to as the "Pancho Villa" of Sardinia in Italian-language broadcasts by Radio Havana and Radio Tirana (Albania).
34. Interview, *Il Giornale Nuovo*, February 9, 1979.
35. This note, signed "Giangi," was found among Dr. Negri's documents after his arrest in April 1979. See *Processo all'Autonomia* (Autonomy on Trial), compiled by Negri's defense lawyers (p. 173).
36. Sibilla Melega, interview, *La Repubblica*, April 8, 1979.
37. Breguet, departing for Haifa from Ticino, Switzerland, was arrested in Israel in June 1970.
38. The girl, Maria Angeloni, is named by Judge Viola in *Il Criminalizzazione* (p. 66). She and her companion, the Greek Cypriot George Tsecuris, blew themselves up accidentally in a Volkswagen parked in front of the embassy on January 9, 1970.
39. The Florence Conference was reported many years later in the Italian press (in *Corriere della Sera* and in *La Stampa* [Turin], December 29, 1979).
40. Richard Burt reported this in *The New York Times*, April 28, 1978.
41. Viel's testimony at the Red Brigades trial.
42. Röhl, *Fünf Finger*.
43. Viola, in *Il Criminalizzazione*, p. 126.
44. *Il Giornale Nuovo*, April 1, 1979.
45. The full text of the tape is given by Viola, in *Il Criminalizzazione*, pp. 140–48. It was recorded by Antonio Bellavita, who then and since has edited the Red Brigades' house organ, *ControInformazione*. Bellavita lives in Paris, where the French courts have refused an Italian request for his extradition.

3 THE STRANGE CAREER OF HENRI CURIEL

1. "International Terrorism in 1978," CIA Annual Report, March 1979, p. 3.
2. Reported in the *Sunday Times* (London), November 20, 1977.
3. *Le Point*, June 21, 1976. Suffert was sued for defamation of char-

acter by Curiel's family in 1980, but they lost the case. Suffert himself retracted nothing on the witness stand. (*Le Point*, June 9, 1980.)
4. *Le Point*, June 21, 1976.
5. Ibid.; also cited in the *Economist Foreign Report*, November 16, 1977 and confirmed to me by confidential police sources.
6. Police sources.
7. *Le Point*, June 21, 1976; *Annual of Power and Conflict*, 1976–77, p. 17; police sources.
8. *Le Point*, June 28, 1976 (on Joyce Blau's Kurdish studies).
9. For further explanation, see chapter six on the Tucumán Plan for a Europe Brigade.
10. Christopher Dobson and Ronald Payne, *The Carlos Complex*, pp. 90–91; Colin Smith, *Carlos: Portrait of a Terrorist*, p. 171.
11. *Le Point*, June 21, 1976; Dobson and Payne, *The Carlos Complex*; Smith, *Carlos*.
12. For Haberman, see *Le Point*, June 21, 1976; for Japanese Red Army, see *Economist Foreign Report*, November 2, 1977; Curiel's comment in *Sunday Times* (London), November 20, 1977.
13. *Economist Foreign Report*, November 16, 1977.
14. Police sources.
15. *Libération* (Paris), June 21, 1976, and May 20, 1977.
16. *Times* (London) and *Daily Telegraph* (London), both May 5, 1978; Dobson and Payne, *The Carlos Complex*, p. 85.
17. *Economist Foreign Report*, June 21, 1978.
18. French Communist Party sources, reluctant to be named.
19. André Marty, *L'Affaire Marty* (published 1955), p. 48 (extracts of Marty's letter to the French Communist Party, December 2, 1952).
20. *Economist Foreign Report*, June 21, 1978.
21. Ibid.
22. *Sunday Times* (London), November 20, 1977.
23. *Le Point*, June 21, 1976; *Daily Telegraph* (London), May 5, 1978.
24. Ibid. (both).
25. Jean Montaldo, *Les Secrets de la Banque Soviétique en France*.
26. *Le Point*, June 6, 1977, p. 183.
27. Ibid., p. 177.
28. *Sunday Times* (London), November 20, 1977.
29. *Le Point*, June 6, 1977, p. 178.
30. *Economist Foreign Report*, January 18, 1978; confirmed to me by police sources.
31. Ibid., June 21, 1978.

4 "ANNABABI"

1. Quoted by Maître Bernard Rambert, Krause's Swiss defense lawyer, *La Suisse* (Geneva), July 26, 1977.
2. CIA Annual Report, 1978. The authoritative Zurich daily *Neue Zürcher Zeitung*, January 25, 1978, describes her as the "chief" of the band known as "Annababi's group."
3. *Neue Zürcher Zeitung*, December 1, 1978.
4. Ibid., September 30, 1977.
5. The full charges against Krause, based on von Arb's and Staedeli's confessions, are included in the sentence of the Zurich court, convicting her two Swiss accomplices, issued September 27, 1977. (Egloff had been tried some months earlier.)
6. The confessions of von Arb and Staedeli fixed the first meeting with Roberto Mander and Brigitte Heinrich on May 1, 1973.
7. Per von Arb's and Staedeli's confessions, Mander and Heinrich then went again to Zurich in December 1973 to pick up four hand grenades, returning a month later to pick up ten mines (as reported in Keesing's Contemporary Archives, March 3, 1979). Five of these mines were recovered by German police in the raid on Baader-Meinhof safe-houses in Hamburg and Frankfurt on February 4, 1974. See also Zurich court sentence, p. 52.
8. *Newsweek*, July 18, 1978.
9. Interview, *Panorama*, September 8, 1977, cited in Ida Faré and Franca Spirito, *Mara e le Altre*, p. 45.
10. *Le Nouvel Illustré* (Geneva), February 14, 1979.
11. *Neue Zürcher Zeitung*, September 30, 1977.
12. From Swiss police sources. This and all subsequent quotations from the defendants are cited from their confessions to police interrogators and testimony in court.
13. Zurich court sentence, p. 53.
14. One of the Japanese hit-men stranded in Switzerland at the time was Kazuo Tohira, stuck in Geneva until he could meet with Carlos in Amsterdam.
15. Reported soon after Carrero-Blanco's death, in December 1973, by *ABC* (Madrid); reaffirmed in *Le Nouvel Illustré*, February 14, 1979; and confirmed to me in Berne by a spokesman of the Swiss Federal Department of Justice.
16. Zurich court sentence, p. 50, says that this first consignment was in June or July 1974. Krause's request for the arms was confirmed again by von Arb during the Italian trial for the same episode (*Corriere della Sera* [Milan], November 27, 1979).
17. *International Herald Tribune*, August 29, 1980.
18. Volker Speitel, in *Der Spiegel*, July 28, 1980.

19. Von Arb's confession to police before trial; confirmed in Zurich court sentence, pp. 60 and 54.

20. On July 11, 1979, Haag was convicted in West Germany and sentenced to fourteen years for formulating the Stockholm raid plans, recruiting the assault team, and procuring these specific weapons in Switzerland. The press release of the Stuttgart court of appeals cited the Zurich court sentence, p. 60, on Krause's personal delivery of these weapons to Haag in Waldshut, West Germany, on January 31, 1975.

21. Sources for discovery of some items provided by the Swiss take-out service are as follows: in the Hamburg and Frankfurt Baader-Meinhof safe-houses, Zurich court sentence; on the Catalan *Talgo* Express, Zurich court sentence, pp. 49, 50, 51, 52, 53, 54, 60, and 61; for grenades in Aqui, where Curcio's wife Mara Cagol was killed in the shootout, see Vincenzo Tessandori, *Br—Imputazione: Banda Armata*, p. 260; in the Red Brigades' safe-house for the Moro hit, Attorney General Guido Guasco's *requisitoria* on the Moro case; in the Rome-Prati hideout of Valerio Morucci, on Viale Giulio Cesare, Guasco's *requisitoria*; and for grenades at the Red Brigades' safe-house in Robbiano di Mediglia, see indictment by Judge Bruno Caccia, preparing the GAP-Feltrinelli trial.

22. On May 4, 1979, in Hamburg.

5 A TOURIST'S GUIDE TO THE UNDERGROUND

1. Dr. Michael Naumann of *Die Zeit*, who was a professor of hers at Bochum, told me this in Hamburg, May 1979.

2. Jillian Becker, *Hitler's Children*, p. 300.

3. *Quick*, August 11, 1977.

4. Ibid. She left for Aden on March 3, 1975.

5. Interview, *La Suisse* (Geneva), June 28, 1978.

6. Ludwina Janssen's story reported in Christopher Dobson and Ronald Payne, *The Terrorists*, pp. 72–73; a fuller account is in *Rheinplatz* (Ludwigshafen), August 24, 1978.

7. Interview, *Der Spiegel*, August 7, 1978; *Lotta Continua*, October 5, 1978; and in Klein's subsequent book, *Rückkehr in die Menschlichkeit*. CBS cited the South Yemen training center for West Germans, South Moluccans, and the IRA, as noted in the *Congressional Record*, April 26, 1978. The South Moluccan presence was also cited in *The New York Times*, May 26, 1977.

8. Schmucker's 1973 court testimony is quoted at length in Ovid Demaris, *L'Internationale Terroriste*, p. 286.

9. Michael "Bommi" Baumann, *Come è Cominciata*, p. 93.

10. Interview, *Lotta Continua*, October 6, 1978.

11. Gabriele's possession of the Palmer ransom money (or $20,000 of it) was reported in all Swiss papers, including *La Suisse*, December 24, 1977. The two young Austrians, Thomas Gratt and Othmar Kepplinger, were arrested at Tessin in November 1977.

12. *La Suisse*, June 11, 1978.

6 OPERATION LEO

1. *Der Spiegel*, no. 32, 1979. Press statement of attorney general's office, Düsseldorf, summing up charges for impending trial of Norbert Kröcher and his accomplice Manfred Adomeit, June 22, 1979.

2. Confidential intelligence source.

3. *Annual of Power and Conflict*, 1978–79, p. 78.

4. Reported in *Kristeligt Dagblad* (Copenhagen), August 15, 1969.

5. "Sweden's Maoist Subversives," *Conflict Studies*, no. 58 (London: Institute for the Study of Conflict, May 1975), p. 14.

6. Arrested in February 1975 and shipped back to Japan, Jun Nishikawi made a full confession, according to reliable police sources.

7. Many of the following details are to be found in *Operation Leo*, a painstaking and comprehensive study by Hans Hederberg. This book, warmly recommended to me by West German authorities dealing with Norbert Kröcher's case, provides details published nowhere else.

8. Jillian Becker, *Hitler's Children*, p. 315.

9. Colin Smith, *Carlos: Portrait of a Terrorist*, p. 194. Smith reports that Carlos and Moukarbal flew to Stockholm from Brussels on April 20, 1975, returning to Paris two days later.

10. Becker, *Hitler's Children*, p. 344.

11. Hederberg, *Operation Leo*.

12. John Barron, *KGB*. See Barron's chapter 6, "The Plot to Destroy Mexico," pp. 230–57.

13. *Annual of Power and Conflict*, 1973–74, p. 41. Armando's version is told in Hederberg, *Operation Leo*. Cuban details confirmed to me by three separate Western security services.

14. Allan Hunter's case reported in the *Guardian* (London), April 5 and 18, 1977, and *Times* (London), April 5, 1977.

15. Hederberg, *Operation Leo*. Also confirmed to me by Western security sources.

16. The background story of the Martinez brothers was told to me by two highly placed intelligence sources, neither willing to be

quoted but both unmistakably in a position to know. An off-duty CIA analyst in Western Europe confirmed the most cogent details.

17. Upon the arrest of Juan Paillacar, on April 9, 1979, the Italian press carried reports of his Cuban guerrilla training. I had been told of this a year earlier, by a prominent official in the Italian Ministry of the Interior, when Paillacar's whole underground Latin American band in Rome was under close police scrutiny during the hunt for Aldo Moro. Paillacar's "advisory" role in Norbert Kröcher's Stockholm plot was disclosed to me at that time.

18. Paillacar's Latin American band worked with the underground Azione Rivoluzionaria (see *La Repubblica* [Rome], April 10, 1979, and August 15, 1979; *Il Giornale Nuovo* [Milan], November 6, 1979). The nine Cuban-trained "instructors in terrorism" were said by Italy's military intelligence service SISMI to have been *operating in Italy since August 1975 (Corriere della Sera* [Milan], November 13, 1979). All were expelled from Italy rather than be brought to trial (*Corriere della Sera,* November 12, 1979).

19. Hederberg, *Operation Leo.*

20. Ibid.

21. Ibid.

22. Argentina's Tucumán province had become a rural front for the Trotskyite guerrilla ERP in 1974 (*Annual of Power and Conflict,* 1976–77, p. 124). The ERP had one hundred camps there, several communications centers, field hospitals, and an intelligence center (*Annual of Power and Conflict,* 1977–78, p. 117). The contents of the documents discovered in May 1975, revealing details of the Tucumán Plan for a Europe Brigade, were told to me by one of the best-informed intelligence analysts in Europe.

23. The Guanabo training camp is described in the *Economist Foreign Report,* March 23, 1977.

24. Ibid.

25. Sources for the JCR's presence in Paris and Portugal are the same intelligence analysts cited in *n.* 22, above, and *Annual of Power and Conflict,* 1976–77. The JCR press conference was reported in *Diário de Noticias,* April 4, 1975. The second press conference in Oporto, Portugal, on June 4 of that year is also reported in the same newspaper.

26. "Portugal: Revolution and Backlash," *Conflict Studies,* no. 61 (September 1975).

27. *Der Spiegel,* no. 32, 1979.

7 THE PALESTINIANS COME TO EUROPE

1. Vittorio Lojacono, *I Dossier di Settembre Nero*, p. 146.
2. Oriana Fallaci, *Interviste con la Storia*, published in 1974, containing interviews going back to 1970.
3. Feltrinelli's reported encounters with Prince Borghese in Davos, Switzerland, were the subject of two confidential reports by Italy's secret services, in the autumn of 1971 and again in February 1972. Both the Red and Black underground leaders were fugitives from Italian justice at the time. See Gianni Moncini, *Il Giornale Nuovo* (Milan), February 6, 1980.
4. Reported in *Settembre Nero*, edited by a group of Socialist journalists in Italy's Stampa Club (p. 67). Also cited in *Epoca*, November 2, 1974, in a carefully documented report by Sandra Bonsanti (whose reporting on Black terrorism in 1974 got her involved in a libel suit that she won without difficulty). In his *Terrorismo Internazionale* (p. 54), Andrea Jarach gives a few names of ex-Nazi instructors who after the conference went off to help out in the Middle East. They include Erich Altern, alias "Ali Bella," a former regional leader of the Gestapo's Jewish Affairs Section in Galicia, and Willi Berner, alias "Ali ben Keshir," a former SS officer in the Mauthausen concentration camp. See also *Gente*, September 21, 1970.
5. This ex–SS officer was Jean Roberts Debbaudt, cited in *Settembre Nero*, p. 65.
6. The Munich gathering called itself the first National European Congress of Youth and was the largest Nazi-Fascist meeting in Europe since the war. German police were apparently unaware of the meeting until delegates began to hand out leaflets in praise of Black September. Several of the Italian delegates present were interviewed personally by correspondent Sandra Bonsanti on returning to Rome (published in *Epoca*, November 2, 1974, and elsewhere).
7. I have an authentic copy of the poster, suitably printed in red and black. It shows Sirhan behind bars, with the added caption: "But the true culprit, Zionism, is still at large."
8. The Hilton hotel meeting was reported by Sandra Bonsanti in *Epoca*, November 2, 1974, where she provided several names of the thirty Europeans present. Aldo Gaiba, a founder of the Italy-Libya Association (along with Claudio Mutti—see chapter fourteen), called on Bonsanti that November 7 to rectify just a few details. He confirmed his own presence at the meeting, representing the neo-Fascist Lotta di Popolo, inextricably tied to the Nazi-

Maoist terrorist Franco Freda, who would later get a life sentence for the bombing of Milan's Bank of Agriculture in 1969. Another neo-Fascist group closely tied to his own was Avanguardia Nazionale, later outlawed. All three groups had signed the manifesto issued at the Black International's meeting in Munich in 1972. Lotta di Popolo, in particular, was known to receive a monthly subsidy from Colonel Qaddafi.

9. The Malga Croun camp in Italy's Trento region was run by the fascist Avanguardia Nazionale, to "forge young Palestinians" (Lojacoano, *I Dossier di Settembre Nero*, p. 64).

10. Ibid., pp. 144–45; Jarach, *Terrorismo Internazionale*, p. 54.

11. In reality, gentle poet or not, Zwaiter was the terrorist Black September's representative in Rome. See *Le Nouvel Observateur's* article on the Black Orchestra (meaning the interlocking Black terrorist structure in Europe), cited in *Epoca*, November 2, 1974. For other skeptical views of Zwaiter's peace-loving role, see David Tinnen and Dag Cristensen, *The Hit Team*, pp. 78–79.

12. Lojacono, *I Dossier di Settembre Nero*, pp. 144–45.

13. The founders of Black September were Ghassan Kanafani, Bassan Abu Sharif, and Wadi Haddad of George Habash's PFLP, together with Hassan Salameh, Abu Daoud, Abu Yussef, and Abu Jihad of Arafat's Fatah. See Jarach, *Terrorismo Internazionale*; *Settembre Nero*; and Lojacono, *I Dossier di Settembre Nero*, pp. 41–44.

14. Salameh's planning of the Olympics massacre is described in Tinnen and Cristensen, *The Hit Team*, pp. 46, 96–98, and in John Laffin, *Fedayeen*, p. 149.

15. Lojacono, *I Dossier di Settembre Nero*, p. 119.

16. Ovid Demaris, *L'Internationale Terroriste*, pp. 34–35; Christopher Dobson and Ronald Payne, *The Carlos Complex*, pp. 28–29; Colin Smith, *Carlos: Portrait of a Terrorist*, p. 101.

17. François Arnoud in *Gente* on September 21, 1970, claimed author's rights in a Swiss court for a book based on Martin Bormann's papers, and a Cologne court in 1956 confirmed his rights to the posthumous works of Goebbels. His relations with Hassan Salameh are described in Lojacono, *I Dossier di Settembre Nero*, pp. 118–19, and Jarach, *Terrorismo Internazionale*, pp. 58–59. Salameh's handling of Black September's $100 million or so of funds channeled to Switzerland is described in Laffin, *Fedayeen*, p. 149.

18. Tinnen and Cristensen, *The Hit Team*, p. 46.

19. Hans-Joachim Klein says that Carlos first met members of the PFLP in Moscow (*Lotta Continua*, October 6, 1978). Carlos met

Boudia at Lumumba University there, according to Demaris, *L'Internationale Terroriste*, p. 34. In *Carlos*, Colin Smith says that Carlos "came to Habash highly recommended by his man in Moscow" (p. 78).

20. Interviews with Arafat and Habash, March 1972, in Fallaci, *Interviste con la Storia*.

21. PFLP defines itself "Leninist" in Bichara and Khader, eds., *Testi della Rivoluzione Palestinese, 1968–1976*, p. 236; Habash quoted in Demaris, *L'Internationale Terroriste*, p. 231.

22. The Baddawi conference is described in most informed works on international terrorism. See Paul Wilkinson, "Terrorism: International Dimensions," *Conflict Studies*, no. 113, p. 8 and *L'Avenir n'est ecrit nulle part*, by former French Interior Minister Michel Poniatowski (p. 202).

23. Smith, *Carlos*, p. 71.

24. Bassam Abu Sharif, chief spokesman for Habash's PFLP, was quoted in the *Washington Star*, January 20, 1979, as saying that his group had "been in touch with the Iranian people's struggle for the past seven years." He added that the PFLP had provided Iranian terrorists with training "in everything from propaganda to the use of weapons."

25. The pact was signed in Dublin, May 27, 1972. See Wilkinson, "Terrorism: International Dimensions," *Conflict Studies*, p. 8, and Stefan Possony and Francis Bouchey, *International Terrorism—The Communist Connection*, p. 35. The first IRA guerrillas in Jordanian camps were reported in 1968 (see U.S. Congress, House Committee on Internal Security document, August 1, 1974).

26. Dobson and Payne, *The Carlos Complex*, pp. 187–90; Smith, *Carlos*, p. 112.

27. Demaris, *L'Internationale Terroriste*, pp. 39, 41, and Dobson and Payne, *The Carlos Complex*, p. 192.

28. *The New York Times*, September 18, 1972.

29. Interview, in Fallaci, *Interviste con la Storia*.

30. United Press International, in a story dated January 22, 1974, reports that the Palestinians held a "series of meetings" secretly in Dublin, at one of which, in December 1973, they offered training in Lebanon and £1 million worth of modern weapons for distribution among European terrorist groups. The lion's share went to the IRA, but some also went to the French, the Italians, and the Spanish Basques, said UPI. Intelligence sources confirm this report.

8 "CARLOS"

1. The Interview ran in two parts, starting December 1, 1979; reproduced in part in *Le Figaro* (Paris), December 15, 1979.

2. Christopher Dobson and Ronald Payne, *The Carlos Complex*, p. 36; Michel Poniatowski, *L'Avenir n'est ecrit nulle part*, p. 203.

3. Poniatowski, *L'Avenir n'est ecrit nulle part*, p. 203. *Annual of Power and Conflict*, 1976–77, pp. 16–17, indicates that Carlos was originally recruited by the KGB in Venezuela. In *The Carlos Complex*, Dobson and Payne speak of his "Ecuadorian" instructor "Antonio Dages Bouvier" (p. 36). In *Carlos: Portrait of a Terrorist*, Colin Smith reports on Bouvier's later presence in Europe (p. 103).

4. *Annual of Power and Conflict*, 1976–77, reports Carlos's return to Moscow for these four specialized advanced courses, around 1974. In *The Carlos Complex*, Dobson and Payne report Carlos's stint at these special courses with PFLP comrades in 1974 (p. 39). The latter report came from an Arab terrorist imprisoned in Israel who swore he had seen Carlos in the Moscow camp.

5. Ovid Demaris, *L'Internationale Terroriste*; Dobson and Payne, *The Carlos Complex*; Smith, *Carlos*; and *Lotta Continua*, October 6, 1978.

6. Dobson and Payne, *The Carlos Complex*, reports Carlos's detour to East Berlin on the way back from Moscow (p. 40). John Laffin, *Fedayeen*, reports the early terrorist support system (p. 149). The *Washington Post* reported (September 7, 1975) that "the Baader-Meinhof Gang constantly received support from the East German secret police. False papers and identity cards, money, arms, ammunition, and training were specific forms of support." *Annual of Power and Conflict*, 1973–74, p. 8, reports that the PLO opened an office in East Berlin on August 14, 1973. Its secret agreement with the East German Communist Central Committee for special facilities is reported in note 5 of chapter sixteen.

7. For Antonio Dages Bouvier and Nydia de Tobon in London, see Smith, *Carlos*, pp. 187 and 158–63; Dobson and Payne, *The Carlos Complex*, pp. 72–74.

8. Dobson and Payne, *The Carlos Complex*, p. 41. The episode on the Lebanese corniche was told to me by highly responsible intelligence sources—not Israelis, as it happens.

9. Interviews in *Der Spiegel*, August 7, 1978; *Lotta Continua*, October 5–6, 1978; and in Klein's book *Rückkehr in die Menschlichkeit*.

10. Dobson and Payne, *The Carlos Complex*, pp. 83–84.

11. *The New York Times*, July 11, 1975.
12. In *The Carlos Complex*, p. 83, Dobson and Payne say that Poniatowski "wanted to name the Soviet Union as well, but was restrained on the orders of President Giscard D'Estaing, who was about to make a visit to Moscow and had no wish to embarrass the Russians on the eve of it." Also in Smith, *Carlos*, pp. 14–15.
13. Smith, *Carlos*, p. 128.
14. Details of the Schönau operation were described to me by two members of Austria's Anti-Terror Squad on my visit to Vienna in May 1978. The operation is also recounted in Smith, *Carlos*, pp. 127–38.
15. The presence of this KGB agent, in a directorial capacity, for such a major international terrorist undertaking, has been confirmed by the highest authorities. The Israeli Defense Ministry claimed, after Israel's commando rescue mission, that Bouvier had taken "command of the entire action at Entebbe" (Dobson and Payne, *The Carlos Complex*, p. 233).
16. The full story is told in *The New York Times*, September 17, 1976.
17. Dobson and Payne, *The Carlos Complex*, p. 40.

9 THE LONGEST WAR: THE PROVISIONAL IRA

1. Maria McGuire, *To Take Arms*, p. 110.
2. *ControInformazione*, November 1978.
3. Associated Press dispatch of August 27, 1979, in *International Herald Tribune*, August 28, 1979.
4. John Barron, *KGB*, p. 255.
5. McGuire, *To Take Arms*, p. 71.
6. See chapter four of *To Take Arms*, where the full story of the Czech arms shopping trip is given.
7. See U.S. Congress, House Committee on Internal Security document, August 1, 1974.
8. *Corriere della Sera* (Milan), December 29, 1979.
9. Stefan Possony and Francis Bouchey, in *International Terrorism— The Communist Connection*, p. 35, refer to Victor Louis's visits as reported in the *Daily Telegraph* (London), June 1974. Barron, *KGB*, sums up the KGB's role, naming the first three agents (pp. 254–55). The fourth Dublin agent is named in Brian Crozier, *Strategy of Survival*, p. 137. The reference to the DGI's operational plan is in Barron, *KGB*, p. 151.
10. Crozier, *Strategy of Survival*, p. 146. *Annual of Power and Conflict*, 1974–75.
11. *An Phoblacht*, October 26, 1977.

12. For Devlin and Farell quotations, see Ovid Demaris, *L'Internationale Terroriste*, pp. 365–66 and 370.
13. *An Phoblacht*, April 12, 1977.
14. Signed during a visit to the Continent by the IRA's Malachy McGurran, who had been assigned to supervise arms-running operations at the Florence conference sponsored by Feltrinelli and Potere Operaio in October 1971.
15. United Press International, in a story dated January 22, 1974, reported that the Palestinians held a "series of meetings" secretly in Dublin, at one of which, in December 1973, they offered training in Lebanon and £1 million worth of modern weapons for distribution among European terrorist groups. The lion's share went to the IRA, said UPI. There are similar reports on Dublin meetings from multiple Western intelligence sources. The authoritative left-wing Basque historian Francisco Ortzi, in *Historia de Euskadi*, p. 391, refers to one such meeting on May 1, 1972, attended by the Basque ETA, the IRA Provisionals, the French Breton Liberation Front, and Habash's PFLP. The left-wing French weekly *Politique Hebdo* of June 1972 reported that such a meeting was held "somewhere in Ireland" that April. *Die Zeit*, December 7, 1974, reports a Dublin terrorist summit held in December 1973, attended by Black September, the Italian Red Brigades, the West German Red Army Fraction, the Basque ETA, and the Breton Liberation Front, dealing with weapons exchange, false documents, safe-houses, and courier routes.
16. Demaris, *L'International Terroriste*, p. 370.
17. *Daily Mail* (London), April 2, 1973.
18. *An Phoblacht*, February 20, 1976.
19. Interview with Washington correspondent of *Daily Telegraph* (London), September 3, 1979.
20. *Daily Mirror* (London), January 1975.
21. Both routes detailed in Demaris, *L'International Terroriste*, pp. 367–68, who cites *Daily Mirror* (London) report of January 1975.
22. Jillian Becker, *Hitler's Children*, p. 199.
23. José Maria Portell, *Euskadi: Amnistía Arrancada*, p. 251. See chapter ten for fuller statement on the ETA position.
24. See chapter twelve for Turkish People's Liberation Army statement on inciting to militarization.
25. See chapter two for Feltrinelli's statement.
26. *Brigate Rosse*, edited by Soccorso Rosso, the Red Aid legal assistance group, p. 104.
27. McGuire, *To Take Arms*, pp. 7 and 144.
28. *An Phoblacht*, June 15, 1977.

29. Ibid., June 22, 1977.
30. In *L'Europeo*, September 13, 1979, O'Bradaigh rejected this "unacceptable confederation." In a front-page interview with *Il Giornale Nuovo* (Milan), September 2, 1979, O'Bradaigh explained his views on dismantling both the Irish Republic and Ulster.
31. Same interview, *Il Giornale Nuovo*, September 2, 1979.
32. *Sunday Independent* (Dublin), September 19, 1976.
33. *An Phoblacht*, April 12, 1977.
34. *ControInformazione*, November 1978.
35. Ibid.
36. See Patrizio Peci's confession, chapter eleven.
37. Interview in *La Repubblica* (Rome), October 24, 1979.
38. *Irish Times* (Dublin), November 21, 1978.

10 TERROR IN BASQUELAND

1. See chapter four, *n.* 14, for provenance of dynamite via Petra Krause group.
2. Julen Agirre, *Operation Ogro: The Execution of Admiral Luis Carrero Blanco.*
3. José Maria Portell, *Euskadi: Amnistía Arrancada*, p. 265.
4. Ibid., p. 70.
5. Ibid., pp. 88–109 and 146–50.
6. José Maria Portell, *Los Hombres de ETA*, p. 265.
7. "Peixoto's" letter in photocopy, in Portell, *Euskadi: Amnistía Arrancada*, p. 192. For the "Month of Urban Guerrilla Warfare," see ibid., p. 218.
8. Ibid., p. 148.
9. Estimate by U.S. consulate, Bilbao, in 1979; similar report given me by editors of *Cambio 16* (Madrid).
10. Communiqué of the Basque General Council, January 9, 1979.
11. Portell, *Euskadi: Amnistía Arrancada*, p. 285.
12. Ibid., p. 251.
13. Portell, *Los Hombres de ETA*, p. 88. Portell says that the fact was confirmed by Jaime Caldevilla, Spain's former information counselor in the Spanish embassy, Havana, in April 1973.
14. After its fifth *asamblea*, in a declaration representing "the most important theoretical leap in all ETA's history," says Francisco Letamendia Ortzi, in *Historia de Euskadi*, p. 383.
15. Spanish secret service reports.
16. Ortzi, *Historia de Euskadi*, p. 391. The pact was signed in Dublin on May 1, 1972, and included the French Breton Liberation Front.
17. Ibid. Also see chapter nine, *n.* 15.

18. See chapter nine's references to documents related to Italy's Organized Autonomy and The Organization. Charges against Professor Antonio Negri, awaiting trial for organized subversion in Italy, include the following excerpts allegedly written by him, published by his April 7 College of Defense in *Processo all'Autonomia* (Autonomy on Trial). "We are here to set up multiplying mechanisms both from the point of view of policy and action" (in a letter sent to Negri from "abroad," p. 180). "The communist order of the day to be imposed wherever the struggle exists; Basques, Bretons, Catalans, Irish . . . have already organized their defense . . . the first step toward unification and requalification of these groups of the revolutionary advance guard . . . [requires] great effort to recuperate them for the Europe Project" (p. 179). "Dear Comrades. . . . We have reached agreement on three points: [one of which is] preparation of an international conference to launch the theme of insurrection in Europe, and deepen contacts between national groups" (letter from Potere Operaio's "International Office" in Zurich, p. 179).

19. See chapter seven, *n*. 31; chapter nine, *n*. 15.

20. *ABC* (Madrid), August 3, 1978, carried a lengthy report by Alfredo Semprun on the secret *asamblea* and the subsequent guerrilla training in Algeria. The information was confirmed to me by highly responsible Spanish and American sources.

21. Ibid. (both *ABC* and Spanish and American sources).

22. Pooled information of Western intelligence services on Libya-Algeria agreement. Camps in Libya are described in chapter fourteen.

23. The Breton's attacks shot up from almost none to their apotheosis with the fire-bombing of the Palace of Versailles, presumably part of their program to "annihilate capitalism." In Corsica, terrorist attacks rose from 111 in 1974 to 238 in 1976 (*Annual of Power and Conflict*, 1978–79, p. 31).

24. *L'Espresso* (Rome), April 10, 1980, in a report by this weekly's expert on terrorism, Mario Scialoia.

25. Dr. Hans Josef Horchem, of West Germany's Anti-Terrorist Office for the Defense of the Constitution, in a conversation with me in Hamburg.

26. Attorney General Guido Guasco noted the Yugoslav meeting formally in his indictment of several score Italians implicated in the Moro case, December 13, 1979. Among the participants were the West German Red Army Fraction, the IRA, the Japanese Red Army, and ETA (*Economist Foreign Report*, December 6, 1979).

27. Confirmed to me by Spanish, German, Italian, and American intelligence sources.
28. They were Franco Pinna, Orianna Marchionni, Enrico Bianco, and Pierluigi Amadori (all Italian papers, March 30, 1980).
29. She was Olga Girotto (all Italian papers, March 31, 1980).
30. *La Stampa* (Turin), April 1 and 3, 1980; *Paese-Sera* (Rome), April 1, 1980; *La Repubblica* (Rome), April 2 and 3, 1980; *L'Aurore* (Paris), March 31, 1980; *Corriere della Sera* (Milan), April 3, 1980.
31. *International Herald Tribune*, February 18, 1980; *Corriere della Sera*, April 3, 1980.
32. *Annual of Power and Conflict*, 1978–79, p. 70, cites November 24, 1978, reports in two Madrid papers, *Cambio 16* and *Informaciones*, revealing KGB meeting with "Anchon." These reports were evidently based on information provided by Spanish security services, which also confirmed them to me.
33. *El País* (Madrid), January 23, 1979.
34. Dispatches by the Associated Press and Agence France Presse from Madrid, September 12, 1979.

11 THE ISHUTIN SOLUTION

1. Adam B. Ulam, *In the Name of the People*, pp. 154–58.
2. Fioroni's lengthy interrogation by the Italian magistracy, published in *Lotta Continua*, January 8, 1980, presumably in full (though it, or he, must have left some things out).
3. Text of "Saetta's" reply, signed "Elio" (Piperno's other game-name), published in *La Repubblica* (Rome), January 6, 1980.
4. The receipt, made out to Carlo Fioroni, was found in 1975 (*Corriere della Sera* [Milan] May 13, 1978). De Vuono had just finished serving three years for theft when he undertook the Saronio kidnapping, *Corriere della Sera* said.
5. In Fioroni's letter of October 24, 1978. I have a copy.
6. *Paese-Sera* (Rome), October 10, 1978.
7. *La Repubblica,* October 9, 1978.
8. Fioroni's interrogation, confirmed by a major witness, Mauro Borromeo, arrested on the strength of his testimony. Borromeo, the administrative director of Milan's Catholic University, confirmed that he had been at dinner with other leaders of The Organization—and Saronio—on the night of the kidnapping (*La Stampa* [Turin], December 30, 1979; *Corriere della Sera*, December 23, 1979).
9. Following Fioroni's confession, Marco Boato, the famous former

national student leader of 1968, appealed to his old comrades in *Lotta Continua*, December 29, 1979, "to remove all shadow of doubt" about Alceste Campanile's death. This, he said, would be a political response to "the terrifying weakness produced by terrorism in all ranks of the left." Boato spoke in this context of "a horrendous crime made to pass as the outcome of militancy and a revolutionary theory." The Campanile case, never solved, was reopened by the courts only to be closed again for lack of evidence.

10. In Judge Gallucci's rejection of an appeal for provisional liberty, for Professor Antonio Negri and other "Autonomy" leaders under arrest, July 7, 1979, reported in *Autonomy on Trial*, published by Negri's April 7 Defense College, p. 278.

11. *Brigate Rosse*, edited by Soccorso Rosso (Red Aid), p. 275.

12. Antonio Negri, *Dominio e Sabotaggio*, p. 65.

13. Cited in *Autonomy on Trial*, p. 170.

14. *Dominio e Sabotaggio*, p. 43.

15. *L'Europeo*, January 1, 1980.

16. *Autonomy on Trial*, pp. 257-58.

17. Ibid., pp. 258–59.

18. Ibid., p. 260.

19. The details of Front Line's transformation can be traced through *Autonomy on Trial* and Fioroni's confession. Fioroni, in prison when Front Line itself emerged as such, told his interrogators that its communiqués alone made its origins clear to him (*La Repubblica*, December 28, 1979). Confirmation of its transformation by other witnesses at the time is too massive to report here. The stages of transformation in The Organization's occult military arm went from Potop's Illegal Works Department in September 1971, to FARO in December 1971, to Centro-Nord over the next couple of years, to Front Line in 1976.

20. *Il Giornale Nuovo* (Milan), July 10, 1979; *Potere Operaio*, September 25, 1971, October 25, 1971, November 1971 (no. 44), and December 1971 (no. 45).

21. *Autonomy on Trial*, p. 162.

22. Ibid., p. 269.

23. Ibid., p. 263.

24. Among these was Mauro Borromeo, who confirmed that a meeting had taken place between Negri and Curcio in the summer of 1974, in his own country house in Bellagio (*La Stampa*, December 30, 1979).

25. Ibid.

26. *ControInformazione* was identified as the Red Brigades' house organ after a police raid on the Brigades' safe-house in Robbiano di Mediglia in 1974. A document found there, dated November 1973, addressed to "the Comrades of *ControInformazione,*" spelled out the "terms of our collaboration" (the Red Brigades', that is), after the first ("Zero") issue. "Every member of the editorial staff must pronounce an explicit commitment of political homogeneity" with the Red Brigades, the letter read. The Brigades would assume the publication's financing, provided its policy "coincided exactly" with the Brigades' "armed strategy." "No other component of the democratic area" could "be inserted into the editorial staff" of the magazine. In short, *ControInformazione* was financed and *exclusively staffed and edited* by Red Brigades members or others whose views "coincided exactly." (The document is cited by Examining Magistrate Bruno Caccia, preparing the first classic trial of the Red Brigades in *La Criminalizzazione della Lotta di Classe*, p. 326).

   Professor Negri admitted under interrogation to having directed *ControInformazione* for its "zero" issue only. Later, he conceded his connections with the review for issues one and two. Judge Gallucci confronted him with evidence purporting to show his continuing collaboration for issues three, four, five, and six (*Autonomy on Trial*, pp. 141, 162, 266–67, and 167).

27. *Autonomy on Trial*, pp. 162, 141, 269, and 162.

28. Ibid., pp. 268 and 162.

29. Ibid., p. 179.

30. Ibid., p. 180.

31. The arrests were made in Cairo on April 26. One of the ringleaders was Sergio Mantovani, a Swiss in close contact with the Eco-Libro bookshop's owner, Giorgio Bellini, who had put up Petra Krause occasionally during her Zurich stay. Mantovani's co-leader was a Palestinian named Mohammed Aref al-Moussa, previously expelled from Rome University (*Daily Telegraph* [London], April 27, 1978). Al-Moussa, who confessed in full to the Egyptian police, was murdered in Madrid a year later. The band's plot is cited in Attorney General Guido Guasco's indictment in the Moro case, December 13, 1979.

32. *Autonomy on Trial*, p. 198; also Attorney General Guasco's indictment.

33. Dr. Negri delivered a report on the Palestine Resistance. *La Repubblica*, December 29, 1979.

34. *Autonomy on Trial*, p. 198.

35. A specific charge in the indictment of Morucci was his having

taken delivery of one such Swiss consignment in Zurich, on February 14, 1974 (Attorney General Guasco's indictment). Fioroni, who claimed to be procuring weapons for The Organization on his trips to Switzerland in 1973, received at least one check for 500,000 lire (about $800 at the time) from Toni Negri, on October 4, 1973. Negri admitted this under interrogation (*Autonomy on Trial*, pp. 269–70).

36. See Zurich court sentence, p. 52.
37. Attorney General Guasco's indictment, December 13, 1979.
38. *Panorama*, December 3, 1979.
39. See *Il Giornale Nuovo*, January 11, 1980; May 22, 1980; and September 18, 1980.
40. I have a photocopy of General Sejna's list. Here it is, with whatever errors and omissions, as he wrote it: Fabrizio Pelli; Franco Troaino; Budio Bianchi; Luciano Ferrari; Ferruccio Gambino; Semino; Clemente; Briglia, Roberto; Spazzali; Viale; Cesare Capellino; Franceschini.

    Renato Curcio, co-founder (with Franceschini) of the Red Brigades, was reported by *The New York Times'* Richard Burt to have been trained in Czechoslovakia as well. Burt's article, evidently based on high-level American security sources, appeared in the *Times*, April 26, 1978.
41. *Panorama*, September 15, 1980.
42. *Il Giornale Nuovo*, April 16, 1980. This newspaper had clearly seen the text of Peci's interrogation, carefully paraphrasing it to avoid prosecution for violating judicial secrets. (A correspondent for Rome's *Il Messaggero*, who published the text as such—omitting all textual references to the Red Brigades' international ties—landed in jail that May.) It was common knowledge in Rome that the text of Peci's interrogation was circulating among all Italy's newspaper offices. Reportedly, it was on sale for 2 million lire ($2,500) to anybody who could get the money up.
43. *Corriere della Sera*, April 16, 1980; *La Repubblica*, April 16, 1980; *La Stampa*, April 19, 1980.
44. Ibid. (all three).
45. Story of Pifano's capture: all Italian papers, November 9, 1979. Sabeh Abu Anseh was an agent of Habash's PFLP in Italy since 1975: all Italian papers, November 9, 1979; *Panorama*, December 3, 1979. PFLP's letter to the Italian government and the President of the Chieti court trying Pifano: all Italian papers, January 11, 1980. *Il Messaggero* of that date reported that the letter was delivered by hand, by the Radical Deputy Mauro Mellini.
46. Pifano's open letter to *Lotta Continua*, May 2, 1980.

47. *Washington Post*, February 2, 1979.
48. *L'Espresso* (Rome), March 4, 1979.
49. The horse was named Carnauba and in its day was considered to be the best three-year-old (*L'Unità* [Rome], December 30, 1979).
50. *La Repubblica*, December 11, 1978. This was the first joint Mafia-Red Brigade snatch, on January 12, 1977, just over a year before Moro himself was snatched.
51. Ibid. Casirati, the "honest crook" who also told all about The Organization after Fioroni did, complained that The Organization's criminal connections with the underworld were hurting other honest crooks like himself. First of all, they were being hounded in jail because of suspected connections with the "politicals." Secondly, they were cheated by the "politicals" themselves, who promised them "a Utopian mirage of a society without prisons" (*Corriere della Sera*, January 29, 1980).
52. In the Bergamo area of Lombardy alone, five members of Organized Autonomy were arrested on April 24, 1980, accused of fifty terrorist acts connected with both Front Line and the Red Brigades (*Corriere della Sera*, April 25, 1980).
53. The court found that terrorist acts committed and arms stored by the defendants were designed to "subvert the state order" (*Corriere della Sera*, July 28, 1980).
54. Ibid., July 5, 1979.
55. Valerio Morucci, who had started out as Potop's first underground military commander and gone on to become the Red Brigades' Rome column commander, helping to catch and kill Aldo Moro, had broken with the Brigades' strategic high command after the Moro hit. A lengthy criticism of the Brigades' Stalinist elitism was found in his hideout when he was arrested in August 1979. Oreste Scalzone, starting out at the same high level in the Potop mother cell, added his protest from prison that August, speaking of the Red Brigades as "an emanation of the Soviet KGB" (*La Repubblica*, August 20, 1979).

12 TURKEY: THE ANARCHY

1. The PLO leader was Hani al-Hassan (reported in *Corriere della Sera* [Milan], March 14, 1979). *Il Manifesto* (Rome), April 7, 1979, reports him as having said, "Turkey will be next to explode."
2. Associated Press dispatch from Ankara, March 15, 1979.
3. *International Herald Tribune*, July 24, 1979. *Annual of Power and Conflict*, 1978–79, pp. 108–9, says that the republican government of Premier Bulent Ecevit first claimed the riots were provoked

against "defenseless leftists" but later confessed to left-wing provocation as well.

4. *International Herald Tribune*, July 24, 1979.
5. *Annual of Power and Conflict*, 1977–78, p. 73.
6. *Financial Times* (London), October 13, 1978.
7. John Barron, *KGB*, pp. 56, 79, 175–76, and 256.
8. Ibid.
9. Jacob M. Landau, *Radical Politics in Modern Turkey*, pp. 41–42; *Ortam* (Istanbul) April 19–26, 1971. The CIA Annual Report published in April 1976 says (p. 14): "Palestinian training camp facilities in Syria have been used by the Turkish People's Liberation Army. To reciprocate for this aid, Turkish terrorists have attacked Israeli targets in Turkey." An AP dispatch on April 1, 1972, says, "The Turkish People's Liberation Army is mostly trained in Arab camps in Syria, getting money from East Germany and arms from the Arabs."
10. Barron, *KGB*, 175–76. The Turkish senator spreading the forgery was Hadar Tunckanat, who produced his "documents" on July 7, 1968, including fake photostats of U.S. intelligence intervention. The second "document" was a forged letter to the U.S. defense attaché in Ankara, Colonel Donald Dickson. The third "proof" was an official-looking press release.
11. Landau, *Radical Politics in Modern Turkey*, pp. 38–41. See also *Annual of Power and Conflict*, 1972–73, p. 28.
12. Landau, *Radical Politics in Modern Turkey*.
13. Barron, *KGB*, pp. 56 and 27. The occult military arm of Dev Genç was the Turkish People's Liberation Army, founded in January 1971 by Mahir Cayan.
14. The *Observer* (London) estimated that three hundred youths were in Colonel Turkeş's neo-Nazi camps on August 19, 1969. Their acts of violence then were limited to smashing a few windows in left-wing students' quarters in Ankara, the *Observer* said.
15. *International Herald Tribune*, July 27, 1980.
16. *Annual of Power and Conflict*, 1973–74, pp. 26–27.
17. AP dispatches, Ankara, March 27 and 30, 1972.
18. *Annual of Power and Conflict*, 1972–73, p. 27. Landau, *Radical Politics in Modern Turkey*, pp. 44–45.
19. Christopher Dobson and Ronald Payne, *The Carlos Complex*, pp. 48–49.
20. Landau, *Radical Politics in Modern Turkey*, p. 43.
21. *Annual of Power and Conflict*, 1977–78, p. 74. *Economist Foreign Report*, September 28, 1977.
22. In an interview with *Yanki*, July 11, 1978.

23. *Il Giornale Nuovo* (Milan), August 8, 1979, and *Corriere della Sera*, August 8, 1979.

24. Ecevit was generally described this way in the European press. *La Repubblica* of Rome called him "The Allende of the Bosporus" (October 17, 1979).

25. Dennis Redmont, in an Associated Press report from Ankara, April 1979.

26. *New York Times* report, carried by the *International Herald Tribune*, April 8, 1980.

13 THE MAGNETIC POLES (I): CUBA

1. John Barron, *KGB*, pp. 150–51. The story has been told in more or less the same terms by a dozen writers specializing in Cuban affairs.

2. Barron, *KGB*, pp. 25–26. Barron says that "the United States learned, through a penetration of the KGB, that in 1968 the [Soviet] Central Committee reversed the previous Soviet policy of shunning the Palestinians. Soviet assistance to them, in the form of training and arms, has increased as the Soviet position in Egypt has weakened."

In the CIA Annual Report of April 1976, David Milbank writes that the Russians "began channelling funds, weapons and other assistance to Fedayeen groups . . . in 1969."

The Arab Communist meeting in Moscow in July 1968 is reported in *Fedayeen*, by the experienced Middle East journalist John Laffin. On p. 36, he notes: "Arab communists attending the July 1968 conference in Moscow were instructed to establish close contacts with the Fedayeen. The collection of intelligence was an important objective. But their main task was to investigate the possibilities of bringing the Palestinian organizations under their influence." Laffin adds that "by 1970, promising Fedayeen were being sent to officers' Special Schools in Egypt, Algeria, Syria, Libya, Iraq, China, North Vietnam and Cuba," receiving "political indoctrination based on Marx, Engels, Lenin and Stalin."

3. The Zanzibar National Party opened an office in Havana in December 1961, when John Okello and a sizable number of his followers arrived for training. Other Zanzibaris joined Okello there in August 1962. See *Cuba: The Technology of Subversion* by Alfonso Tarabocchia, chief investigator for the United States Senate Internal Security Subcommittee (pp. 34–35).

4. Ibid., p. 35.

5. Ibid. Tarabocchia refers to Cuban revolutionary ties going back to the 1870s, when Cuban insurrectionists were exiled to the island of Fernando Po off the coast of Spanish Equatorial Guinea. Using this pretext, Cuba began to infiltrate the island with "historians" starting in 1962, "helping to stir anti-Spanish sentiment, leading to Nguema's coup in 1969." Guerrilla training for the inhabitants had been available in Havana since January 1962, Tarabocchia says.

6. In Editorial Research Reports, May 20, 1977, Richard Schroeder reports the presence of numerous Cuban "advisers and technicians in Equatorial Guinea." Jean-François Revel wrote that the Cubans were "counseling" Nguema on the eve of his fall (*L'Express*, August 1979). The *Economist Foreign Report*, November 30, 1977, claims that there were three to four hundred Cubans in Equatorial Guinea that year, half of them military personnel. Lamb's report ran in the *International Herald Tribune*, January 28, 1980.

7. Editorial Research Reports, July 19, 1967.

8. Castro's radio announcement on December 2, 1961, caused a sensation. His non-Communist affiliation had been widely accepted internationally. See Editorial Research Reports, July 19, 1967.

9. Barron, *KGB*, pp. 150–51.

10. *Time*, September 17, 1979.

11. Barron, *KGB*, p. 150; testimony of former DGI agent Orlando Castro Hidalgo to U.S. Senate Subcommittee on Internal Security, October 16, 1969.

12. Brian Crozier, "The Surrogate Forces of the Soviet Union," *Conflict Studies*, no. 92 (February 1978).

13. Hidalgo's testimony before the Senate subcommittee, October 16, 1969.

14. Suzanne Labin, *La Violence Politique*, p. 130.

15. Tarabocchia, *Cuba: The Technology of Subversion*, p. 16.

16. The *Cookbook*'s contents were described to me by an off-duty U.S. government official with notable Cuban expertise. I later found a copy.

17. Stefan Possony and Francis Bouchey, *International Terrorism— The Communist Connection*, p. 47.

18. In August 1976, the CIA estimated that three hundred Arab *fedayeen* were training in Cuban camps (Jacques Kaufmann, *L'Internationale Terroriste*, p. 227). Same estimate given by the *Christian Science Monitor*, March 15, 1977. George Habash was

received by Castro in Havana on April 22, 1978, and requested training for five hundred more *fedayeen* in the PFLP. Reporting the impending visit, John Cooley of the *Christian Science Monitor* observed (April 20, 1978): "Dr. Habash, who disavowed international terrorism in an interview with this reporter last month, now is paying his first visit to Havana for talks with Cuban leader Fidel Castro."

Arafat, who had maintained a PLO office in Havana since 1974, undertook in the summer of 1978 to sign a formal military pact with Castro that September (*Jerusalem Post*, July 27, 1978; *Economist Foreign Report*, June 28, 1978).

Naif Hawatmeh, most orthodox pro-Soviet of the Palestine Resistance forces, visited Havana with a delegation on January 4, 1977 (BBC), to meet directly with the Cuban Communist Party's Central Committee.

19. A confidential memorandum from a staff member of the Institute for the Study of Conflict, London, 1975.
20. The Cuban role is cited in the *Annual of Power and Conflict*, 1978–79, pp. 375–76. The left-wing Lebanese daily *al-Liwa* and Kuwait's *al-Anbaa* also report this, as well as the arrival of five hundred Cuban troops by airlift from Ethiopia for the battle (*Il Giornale Nuovo* [Milan], April 29, 1978).
21. For a fuller list of eyewitness reports on South Yemen guerrilla training see chapter five, and its note 6. Oman's Dhofar insurgency and its Soviet-Cuban backers are reported in the *Annual of Power and Conflict*, 1976–77, pp. 249–51. That the first Cuban presence in South Yemen was in 1973 was reported by (among others) *Corriere della Sera* (Milan), October 13, 1979.
22. Alfredo Semprun's report in *ABC* (Madrid), August 3, 1978.
23. The many press reports estimated in this range; this particular estimate is from *Corriere della Sera*, October 22, 1979.
24. Ibid.
25. Cited in Kaufmann, *L'Internationale Terroriste*, p. 277.
26. As reported by the *International Herald Tribune*, August 20, 1980, Beaufort Castle, just north of the Litani River, subsequently became a major missile- and rocket-launching base for Rejection Front attacks on Israeli settlements across the Lebanese frontier. On August 19, 1980, the Israelis carried out a major commando raid, penetrating inland from the Lebanese coast for the first time, to knock out this guerrilla artillery base.
27. *Economist Foreign Report*, March 23, 1977.
28. Ibid.

29. *Corriere della Sera*, October 22, 1979.

30. *Annual of Power and Conflict*, 1978–79, p. 5.

31. I was given this information personally in NATO headquarters in March 1979.

14 QADDAFI, THE DADDY WARBUCKS OF TERRORISM

1. Interview to the BBC on June 17, 1980.

2. Mutti was expelled from the neo-Fascist MSI (Italian Social Movement) for extremism in 1964. He went on to operate through Lotta di Popolo, which had a regular monthly allowance from Qaddafi, in the early seventies. He was the first to translate and publish Qaddafi's Green Book in Italy and wrote an ecstatic volume titled *Qaddafi, Templar of Islam*. He was jailed on August 29, 1980, for complicity in planting the Bologna railway station bomb, which killed eighty-four people that August 2. Mutti's founding of the Italy-Libya Association in 1973 was reported in *Paese-Sera* (Rome), August 25, 1974, a fact rediscovered by a dozen Italian papers after the Bologna bombing. He was also under indictment for abetting the prison escape of his close friend Franco Freda, sentenced to life for the bomb that killed seventeen people in Milan's Bank of Agriculture in December 1969.

3. Andrea Jarach, *Terrorismo Internazionale*, p. 144; *Il Giornale Nuovo* (Milan), August 8, 1980.

4. Jarach published a photocopy of this poster in *Terrorismo Internazionale*.

5. Libya formally suspended these payments on January 25, 1973. See Brian Crozier, "Libya's Foreign Adventures," *Conflict Studies*, no. 41 (December 1973).

6. Undersecretary Newsom was testifying before a U.S. Senate commission investigating Billy Carter's adventures in Libya; Reported in *Il Giornale Nuovo*, August 9, 1980, and *Corriere della Sera* (Milan), August 6, 1980.

7. *The New York Times*, September 13, 1975.

8. *Jeune Afrique*, February 13, 1980.

9. Ibid., and *L'Europeo*, April 1, 1980.

10. *La Stampa* (Turin), February 5, 1980; *Il Giornale Nuovo*, May 5, 1980; *La Repubblica* (Rome), February 18, 1980; *Panorama*, May 5, 1980; *L'Europeo*, April 1, 1980; *Le Nouvel Observateur*, February 1980; *Jeune Afrique*, February 13, 1980.

11. Christopher Dobson and Ronald Payne, *The Terrorists*, p. 71.

12. *Jeune Afrique*, February 13, 1980.

13. *International Herald Tribune*, October 13, 1979.
14. *Neue Zürcher Zeitung*, June 22, 1979.
15. In Hans-Joachim Klein's clandestine interview with *Lotta Continua*, October 5, 1978.
16. Archimedes Doxi, a Greek leftist who requested asylum in Sweden in March 1975, said he had worked for the PFLP in Paris (the Carlos network) and had carried the two Strela missiles to Rome for the aborted hit in 1973 (pooled information from Western intelligence services).
17. Vittorio Lojacono, *I Dossier di Settembre Nero*, pp. 365-69.
18. Jarach, *Terrorismo Internazionale*.
19. Aldo Moro's letters from a Red Brigades prison, those in particular addressed to Christian Democratic leader Flaminio Piccoli, former assistant justice minister Erminio Pennachini, and assistant justice minister Renato dell'Andro. Published in *Corriere della Sera*, September 13, 1978.
20. *International Herald Tribune*, October 13, 1979.
21. Cairo's *al-Akhbar*, quoted in *Miami Herald*, April 24, 1977.
22. *Washington Post*, May 25, 1976; *Christian Science Monitor*, June 21, 1977; *Corriere della Sera*, March 31, 1979, and July 21, 1980; *L'Espresso* (Rome), June 1, 1980.
23. *The New York Times*, January 12, 1979.
24. Brian Crozier, "The Surrogate Forces of the Soviet Union," *Conflict Studies*, no. 92 (February 1978), p. 4; *Annual of Power and Conflict*, 1976-77, p. 14; *L'Espresso*, June 1, 1980.
25. *The New York Times*, May 29, 1975.
26. Ibid., June 20, 1978.
27. *Newsweek*, June 18, 1979.
28. *Washington Post*, June 28, 1977.
29. BBC Monitoring Service, February 4, 1979.
30. I have the full texts of the Lisbon Congress proceedings, dated November 2-6, 1979.
31. *Corriere della Sera*, May 20, 1980.
32. Maurizio Chierici, *I Guerriglieri della Speranza*, p. 80.

15 THE MAGNETIC POLES (II): THE PALESTINE RESISTANCE

1. John Barron, *KGB*, p. 57, reports on the shipment of thirty Palestinians to the Soviet Union in the summer of 1970 "to convert them into controlled agents while training in guerilla warfare."
2. John Laffin, *Fedayeen*, p. 79. The Olympics hit-planning in Sofia was revealed to the world over Jordanian television by Black September leader Abu Daoud, who, on his arrest in Jordan, Feb-

ruary 20, 1973, said he had been in the Bulgarian capital at the time. He was there "to buy weapons," he explained, and had lent his passport to a Palestinian sent to scout the terrain in Munich (*I Guerriglieri della Speranza*, by Maurizio Chierici of *Corriere della Sera*, pp. 120–21).

3. The use of Bulgaria as a staging post for Russian-made weapons distributed to various international terrorist formations is illustrated also by regular arms shipments to the Turkish underground from Varna, Bulgaria, as reported in chapter twelve. When the Turkish People's Liberation Army leaders fled Turkey for Paris, headed by the widow of the army's founder, Mahir Cayan, they stopped off in Bulgaria to on-load a large consignment of arms and explosives for future use in Paris. Driving westward, they were stopped at Modane, on the Italian-French border, on a tip from the Israeli Mossad. Their confession led to a French police raid on their key safe-house, in Villiers-sur-Marne, near Paris, shared by Carlos. See Christopher Dobson and Ronald Payne, *The Carlos Complex*, pp. 48–49.

4. Laffin, *Fedayeen*, pp. 50–51.

5. Vittorio Lojacono, *I Dossier di Settembre Nero*, pp. 149–51.

6. Ibid.

7. The attack occurred May 20, 1970, close to Israel's frontier with Lebanon, near the Kibbutz Moshov Avivim.

8. This was during Arafat's visit on July 24, 1978 (*Economist Foreign Report*, September 6, 1978). The Lebanese weekly *al-Sayif* (August 13, 1978) reported that Arafat "got Russia's promise not to abandon the PLO."

9. The interview, with the PLO's Zehdi Labib Terzi, was conducted by the Public Broadcasting Service's Marilyn Berger and broadcast August 25, 1979. Terzi added, "Well, the Soviet Union and all the Socialist countries . . . they give us full support—diplomatic, moral, educational, and also they open their military academies to some of our freedom fighters."

10. *Die Welt* (Hamburg), January 31, 1978. *Al-Azmal* (Beirut) reported on February 9, 1978, that "these shipments comprise sophisticated Soviet weapons including anti-aircraft and ground-to-ground missiles." *Al-Manaar*, an Arabic publication in London, stated on February 12, 1978: "Large quantities of Soviet arms reached Palestinian organizations at the end of last week . . . transferred under the aegis and protection of the Soviet navy in the Mediterranean. . . . The terrorists received improved missiles from the USSR, and several experts arrived in southern Lebanon to instruct the Palestinians in their use."

11. Address to the Jerusalem Conference on International Terrorism, July 2–5, 1979.

12. This is a composite description furnished by several dozen *fedayeen* under arrest in Israel after assault missions following their training in Soviet camps. It is borne out in good part by interviews with three such *fedayeen* granted to Herbert Krasney of the Canadian Broadcasting Corporation. His views were presented by the Public Broadcasting Service and published in full by *New York*, July 24, 1979.

13. This listing was provided in full by two separate intelligence services and has been confirmed in bits of various news reports between 1978 and 1980. For instance, the *Christian Science Monitor* reported on July 28, 1978, that, according to the leftist Cairo paper *al-Ahali*, thirty-two Palestinian pilots and sixty technicians had recently completed training courses in the Soviet Union, East Germany, and Czechoslovakia. See also Christopher Dobson and Ronald Payne, *The Terrorists*, p. 77.

14. As cited in *n*. 12 above. See also *The New York Times*, October 31, 1980, on Russian training of Palestinians.

15. *Jerusalem Post* account, similar reports in all Israeli papers.

16. *Annual of Power and Conflict*, 1978–79, estimated the combined Palestinian guerrilla forces at around fourteen thousand for 1978. The same annual's estimate at the end of 1974 was seven thousand.

17. *Annual of Power and Conflict*, 1978–79, p. 348.

18. *The New York Times*, June 9, 1980.

19. An Associated Press dispatch of April 25, 1980.

20. *New York Times*, February 21, 1979. The criticism was voiced by Saleh Khalef, known as "Abu Iyad," Arafat's second-in-command. "We openly declare that we stand on the side of Vietnam against the Chinese invasion," he said.

21. Khaddumi was quoted by the Bulgarian news agency BTA as making this statement at an official banquet in his honor in Sofia (*Il Giornale Nuovo* [Milan], January 14, 1980).

22. *International Herald Tribune*, in a United Press International dispatch of March 21, 1980, says that President Bani-Sadr announced Arafat's "first word" of the Soviet Afghanistan invasion to Ayatollah Khomeini in this way. *La Repubblica* (Rome), March 12, 1980, says that Arafat claimed the Soviet presence in Afghanistan would be "absolutely temporary."

23. *International Herald Tribune*, June 7, 1980; *Il Giornale Nuovo*, June 14, 1980 (from a *New York Times* Beirut dispatch).

24. Dispatch from Beirut by Nicholas Gage of *The New York Times* in *International Herald Tribune*, June 9, 1980.
25. *France-Soir* (Paris), May 29, 1980; *Corriere della Sera* (Milan), June 6, 1980; *La Repubblica*, May 29, 1980.
26. *Panorama*, June 16, 1980.
27. Confidential report by DIGOS, Italy's civilian security police, to Judge Ferdinando Imposimato, investigating the Moro case. The report cited a standing liaison committee between the Italian Red Brigades and the PFLP's Bassam Abu Sharif agreed upon in Baghdad at the end of July 1978, after earlier contacts between the two groups in Baghdad and Tripoli (*La Repubblica*, February 2, 1980).
28. *Panorama*, June 16, 1980.

16 THE BENEFICIARY

1. Address to the Jerusalem Conference on International Terrorism, July 2–5, 1979.
2. Interview with Roberto Gervaso, *Corriere della Sera* (Milan), August 25, 1979.
3. *Annual of Power and Conflict*, 1978–79, p. 13.
4. "The Baader-Meinhof Gang members constantly received support from East German secret police. False papers and identity cards, money, arms, ammunition and terrorist training were the specific forms of support" (*Washington Post*, September 7, 1975). "Warsaw Pact members' assistance to terrorists originates in Pankow [East Germany] and Prague," said the CIA in "International and Transnational Terrorism," April 1976, p. 21 of the CIA's Annual Report. "North Korean diplomats help coordinate the activities of terrorists in Europe through an agent in East Germany," said the *Christian Science Monitor*, March 5, 1977. Arafat thanked the East Germans for their aid to the Palestine Resistance in a visit to East Berlin: "You too, dear comrades in the German Democratic Republic [are] our true friends in the Socialist camp," he is quoted as saying in Beirut's *al-Anwar*, April 9, 1978.
5. The arrangements were made after Arafat's visit to Moscow in July 1972. East Germany was thereupon instructed to become the Warsaw Pact's aid center for Palestinian guerrillas abroad. In February 1973, Arafat himself met in East Berlin with a delegation headed by Comrade Kromirek of the Party's Politburo there, to discuss such cooperation. (Black September, co-sponsored by Arafat's Fatah, was still in full swing in Western Europe then,

having just pulled off the Olympic Games hit in Munich.) The East Germans agreed to let the PLO open its East Berlin office "to reinforce collaboration between the Palestinian people and German people in the common struggle against Zionism and imperialism." The accord provided for East German political, military, and civilian aid. The PLO's office opened at Fischerinsel 6, headed by Nabil Qalailat. (Pooled information from Western intelligence services' Middle East watchers.)

6. *Le Point*, May 12, 1980; *Le Matin* (Paris) and *Il Giornale Nuovo* (Milan), May 7, 1980.
7. *L'Espresso* (Rome), June 8, 1980.
8. General Miceli raised this in the Chamber of Deputies, May 19, 1978.
9. *L'Espresso*, June 8, 1980.
10. *Panorama*, to which the message was addressed, June 9, 1980.
11. *The New York Times*, April 28, 1978, in a report by Richard Burt.
12. Giorgio Bocca, *Il Terrorismo Italiano 1970–80*.
13. *The New York Times*, April 28, 1978.
14. Citation by *Il Giornale Nuovo*. As far as I know, the item was not carried in other Italian papers.
15. Volker Speitel, in *Der Spiegel*, July 28, 1980.
16. Jukov, Vice-President of the "Soviet Committee for Peace," gave this assurance to former Premier Andreotti on a visit to Rome (*Il Giornale Nuovo*, May 30, 1980).

EPILOGUE
1. Soccorso Rosso, eds., *Brigate Rosse*.
2. *Corriere della Sera* (Milan), December 1, 1978.
3. *Panorama*, June 3, 1980.
4. *Lotta Continua*, June 1980.
5. *ControInformazione*, June 18, 1980.
6. *La Repubblica* (Rome), June 30, 1980.
7. *Panorama*, June 30, 1980.
8. Ibid.
9. *Panorama*, June 9, 1980.
10. *ControInformazione*, June 18, 1980.
11. Ibid.
12. *Washington Post*, March 9, 1980.

BIBLIOGRAPHY

L'Affare Feltrinelli. Con testimonianza di Carlo Ripa di Meana. Milan: Stampa Club, 1972.

Agirre, Julen. *Operation Ogro: The Execution of Admiral Luis Carrero Blanco.* New York: Times Books, 1974.

Alexander, Yonah. *Terrorism in Italy.* New York: Crane, Russak, 1979.

Almanac, Turkey, 1978. Ankara: Turkish Daily News, 1978.

The Anarchists' Cookbook. Secaucus, N.J.: Lyle Stuart, 1978.

Annual of Power and Conflict 1972–73, 1973–74, 1974–75, 1975–76, 1976–77, 1977–78, 1978–79. London: Institute for the Study of Conflict.

Bakunin, Michele. *Lettera ai Compagni d'Italia.* Privately printed in Italy.

Barron, John. *KGB.* New York: Reader's Digest Press, 1974.

Bassiouni, Cherif. *International Terrorism and Political Crimes.* Springfield, Ill.: Charles Thomas, 1975.

Baumann, Michael "Bommi." *Come è Cominciata.* Milan: La Pietra, 1975.

Becker, Jillian. *Hitler's Children.* London: Panther Books, 1978.

Bell, J. Bowyer. *The Secret Army: The Ira 1916–1974.* Cambridge, Mass.: MIT Press, 1970.

Beltza. *Del Carlismo al Nacionalismo Burgués.* San Sebastián: Editorial Txertoa, 1978.

———. *Nacionalismo Vasco y Clases Sociales.* San Sebastián: Editorial Txertoa, 1976.

Bichara and Khader, eds. *Testi della Rivoluzione Palestinese 1968–1976.* Verona: Bertani, 1976.

Bocca, Giorgio. *Il Terrorismo Italiano 1970–80.* Milan: Rizzoli, 1978.

Boulton, David. *The Making of Tania: The Patty Hearst Story.* London: New English Library, 1975.

Bruni, Luigi. *ETA.* Edizioni Filorosso.

Burgos: Juicio a un Pueblo. Zarauz, Spain: Hordago, 1978.

343

Cantore, Romano; Rosella, Carlo; and Valentini, Chiara. *Dall'Interne della Guerriglia*. Milan: Arnoldo Mondadori, 1978.

Chaliand, Gerard. *The Palestinian Resistance*. London: Penguin (in association with Cedric Chivers), 1972.

Chierici, Maurizio. *I Guerriglieri della Speranza*. Milan: Arnoldo Mondadori, 1978.

CIA Annual Report 1976, 1978, 1979. Washington.

Cleaver, Eldridge. *Post-Prison Writings and Speeches*. London: Jonathan Cape, 1969; New York: Vintage, 1969.

Conflict Studies nos. 28, 33, 41, 46, 58, 61, 63, 65, 92, 113, 120. London: Institute for the Study of Conflict.

Conrad, Joseph. *The Secret Agent*. London: Pan, 1907; New York: Doubleday, 1953.

Contemporary Terrorism. Selected Readers. Gaithersburg, Md.: International Association of Police Chiefs, 1978.

Criminalizzazione della Lotta di Classe. A cura di Guiso, Bonomi, Tommei. Verona: Bertani, 1975.

Crozier, Brian. *Strategy of Survival*. New Rochelle, N.Y.: Arlington House, 1978.

Demaris, Ovid. *L'Internationale Terroriste*. Paris: Olivier Orban, 1978.

Dobson, Christopher, and Payne, Ronald. *The Carlos Complex*. London: Coronet Books/Hodder & Stoughton, 1977.

———. *The Terrorists*. New York: Facts on File, 1979.

Dostoievski, Feodor. *The Possessed*. New York: New American Library, 1962.

Editorial Research Reports. Washington: Congressional Quarterly.

Fallaci, Oriana. *Interviste con la Storia*. Milan: Rizzoli, 1974.

Faré, Ida, and Spirito, Franca. *Mara e le Altre*. Milan: Feltrinelli, 1979.

Feltrinelli, il Guerrigliero Impotente. Rome: Edizioni "Documenti."

Finetu, Ugo. *Il Dissenso nel PCI*. Milan: Sugar Co., 1978.

Forest, Eva. *Diario y Cartas Desde La Cárcel*. Zarauz, Spain: Hordago, 1978.

———. *Testimonios de Lucha y Resistencia*. Zarauz, Spain: Hordago, 1979.

Formare l'Armata Rossa. Collected works RAF, Baader-Meinhof Gang. Verona: Bertani, 1972.

Guiso, Giannino. *La Condanna di Aldo Moro*. Milan: Sugar Co., 1979.

Hallier, Jean-Edern. *Chaque Matin qui se lève est une leçon de courage*. Paris: Editions Libres-Hallier, 1978.

Halpern, Ernst. *Terrorism in Latin America*. The Washington Papers, no. 33. London and Beverly Hills, Calif.: Sage Publications, 1976.

Hederberg, Hans. *Operation Leo.* Stockholm: Raben and Sjogren Boktorlag AB.

Ibarzabal, Eugenio. *50 Años de Nacionalismo Vasco.* San Sebastián: Ediciones Vascas, 1978.

Isman, Fabio. *I Forzati dell'Ordine.* Venice: Marsilio, 1977.

Jarach, Andrea. *Terrorismo Internazionale.* Florence: Vallecchi, 1979.

Kaufmann, Jacques. *L'Internationale Terroriste.* Paris: Librairie Plon, 1976.

Khaled, Leila. *The Autobiography of Leila Khaled.* London: Hodder & Stoughton, 1973.

Klein, Hans-Joachim. *Rückkehr in die Menschlichkeit.* Hamburg: Rowohlt, 1979.

Kubeissi, B. al-. *Storia del Movimento dei Nazionalisti Arabi.* Milan: Jaca Book, 1977.

Labin, Suzanne. *La Violence Politique.* Paris: France-Empire, 1978.

Laffin, John. *Fedayeen.* London: Cassell, 1978.

Landau, Jacob M. *Radical Politics in Modern Turkey.* Leiden, Netherlands: E. J. Brill, 1974.

Laqueur, Walter. *Terrorism.* London: Weidenfeld and Nicolson, 1977.

Lenin, Vladimir. *Scritti sulla Violenze.* Verbani, Italy: MOB, n.d.

Levergeois, Pierre. *J'ai choisi la D.S.T.* Paris: Flammarion, 1978.

Lewis, Geoffrey. *Turkey.* London: Ernest Benn, 1955.

Lojacono, Vittorio. *I Dossier di Settembre Nero.* Milan: Bietti, 1974.

Manzini, Giorgio. *Indagine su un Brigatista Rosso.* Turin: Giulio Einaudi, 1978.

Marighella, Carlos. *Piccolo Manuale del Guerrigliero Urbano* (Mini-Manual for Urban Guerrillas). Italian translation, privately printed.

McGuire, Maria. *To Take Arms.* London: Macmillan, 1973.

Montaldo, Jean. *Les Secrets de la Banque Sovietique en France.* Paris: Albin Michel, 1979.

La Morte di Ulrike Meinhof. Rapporto Commissione Internazionale d'Inchiesta. Naples: Libreria Tullio Pironti, 1979.

Moss, Robert. *Urban Guerrilla Warfare.* Adelphi Papers, no. 79. London: International Institute for Strategic Studies.

Mucchielli, Roger. *La Subversion.* Paris: C.L.C., 1976.

Negri, Antonio. *Crisis e Organizzazione Operaia.* Milan: Feltrinelli, September 1974.

———. *Dominio e Sabotaggio.* Milan: Feltrinelli, January 1978.

———. *Proletari e Stato.* Milan: Feltrinelli, March and December 1976.

Nortarnicola, Sante. *L'Evasione Impossibile*. Milan: Feltrinelli, 1972.

O'Brien, Conor Cruise. *States of Ireland*. London: Hutchinson, 1972.

Orlando, Federico. *P 38*. Milan: Editoriale Nuova, 1978.

Ortzi, Francisco Letamendia. *Historia de Euskadi*. Barcelona: Ruedo Ibérico, 1978.

Pansa, Giampaolo. *Storie Italiane di Violenza e Terrorismo*. Bari, Italy: Laterza, 1980.

Poniatowski, Michel. *L'Avenir n'est ecrit nulle part*.

Portell, José Maria. *Euskadi: Amnistía Arrancada*. Barcelona: Dopesa, 1977.

————. *Los Hombres de ETA*. Barcelona: Dopesa, 1974.

Possony, Stefan, and Bouchey, Francis. *International Terrorism—The Communist Connection*. Washington: American Council for World Freedom, 1978.

Potere Operaio. Special issue, March 26, 1972.

Processo all'Autonomia (Autonomy on Trial). A cura del Comitato 7 Aprile. Viterbo, Italy: Lerici, 1979.

Red Army Fraction. *La Guerriglia nella Metropoli*. Verona: Bertani, 1979.

Ricci, Aldo. *I Giovani non Sono Piante*. Milan: Sugar Co., 1978.

Röhl, Klaus Rainer. *Fünf Finger sind Keine Faust*. Hamburg: Kiepenheuer & Witsch, 1977.

Ronchey, Albero. *Libro Bianco sull'Ultima Generazione*. Milan: Garzanti, 1978.

Sale, Kirkpatrick. *SDS*. New York: Vintage, 1974.

Salvi, Sergio. *Patria e Matria*. Florence: Vallecchi, 1978.

Secchia, Pietro. *Chi Sono I Comunisti*. Milan: Gabriele Mazzotta, 1977.

————. *La Resistenza Accusa*. Milan: Gabriele Mazzotta, 1973.

Settembre Nero. A cura di Bergamaschi, Laurora, Salvatori e Trovatore. Milan: Stampa Club, 1972.

Silj, Alessandro. *Mai Piu Senza Fucile!* Florence: Vallecchi, 1977.

Smith, Colin. *Carlos: Portrait of a Terrorist*. London: Sphere Books, 1976; New York: Holt, Rinehart and Winston, 1977.

Snow, Peter, and Phillips, David. *Leila's Hijack War*. London: Pan, 1970.

Soccorso Rosso, eds. *Brigate Rosse*. Milan: Feltrinelli, 1976.

Sterling, Claire. "Italy: The Feltrinelli Case." *Atlantic Monthly*, July 1972.

Stevenson, William. *Ninety Minutes at Entebbe*. New York: Bantam, 1976.

Tarabocchia, Alfonso. *Cuba: The Technology of Subversion*. Gaithersburg, Md.: International Association of Police Chiefs, 1976.

Terrorismo y Justicia en España. Madrid: Centro Español de Documentación, 1975.

Tessandori, Vincenzo. *Br—Imputazione: Banda Armata*. Milan: Garzanti, 1977.

Tinnen, David, and Cristensen, Dag. *The Hit Team*. New York: Dell, 1977.

Transnational Terror. Palo Alto, Calif.: Hoover Institution on War, Revolution, and Peace, 1975.

Ulam, Adam B. *In the Name of the People*. New York: Viking, 1977.

Wilkinson, Paul. *Terrorism and the Liberal State*. London: Macmillan, 1977.

INDEX

Firk, Michèle ("Isabelle Chaumet"), 51, 63
France, 219, 265
  as haven for political exiles, 52–53, 54, 196
  intelligence service (SDECE), 12, 68, 287
  see also DST
France, Terre d'Asile (France, Land of Asylum), 50, 55, 111
Franceschini, Alberto, 307, 331n40
Franco, Francisco, 11, 72, 115, 141, 163, 172, 173–74, 175, 176, 178, 180, 182, 191, 192, 195, 199
FRAP, 72
Freda, Franco, 116, 321n8
Free French Mission, 60, 67–68
French Foreign Legion, 203, 207
French Red Brigades, 195, 198
Front Line, 8, 196, 197, 203, 211, 216, 217, 218, 221, 224–25, 293, 302, 303, 329n19

Gafsa operation, 260–61
Gaiba, Aldo, 320n8
Gallardo, Antonio Ramirez, 172
Gallucci, Achille, 210, 330n26
Gambino, Ferruccio, 331n40
GAP, *see* Proletarian Action Group
Gauche Proletarienne (Proletarian Left), 42
Gazit, Shlomo, 278
German Democratic Republic (East Germany), 14
  guerrilla instructors, 92, 159, 254, 263, 281
  role in international terrorism, 287–88
Gezmis, Denis, 238–39
Ghotbzadeh, Sadegh, 55
Giai, Fabrizio, 303, 306
Giovannone, Stefano, 266, 285
Giscard d'Estaing, Valéry, 144, 324n12
Glavatsky, N. V., 156
Gökbulut, Erdoğan, 230
Gonzales, Hortensia, 172
Goriaran, Osmany Cienfuegos, 15
GRAPO, 55, 169, 178, 196
Gratt, Thomas, 318n11
Great Britain, 3, 200, 265
  Communist Party, 156
  intelligence service (MI6), 12, 64
  and IRA, 151, 164–70
  Labour Party, 294
  political asylum in, 137
  Soviet agents in, 138
Gromyko, Andrei A., 274, 277
Gross, Richard, 54
GRU, 221, 234, 275
Grubyakov, Vasili Federovitch, 236
Guasco, Guido, 79, 197, 330n31
Guerrilla International, 192

Guerrilla training camps, 3, 14, 15, 39, 41, 116, 172, 193, 196, 220, 236, 273
  Algeria, 195
  Cuba, 14, 15, 20–21, 45, 105, 249–50, 252, 253, 255–56
  Czechoslovakia, 220, 221, 290–91
  IRA at, 155, 159, 161
  Iranians in, 124
  Ireland, 194
  Libya, 254, 262–64, 267
  Palestine, 253
  payment for training in, 15, 91, 122–23, 126
  Russia, 34, 44, 89–90, 121, 248, 278–80, 281
  South Yemen, 88, 284
  Syria, 254–55, 333n9
Guerrilla warfare, 202, 203
  urban, 18, 22–23
  see also Marighella, Carlos: *Mini-Manual for Urban Guerrillas*
Guerrillas, *see* Terrorists
Guevara, Ernesto "Ché," 8, 9, 29, 36, 37, 39, 40, 72, 248, 252
Güneş, Elvan, 229

Haag, Siegfried ("Khaled"), 77–78, 80, 91, 92, 100, 101, 106, 108, 159, 317n20
Habash, George, 12, 38–39, 41, 54, 74, 90, 98, 196, 200, 222, 236, 240, 253, 261, 277, 282, 285
  and Carlos, 137, 148
  in Cuba, 253
  and ETA, 194
  and export of Palestinian terrorism to Europe, 113–14, 115, 117, 118, 120, 121, 122, 128–29, 130, 281
  and IRA, 158–59, 165
  and Japanese terrorists, 125–26
  and Jibril, 276
  and Kurds, 244–45
  and Qaddafi, 271
  and training camps, 123–24, 155
Haberman, André ("Jean-Baptiste"), 56
Haddad, Wadi, 90, 91, 92, 93, 98, 99, 117, 118, 120, 123, 126, 128, 130, 132, 138, 146, 236, 253, 264, 271, 281
  and Carlos, 137, 140, 148
  central role of, 140
  and ETA, 194
  and IRA, 158–59
Haig, Alexander, 174
Haiti, 55, 58, 248
Halabi, Akram, 273, 274
Hallier, Jean-Edern, 42
Hamchari, Mahmoud, 119
Hausner, Siegfried, 101
Hawatmeh, Naif, 128, 253, 261, 271, 276, 277, 281, 282, 336n18
Hearst, Patty, 17
Heath, Edward, 139